GENOCIDAL LIBERALISM

GENOCIDAL LIBERALISM

THE UNIVERSITY'S JIHAD AGAINST ISRAEL & JEWS

Richard L. Cravatts

DAVID HOROWITZ FREEDOM CENTER

Published in the United States by the David Horowitz Freedom Center
P.O. BOX 55089
Sherman Oaks, CA 91499-1964
www.frontpagemag.com

Distributed by Publications Management Company
P.O. Box 15302
Boston, MA 02215
(617) 521-2412
(617) 521-3880 Fax

ISBN-13: 978-0615566382
ISBN-10: 0615566383

Manufactured in the United States of America

Author photograph by Aaron Washington
Cover design by Jasmine Hairsine-Padmore

First Edition

For Sara, who got the recipe

CONTENTS

Contents

PART ONE
THE IDEOLOGICAL ROOTS OF ANTI-ISRAELISM

Chapter 1

How the Academic Left Came to Hate Israel & Why It Matters

Writing some years ago about Tony Judt, a professor who controversially wrote that Israel was an "anachronism" and should be eliminated, former presidential speechwriter David Frum coined a new phrase for describing this troubling trend on campuses of Left-leaning academics who persistently vilify Israel. His term was "genocidal liberalism," the notion that this was truly a new mutation of anti-Semitism, and that those on the Left who, in their obsessive reverence for everything Palestinian and their chronic and deadly Israel hatred, were in essence working toward the elimination of the Jewish state.

Professor Judt's fulminations were perverse but unfortunately not uncommon on today's college campus.

Coupled with harsh and relentless criticism of Israel—and more particularly with Zionism—is the common technique of Israel's detractors of hurling accusations against the State that are historically inaccurate, derogatory, slanderous, or merely lies and exaggerations to help further isolate Israel from the world community of approved nations.

Thus, on campus today Israel is regularly, though falsely, condemned for being created "illegally"—through the "theft" of Palestinian lands and property—and thus has no "right to exist." The government is accused of a "brutal," illegal "occupation" of Palestinian lands, especially Gaza and the West Bank, of being a "colonial settler state," a Zionist "regime," a land-hungry nation building an "apartheid wall" as a further land grab, a usurper of property that was lived on and owned by a Palestinian "people" "from time immemorial." Zionism is regularly equated with Nazism, and the perceived offenses of Israel's government and military are likened to Nazi crimes against humanity; the notion is that Israel is creating a "Holocaust in the Holy Land" through "ethnic cleansing," an ongoing "genocide" of Arabs, and the elimination of the rights of an innocent, "indigenous people" who merely seek self-determination and the peaceful creation of a Palestinian homeland. The very existence of Israel is described as being the "greatest threat to world peace," the core cause of Muslim anger toward the West, the root of the Palestinians' suffering, and the nation has even been referred to publicly as a "shitty little country" by the French ambassador to Britain.

These beliefs permeate the vocabulary of Israel-hatred on campus, and are dangerous and troubling not merely because they vilify the Middle East's only democracy and America's principal ally in that region; they are of concern because they are based on misrepresentations of history, exaggerations of current conditions in Israel, the West Bank, and Gaza, and, most seriously, involve a complete inversion of truth which enables Israel-haters to load cruel and destructive invective on Zionism without apology, while in reality they are promulgating vile, disproportionate opprobrium that frequently shows its true face as raw anti-Semitism.

In *The Return of Anti-Semitism* Gabriel Schoenfeld notes how the very language itself has become a form of "turnspeak," that the ". . . language in which such accusations are leveled is extravagantly hateful, drawn from the vocabulary of World War II and the Holocaust but grotesquely inverted, with the Jews portrayed as Nazis and their Arab tormentors cast in the role of helpless Jews."[1]

Phyllis Chesler, author of *The New Anti-Semitism*, similarly suggests that it is the academics who lead the charge against Israel, and they have successfully contorted the language of dialogue to vilify the nation repeatedly, that "the intelligentsia tell us that Israelis are the 'new Nazis' and 'worse than Nazis.' This is a new form of Holocaust denial. It lets Europeans off the hook: they no longer must wrestle with their own formidable colonial pasts and their persecutory-collaborationist-bystander roles in the Holocaust."[2]

All of these alleged transgressions on the part of Israel are often further conflated with the academic Left's view that the "brutal occupation" of Zionism has unleashed these "crimes against humanity" through U.S. complicity, that as its proxy in the Middle East, Israel tarnishes America through its misdeeds and mirrors the U.S.'s own imperialistic, militant, and anti-Muslim impulses. Thus, Israel haters on campus are frequently the same individuals who regularly rant against the evils of the United States, as well, and who despised President George Bush and the cabal of neo-conservatives who, they believe, surreptitiously drew the United States to war in Iraq for the ultimate benefit of Israel, and who, in the Left's view, represented jingoism, patriotism, and a fundamental belief in the righteousness of democratic ideals of freedom—notions that are viewed as dangerous and anachronistic by many liberal academicians.

It was not always thus. Prior to the 1967 war, Israel still garnered sympathy and admiration from the non-Muslim world that saw its pluck and ability to bring a vibrant democracy to the desert as being enviable and praiseworthy. Still weak and living in a perilous realm surrounded by hostile, totalitarian regimes, Israel could count on the liberal Left for support and an ideological nod of approval. But thanks to is actual ascension to a status as a militarily and economically powerful nation, coupled with the successful propaganda war waged against it by its Arab neighbors and jihadist foes, many of Israel's sympathizers began to lose their affection for their former Middle East favorite and instead began conflating their negative views of the United States, capitalism, and imperialism (defined as "occupation" in the case of Israel) with the Jewish state.

There is also clearly a double standard on the part of the academic Left where Israel is involved, an inclination by apologists for the Third World's failures and excesses to overlook these blatant flaws and transfer their collective condemnation on Western nations—and Israel—precisely, so they seem to believe, because those countries should know better. In fact, says Richard Baehr, chief political correspondent of *The American Thinker*, many of liberals' favorite causes are routinely and chronically violated by those very nations on whose behalf they work so hard to excuse the behavior of. "Many on the left," he said, "seem to be unconcerned about how illiberal and unprogressive are the attitudes and behaviors of those they champion in this conflict; the forever aggrieved Palestinians and their Arab and Muslim allies. They are loath to defend Palestinian (or Saudi) behavior on such issues as women's rights, gay rights, tolerance for secularists and other non-Muslim believers, freedom of speech and the press, and so on. Because cultural relativism reigns supreme on the left, the progressives refuse to judge a non-western culture by western standards (or alternatively, it is just too inconvenient to do so). Only Israel can be judged by western standards (perfection in its case) and always found wanting."[3]

What troubles defenders of Israel the most as they witness this onslaught of vilification, of course, is the singular obsession many academics have with Israel, and only Israel, from among the world's countries. This double standard leads many to believe that something else is going on here below the surface besides mere concern for the aggrieved Palestinians. In fact, to observers like Phyllis Chesler, the singling out of Israel for condemnation while other, worse countries (such as China, North Korea, Rwanda, and others that she mentions), receive silence or apologetics, exposes the academics' actual sentiments. Referring to the call for an academic boycott against Israel's scholars, Chesler suggested that "Such obsessive anti-Zionist stands by intellectuals are examples of Jew-hating," since "Western intellectuals have not even-handedly condemned academics from . . ." the other transgressing nations she lists.[4]

Why the animus against democratic Israel in academe as the nation defends itself from an unending campaign of aggression from Arab countries? One trend that has permeated the university—and which has had a subsequent influence on the way Israel is perceived—was the coming of two watchwords of higher education: *diversity* and *multiculturalism*. Diversity has seen administrations bending over backwards to accommodate the sensitivities of minorities and perceived victims of the majority culture—usually at the expense of fairness and rationality. Multiculturalism has brought with it a type of moral relativism in which every country or victim group is equal, regardless of what vagaries, weaknesses, or fundamental evil may underpin its social structure.

But in their zeal to construct an academic setting that reflects the true diversity of the nation—and simultaneously attempts to redress past discrimination and exclusion—universities have created campuses that have evolved in an entirely opposite direction. Rather than helping students adapt to the real diversity of society outside the campus walls, the diversity 'movement' in the hands of liberals has served to create balkanized campuses where victims of the moment segregate themselves into distinct and inward-looking racial and cultural groups—exactly the opposite intention of the diversity credo.

In fact, as Alan Charles Kors and Harvey A. Silverglate suggested in their insightful study, *The Shadow University: The Betrayal of Liberty on America's Campuses*, diversity and multiculturalism programs, as practiced by universities, are frauds, the very use of which terms has, in their view, "become a politicized perversion of language." "All that the social engineers of diversity mean," they say, "is the appreciation, celebration, and study of those people who think exactly as they do about the nature and causes of oppression, wherever they are found and however nonrepresentative those thinkers might be of the broader groups they purportedly represent."[5]

Students from 'underrepresented' minority groups, who may well initially arrive at campuses thinking of themselves as part of mainstream society, are taught, in the name of diversity, to think of themselves differently: as part of a racial, cultural, sexual, or political subset of American life. If they have not previously been aware of their victim status, then indoctrination about diversity, as Charles W. Sykes points out in *A Nation of Victims*, quickly helps them assume that identity and exploit it for social gain. "In the society of victims," he wrote, "individuals compete not only for rights or economic advantage but also for points on the 'sensitivity' index, where 'feelings' rather than reason are what count."[6]

More cynically, programs to promote campus diversity and multiculturalism have essentially become tools by liberal ideologues to construct a world view that is anything but truly diverse. Jay Bergman, a history professor at Central Connecticut State University in New Britain, bemoaned this very point when he commented that "what is perhaps most striking about the obsession with diversity is that most of those who favor it seem to have no interest in fostering intellectual diversity [and] the inclusion of conservative opinions, which are woefully underrepresented on college campuses."[7]

The language of multiculturalism on campuses is sprinkled with the linguistics of oppression, coaxing students in newly-identified victim groups to see themselves as deserving of protection and special political, racial, and cultural recognition. SUNY Corland's Center for Multicultural and Gender Studies, for example, announced in its mission statement quite openly that the "central operating assumption is that all oppressed groups share a similar, though not identical, body of experiences that promotes a common bond. While the separate identities of groups must be acknowledged and respected, the center *strongly endorses the need for these groups to work collectively in pursuing social justice* [italics added]," the implication being, once again, that social justice is achieved for oppressed groups when powerful (read: "white") groups are identified as the racist elitists they are, and when they begin to relinquish authority and privilege to self-identified victim groups.

The obsessive reverence for multiculturalism on the part of universities has also meant that liberal faculty members have come to embrace attitudes that give equal value to very different cultures and nations, a factor which has led—as it did before when the Left embraced the ideology and overlooked the barbaric excesses of Communism—to a dangerous acceptance of radical Islam as equal to and compatible with the culture, values, and ethics of Western democracies. In his examination of the traditional impulse from the Left to align itself with political movements with opposite values of America, *United in Hate: The Left's Romance With Tyranny and Terror,* Jamie Glazov saw a direct causal link between an acceptance of defective ideologies by the Left as part of the process by which they reject democratic Western ideal and a slavish fondness for what he characterizes as the "Left's sacred cow of multi-culturalism."[8]

Thus, the decades-old emphasis on bringing multiculturalism to campuses has meant that faculty as well as students have been seeped in an ideology which refuses to demarcate any differences between a democratic state struggling to protect itself and aggressive, genocidal foes who wish to destroy it with their unending assaults. For the multiculturalist Left, the moral strengths of the two parties are equivalent, even though the jihadist foes of Israel, for example, have waged an unending struggle with the stated aim of obliterating the Jewish state through the murder of Jews.

Thus, this inclination to worship multiculturalism forces liberals to make excuses for those cultures which have obvious, often irredeemable, moral defects, such as the Islamist foes who currently threaten Israel and the West. "The believer cannot accept the truth about Islamism or much of Islam," observed Glazov, "because he would then have to concede that not all cultures are equal, and that some cultures (e.g., America's, with its striving for equality) are superior to others (e.g., Islam's structure of gender apartheid). For the believer to retain his sense of purpose and to avoid the collapse of his identity and community, such thoughts must be suppressed at all cost." One way these truths are "suppressed," as Glazov put it, in those instances when liberals make their morally imbecilic judgments about the essential worth of clearly defective cultures, is the construction of a curious double standard when looking at cultures other than their own, Western models. As commonly happens when liberals appraise the relative merits of their own countries and others, one set of expectations are used to measure Third-world countries and their leaders, and a totally different, far more stringent (if not unreasonable) set is used when evaluating the behavior and values of the United States, the EU, or Israel. This cynical, nearly hypocritical, view has meant that the Left frequently denounces Western democracies as imperialistic, racist, militaristic oppressors, precisely because they wish them to evolve to a purer, newly-structured society and feel that they have the collective insight and moral strength to effect this change as they strive for social justice.[9]

At a 2003 "peace rally" at Columbia University held to denounce America's initiation of the liberation of Iraq from Saddam Hussein's treachery, for example, many were stunned and mortified when Columbia anthropology professor Nicholas De Genova proclaimed to the gathered crowd of some 3000 that, "Peace is not patriotic. Peace is subversive, because peace anticipates a very different world than the one in which we live—a world where the

U.S. would have no place." And then, in what could be considered a nearly seditious rant, De Genova asserted the insidious, perverse notion that "The only true heroes are those who find ways that help defeat the U.S. military. I personally would like to see a million Mogadishus," alluding to the 1993 ambush and slaughter of American forces in Somalia.

That professor De Genova could make such seemingly insidious remarks publicly suggests the moral incoherence endemic to Leftist thought, and gives credence to political theorist James Burnham's observation in his 1964 work, *Suicide of the West*, that liberalism "is the ideology of Western suicide," precisely because of its failure to confront the threat of enemies who do not share liberals' confidence in the moral redemption of mankind through social equanimity. Like his fellow travelers on the Left, De Genova conceives of and eerily echoes the language of what Burnham described as a "new and better world," a place where "the soul may take refuge from the prosaic, unpleasant world of space and time" and where "the abandonment of a million of one's own countrymen and the capitulation to a band of ferocious terrorists become transformed into what is called 'liberation'."[10]

The visceral hatred by the Left toward their favorite hobgoblins, imperialist America and its codependent oppressor, Israel, finds similar expression from other morally-defective professors, such as University of Michigan's conspiracy-frenzied Juan Cole, who whose regular rants in his blog, *Informed Comment*, take swipes at Israeli and American defense, while simultaneously excusing Arab complicity for violence or terror. In fact, according to Cole, it is the militancy of the West that causes the endemic problems in the Middle East, and makes America guilty for its moral and financial support of Israel. "When Ariel Sharon sends American-made helicopter gunships and F-16s to fire missiles into civilian residences or crowds in streets," Cole wrote in 2004, "as he has done more than once, then he makes the United States complicit in his war crimes and makes the United States hated among friends of the Palestinians. And this aggression and disregard of Arab life on the part of the proto-fascist Israeli Right has gotten more than one American killed, including American soldiers."[11] There is, of course, no mention in Cole's fantasies about why American or Israeli soldiers would be involved in military actions in the first place, affirming the view that it is Western imperialism and oppression that disrupt and embroil the otherwise taciturn political state of the Arab world.

This cultural condescension, the disingenuous lie from the Left that all cultures are equal, but some are more or less equal, to paraphrase Orwell, leads liberals into the moral trap where they denounce Israel's military self-defense as being barbaric, criminal, and Nazi-like (because Israel is a powerful, democratic nation) and regularly excuse or apologize for genocidal Arab terrorism as an acceptable and inevitable result of a weak people suffering under Western oppression. Violence on the part of the oppressed is accepted by liberals because it is deemed to be the fault of the strong nations whose subjugation of those defenseless people is the very cause of their violent resistance. In fact, when Leftist professors, such as Columbia University's Joseph Massad, apologize for Palestinian terror, he justifies it by characterizing the very existence of Israel as being morally defective, based, in his view, on its inherent racist and imperialist nature. For him, nations which are racist and imperialistic cannot even justify their own self-defense, while the victims of such regimes are free to "resist," based on the Left's notion of universal human rights—but especially for the weak. "What the Palestinians ultimately insist on is that Israel must be taught that it does not have the right to defend its racial supremacy," Massad wrote during the 2009 Israeli defensive incursions into Gaza, "and that the Palestinians have the right to defend their universal humanity against Israel's racist oppression."[12]

Conflated with the exclusion of nearly all but liberal thought on campus is the darker side of diversity: as victim groups become aware of their supposed classification as 'authentic' victims, they are prone to contradict the stated goal of diversity by limiting real dialogue and interchange between opposing points of view. Thus, while diversity proponents adamantly defend free speech in order to promulgate their own world views, they frequently move to stifle the speech of others, usually conservatives—through calls for censorship, newspaper theft, and speech codes—and exempt themselves from having to live by the suppressive rules they write for others. In an article in the school's *Massachusetts Daily Collegian*, for example, a University of Massachusetts at Amherst student made the oft-expressed claim that designated victim groups could not be held accountable for any negative thoughts they might harbor against other races or cultures—justifiable or not. "People of ALANA [African, Latino, Asian, and Native American] descent cannot be racist," the column observed, "because we don't hold the economic power in this country, though we may feel anger which is provoked by racists."[13]

There is another, related irony to the bleating on campuses about the virtual sanctity of the notion of diversity: while faculty and administrators have been claiming a fervent desire to create ideological diversity in academia, research studies have indicated that, in reality, nothing even close to this aspiration has been realized. In fact, in one of these investigations conducted by Daniel B. Klein and Charlotta Stern in 2003, "How Politically Diverse Are the Social Sciences and Humanities?," the authors identify the existence of what they identify as highly-biased campuses where Democrats (liberals) outnumber Republicans (conservatives) at alarming rates of disparity, with "results [that] support the view that the social science and humanities faculty are pretty much a one-party system." The study found that the ratios between Democrats and Republicans in the different academic departments ranged from a low of 3-to-1 in Economics to a shocking 30.2-to-1 imbalance of Democrats to Republicans among Anthropology faculty. The other distressing Democrat to Republican ratios included those in departments of Political Science (at 6.7-to-1), History (at 9.5-to1), Philosophy (at 13.5-to1), and Sociology (at 28-to1), *with the average of the six ratios being 15.1-to-1*. Professor Klein conducted a parallel study of 23 academic departments at University of California, Berkeley and Stanford University and found similar stark indications that liberal bias had infected entire campuses, supporting again what they call the "'one-party campus' conjecture:" "For UC-Berkeley," the study stated, "we found an overall Democrat:Republican ratio of 9.9:1. For Stanford, we found an overall D:R ratio of 7.6:1. Moreover, the breakdown by faculty rank shows that Republicans are an 'endangered species' on the two campuses."[14]

"In the U.S. population in general, Left and Right are roughly equal (1 to 1), like male and female among college students," Klein and Stern wrote, meaning that the Left-leaning ideological bias of faculty members—particularly in the social sciences and humanities—suggests a disturbing imbalance in their resulting worldviews, and a greater likelihood that their teaching, and political views, will reflexively embrace anti-American, anti-democratic, and anti-Israel attitudes. The voting habits are not the issue here; what is significant is that campuses that have been ideologically hijacked by Left-leaning faculty tend to recruit and grant tenure to like-minded professors, publishing their work, rewarding their scholarship, and balkanizing academia so that competing scholarship from conservative faculty is either entirely absent or, when even represented, is marginalized.

More importantly, faculty attitudes about politics have a direct effect on how they help form a university's collective moral consciousness, particularly when universities are regularly asked to take stands for the cause of the moment on behalf of radical faculty. In 2003, for instance, when some 106 of Columbia's faculty signed the "Columbia/Barnard Arms Divestment Petition" against Israel that called for divestment and would deprive Israel of the means to defend itself, a startling 20 faculty members from the Anthropology Department (one of Columbia's smallest academic departments), twenty percent of the total, were signatories on that petition, a not unexpected response given the findings of Klein's study that showed a ratio of over 30 to 1, Democrats to Republicans, in departments of Anthropology in the schools they evaluated.

The reverence for diversity, regardless of the failure of universities to achieve anything coming close to actual, substantive diversity in their classrooms, has nonetheless led to a heightened level of group identity on campuses, with racial victims having an especially protected place at the diversity table. While proponents of diversity initially hoped in their enlightened, if not naïve, way that disparate ideas and cultural backgrounds would coexist with more or less equal footing, additional protections were eventually implemented to provide "historically victimized" groups—blacks, gays, native Americans, among them—with special rights and social entitlements. And of all the issues on campus, racism continues to be the most highly-charged and politically sensitive among liberal professors and students.

The charge of racism also enables liberals to excuse the moral transgressions of the oppressed, and, as an extension of that thinking, to single out Israel and America for particular and harsh scrutiny owing to their perceived "institutionalized" racism and greater relative power. The self-righteousness the Left feels in pointing out Zionism's essential defect of being a racist ideology insulates it from having to also reflect on Arab transgressions, since, as Ruth Wisse has pointed out in *If I Am Not For Myself: The Liberals Betrayal of the Jews*, liberals can excuse their own betrayal of Israel by holding it fully responsible for the very hatreds it inspires. "Ascribing to Israel the blame for its predicament, democratic countries can pursue their self-interest free of any lingering moral scruple," she said. "Israel is examined for its every moral failing to justify policies of disengagement, while the moral failings of Arab countries are considered no one's business but their own, so that their blatant abuses of human rights should not get in the way of realpolitick."[15]

This "unholy alliance" between jihadists and Leftists, which might seem initially incompatible, serves both sides well: Arab nations, who wish to deflect the pathologies of their own societies, savor being able to assign the West's worst appellation of 'racist' to Israel, and campus liberals at the same time fulfill their Marxist dreams of trying to envision and help create what Wisse called the "ideal of the egalitarian state," something that the Left had hoped that Communism would create, but which ultimately failed to be established anywhere and in the pursuit of which some 100 million souls perished during the twentieth century.

The notion that Israel is a racist state has also gained resonance among African-Americans on campus, who since the Civil Rights era have enjoyed only a tenuous relationship with Jews, and who have also embraced some of the negative attitudes about Israel and Jews in general, fanned on, in part, by such luminaries as Louis Farrakhan of the Nation of Islam. Minister Farrakhan, it will be remembered, characterized Judaism as a "gutter religion," deemed Hitler "a great man," and, lest there be any doubt where his sympathizes lie regarding Israel, decided that the "plight" of American blacks puts them "in the same position" as the Palestinians. While Farrakhan's own visits to campuses are rare, Nation of Islam spokesman Khalid Abdul Muhammad's 1993 speech at Kean College in New Jersey left no doubt about the sentiment deemed appropriate to deliver to the crowd at the black student-sponsored event:

> Who are the slumlords in the Black community? The so-called Jew. . . Who is it sucking our blood in the Black community? A white imposter Arab and a white imposter Jew. . . . You see everybody always talk about Hitler exterminating 6 million Jews. That's right. But don't nobody ever ask what did they do to Hitler? What did they do to them folks? They went in there, in Germany, the way they do everywhere they go, and they supplanted, they usurped. . . .[16]

That image of a "white" Jewish "imposter" Arab, of course, reaffirms the notion of the Jew having no real connection to Israel, that the presence of Jews in Palestine is yet another indication of colonialism, "supplanting," and "usurpation." The frequent condemnations, on and off campus, that Zionism is equivalent to racism and that Israel is an "apartheid" country (a charge given credence by such luminaries as former President Jimmy Carter, among others), as suggested in a 2003 *Yale Herald* opinion piece by a student Robert Spiro, could be part of the reason that among some black students an affinity for the oppressed Palestinians seemed natural and an extension of their own perception as victims of American racism at the hands of white bigots. "Black students," Spiro said, "have been convinced that the Israeli-Palestinian conflict is at heart an attack on 'peoples of color,' an assault on downtrodden minority groups. Since blacks identify themselves with Palestinians, they have taken up the anti-Zionist (and subsequently anti-Jewish) cause."[17]

Coupled with academia's fervent desire to make campuses socially ideal settings where racial and cultural strife cease to exist is the other newly-popular impulse to inculcate students with a longing for what is called "social justice," a nebulous term lifted from Marxist thought which empowers Left-leaning administrators and faculty with the false ethical security derived from feeling that they are bringing positive moral and ethical precepts to campuses.

For the Left, according to David Horowitz, a former radical leftist turned conservative, social justice is "the concept of a world divided into oppressors and oppressed."[18] Those seeking social justice, therefore, do so with the intention of leveling the economic, cultural, and political playing fields; they seek to reconstruct society in a way that disadvantages the powerful and the elites, and overthrows them if necessary—in order that the dispossessed and weak can acquire equal standing. In other words, the Left yearns for a utopian society which does not yet exist, and is willing to reconstruct and overturn the existing status quo—often at a terrible human cost—in the pursuit of seeking so-called "justice" for those who, in their view, have been passed over or abused by history. According to Horowitz, this "radicalism is a cause whose utopian agendas result in an ethic where the ends outweigh and ultimately justify the means," a view which has meant that Western leftists have come to share a sympathy for the tactics and ideology of jihadists who seek to overturn Western ideals in their pursuit of an Islamic caliphate, what Horowitz calls an "unholy alliance" of the Left and Islamists in their pursuit of social justice.

"Like the salvationist agendas of jihad," he wrote, "the Left's apocalyptic goal of 'social justice' is the equivalent of an earthly redemption. A planet saved, a world without poverty, racism, inequality, or war—what means would not be justified to achieve such millennial ends?"[19] For that precise reason, Israel is continually slandered as a racist state, an aggressive, militaristic regime that inflicts disproportionate suffering on the hapless Palestinians, lubricating the argument that this inequality is inherently and inexorably wrong, that it must be corrected and made just. Thus, when such radical student groups as Students for Justice in Palestine have as their core mission, as their name implies, bringing their own vision of justice to the Middle East, it is justice *only* for the oppressed, the Palestinians, and not for the oppressor, Israel, whose position of power was made possible, Horowitz suggested, only because of a "hierarchy of class and race [which] exists globally."[20]

For the Left, social justice is solely for the disenfranchised, the 'victims' of unjust Western societies, those whose suffering is ostensibly caused by and is the fault of imperialistic, capitalistic, militant, hegemonic nations—America and Israel foremost among them. And on campuses, where liberal professors have nearly made sacred the politics of race and class and have identified specific sets of favored victim groups for whom justice will be sought, the cult of "victimhood" has even led to compulsory instruction on the mechanics of achieving social justice for the weak in society.

A September 11, 2007 report prepared by the Princeton, New Jersey-based National Association of Scholars, "The Scandal of Social Work Education," for instance, revealed the alarming extent to which students in social work programs at universities across the country were not only being encouraged to embrace a politicized role for social work, but were actually being required, in many instances, *as part of their educational requirements*, to adopt a mandatory ideology in which the bringing about of "social justice" for certain groups means giving them the perpetual mantle of "victimhood," together with a status of being subject to exploitation, oppression, and abuse by other, stronger social groups.[21]

Thus, the NAS report found from its observation of courses and programs accredited by the Council on Social Work Education "that even within the ideologically colored environment of the contemporary university, social work education constituted an especially advanced case of politicization, in which dogma, tendentiousness, and coerced intellectual conformity were becoming integral to the definition of the field." The report also revealed that CSWE-approved programs, at such schools as Arizona State University, Berkeley, UCLA, the University of Central Florida, the University of Houston, the University of Michigan, the University of Minnesota/Twin Cities, the University of Texas/Austin, the University of Washington, and Wayne State University, for example, mandated that students "embrace and/or prepare students to advocate for social and economic goals described by decidedly liberal/left formulations as 'social and economic justice,' 'distributive justice,' and 'nondiscriminatory social and economic systems,' as well as to have students understand something referred to as 'the global interconnections of oppression,'" this latter view ideal for conflating, at least in liberal imaginations, the shared complicity of America and Israel in their long-term oppression of the indigenous people of Palestine.[22]

The new academic dialogue over the concept of social justice obviously found a fitting locus with concern for the Palestinian cause, since, as the report also noted, the concept of social justice had been "frequently used to justify new entitlement rights for individuals and whole categories of people, i.e., legally enforceable claims of individuals or groups against the state itself," particularly applicable on highly-politicized campuses when, as in the case of the Palestinians, that claim was statehood and that state was Israel. Compassion for the dispossessed and the weak on the part of the Left has also seen the growth of a whole different set of ethical standards by which the actions of powerful nations—primarily Israel and the U.S—are judged as compared to weaker, developing, sometimes clearly inferior nations, based on their political and international behavior.

Ron Radosh, professor emeritus of history at CUNY and an adjunct fellow at the Hudson Institute, observed that the Israeli/Palestinian conflict was the exact cause on which the capitalism- and imperialism-hating Left could focus their attention. "It is clear that having had only limited success with organizing around domestic issues such as the movement for a 'living wage,' or calling for an end to 'Third World sweatshops,'" he said, "the Israeli counteroffensive against terrorism which by necessity is based on a military response to the brutal killing of innocent civilians serves just that purpose.

And by resurrecting the old and discredited shibboleths that 'Zionism is racism' and that Israel is the moral equivalent of the apartheid regime in the old South Africa, they have what they regard as the perfect mechanism for achieving their ends."[23]

But in the mind of the academic Left, coming out of years of seeking social justice and diversity for everyone by applying low standards to all, there are no superior national behaviors; all nations are equal in value and in the same world opinion. This contorted reason is commonly referred to as "moral relativism," and is a seminal cause of the way Israel's actions in defending itself against genocidal Arab aggression over 60 years are seen to be no different than the homicide attacks on Israeli civilians initiated by its enemies. Journalists promiscuously refer to the sad "cycle of violence," something that classics professor Bruce Thornton of California State Fresno called "a morally moronic notion," which equates the violence on both sides of the Palestinian/Israeli conflict, as if each Arab attack is somehow a rational and understandable reaction to Israel's occupation and efforts at self-defense.

Professor Thornton also saw an intellectual defect on the part of Left-leaning academics who serve up these apologies for terror on behalf of the heroic self-determination of the Palestinians, and who see homicidal attacks on Israeli civilians at cafes and on buses as being the same rational actions as the defensive measures of the Israeli government in trying to protect its populace from attack. Leftists not only see as equivalent acts of violence from both sides, they give greater credibility to the nihilistic violence of terror due to what Thornton called "the sentimental Third-Worldism that idealizes the non-Western 'other,'" and another troubling trend in the politics of the Left, what he observed as "the juvenile romance with revolutionary violence."[24]

Part of the academic Left's conflation of America's wrongdoing with Israel's is the manner in which both powers are seen as complicit by the anti-globalization movement, which conveniently assigns blame to the U.S. and Israel, among others, for the failure of Third-World societies to prosper under the unfair and oppressive pressure of unrestrained global capitalism. Writing in *Foreign Policy*, Mark Strauss observed that the anti-globalism movement has helped disparate political groups, each with its own agenda, focus on a common enemy—imperialist, colonial superpowers—with Jews and Israel represented prominently in that murky view. "The backlash against globalization unites all elements of the political spectrum through a common cause," Strauss wrote, "and in doing so it sometimes fosters a common enemy—what French Jewish leader Roger Cukierman calls an anti-Semitic 'brown-green-red alliance' among ultra-nationalists, the populist green movement, and communism's fellow travelers."[25]

Strauss noted that the anti-globalism narrative, which positions Israel as an imperialist European-born regime that deprived an indigenous people of both their land and resources, conforms to the opinions of other Israel-haters who hold the same notion, coupled with the added view that this colonial "project" is subsidized and further exploited with the support and moral complicity of the similarly imperialistic United States. "Israel enjoys a unique pariah status among the antiglobalization [sic] movement because it is viewed as the world's sole remaining colonialist state—" said Strauss, "an exploitative, capitalist enclave created by Western powers in the heart of the developing world."[26]

On campuses where a coddled and insulated professoriate often express antipathy for the perceived ills of capitalism, the demonizing of Israel on the basis of its economic vagaries is further evidence to the academic Left that Israel's very existence is not at all about self-determination (something they grant acceptable only to the Palestinians) and all about greed, globalism, colonialism, exploitation, and undeserved political and economic might. Not unnoticed to Strauss and others is that these same accusations, hurled so regularly at Israel, are a core part of the classic accusations that have followed Jews through many centuries and in various societies in which they are sometimes tolerated, sometimes reviled.

While critics of Israel regularly and passionately deny any ill-will towards Jews in general, and instead claim to be merely commenting on some failures in the Israeli government's policies, the extreme vitriol and condemnation often evolves into a new type of Jew-hatred, ushering along the old hatreds and suspicions, central to the anti-globalism crowd as well. "The new anti-Semitism is unique," said Strauss, "because it seamlessly stitches together the various forms of old anti-Semitism: The far right's conception of the Jew (a fifth column, loyal only to itself, undermining economic sovereignty and national culture), the far left's conception of the Jew (capitalists and usurers, controlling the international economic system), and the 'blood libel' Jew (murderers and modern-day colonial oppressors)."[27]

This "trifecta" of hatred is no longer blatantly expressed towards Jews and thus not exposed as naked anti-Semitism; instead, the same themes of Jew-hatred are now conveniently channeled through the Jew of nations, Israel. In the Arab world, specifically, the three strains of divergent Jew-hatred are regularly exploited as part of the ideological war against Israel, along with the deranged fantasies of what Jews represent, as manifested in such Middle Eastern bestsellers as the czarist forgery, the *Protocols of the Elders of Zion*. Here, the far Right's notion, a remnant of European fascism, that the self-serving Jew threatens world peace because of his truculence and obsession with Zionist ideology is given credence to an Arab audience, who, prior to 1948, had only scriptural motivation for loathing Jews, traced to Mohammed's experience with having been rebuffed by a Judaism which would not embrace Islam. Like those from the far Left, Arabs, too, now point to the *Protocols* as one bit of proof that the Jew manipulates government in his rapacity and longing for world domination, and that his insatiable desire for more land is confirmed in his continuing, and widening, "occupation" and "theft" of Muslim lands. And the European medieval blood libel against the Jew—first aimed at Jews for having killed Christ, and later for their role in murdering Christian children to harvest blood for matzos—has now reappeared in full array in the Arab world, where supposed "scholars" appear on state-sponsored television programs to reveal the bloodthirstiness of Jews who now kill Muslim children for their blood, or by the accusations of Israel-haters in the West who condemn Israel's military self-defense as "barbaric," "genocidal," or a "crime against humanity," yet another example of how, in the minds of their enemies, Jews will not hesitate to spill the blood of non-Jews because of their perfidious nature and due to their zeal to achieve world domination.

Paul Hollander, author of *Anti-Americanism: Irrational and Rational,* pointed out a perverse inclination on the part of some on the Left to embrace the troubling impulse of violent responses to political causes when he wrote that "Many Western intellectuals had a longstanding and barely (if at all) suppressed admiration for what they saw as the morally superior, passionate, invigorating, authentic use of violence in a wholesome, liberating cause. . . Political (and sometimes non-political) violence came to be seen as the magic device with which to bridge the gap between theory and practice, rumination and action, good intentions and genuine commitment."[28]

This rationalization, that violence is an acceptable, if not welcomed, component of seeking social justice—that is, that the inherent "violence" of imperialism, colonialism, or capitalism will be met by the same violence as the oppressed attempt to throw off their oppressors—is exactly the style of self-defeating rationality that in this age has proven to be an intractable part of the war on terror. America-hating and Israel-hating academics have not infrequently wished for harm to come to these countries at the hands of the victim groups to whom they readily give their sympathies. They frequently, and mistakenly, ascribe to poverty and helplessness the inclination to lead to terrorism on the part of otherwise weak and oppressed individuals. And, like Leftist apologists for revolutionary violence in earlier examples of resistance, they see an opportunity for the tables to be turned on the oppressors and an equal distribution of suffering to be brought about in the resulting power shift.

This trait, in which Leftists flirt with a romanticized idea of insurrection and violence, seems to confirm Glazov's thesis that the Left's current "romance with Islamism is just a logical continuation of the long leftist tradition of worshipping America's foes. . . ," with Islamism now viewed by the Left as a "valiant form of 'resistance' against American imperialism and oppression." For Glazov, sympathy for jihadists is part of an enduring ideological legacy, and "the Left clearly continues to be inspired by its undying Marxist conviction that capitalism is evil and that forces of revolution are rising to overthrow it—and must be supported."[29]

Stanford University's Joel Beinin, for instance, a self-avowed Marxist and former president of the Middle Eastern Studies Association, specifically excused Palestinian violence during the first Intifada in a piece entitled *Was the Red Flag Flying There?* "Palestinian attacks on civilians (and even armed soldiers) were widely condemned as terrorism by international opinion and media," Beinin wrote, but terrorism was clearly the "Palestinians' primary weapon of resistance" given the political impediment they faced; namely, the "colonialist thrust of the Zionist project,"[30] and the complicity of hegemonic, imperialist powers in inspiring the terror wrought against them.

Similarly, Joel Kovel, the rabidly anti-Zionist Bard College professor who was finally fired by the school in 2009 because of his ideological excesses, has seen terrorism as the logical, and excusable, end result of occupation—something for which, in his view, not only Israelis but all Jews must share in the blame. "Why have a substantial majority of Jews," he wrote in *Tikkun Magazine*, "chosen to flaunt world opinion in order to rally about a state that essentially has turned its occupied lands into a huge concentration camp and driven its occupied peoples to such gruesome expedients as suicide bombing?"[31]

Some students, themselves, have absorbed the liberal moral relativism of their professors, the first step in justifying the use of terror in struggles for self-determination on the part of the oppressed. Andrew Dalack and Julia Eden Ris, members of University of Michigan's Students Advocating Freedom and Equality, for example, wrote in *The Michigan Daily* their opinion that Arab terror only reflected Israeli terror, that "violence on the part of the Palestinians is only one of the forms of resistance to another form of violence demonstrated by Israeli occupation. This includes Israeli military incursions into Palestinian neighborhoods, harassment of Palestinians at more than 500 checkpoints inside the West Bank and the construction of a militarized apartheid wall."[32]

The aspect of liberalism that allows the terrorist to have equal moral weight with a democratic society attempting to protect itself from terrorism also, of course, enables those on the Left to ignore other values and beliefs, as well, particularly if they are inconsistent with a worldview that would actually hold victim groups responsible themselves for their moral and ethical lapses. In a philosophical universe where there is no difference between a uniformed soldier defending his country and a homicidal maniac slaughtering civilians on a crowded bus, there is little room for faith, religious values, and ethics. In fact, woefully absent and specifically derided at most campuses is any fondness for religion, an antipathy that accompanies a diminution in the value of modern democratic societies. As they hate the West, liberals, too, hate its values and religious traditions, preferring instead to ennoble Third World faiths while they deride, scoff at, and general marginalize Judeo-Christian traditions. The idea of a state founded by a religious group—the Jews—is yet another reason that Israel's very existence has found disfavor with what commentators call the "secular humanists" for whom personal value systems are the new faith.

Even when the fundamentalism of Islam has been linked to terror and fanaticism, Tzvi Fleischer observed, that religious fervor is not ridiculed by the same America- and Israel-haters, such as MIT's Noam Chomsky, who prefer to give ideological support to totalitarian, Islamofacist movements rather that democratic societies. "Philosophically, of course, anarcho-socialist Chomsky has almost nothing in common with Hezbollah, which seeks to establish an Iranian style theocracy dominated by coercive enforcement of sharia religious law," said Fleischer. "He wouldn't be caught dead supporting a Christian group with the same violent theocratic tendencies. But as Chomsky and many on the far Left have demonstrated many times, for them, anti-Americanism trumps everything else."[33] Hollander reinforces the same point when he suggested that part of the reason Israel is blamed for defensive actions against terror while the terrorists are frequently excused is that the religious impulses that fueled Zionism are suspect while those of the Muslim victims of Zionism are acceptable. Leftists have always been suspicious of fundamentalist forms of religion, Hollander said, and particularly the strains that defined the Christian Evangelical movement in America. "Islamic religious fanaticism is quite another matter," Hollander said, however, "since it is a product of the Third World and the cultural diversity it represents and as such deserving of respect."[34]

There is, of course, a particular irony that many on the Left, whose devotion to and support of a Jewish state was almost an integral component of liberal thought, including among many Jews themselves, have now boxed themselves in to a paradoxical situation in which they have had to distance themselves from the idea of Israel in order to preserve their own conception of what being a liberal means. In fact, as Ruth Wisse recounted in *If I Am Not For Myself*, from the founding of Israel in 1948 until the occupation brought about by the six day war in 1967, and then until 1975 when the UN declared that Zionism was racism, liberals felt complacent in their ideological support for the Jewish state, since, as Wisse wrote, "Jews figured as unquestionable victims and underdogs," and thus qualified for liberal devotion and protection. Once Arab intransigency had begun to demonize Israel in the eyes of the world, and once the Palestinian narrative supplanted the victimology of the Jews, liberals faced a fuzzy moral incoherence: it became difficult for them to defend the existence of a Jewish state that now stood for oppression rather than victimhood, that was now, according to the Arab world, denying another people of their own self-determination, inspiring violence from the people being dispossessed by Jews, and that was, in fact, beginning to make anti-Semitism a reality again, even so soon after the Holocaust.[35]

In fact, the continual pattern of violence in the Arab world against Israel agitated liberals greatly, and made them condemn Israel, not its foes, for having inspired Arab rage, with the assumption that only peoples with justifiable grievances are moved to violent ends to solve their woes. The Jew-hatred that became the core Arab pathology was something that Wisse said "discomfits liberals by forcing them to abandon their pacific, generous, optimistic view of the world in order to take account of a specific, aggressive, and declared intention of destroying—yet again—the Jews."[36]

This explains why the Left has regularly glossed over terroristic behavior on the part of Islamists—Hamas, Hezbollah, Fatah, the Al Aksa Brigades, or others—and has romanticized this violence as "resistance." But that idealized world requires that state actors behave in rational ways, something that is clearly absent in conflicts in which theology, apocalyptic views of the world, a longing for martyrdom, or genocidal ethnic hatred guide geopolitical struggles. In fact, said Wisse, the more hostile the Arab foes of Israel became, the more difficult it became for liberals to absolve Israel for creating the very violent urges that were arising to eliminate it. "By blaming Israel for Arab complaints," she wrote, "liberals anticipate a reasonable, pacific solution to the conflict. . . The democratic Jewish state is subject to 'rational' persuasion; not so the Arabs. The more determinedly, and by Western standards, irrationally, Arab governments and their agents pursue their anti-Israel campaign. . . the more desperately the liberal imagination tries to blame the Jews for incurring Arab displeasure."[37]

Most curious has been the betrayal of Israel by some liberal Jews themselves, who, poisoned by a pathology that enables them to deflect the hatred of others by absorbing it themselves, have reacted by attacking the Jewish state, the hatred of which is unavoidably tarring them, as Jews, in a prejudice they are unwilling to have be directed at them. Because as liberals they stand for a world in which equanimity is achieved between nations, at no particular people's expense, the increasing vilification of Israel as an impediment to Middle Eastern harmony has caused some Jewish liberals to have to distance themselves from open support of Israel. More dangerously, in their zeal to confirm that their liberalism is pure and that they still reflexively support victims, not oppressors, some Jews themselves have betrayed Israel and Zionism, to use Wisse's words, by attacking today's core source of Jew-hatred: Israel. Rather than confront the lies and distortions promulgated by the Arab world against Israel over its alleged racism, barbarity, imperialism, cruelty, and lack of morality, anti-Israel liberal Jews accept the spurious new narrative completely, and in fact often abet it with their own condemnations of the Jewish state. For Wisse, this political behavior could "more accurately be described as the desire to disassociate oneself from a people under attack by advertising one's own goodness,"[38] a psychological pattern that has manifested itself conspicuously on campuses.

Normal Finkelstein, as one example, late of DePaul University and the author of the invidious screed, *The Holocaust Industry*, has made a career as an ideological hit man against Israel, using the fact that his parents were Holocaust survivors to inoculate himself from charges of anti-Semitism, even while he demeans the Holocaust, praises Hezbollah as morally upright freedom fighters yearning for peace, and promiscuously lectures on college campuses about the irredeemable evil of Israel, the racist character of Zionism, and the complicity of Jews who actually support the Jewish state. Finkelstein's mentor, MIT's Noam Chomsky, who Harvard's Alan Dershowitz has called the "godfather" of anti-Israel thought, when he is not lecturing on the evils of American capitalism and its ruthless lust for 'empire,' busies himself by blaming Israel for every problem of the Middle East's highly dysfunctional, authoritarian regimes. Nor was he the least bit embarrassed in 2006 when he visited Lebanon to hold court with Sheikh Hassan Nasrallah, Hezbollah's homicidal secretary general, and assured viewers watching his guest appearance on Al Manar TV that his support for a terrorist organization that had murdered Israelis and Americans was unflagging. "Hezbollah's insistence on keeping its arms is justified," Chomsky crowed. "I think [Hezbollah leader Sheik Hassan] Nasrallah has a reasoned argument and [a] persuasive argument that they [the arms] should be in the hands of Hezbollah as a deterrent to potential aggression, and. . . until there is a general political settlement in the region, [and] the threat of aggression and violence is reduced or eliminated, there has to be a deterrent."[39]

Professor Jennifer Loewenstein, Director of Middle Eastern Studies at the University of Wisconsin, glorified Palestinian resistance and the yearning for Arab self-determination while describing Israel as a nation that "speaks with a viper's tongue over the multiple amputee of Palestine whose head shall soon be severed from its body in the name of justice, peace and security."[40] Then there was New York University's notorious Tony Judt, who claimed that Israel is "an oddity among nations," which no one wants to have in existence "because it is a Jewish *state* in which one community—Jews—is set above others, in an age when that sort of state has no place," and which ultimately means that as a Jew, Judt will have to suffer the moral scolding of the world's anti-Semites on behalf of Israel's sin of merely existing—something he is disinclined to do.[41] Echoing one of Israel-haters' current favorite slanders is Richard Falk, professor emeritus of International Law and Policy at Princeton University and the UN's preposterously-titled "Special Rapporteur on the situation of human rights in the Palestinian territories occupied since 1967," who wondered aloud if it was "an irresponsible overstatement to associate the treatment of Palestinians with this criminalized Nazi record of collective atrocity?" on the part of Israel, and then quickly answered his own question by saying, "I think not."[42]

Two of the other national traits that liberals derisively ascribe both to America and Israel are their religious underpinnings and tradition, and their ability to deploy military forces in pursuit of self-defense. This revulsion on the part of the Left with Judeo-Christian religion and militarism—both of which impulses they ascribe to the cause of many of the ills of the world—forms the basis for imagining what Israel is like in the minds of many of its detractors: an oppressive, glum, faith-based militaristic regime subjugating an innocent indigenous people with its zeal, greed, and power. In the frenzied imagination of Israel-haters, such as Columbia's odious Hagop Kevorkian Professor of Iranian Studies and Comparative Literature, Hamid Dabashi, this militarism has become an existential curse on Israelis, a self-inflicted pathology that for Dabashi, of course, has no relation to the fact that the Jewish state has survived in a sea of hostile foes who have sought its destruction for over 60 years. For Dabashi, Israel is a form of mechanized, militarized evil, a soulless state created solely to dominate a defenseless people. "What they call 'Israel' is no mere military state," he wrote in Egypt's *Al-Ahram Weekly*, a state-sponsored newspaper which regularly features insidious anti-Semitic and anti-Israel propaganda. "A subsumed militarism, a systemic mendacity with an ingrained violence constitutional to the very fusion of its fabric, has penetrated the deepest corners of what these people have to call their 'soul,'" Dabashi continued. "What the Israelis are doing to Palestinians has a mirror reflection on their own soul—sullied, vacated, exiled, now occupied by a military machinery no longer plugged to any electrical outlet. It is not just the Palestinian land that they have occupied; their own soul is an occupied territory, occupied by a mechanical force geared on self-destruction."[43]

This dark and twisted characterization has meant that Israel is perceived in exactly that way by many outside the university, as well, something that has proven to be such a problem that in a recent survey to determine people's attitudes about the favorability of countries, the National Brands Index conducted by Simon Anholt, Israel finished last from among 35 other countries. As part of the psychological repositioning process, the task is for Israel to sidestep negative perceptions which comprise the current bundle of people's emotional and rational connections to the country and start to tell a different brand story. Researchers in another survey by The Brand Israel group found that younger, non-Jewish Americans, in particular, had a singular view of Israel being "militaristic" and "religious," and none of these aspects were seen as positive associations, according to David Saranga, consul for media and public affairs at the Israeli Consulate in New York. "Israel is not perceived as a fun place where people live,"[44] he said, signaling a complete turnaround from the early years when Israel's military competency and the religious orientation were at least perceived favorably as part of the country's cultural dethos.

This nearly total rejection by the Left of any recognition of goodness on the part of Western countries, favoring without hard judgments severely flawed societies of the Third World is, according to commentator Melanie Phillips, symptomatic of academics' belief in their own moral superiority, a feature which, at least in their own minds, gives them a more genuine and principled worldview. "In the grip of a group-think that causes them to genuflect to victim-culture and the deconstruction of western morality and the concept of truth," Phillips said, "a dismaying number of our supposedly finest minds have been transformed from people who spread enlightenment to those who cast darkness before them."[45]

And once the Left had ideologically captured university campuses, the stage was set for the spread of a poisonous, malignant hatred against Israel, which would begin to play itself out with a radicalization of student groups, divestment campaigns, anti-Semitic speakers and events, corrupted, biased Middle Eastern studies programs, and a general feeling that the cause of the Palestinians was so sacrosanct that it was worth sacrificing and destroying the Middle East's only democracy in the pursuit of that supposedly noble cause.

Chapter 2

Liberal Academia's Embrace of 'Palestinianism'

I f Israel was to be persistently vilified by its enemies in the court of public opinion, in the minds of its ideological foes it had to be set against a countervailing force, a competing example of self-determination whose righteousness and purity could effectively cancel out Israel's own struggle to establish and preserve its nationhood. For the Jewish state's Arab foes, that force was to be found in the creation of a fictive people, an invented nation—the Palestinians. Although now the Palestinians' existence and authenticity is rarely even questioned any more, those who care to look back only to before the Six Day War of 1967 see that no group called Palestinians, either self-defined or identified by the outside world, ever existed, nor had any nation by that name ever occupied lands in historic Palestine or any of the territory that eventually became Israel.

A March 31, 1977 interview with Palestine Liberation Organization executive committee member Zahir Muhsein in the Dutch newspaper *Trouw* revealed as much, with his very forthright, perhaps unintended, confession that the invention of the Palestinian and the notion of a Palestinian state was principally a tactic in the ideological war against Israel. "The Palestinian people does not exist," Muhsein admitted at the time. "The creation of a Palestinian state is only a means for continuing our struggle against the state of Israel for our Arab unity. In reality today there is no difference between Jordanians, Palestinians, Syrians and Lebanese. Only for political and tactical reasons do we speak today about the existence of a Palestinian people, since Arab national interests demand that we posit the existence of a distinct 'Palestinian people' to oppose Zionism."[1] In fact, those people now called Palestinians by the world were perceived by their Arab brethren as being largely comprised of Syrians, since "Palestinians" living in the British Mandate could be Jewish Palestinians or Arab Palestinians, defined primarily by their residency in the geographical area of biblical Palestine. When the Soviet Union helped found the Palestine Liberation Organization in 1964, with Yasser Arafat at the helm, the intention was to "liberate" the *lands* of Palestine between the Jordan River and the Mediterranean Sea, not a *people* who were then identified as being a people with a distinct national identity.

But if a convincing argument was to be made by Arab propagandists that Zionism, in its quest to create a Jewish state in Palestine, had dispossessed another "people" with ancestral and historic ties to the same land, the notion of a Palestinian nation and people had to be conjured up as a group whose suffering and victimization could outshine that of the Jews who had created their own state with remembrance of the Holocaust still seared on the world's conscience. Positioned as colonial settlers who arrived from Europe to subjugate an indigenous population of "Palestinians" who had lived on that land, in Joan Peters' phrase, "from time immemorial," the Zionists were cast as usurpers of Muslim land who were oppressing hapless victims of Western imperialistic dreams—and even more so after the 1967 war when Israel's remarkable conquests and acquisition of broad swathes of new territory seemed to confirm the disproportionate strength of the Zionism regime against the weaker Palestinian Arabs.

For the PLO and their Arab sympathizers, the intention was simple and straightforward: drive the Jews into the sea and reclaim what was believed to be, once and forever, Muslim land. But that Islamic imperialism, as Professor Efraim Karsh has termed it in his book by the same name, was not a tactic that could be embraced comfortably by most in the West, nor by academics on the Left looking for the next liberation movement on which to fasten their ideological support. The newly-minted Palestinians became the perfect symbol of the struggle by the weak and oppressed of the Third World to seek self-determination and freedom from the powerful, colonizing, imperialistic superpowers, and the cult-like obsession with their cause has been referred to as "Palestinianism," "a new political and religious cult," by author Bat Ye'or and others.[2]

Ye'or, a scholar of dhimmitude, is more concerned than other commentators about the potential lethality of Palestinianism to the West, thinking, like political scientist James Burnham before her about other totalitarian movements, that it involves a kind of cultural and national "suicide of the West" in accommodating Islamic supremacism. In the first place, by having as one of its principal aims to eliminate Israel, it seeks to rewrite history and impose its Islamic values on the Middle East and eventually the West, as well. According to Ye'or, "Palestinianism condenses jihadist values. It promotes the destruction of Israel, the denial of Hebrew biblical history and hence Christianity. It preaches Islamic replacement theology and the Arabization and Islamization of the Holy Land's biblical archeology."[3] Through European appeasement and a slavish devotion to the aims of Islamic movements, Palestinianism gained traction, especially as it became the cause of the moment on campuses in Europe and America and the ideological creed of the EU, the United Nations, anti-Israel NGOs, and others in the international community.

But its danger is based on the divergent objectives of those who promote and embrace it. For Europe, it has become a craven way of insuring self-defense: Palestinianism, said Ye'or, is "the most cherished European ideology because it is the very guaranty of its security against terror—that has determined European support for jihadist tactics." That tenuous relationship has created an unholy alliance between Europe and the Arab world, one which involves, in Ye'or's words, "the building of an idealized 'Islamo-Christian Civilization,' the dawn of a messianic universal peace whose blessing over the whole world is impeded by Zionism and Israel."[4]

For the Arab world, of course, the nurturing of Palestinianism has a more insidious and deadly purpose: the vilification of Israel as a technique of eliminating it, and, simultaneously and as part of that same effort, a stealth jihad to undermine the values and hegemony of the West. In a review of Ye'or's book, *Eurabia: The Euro-Arab Axis,* in which she examines this dangerous phenomenon, classics professor Bruce Thornton of California State University, Fresno noted that while the Left's obsession with "Palestinianism also expresses various cultural pathologies of Western societies, such as Western self-loathing, the idealization of the non-Western 'other,' the glamour of guerilla resistance, refugee pathos, and a sentimentalized post-colonial guilt," its "ultimate goal. . . is not the establishment of a Palestinian state but the prosecution of *jihad* against the West."[5]

Central to this propaganda campaign to enshrine Palestinianism—in which the suffering of the Palestinian will finally trump the historic suffering and dispossession of the Jews—is the wholesale, deliberate appropriation of the language and symbols of the Jews by foes who wish to eradicate, not only the Jewish past, but the very existence of the Jewish state. Thus, the actual genocide of European Jewry during the Holocaust is either minimized or denied by the Arab world at the same time that Israel is denounced for committing a new "holocaust" against the Palestinians through ethnic cleansing, the oppression of occupation, and war crimes.

Palestinians regularly refer to themselves as being dispersed in a Diaspora, what they call their own "Nakba," a catastrophe, just as Jews had traditionally spoken of their own scattering from their homeland after the destruction of the Second Temple. While Arab aggression and homicidal impulses against Jews have been unrelenting—before and since the creation of Israel—the Palestinians have successfully been cast as the perennial victim of Jewish supremacism, even though the irredentist aims of the Islamists to establish a Muslim-only state in historic Palestine is the very form of self-determination that is repeatedly decried on the part of Israel for being racist, inhumane, internationally criminal, and morally unacceptable.

In the West Bank, where in April, 2009 an Arab was sentenced to death for selling land to a Jew, it is Israel that is accused of being an "apartheid state," and the organic growth of Jewish neighborhoods in Biblical Judea and Samaria are referred to as "illegal settlements" that are pointed to as being the main impediment to Middle East peace and an obstacle to the creation of a Palestinian state. The terrorism and violence against Israel by its Arab neighbors is regularly ascribed to the brutal occupation and defined as mere resistance, but the occupation was a necessary defensive response to Arab aggression against the Jews that had begun in the 1920s—long before the dreaded occupation had occurred. In this perverse historic inversion, Israel is stripped of its moral legitimacy and all of it is transferred, in the eyes of the West, to the Palestinians. Israel, the Middle East's only democracy, with a multi-racial, heterogeneous population, is condemned as a racist state.

The charge of racism against Israel, of course, has been increasingly uttered by the Jewish state's enemies, particularly after the 1975 United Nations' invidious proclamation that "Zionism is racism," thereby branding the very ideological existence of Israel as a racist act. This charge was widened in an unrelenting propaganda war that was successful in painting Israel as a "settler nation" of white Europeans who dispossessed a native population of colored people. As terror against Israel continued, and especially since Yasser Arafat's 2000 second Intifada, the image of a minority of racist Zionists oppressing a Palestinian majority began to resonate in the collective imagination of Israel's critics, particularly on campuses where Leftists took comfort in the fact that their moral stand had helped dismantle the actual apartheid system of South Africa. In a campus environment where racism was the twentieth century's greatest ideological sin, the ability to brand Israel as an illegitimate and racist state was an irresistible way for liberals to find a new cause of the moment by which to nourish their own righteousness.

"This issue [of Israel] boils down to racism," wrote Julian Perez, a member of Yale University's Students For Justice in Palestine in the *Yale Daily News*, supporting this widely-held view of Israel's essential racist ideology. "An entire indigenous population is being denied their human rights by a colonial state that is based on religion and ethnicity," he concluded, promulgating the myth that Palestinian Arabs were indigenous to the region that became Israel, and that the existence of the Jewish state further denies Arabs rights they would otherwise be enjoying absent the existence of Israel.[6]

Of the many libels from the world community against Israel, perhaps none has gained such traction on campuses as the accusation that the Jewish state now practices apartheid, that the checkpoints, security barrier, Israeli-only roads, barricades, and other remnants of occupation are tantamount to a racist system which victimizes the indigenous Palestinians, just as South African apartheid oppressed and devalued indigenous blacks while stripping them of them civil rights. The same Left-leaning activists from universities who carried the banner against the South African regime have now raised that same banner—with the same accusatory language—and superimposed on Israel the notion that yet another apartheid regime is oppressing Third-world victims.

This chorus of denunciation against the new Zionist apartheid regime has been given ideological and moral support, as well, by such high-visibility figures as South African archbishop Desmond Tutu who, when visiting Israel, commented that "I've been very deeply distressed in my visit to the Holy Land; it reminded me so much of what happened to us black people in South Africa. I have seen the humiliation of the Palestinians at checkpoints and roadblocks, suffering like us when young white police officers prevented us from moving about."[7] Similarly, former president Jimmy Carter instigated additional condemnation against Israel on college campuses with the publication of his book, provocatively entitled *Palestine: Peace, Not Apartheid*, which left little to the imagination about what his view toward the conflict was. In a 2006 interview on National Public Radio, for instance, he repeated the misrepresentation that Israel had usurped Palestinian land and suggested that the current system in the occupied territories was tantamount to apartheid:

> I have spent a lot of time in Palestine in recent years. . . . The Palestinians have had their own land, first of all, occupied and then confiscated and then colonized. . . They have been severely restrained in their movements. . . The Israelis have built more than 200 settlements inside Palestine. They connect these

settlements with very nice roads for the Israeli settlers, and then superhighways and so forth going into Jerusalem. Quite often the Palestinians are prevented from even riding on those roads that have been built in their own territory. So this has been in many ways worse than it was in South Africa.[8]

This ideological cover from some of the Left's favorite spokesmen has trickled down to campuses where the same language is frequently heard as part of student-run protests, divestment campaigns, and Israel-bashing in general. "Racism and discrimination rear their ugly heads in many countries but these crimes rarely, if ever, constitute apartheid," wrote student Eugene Gu in the *Stanford Daily*. "However," he continued, at last identifying the sole, horrific example where apartheid *does* exist in the world, "the situation in the Israeli-occupied territories has become so appalling, the problem so dire, and global censure so unanimous that it constitutes one of those rare occasions where the use of such a strong word is not only justified but also a matter of truth and accuracy."[9]

Former Bard professor, Joel Kovel, the rabid anti-Zionist whose ideology is focused on dismantling Israel completely through the creation of a single, bi-national state, was even more direct in his denunciation of Israel's existential sins, including the U.S.'s complicity in the oppression of the Palestinians under what he, too, describes as an apartheid system. "The recent efforts of activists to publicize the parallels between Israel and apartheid South Africa, then, are an essential element in the one-state strategy," he told an interviewer. "The anti-Israeli-apartheid campaign is energizing forces of opposition across the world to build a powerful political movement to oppose Zionism and its lobbyists in the major capitalist/imperialist countries. This is significant because Israel simply cannot sustain itself without the support of the capitalist/imperialist powers, the United States in particular. Its current prosperity is entirely dependent on them."[10]

This kind of language helps reinforce the Left's notion that the imperialism of Western nations is once again responsible for setting up racist, oppressive caste systems in developing countries, systems that have to be dismantled through protest, resistance, and divestment campaigns. It has also formed the basis of divestment petitions which become "working documents" in the strategic vilification of Israel. A January, 2003 document created by New Jersey Solidarity and the Rutgers University Campaign for Divestment from Israeli Apartheid, "Acting for Human Rights, Taking a Stand for Justice," for instance, proclaimed that "The world, and specifically the United States, can no longer be silent about the criminal Israeli regime. Conceived by colonial powers without the consent of the indigenous Palestinian people, the State of Israel has continued to pursue its institutionalized policies of racism, discrimination and oppression." What's more, the petition claimed, the United States, in providing continuous financial support for Israel, was directly responsible for the social injustices taking place in the occupied territories. "Unlike other countries receiving foreign aid," the petition continued, "Israel's aid is unencumbered with restrictions—thus, it may be used directly to promote settlements, engage in military incursions inside the occupied territories, and other acts in violation of international law."[11]

Abetted by the Arab world, which has also perennially defined Israelis as European interlopers with no racial connection to the Levant, campus Leftists are now willing to sacrifice the very survival of the Jewish state because they feel that charge of racism against Israel is more incompatible with their closely-held beliefs in a perfectible world than the rejectionist and genocidal efforts of the Arab world which in fact have necessitated Israeli security measures—the separation wall, indeed, the occupation itself—all of which are pointed at as indications of exactly how racist Israel's behavior actually is against the Palestinians.

The much-reviled security barrier, which Israel began building around the West Bank in 2005 as a tactic to reduce terror attacks on its citizenry (and which has been successful in reducing the frequency of those attacks by ninety percent) is, in the eyes of Israel's critics, not a means of defense, but what is promiscuously termed the "apartheid wall," a type of racial fence built merely to create Palestinian "Bantustans," which segregates Jews from Arabs, and which is, for many, emblematic of Israel's never-ending ambition to "steal" Arab land, disrupt Palestinian life, and expand its Zionist dream to ever-broader borders.

"Today in Palestine," wrote Humza Chowdhry, a graduate student at San Jose State University in the school's newspaper, the *Spartan Daily*, "an apartheid wall continues to be constructed around the region with land grabs at every corner cutting through college campuses and dividing families."[12] In language which is echoed with the same refrain on campuses and throughout the Arab world, Israel is regularly called an "apartheid regime," with the security barrier its most visible and damning bit of evidence supporting that charge, but with checkpoints, the Gaza blockade, Israeli-only roads, Jewish settlements, and special privileges for Jewish Israelis also seeming to give proof to the distorted comparison of Israel and South Africa.

But the apartheid comparison is a simple and powerful way for Israel's campus enemies to heap yet another moral condemnation on the Jewish state, particularly because it reenergizes the campus liberals who made South African apartheid their cause of the moment during the 1990s. Even though Arab citizens of Israel enjoy more human and civil rights than their brethren in any other Arab nation, the apartheid accusation is effective because it once again points to the social disparity between Israelis and Third-world Arabs, Israeli citizens or not. Israel's need for self-defense, in the mind of its detractors, does not even justify the "apartheid wall," since as a strong Western democracy it presumably should not have established its illegitimate state on Arab lands in the first place, nor should it be surprised when those indigenous inhabitants try to reclaim their stolen property by using terrorism as their only available tactic against an oppressive, militarily-strong regime.

In fact, according to some critics, the Palestinians' failure to create a state of their own, complete with a functioning civil society, is laid at Israel's feet, as well. Why? Because "Israel is suffocating the Palestinians," suggested Carnegie Mellon student (and frequent contributor) Hanadie Yousef in the University's newspaper *The Tartan*. "There are numerous checkpoints in Palestinian territory that prevent travel from one town to another. The wall is being constructed on Palestinian farmland, and is further preventing the practically nonexistent export of Palestinian goods. Fifty percent of Palestinians are jobless, a direct result of the Israeli occupation of Gaza and Gaza's perpetual state of oppression."[13]

Radical faculty members write similar accusations against Israel, ascribing most of the blame for failed Palestinian self-determination to the Jewish state in its efforts to defend its citizenry. Like many in the international community who regularly decry the construction of illegal "settlements" in the West Bank, Princeton University assistant professor of history Nick Guyatt sees Israel's self-protection as unnecessary, yet another artificial step taken to impede Palestinian statehood and economic viability. "Each settlement in the Occupied Territories demands special roads, military defenses and other infrastructure which demoralizes and oppresses Palestinian communities," he wrote in the *Daily Princetonian*. "Each settlement represents an obstacle to the realization of Palestinian national aspirations, as well as a violation of international law."[14]

Not only is Israel responsible for hampering the viability of the Palestinian state, its claims that it is under siege by its enemies is said to be overstated, as well. "Some would say the apartheid state of Israel is 'protecting itself,' but from what?," asked Mr. Chowdhry in his *Spartan Daily* letter. "The Zionist regime has nuclear weapons and F-16s courtesy of the United States. By contrast, Palestinians have their bodies as their F-16s."[15] Thus, the charge of apartheid is valuable to Israel's detractors, for it both devalues the nation by accusing it of perpetuating the Left's greatest crime—racism—in the form of apartheid, which Israel enforces with the complicity of the United States, while simultaneously absolving Arabs of responsibility for the onslaught of terror they continue to inflict on Israel. By pointing to the weakness of the oppressed Palestinians against the superior military and economic might of Israel, the notion that the wall was built as a security measure is made to look ridiculous, as if Israel has nothing to fear by being surrounded by a sea of jihadist foes bent on its destruction.

And who is the co-villain in this racist oppression? The United States, of course. "For enemies of U.S. imperialism," wrote Paul Pryce, a member of the University of Washington's International Socialist Organization, "the lesson is clear: to oppose American occupation in the Middle East is to oppose Israel. If we want to see an end to [former President George W.] Bush's wars for oil, we must build an antiwar movement that challenges the so-called 'war on terror,' and defends the right of Palestinians and Lebanese to resist Israel's aggression."[16]

"The majority of the money to build this wall," wrote a University of California, Davis student member of Students for Justice in Palestine in the School's *International Affairs Journal*, "has come from U.S. tax dollars given to the Israeli war-machine to continue its inhumane policies of occupation and apartheid. If the international community cannot stop the construction of the Apartheid Wall and other illegal Israeli practices then humanity is at stake," he concluded, thereby placing the responsibility for the virtual survival of mankind on the shoulders of Israel and the United States, and seeing in the construction of a terror-preventing barrier a malignant, human rights-threatening event.

The student then imputed a second, even darker, motive in Israel's decision to construct the separation barrier: it was not to reduce deaths among Israeli civilians from terrorist attacks; instead, it was to create an impediment to state-building on the part of the Palestinians, who, it will be remembered, have repeatedly turned down offers of a state of their own.

So in a perverse but convenient moral twist, the Left can make the claim for righteousness in seeking to address the ills of racial prejudice, oppression, and exclusivism while simultaneously giving expression to Jew-hatred, anti-Israelism, and anti-Americanism. "American and European leftists claim to hate racism and racial oppression," noted conservative commentator David Horowitz when he observed in a 2005 article how progressives were unfazed by actual ethnic cleansing when long-standing Jewish settlements in Gaza were dismantled in order to make it *Judenrein*, Jew-free. "But when it comes to the racial oppression of the Jews they hate the Jews more than they hate racism or oppression. . . . And why do they hate the Jews? They hate the Jews because Israel is America's only real ally in the entire Third World—the world of ethnic minorities and the oppressed. They hate the Jews because the Jews expose their hypocrisy in supporting mayhem and murder and tyrannical oppression in the name of compassion and social justice."[17]

This view of the Jew, or of Israel, the Jewish state, as a political destablizer, is, of course, also central to the notion that the victims of that manipulation are the dispossessed and weak for whom liberal academics tirelessly seek "social justice." Any tactics, including terror and violence, are considered appropriate and excusable in the victims' campaign to throwing off the yoke of oppression. And the Palestinian, positioned as one made to suffer daily humiliation and endlessly deprived of a homeland and the right to self-determination, has become the perfect example of the contemporary victim archetype, the Third-World "other," an ever-present, homeless, dispossessed tragic refugee whose plight could be traced directly to supposed colonialism on the part of the "settler" state of Israel.

Saidism and the Academic Roots of Palestinianism

Were it not for Edward W. Said, the Palestinian cause may have echoed through the halls of the United Nations, and influenced diplomacy and statecraft in the Middle East and in the West, but never have captured the imagination of academe. Said, a professor of comparative literature at Columbia University, in 1978 published a provocative and highly-influential book, *Orientalism*, that not only had a profound effect on the direction of Middle East studies here and abroad, but eventually provided a foundation for the intellectual aspect of Palestinianism, and inspired the reverence it has come to receive from the Left and the intellectual elite.

Though he was a Christian who was raised in affluence in Egypt, Said invented a persona for himself, claiming to be himself one of the dispossessed Palestinians whose rights he eventually championed. He served on the Palestinian National Council with Yasser Arafat, threw stones at Israeli soldiers, and railed against Western imperialism and its history of subjugating the East through colonialism, military excursions, and hegemonic influence. And *Orientalism* gave expression to Said's belief that the West's perception of the Middle East—indeed, the way the East was understood—was the product of cultural imperialism, the tendency, in his view, of Western scholars, artists, writers, sociologists, archeologists, and others to define the East based on its presumed cultural, racial, intellectual, social, and political inferiority. Not only was this practice endemic in the West's relations to the East, but it represented an insidious aspect in the study and understanding of the Orient by the Occident, that is, that Orientalism was, in Said's words, "a Western style for dominating, restructuring, and having authority over the Orient." More pointedly, Said announced that no European was even capable of studying the East without superimposing his or her own cultural biases and "intellectual imperialism," leading Said to the breathtaking thesis that "every European, in what he could say about the Orient, was. . . a racist, an imperialist, and almost totally ethnocentric."[18]

Said owed some of his postmodernist thinking to Michel Foucault, whose concept of "discourses" suggested that knowledge was based on a series on "constructs," that this essential artificiality of ideas, history, culture was all subject to questioning and no one narrative was intrinsically superior to or more valid than another. So for Said, the image of the Orient that the West had created was based, not on the verifiable, historic nature of the East, but on a "construct" imposed by the West in its "relationship of power, of domination, of hegemony."[19]

The notion that only those of the Orient could study the Orient impartially came as something of a shock to those Western scholars of the East—esteemed academics like Bernard Lewis, for instance (whom Said regularly derided)—who were now being accused of being incapable of conducting scholarly inquiry because of their ingrained cultural biases. What is more, as Said applied his concept of Orientalism to the Arab/Israeli conflict in which he was increasingly involved, he was able to graft the idea of the West's ethnocentrism and imperialism toward the East on the dynamic between Israel and the Palestinians. Here, Zionism is the "construct," superimposed on the East (and the hapless Palestinians) by the imperialistic West, another form of aggressive Orientalism. The act of dispossession is itself a violent, racist act, Said asserted, based on the assumption that Western colonial settlers can create a narrative which empowers them and deprives the Eastern "other" of his property and history. Orientialism empowered non-Westerners to believe in the inherent racism and imperialism of Western scholarship and politics, and, according to Martin Kramer in his insightful book, *Ivory Towers in the Sand: The Failure of Middle Eastern Studies in America*, is one of Said's lasting contributions to the intellectual climate on campuses when scholars took sides on issues affecting the Middle East. Orientalism, according to Kramer, "also enshrined an acceptable hierarchy of political commitments, with Palestine at the top, followed by the Arab nation and the Islamic world. They were the long-suffering victims of Western racism, American imperialism, and Israeli Zionism—the three legs of the orientalist [sic] stool."[20]

Once the Saidian post-colonialists could neutralize the impact of the West's assessment of the Orient (which for Said and his disciples had come to mean specifically the Middle East), they initiated an entire intellectual enterprise which devalued any scholarship conducted by Westerners, called into question the justice of the imposition of Western culture on non-Western nations, and, in the case of Israel, denounced the creation of this European, colonial settler-state, a cultural "construct" in the midst of passive, less powerful Muslim world. Just as Eurocentric scholars had defined the Orient through the lens of their biased world views, the West had forced the creation of a Eurocentric state of Israel and imposed its racist, imperialist ideology on an unwilling and innocent indigenous population. In fact, that very technique was part of the pernicious aspect of Orientalism, according to Said, through which Orientalists became willing tools of the imperialistic West in its campaigns to subjugate, mollify, and control the East. The Orientalists essentially became agents to the Western powers and, in Said's words, "much of the information and knowledge about Islam. . . that was used by the colonial powers. . . derived from Orientalist scholarship," and "many Islamic specialists were and still are routinely consulted by, and actively work for, governments whose designs in the Islamic world are economic exploitation, domination, or outright aggression."[21]

The negative fallout from this highly-charged intellectual strain still resonates among the campus Left, and, in the view of Professor Bruce Thornton, "Said's incoherent amalgam of dubious postmodern theory, sentimental Third Worldism, glaring historical errors, and Western guilt corrupted not just Middle Eastern Studies departments but other disciplines, too."[22] Northeastern University's M. Shahid Alam, a professor of history, for instance, regularly ranted in the virulent online journal *Counterpunch* about the perfidy of Israel, echoing Said's notion of the hegemonic, racist West imposing its cultural will on the East. "This is the language of racial superiority[,] the doctrine that believes in a hierarchy of races," Alam wrote about Israel, "where the higher races have rights and inferior races are destined for extinction or a marginal existence under the tutelage of higher races. Under the Zionist doctrine, the Jews are a higher race. . . This superiority is also empirically established: the Zionists wanted to take Palestine from the Palestinians and they made it a fact."[23]

Said's charge of Orientalism also stripped Western scholars of their standing in Middle Eastern studies, discrediting them and their potential contribution to scholarly inquiry because of their innate biases and Orientalist orientation. "For a European or America studying the Orient," Said wrote, "there can be no disclaiming the main circumstances of his actuality: that he comes up against the Orient as a European or America first, as an individual second."[24] If Western academics were no longer able to conduct scholarship about the Orient that was authentic and valid, who, then, could? The answer, of course, was clear: Middle Easterners and Arab-Americans, who, after the publication of *Orientalism*, began to fill the academic slots in departments of Middle Eastern studies in increasing numbers in a type of academic affirmative action program. Said's book, said Martin Kramer, "implicitly claimed for them a privileged understanding of the Arab and Islamic East, due not to any individual competence, but to their collective innocence of orientalist [sic] bias. They were unspoiled; they were entitled."[25]

Unfortunately, many of these new academics were also radicalized, and embarked on careers defined by ideology and corrupted scholarship, apologizing for and downplaying the seriousness of the dangerous evolving Islamic movements, condemning the West for impeding the creation of civil societies in the Arab world, and, with increasing and obsessive regularity, demonizing Israel and its chief patron, the United States. Frequently, in their zeal to promote ideology over scholarship, their intellectual output was itself biased, overstated, oppressive—ironically, much like Orientalism in reverse. And the language of academe took on a more vituperative, personal, scathing tone, especially when discussing issues concerning Palestine and Israel. Having been made the mandarins of Middle Eastern studies, these campus radicals invented a new vocabulary for assaulting the West and Israel, avoiding harsh analysis of the endemic flaws of the Middle East and focusing instead on the perceived complicity of the West for having contributed to the Orient's failure to thrive.

But critics of Said, including former Muslim Ibn Warraq, author of *Defending the West: A Critique of Edward Said's* Orientalism, suggested that the Orientalism theory had a wider, more pernicious effect of helping the Arab world avoid analysis of its own faults and explain away its aggression towards the West as being justified in light of perceived oppression it had endured under imperialism. Further, Warraq wrote, "In cultures already immune to self-criticism," "Said helped Muslims and particularly Arabs, perfect their already well-developed sense of self-pity."[26] In fact, the ideology of Orientalism was well-received in the Middle East, precisely because it confirmed what the Arab world wished to believe was the truth about the state of their societies: that the Western powers, in their historical meddling in the affairs and cultures of the Orient, had damaged the social, economic, and civic core of those societies; that in setting up puppet regimes to enforce Western will in the Middle East, the common people were denied autonomy and a civil society; that, in the case of Israel, Palestine had been stolen and permanently occupied, at the expense of the Palestinian Arabs, by the West's outpost, the Zionist regime. To academics who subscribed Said's Marxist vision of a guilty West and an innocent East, their intellectual output began to define the world in Manichean absolutes.

The language of this "scholarship" is often harsh and, when involving Israel, sometimes borders on the kind of raw, anti-Semitic ranting that is ever-present in the state-controlled media of the Arab world. Hamid Dabashi, for instance, Hagop Kevorkian Professor of Iranian Studies and Comparative Literature at Columbia, ensconced in the same department where Said himself once sat, wrote a psychobabble-filled narrative during a visit to Israel which he published in *Al-Ahram Weekly* in which he dehumanizes the entire Jewish state in language that drips with repulsive images and hatred:

> What they call "Israel" is no mere military state. A subsumed militarism, a systemic mendacity with an ingrained violence constitutional to the very fusion of its fabric, has penetrated the deepest corners of what these people have to call their "soul". . . Half a century of systematic maiming and murdering of another people has left its deep marks on the faces of these people. . . There is. . . a vulgarity of character that is bone-deep and structural to the skeletal vertebrae of its culture. No people can perpetrate what these people and their parents and grandparents have perpetrated on Palestinians and remain immune to the cruelty of their own deeds.[27]

This lurid, hateful language used in the critiquing Israel, given academic respectability by an Ivy League professor, has also begun to show itself in the attitudes and language of students—who themselves regularly engage in half-truths, counter-historical appraisals of Middle Eastern history, and emotional outbursts bordering on what, in a different context, might well be considered anti-Semitic hate speech. Mariam Moustafa, for example, a student at what is considered the ground zero of anti-Israelism on campus, the University of California at Irvine, wrote a diatribe in the school's student newspaper, *New University*, on the occasion of Israel's sixtieth anniversary. "Here's to 60 years of claiming peace and unity," she wrote, caustically, "yet ruthlessly murdering Palestinians and other Arabs in neighboring countries. . . Here's to cutting down hundreds upon hundreds of olive trees, many of which had existed in Palestine twice as long as your disgrace of a nation. Lastly, here's to allowing the 4 million [actually, 1.5 million] Palestinians in Gaza to live well below the poverty line, leading to the starvation of many men, women and children who did nothing wrong but be born under your occupation."[28]

Even more dangerous on campus than the seething rage at Israel, and the reverence for everything Palestinian, is how whole academic departments have been blinded by this one-sided, anti-Israel, anti-American ideology, and how, as a result, faculty hiring, curriculum development, fellowships, symposia, and lecture series are shaped by this myopic approach to what passes as scholarship about the Middle East. The legacy of Edward Said is a key component of that sorry state of affairs, but so, too, is the spurious source of much of the funding for endowed professorships, entire research centers and programs, and the bricks and mortar in which much of this activity takes place.

Princeton University's Institute for the Transregional Study of the Contemporary Middle East, North Africa, and Central Asia, for instance, was established with a gift from Prince Moulay Hicham Benabdallah of Morocco, a 1985 Princeton graduate himself. Does the source of a center's funding influence how and what is taught there? Apparently so, based on the topic of some of the annual fellowships offered by the Institute: in 2005, as one example, the fellowship "research theme" was "Society under Occupation: Contemporary Palestinian Politics, Culture and Identity." That theme may or may not have reaped some valid and important scholarship, but it is clear from the fellowship description—replete with omissions about terrorism, distortions about a Palestinian "homeland," and clear anti-Israel bias—that the underlying purpose seemed to invite yet another opportunity to denigrate Israel and enshrine the Palestinian cause, a point of view that no doubt pleases donors with very explicit expectations about the nature of the scholarship their donations are meant to inspire:

> Israel's occupation of the West Bank and Gaza Strip has now persisted for over thirty-seven years, during which time the number of Israeli settlers in the occupied territories has grown to hundreds of thousands and Israeli control over the territories has been strengthened by the use of checkpoints, by-pass roads, military engagement and, most recently, the construction of a wall separating Palestinians from Israel and from one another. Despite living under occupation, as refugees, or outside their homeland, Palestinians have maintained a vibrant cultural and political life. In 2005–2006, the Institute will focus research on contemporary Palestinian life, both under occupation and in the diaspora. We wish to explore Palestinian culture, society and religious life, as well as Palestinian national identity and contemporary Palestinian political, legal and ethical thought. We also hope to examine Palestinians' understanding of dispossession and occupation, and their visions of a post-occupation future.[29]

Charles Jacobs, former president of the David Project, the Boston-based organization that produced the film "Columbia Unbecoming" about the controversies in the University's MEALAC department, has suggested that "Palestinianism and Said-ism [sic]. . . are the orthodoxies spreading throughout the University," that this conflation in academe hampers actual scholarship and is actually as biased and myopic as the scholarly pursuits Said had accused the Orientalists of practicing themselves. This is intellectually perilous, Jacobs thought, because while at the same time "Palestinianism obscures—and is meant to obscure—any academically credible understanding of the region by discounting the plight of ethnic, religious and racial minorities in the Arab world. . . , Said-ism enforces silence about the victims of jihad, dhimmi-tude [sic], and Arab tyranny with threats to label people 'Orientalists'—a curse akin to our culture's most powerful insult, 'racist.' Professors and students influenced by Said are under pressure to speak no criticism of anything done by Arabs or Muslims."[30] The fact that most of the leading intellectual lights of Middle Eastern studies failed to detect the flowering of Islamism, ignored warning signs of jihad, were totally unprepared for the events on September 11, 2001, and then subsequently attacked the War on Terror as an Islamophobic, neoconservative, xenophobic overreaction to justifiable anger against the West all seem to give credence to Dr. Jacobs observation that Saidism, rather than encouraging introspection and analysis, served to retard real scholarly inquiry.

"Obsessed with the obsession" of Palestinianism, as Ruth Wisse put it, the Saidists were blind to the realities of the evolving Arab and Muslim world, and allowed a narrow ideology and a rabid hatred of Israel and the West define how universities would henceforth frame inquiry and discussion of the Middle East.[31]

ẽ Chapter 3

Israel's Academic Ideological Detractors

The West's wide embrace of Palestinianism has been led, for the most part, by the intellectual elites, whose own biases against Israel and the United States serve to animate, and widely promote, the campaign to vilify, defame, and delegitimize Israel. While the ideological antics of anti-Israel student groups, as will be discussed in Chapter 8, are the most visible aspects of the hate-Israel agenda, this acting out and shrill rhetoric from students would be inconsequential were it not for the full intellectual and moral support this movement enjoys from faculty members—those with the prestige and academic muscle to lend credibility and influence to the war of ideas against the Jewish state.

After all, it is faculty members who are able to host academic conferences and symposia in which to demonize Israel. It is senior academics who edit scholarly journals in which the Israeli/Palestinian conflict is debated and critiqued, generally to the detriment of Israel. Professors with radical views of Middle East politics bring those attitudes to the classroom, and often serve as faculty advisors to student groups hosting anti-Israel events and speakers. High-visibility and influential academics from departments of Middle East studies are regularly called upon by the State Department, think tanks, and the media to prepare white papers, policy recommendations, and op-eds in the *New York Times*, *Los Angeles Times*, and *Washington Post*. And since, as discussed, the Left has a disproportionately large representation in college faculties, faculty promotions and tenure are ordinarily offered to like-minded ideologues; and when scholarly books are written about the Israeli-Palestinian conflict, these works invariably are intellectually biased and become part of the continuing 60+ year long propaganda war against Israel.

This liberal slant of university faculties has made it inevitable that many college professors question the integrity of Zionism, if not forthrightly denounce the very existence of Israel as a moral stain on the world that oppresses Arabs and tars the United States as an accomplice in this perceived unjustified oppression. The self-righteous professors who perpetually denounce Israel, though, may or may not have a great moral commitment to the Palestinians at all. In fact, that is often incidental to their primary objective: not to actually assist Palestinian self-determination with constructive, tactical advice and support—which has always been sorely, and visibly, lacking—but to weaken support for Israel with the ultimate intention, shared by Israel's jihadist foes, of eventually eliminating it altogether. The phony rectitude which they use to insulate themselves from critique comforts those who would otherwise see the fundamental moral cruelty of their assaults of Israel. And they are also craven in their self-righteousness for taking such a strident stance against Israel, a point of view and a philosophical approach which requires no courage in the Jew-hating West.

In fact, because the Arab world, the UN, many in the EU, and, sadly, a large portion of the Left in the West shares a similar enmity toward Israel, these academic fellow travelers have found to their delight—as Stephen Walt and John Mearsheimer discovered, for example—that virulent anti-Israelism not only entails little risk for one's academic career, but the exact opposite is true: the more outrageous and morally-imbecilic one's evaluation of the Israeli/Palestinian question is, the more likely that academic notoriety, visibility, and professional success will follow. In other words, academe has created a perverse incentive for academics to elevate Palestinianism and vilify Israel.

The sanctimonious bleating from campuses is unending where Israel is concerned, and the denunciations against it come not just from quarters one might expect, but also from Jewish academics themselves, anti-Zionists who, in a peculiar act of introjection, attempt to psychically expunge themselves from the liberal guilt that condoning Zionism would bring upon them. The anti-Zionist Jew, as Ruth Wisse has suggested, is a logical, though troubling, result of Jewish liberals who, in feeling an affinity for the political underdog—in this case, the Palestinians—have forced themselves to abandon support for the Jewish state, lest they violate their own liberal beliefs. "The paradoxical political behavior of the American Jew," Wisse observed, "could in fact much more accurately be described as the desire to dissociate oneself from a people under attack by advertising one's own goodness."[1]

Of course, "advertising one's virtue" is rampant among the campus Leftists, many of whom feel that, because they seek social justice for the Palestinians and are attempting to strike down the new Israeli version of apartheid, anything they say or do to delegitimize Israel is acceptable, even necessary. Thus, they hector Israel to mend its political ways not only to end Palestinian suffering, but also, they allege, for the good of both Israelis and Diaspora Jews. These fatuous professors, who never have had to face any physical threat more serious than being bumped while waiting in line for a latte at Starbucks, are very willing to scold Israel when it defends itself from unceasing rocket attacks from Gaza meant to murder Israeli civilians. These same professors, many of the vilest critics of whom are from departments of humanities, literature, anthropology, history, and sociology, are, without any expertise in military affairs, eager to advise Israeli officials on the rules of war and denounce the lack of "proportionality" in Israel's attempts to defend its population from jihadist murderers. And so eager are they to publicly assert their righteousness as defenders of the Palestinian cause, they embrace and "eroticize" terroristic violence and willingly align themselves with Israel's deadly foes who seek its annihilation, catering, as essayist David Solway lyrically put it, "to the ammoniac hatred of the current brood of crypto-antisemites posing as anti-Zionists."[2]

Thus, New York University's TONY JUDT, who glibly referred to Israel as an "anachronism" because he could not abide its existence in the Levant amid a sea of totalitarian, dysfunctional Arab states, looked at Israel's security fence and saw, not a protective device for ending the slaughter of Jewish civilians by Islamist madmen who will not accept the existence of Israel at all, but a symbol of the moral imperfection and malediction of Israel itself. "The 'fence,'" he wrote in an incendiary *New York Review of Books* piece, "actually an armored zone of ditches, fences, sensors, dirt roads. . . , and a wall up to twenty-eight feet tall in places—occupies, divides, and steals Arab farmland; it will destroy villages, livelihoods, and whatever remains of Arab-Jewish community." Missing from his description, naturally, is the reason the wall exists in the first place; namely, as a response to unceasing terrorist attacks on Israeli citizens for no reason other than the fact that they were Jewish. Instead, like other disingenuous critics who describe it as the "apartheid wall," in Judt's mind, Israel's intent was simply to steal more Arab land and to inconvenience Palestinians by making it more difficult for them to be murderers. "Like the Berlin Wall," he continued, the security barrier "confirms the moral and institutional bankruptcy of the regime it is intended to protect." It does not confirm the fact that Arabs are perfectly willing to continue their genocidal assault of Jews, of course, nor is his simplistic analogy to the Berlin Wall even relevant, since that wall was designed to keep East Berliners from freely leaving their lands, not as protective means of thwarting assault from mortal foes without.

In reality, however, what distressed Judt the most was not, characteristically, the actual suffering of the Palestinians. No, what bothered Judt was how Israel's actions reflected on him as a Jew and a liberal, as Ruth Wisse had observed in other liberals, and for that he was unwilling to take a moral stand with the Middle East's only democracy. "The behavior of a self-described Jewish state affects the way everyone else looks at Jews," Judt wrote. Then, with same perverse inverted thinking frequently employed by those who either hate Israel or hate America, or both, he ascribes blame for anti-Zionism on the Zionists themselves, or, as is done in the case of the United States when speaking about 9–11, excuses Islamic rage as the product of Western imperialism and hegemony. "The increased incidence of attacks on Jews in Europe and elsewhere is primarily attributable to misdirected efforts, often by young Muslims, to get back at Israel," as if Israel's misdeeds are widely accepted and obvious to everyone, and violent responses to its existence are understandable. And why is it the responsibility of Israel or Jews throughout the world if Muslim youth, living in Europe and the West, no less, and not even in the Middle East feel that they are justified in "getting back at Israel"?

Blaming anti-Semitism on Jews themselves is a long-used, perverse mental trick which, of course, absolves the anti-Semite from the offense of which he himself is guilty but wants to assign to others. But the question Judt and other crypto anti-Semites and apologists for Islamic rage might better ask is: what exactly has Israel done, other than exist, to induce this rage against it? It is far more likely that the loathsome sermons emanating from mosques inciting enmity towards Israel and Jews, not to mention the Jew-hatred manifested in the state-run Arab press, may have contributed to the irrational psychosis that manifests itself in Jew hatred.

What does Judt's conclude from his analysis? "The depressing truth is that Israel's current behavior is not just bad for America, though it surely is," he wrote. "It is not even just bad for Israel itself, as many Israelis silently acknowledge. The depressing truth is that Israel today is bad for the Jews."[3]

That "depressing truth" may be self-evident to Judt and his ilk, but that kind of characterization of Israel invites critique of its own, something that often happens when those who support Israel answer back to such calumnies and accuse Judt, and others, of bias, of moral incoherence, of a misreading or contortion of history and fact, or, sometimes, of apparent anti-Semitism. One well-documented instance of this reaction occurred when Stephen Walt and John Mearsheimer published *The Israel Lobby* (discussed in detail in Chapter 4), a work that purported to reveal the sinister workings of a cabal of pro-Israel Jews and others that negatively affected America's standing in the world. One claim made by the authors was that the dreaded "Lobby," because of its broad political influence, could control discussion about Israel and suppress any critical discussion of Israel and Zionism, a complaint often heard from vociferous Israel-haters who wonder why their noxious ideas never gain traction in the marketplace of ideas. So in a 2007 conference at the University of Chicago titled "In Defense of Academic Freedom," remarkably to defend the odious Norman Finkelstein, Judt and an assortment of the usual suspects in the anti-Israel contingent were empanelled to bray about how academic free speech was being threatened due to the Lobby, and that criticism of Israel was being derailed by ominous foes who opposed spreading calumny and libels about Zionism and Israel.

Judt was quick to announce that those who claimed that the Lobby truly existed were subject to charges of anti-Semitism or worse, but, in his mind, that should not matter—being morally-indignant over Israel's many transgressions was more important. "If you stand up here and say," Judt said at the conference, ". . . that there is an Israel lobby, that. . . there are a set of Jewish organizations, who do work, both in front of the scenes and behind the scenes, to prevent certain kinds of conversations, certain kinds of criticism. . . , you are coming very close to saying that there is a *de facto* conspiracy or, if you like, plot or collaboration to prevent public policy moving in a certain way. . . — and that sounds an awful lot like, you know, the *Protocols of the Elders of Zion* and the conspiratorial theory of the Zionist Occupational Government and so on—well if it sounds like it it's unfortunate, but that's just how it is."

Responding to the charge that accusations about the existence of an Israel Lobby had gained support from some unsavory quarters (David Duke, for example, enthusiastically supported Walt and Mearsheimer's thesis), Judt saw no connection between his own moral incoherence and that of cranks on the far Right and far Left who share similar conspiracist views. "We cannot calibrate the truths that we're willing to speak, if we think they're true," he told the conference attendees, "according to the idiocies of people who happen to agree with us for their reasons." Sharing poisonous ideas with fringe thinkers sometimes "puts you in bed sometimes with the wrong people," Judt contended; nevertheless, he felt that his self-righteousness was superior as part of an upstanding ideological mission to destroy Israel, that "you can't help it if idiots once every 24 hours with their stopped political clock are on the same time as you. You have to say what you know to be true and be willing to defend it on your grounds and then accept the fact that people in bad faith will accuse you of having defended it or aligned yourself with the others on their grounds—that's what freedom of speech means—it's very uncomfortable."[4]

Other courageous academic souls have decided to endure the "very uncomfortable" experience of vilifying Israel beyond all rational limits, as well, including enough Jewish professors, like Judt, that it has led observers, such as Gabriel Schoenfeld, to be concerned that these Israel-hating Jews are exploited by non-Jewish anti-Semites in their own crusades against Israel and Zionism because their poisonous utterances seem acceptable when coming from Jewish sources. "Such 'renegade' Jews," Schoenfeld observed, "play a critical role today in legitimizing the hatred that, coming from non-Jewish voices, might seem unfit for discussion in polite company."[5]

MARC H. ELLIS, a professor of political science at Baylor University in Waco, Texas, is an example of Schoenfeld's 'renegade' Jews, an academic acolyte of Holocaust-minimizing, Israel-hating Norman Finkelstein, who sees the Holocaust as an unfortunate event whose principal purpose was to enable Zionism to create Israel at the cost and to the eternal detriment of the Palestinians. Ellis is Jewish and contemplated the idea that this Jewishness makes him one of the 'chosen people," and even wondered at the seeming contradiction of a Holocaust being visited upon a people supposedly under the protective care of a loving God. But he was also quick to make the odious comparison, ubiquitous in anti-Israel circles, of Israelis having become the new Nazis. "If Jews are set apart," Ellis wrote, "can we also thank God for other times in history, at Auschwitz for example? Does our sense of being chosen and set apart also allow some Jews to act against others, Palestinians for example, in a manner that too closely resembles ways that others have acted against us?"[6]

What is worse, Ellis contended, the ascendency of a politically and militarily powerful Jewish state has created a new reality with which he, and much of the Arab world, have never been able to abide; namely, a resilient and strong Jewish nation arisen from the ashes of the Nazi Final Solution when Jews were solely victims. "Holocaust theology," Ellis wrote, using the word 'theology' in the same cynical way that Finkelstein uses the word 'industry,' "emerging out of reflection on the death camps, represents the Jewish people as we were, helpless and suffering; it does not and cannot speak of the people we are today and who we are becoming—powerful and often oppressive." But while Ellis can abide the fact that Jews—as they are supposedly defined by the existence of Israel—have gained autonomy and strength as a bi-product their negative experiences, that "Holocaust theology argues correctly for Jews to be empowered," he was concerned that this 'theology' "lacks the frame work and skills of analysis to investigate the cost of that empowerment."

Ellis also shared the cruel view that the very existence of Israel is problematic, because of the great suffering, "the Nakba," it unleashed against the Palestinians. "If for Jews the Holocaust remains the ultimate shattering," Ellis wrote, "a further shattering has occurred in response to the Holocaust—the formation and expansion of the state of Israel." Moreover, Israel's treatment of the Palestinians negates any notion that the creation of the Jewish state represented "a reformation of Jewish life." But, Ellis wrote, echoing Judt's idea that Israel is also bad for Israelis and Jews, "for many Jews," the dispersion and oppression of the Palestinian people makes this view impossible to hold, because "when a state is built on exclusivity and necessarily the exclusion of others, then isolation and militarism is the norm. Ingathering can become another form of shattering and Jewish redemption from the Holocaust in the creation of a Jewish state becomes a disaster for Palestinians and for Jews as well."[7]

Compared to the almost polite denunciations against Israel by Ellis and Judt, vitriolic JOEL KOVEL, late of Bard College, another Jewish defamer of Israel, did not try to mask his contempt for Israel when he asserted that he understood "the desire to smash Zionism, for after all, Israel is an abomination [that] has caused endless suffering to innocent people," and the delightful observation that "Zionism is racism and that Israel is racist in the fullest sense of the word." Kovel's perverse desire to see Israel "smashed" means that he was fully willing to embrace the tactic of the weak so often employed against Israel, namely, terrorism. He not only granted Palestinians a legal right to undertake terror that they did not actually enjoy, but he justified the murderous acts of suicide bombers by using the specious argument that when Israel bulldozes a Palestinian militant's house, it is as much a terrorist act as a suicide bombing inflicted on innocent Jewish civilians. "The majority of Palestinian suicide bombers, Kovel asserted in an interview, apparently without the benefit of any actual data, "have been victims of house demolitions. It is this component in armed struggle—the desire to retaliate and to punish others in the way that you have been punished—that has to be overcome." Missing from his analysis, of course, is why homes are bulldozed in the first place, as if the IDF randomly entered Arab property for no reason and leveled homes. It is, naturally, not part of Kovel's appraisal of Israel's existential challenge that Palestinian homes are destroyed because they are lived in by terrorists, or are used a staging areas for lethal rocket launches, or are built over tunnels through which arms are smuggled to kill more Jews.

In fact, when Kovel then offered his view that "if one has been terrorized, the temptation to retaliate with terror is great," he raised a valid point, but had precisely reversed the reality, and sequence of events, of the Arab/Israeli conflict. As much as Kovel and other of Israel's foes wish to believe it, the creation of Israel was not itself an act of violence against the Arab world that would justify, and excuse, 60+ subsequent years of retaliatory terrorist attacks. Terror against Israel was initiated in 1948 and 1967, not to mention in the first and second intifadas; and, yes, Kovel is correct that the "temptation to retaliate" is great, even sometimes necessary, but *for Israel*, not, as he rationalized, for the Palestinians—despite Kovel's counterfactual, but oft-cited contention "that the Palestinian right to resist occupation is enshrined in international law, and that the Palestinian armed struggle against occupation is legitimate." And Kovel was nothing if not compassionate for the Palestinian plight: "If I had a homeland and it was occupied by a foreign force," he said, "I would be part of an armed struggle,"[8] ignoring the fact that the people he now refers to as Palestinians never had a sovereign "homeland" and in the areas that Israel now occupies it does not do so as a foreign power, but as a High Contracting Party with a bundle of rights protected by international law.

In February 2009, Bard, apparently distressed with the rants of this inveterate Israel-hater, released Kovel from his position at the College. In a letter he sent out to Bard faculty in which he decried his firing, Kovel, of course, left no doubt where to assign blame for his unwarranted termination and how it was emblematic of the negative consequences faced by those who spoke against Israel. "If the world stands outraged at Israeli aggression in Gaza," he wrote, concerning Israel's Operation Cast Lead then currently winding down, "it should also be outraged at institutions in the United States that grant Israel impunity. In my view, Bard College is one such institution. It has suppressed critical engagement with Israel and Zionism, and therefore has enabled abuses such as have occurred and are occurring in Gaza. This notion is, of course, not just descriptive of a place like Bard. It is also the context within which the critic of such a place and the Zionist ideology it enables becomes marginalized, and then removed."[9]

The notion, expressed by Kovel and others, that terrorism is not only a legitimate reaction to Israeli oppression, but even has redemptive virtue ingrained in its own violent nature, is another repeated sentiment latent in the Left's sometimes transparent admiration for armed resistance. Nowhere was it more clearly revealed, perhaps, than in a bathetic ode written in the student newspaper in 2002 by the jihad-supporting JULIO CESAR PINO, associate professor of Latin American History at Kent State University, who converted to Islam in 2000. The grotesque poem, "Singing out prayer for a youth martyr," was an exhortation to a teenage girl, Ayat al-Akras, a Palestinian suicide bomber who had made her personal sacrifice for the cause by slaughtering two Israelis civilians in Jerusalem while they were buying groceries:

> You are not a terrorist, Ayat. The real terrorists are those who some 100 years ago hijacked a beautiful religion and transformed it into a real estate venture. Glancing around the world, they saw in Palestine 'a land without a people, for a people without a land,' as their spokesmen and women chant ad nauseaum [sic]. The Zion of the concertina wire, F-16 bomber death planes and tank crews collecting skulls and shedding martyrs' blood. The birthplace of your ancestor, and mine, the Palestinian pacifist Joshua ben Josef, is now a battle zone—with Christians, Muslims and peace-loving Jews trapped inside Bethlehem.
>
> Your last cry, by gesture rather than the spoken word, was 'Stop, thief! This is not your land and we are a people.' I can assure you, Ayat, that the whole world stopped to listen. Even the numbskull who parades as president of the United States heard you, and, following the text written for him by his handlers, expressed astonishment at how a teenager could perpetrate such an act. Simply, it is pronounced "justice" and spelled C-O-U-R-A-G-E.[10]

When he was not busy composing poetry to pay tribute to murderers, Pino apparently also helped spread the word of jihad wherever he could, contributing to a now-defunct website called Global War, self-described as "a jihadist news service [and providing] battle dispatches, training manuals, and jihad videos to our brothers worldwide."[11] After this and a number of other of Pino's hateful rants had been examined in a series of investigative articles by Mike Adams, professor of criminology at the University of North Carolina Wilmington, Pino allegedly took it upon himself to send Professor Adams a personal message, on the sixth anniversary of September 11th, extolling the majesty of Islamic jihad:

> O, Slaves of Zion and Amerika, Arise! The shaheed (martyr) who yearns to die, and has prayed for this moment all his life, has come to rescue you!. . . The martyr is performing an action that is the culmination of a whole life's struggle, and in turn gives meaning to that life. . . The shaheed, May God Be Pleased with Him, is not only the perfect soldier, but the perfect Muslim. All of life is preparation, and striving for, martyrdom. . . The intention for martyrdom is elevated to a higher status than the final act itself. A soldier walking, without shaking, into a field of fire courts death but does not desire it from birth. . . [T]he Muslim knows no continents, regions, nations or tribes but acknowledges the existence of only two groups of human beings; men of faith—his Brothers—and the kaaffir

(unbelievers and apostates), those ungrateful and rebellious beings that, like Satan himself, opted for disobedience. . . The Muslim is commanded in the Quran to 'fight oppression and overcome tribulation, until all religion is for Allah.' This is the true meaning of jihad. . . Jihad is constant battle, in all places and at all times, with those forces, natural and supernatural, that would remove the Muslim from the sacred realm and into the profane . . .The martyr has no time for peace; no time to be cynical, or pessimistic. . . Not by chance did Mohammed Atta's 'Instructions for the Final Night' counsel him [sic] make these his last words before crashing into the World Trade Center. Amen.[12]

Conversion to Islam and an admiration for the Quran, of course, do not in themselves disqualify a history professor from teaching in an unbiased, factual way in his classrooms. But an instructor who glorified murderers, openly and widely called for jihad against the West, and claimed that Israel was responsible for a 'genocide of the Palestinians,' clearly has an ideological agenda, not uncommon among his Leftist fellow travelers, that reveals part of the intellectual rot on campuses. Not surprisingly, one of Pino's students, when evaluating the quality of his teaching on RateMyProfessors.com, without a hint of irony suggested that the content of Pino's instruction "makes noam chomsky [sic] look patriotic."[13]

And like Noam Chomsky, professor Pino and the hate-Israel Left on campus also indict another party in the Arab/Israeli conflict, namely, the United States—both for its material and moral support and for its own perceived offense in oppressing the Palestinians by seeming to side, morally and politically, with Israel. UC Irvine's MARK LEVINE, associate professor of history, shares that view, including his belief that Israeli oppression is not only facilitated by, but also the ideological offspring of, American complicity. In an article with the disingenuous title "We're All Israelis Now?" in September of 2001, just days after the attacks on American soil, LeVine floated the odious notion that, like Israel, the United States was attacked because of what it had done itself to inspire anger from jihadist madmen. "I fear we are more like Israelis than we realize," he wrote, "because even after extreme violence has been perpetrated against us by those whose oppression we have supported and even enforced, we refuse to engage in the honest introspection of what our role has been in generating the kind of hatred that turns commuter jets into cruise missiles." Never mind that Osama bin Laden himself mentioned the Palestinian issue only incidentally in a list of grievances against the West that he himself used as a pretext for the deadly attack. LeVine's thinking once again justifies terror as an expected, and acceptable, tool against sovereign nations, and assigns blame to the victim rather than the perpetrator.

In LeVine's worldview, Israel, like America, essentially receives what it deserves, based on his own peculiar set of moral principles. The United States and Israel are co-villains in the continuing subjugation of the innocent Palestinians, and any violence bubbling up from that cauldron and inflicted on Jewish civilians has as its root the social injustice that Israel itself embodies. "In Israel the violence and terrorism of the latest intifada cannot be understood except as emerging out of decades of occupation, discrimination and dispossession," LeVine suggested. "Yet Israel continues and even intensifies these practices, safe in the knowledge that they have the power and support to ignore the roots of the conflict with Palestinians and avenge the casualties it produces daily. Forgotten in the process is the prophetic injunction to fight oppression and correct injustice, or the warning that 'those who sow injustice will reap calamity.' American tax dollars have overruled both."[14]

The theme of U.S.-Israeli co-dependency in a campaign of imperialist aggression is oft-repeated in the halls of academe, generally with the intention of assigning blame for the failure of peace in the Middle East on the malefaction of Israel and blind complicity with which the United States tolerates or even encourages those outrages. Thus, Hamas's campaign to create an Islamic state inside of Gaza, its efforts to delegitimize the Palestinian Authority as a political entity able to participate in peace negotiations with Israel or even represent the nascent Palestinian state, or its annoying habit of launching thousands of rockets and mortars into Israeli neighborhoods while it uses its own civilians as human shields—all of these actions, not to mention the Arab world's refusal to either recognize Israel or accept a state for the Palestinians in the many instances when it was offered statehood, of course, rarely are mentioned as possible factors in the failure of peace.

It is Israel's actions alone—that and the support of the United States—which are the root cause, wrote University of Wisconsin-Madison's JENNIFER LOEWENSTEIN, Associate Director of the Middle East Studies Program. "Israel has made its view known again and again in the strongest possible language, the language of military might, of threats, intimidation, harassment, defamation and degradation," she wrote during Israel's Cast Lead incursions into Gaza in early 2009. "Israel, with the unconditional and approving support of the United States, has made it dramatically clear to the entire world over and over and over again, repeating in action after action that it will accept no viable Palestinian state next to its borders. . . The more horrific the actions on the ground, the more insistent are the words of peace. To listen and watch without hearing or seeing allows the indifference, the ignorance and complicity to continue and deepens with each grave our collective shame."[15]

Harvard's SARA ROY, a researcher at the University's Center for Middle East Studies (CMES), was inclined to absolve Hamas from any wrongdoing, as well, carelessly overlooking the fact the since 2005, when Israel withdrew every Jew from Gaza, some 8000 rockets had rained down into Israeli neighborhoods, not with the intention of killing soldiers but to murder civilians while they slept, shopped, or went to school. She and Boston University professor Augustus Richard Norton co-authored an article for the *Christian Science Monitor* in which they conjured up the fantasy of a "New Hamas," a now-benign political group the authors felt were deserving of recognition by Western diplomats. And in her own op-ed in the *Monitor*, she only started counting rockets lobbed into Israel from Gaza after, she said, Israel violated some illusory cease fire of which apparently only she and the "new" Hamas were aware. It was only Israel's defensive reaction to the attempted murder of its citizens that prompted Hamas rocket attacks from Gaza, nothing else. "Since Nov. 4," Roy wrote, "when Israel effectively broke the truce with Hamas by attacking Gaza on a scale then unprecedented—a fact now buried with Gaza's dead—the violence has escalated as Hamas responded by sending hundreds of rockets into Israel to kill Israeli civilians. It is reported that Israel's strategy is to hit Hamas military targets," Roy glibly observed, never missing an opportunity to stress the eternal victimhood of the Palestinians, "but explain that difference to my Palestinian friends who must bury their children."[16]

In the morally-imbecilic pantheon of the academic defamers of Israel, perhaps no single individual has emerged as the paradigmatic libeler, the most vitriolic and widely-followed character in an inglorious retinue as NORMAN FINKELSTEIN, late of DePaul University. Finkelstein has loudly and notoriously pronounced his extreme views on the Middle East, not to mention his loathing of what he has called the Holocaust "industry," something he has called an "outright extortion racket;" in fact, he blames Jews themselves for anti-Semitism. Writing in *Beyond Chutzpah: On the Misuse of Anti-Semitism and the Abuse of History*, his off-handed, sardonic response to Harvard professor Alan Dershowitz's own book, *Chutzpah*, Finkelstein accused Jewish leadership, a group he defines as a "repellent gang of plutocrats, hoodlums, and hucksters," of creating a "combination of economic and political power," from which "has sprung, unsurprisingly, a mindset of Jewish superiority." He has called Nobel Prize winner Eli Wiesel, Holocaust survivor and author of *Night*, a "clown." What is more, he continued, echoing the familiar refrain that it Jews themselves who inspire anti-Semitism, "from this lethal brew of formidable power, chauvinistic arrogance, feigned (or imagined) victimhood, and Holocaust-immunity to criticism has sprung a terrifying recklessness and ruthlessness on the part of American Jewish elites. Alongside Israel, they are the main fomenters of anti-Semitism in the world today."[17]

Finkelstein's best known work, *The Holocaust Industry: Reflections On The Exploitation of Jewish Suffering*, cruelly minimizes the magnitude of the Holocaust while simultaneously making the perverse accusation that it is used by Zionists to extract sympathy from the world community and to justify the oppression and subjugation of the Palestinians by Israelis. Despite its popularity with anti-Semites, Islamists, and neo-Nazis worldwide, one critic, Brown University genocide expert Omer Bartov, described the book in a *New York Times* review as "a novel variation on the anti-Semitic forgery, 'The Protocols of the Elders of Zion' . . , brimming with the same indifference to historical facts, inner contradictions, strident politics and dubious contextualizations; and it oozes with the same smug sense of moral and intellectual superiority. . . ."[18] Historian David Greenberg was similarly critical of the level of scholarship in *The Holocaust Industry*, calling it "a hate-filled screed" filled with "pseudo-scholarship, extreme anti-Israel ideology and—there is no way around it—anti-Semitism. And it stinks."[19]

Finkelstein, who was denied tenure at DePaul and then fired (his fourth such experience at a university), has now also adopted the position that this professional set-back is the direct result of being bold enough to speak up against Zionism and Israel, and he has, in his view, been punished into silence accordingly. Despite this analysis of why his professional academic career has stalled, Finkelstein has now become what Washington University professor Edward Alexander called "the dream-Jew of the world's anti-Semites"[20] and regularly visits college campuses nationwide to speak at rallies, anti-Israel events, and symposia and conferences where anti-Israel, anti-American biases infect scholarship and undermine the credibility of the events. In fact, suggested StandWithUs's Roz Rothstein, Finkelstein's "true occupation is as a member of a traveling circus, a freak show of anti-Semites who promote anti-Israel propaganda from campus to campus."[21]

In 2009, for instance, Finkelstein's web site's calendar of appearances included, from January until April alone, some 29 events, sponsored by such a predictable collection of radical anti-Israel campus groups as, among others: Solidarity for Palestinian Human Rights & Colour Connected (University of British Columbia); Palestine Solidarity Network, Canada Palestine Cultural Association, University of Alberta Muslim Students' Association, University of Alberta Political Science Department; Levantine Cultural Center, Middle East Studies Student Initiative and The Center for Global Peace and Conflict Studies/UCI (UC Irvine); Students for Justice in Palestine, Muslim Cultural Student Association (Northwestern); Africana Studies and Research Center (Cornell University); Oxford University Islamic Society; Muslim Law Student Association, Undergraduate Muslim Student Association, Middle Eastern Law Student Association (Wayne State); Fordham Students for Solidarity, Fordham Anti-War Coalition, New School Radical Student Union, Hunter College Campus Anti-War Network; Emory Advocates for Justice in Palestine—Israeli Apartheid Week; Muslim Student Association, Muslim Women of Maryland, and Organization of Arab Students (University of Maryland); and the Palestine Solidarity Committee, Political Science Department, Middle East Studies Program (California State University, Chico).[22]

While Finkelstein was busy demonizing Israel and America at appearances such as these, he coddled homicidal Palestinians and defended the terror of Hezbollah. In a television interview in January 2008, for example, he crowed that he had "no problem saying that I do want to express solidarity with [Hezbollah], and I'm not going to be a coward and a hypocrite about it. I don't care about Hezbollah as a political organization. I don't know much about their politics, and anyhow, it's irrelevant," an odd statement coming from a scholar who pretends to be an expert on the Middle East's politics and the political nature of the players there. And even if the Lebanese people chose terrorist thugs to represent them and do their political will, for Finkelstein that is no issue, specifically since it is Israel upon whom the violence of Hezbollah will be wrought. After all, Finkelstein contended, "There is a fundamental principle: People have the right to defend their country from foreign occupiers, and people have the right to defend their country from invaders who are destroying their country. And that, to me, is a very basic, elementary, and uncomplicated question."

Finkelstein was also quick draw the United States into the conversation, too, suggesting that Hezbollah's resistance was an act of courage in confronting oppression, not terroristic jihad against Western democracies. "Israel and the United States are attacking, because they will not allow any military resistance to their control of the region," Finkelstein said. "That's the problem. If Hizbullah laid down its arms, and said, 'We will do whatever the Americans say,' you wouldn't have a war—that's true. But you'd also be the slaves of the Americans. I have to respect those who refuse to be slaves."[23]

And why were there hostilities in the first place between Lebanon and Israel? According to Finkelstein, "because Israel is determined, with the United States, to put the Arabs in their place and to keep them in their place. Now, how can I not respect those who say 'no' to that?,"[24] meaning that the professor was perfectly willing to let terrorist thugs operate lawlessly inside a sovereign nation to wage war against Israelis and his own countrymen.

In 2009, when Israel was pounding Hamas strongholds to weaken the terrorist underbelly and minimize the likelihood of continuing rocket attacks into Southern Israeli towns, Finkelstein, with apologetics matching those of Sara Roy, wildly proclaimed it was Hamas, not Israel, who had kept the truce and was softening its rhetoric, and it was Hamas, not Israel, who actually wanted peace. Who was the impediment to peace? According to Finkelstein, "Those who are against this settlement are the US or Israel, backed by the US. So when Hamas was becoming moderate and holding to the cease-fire it agreed in June 2008, it was showing herself to be a credible negotiating partner. Hamas was standing by its word," presumably not the words of its charter that proclaims that "Israel will exist and will continue to exist until Islam will obliterate it, just as it obliterated others before it." Even in December of 2009, when the Obama administration was encouraging the quick creation of two states—Palestinian and Jewish—living side by side in peace, Hamas Prime Minister Ismail Haniyeh openly proclaimed that the expulsion of Israel from Gaza was simply a phased process, "just a step toward liberating all of Palestine." And lest anyone be confused about what the actual borders of the envisioned Palestinian state would be if Hamas was drawing the boundaries, Haniyeh articulated the reality that pro-Palestinians never acknowledge, namely, that a Palestinian state will replace, not co-exist with, Israel. "Brothers and sisters," he said, "we will not be satisfied with Gaza. Hamas looks toward the whole of Palestine,"[25] in other words, from the River to the Sea.

Despite its own founding documents, and repeated public statements by its leaders, which commit Hamas to an unending jihad against the Jewish state, Finkelstein sees all the subterfuge and political interference coming from the Israeli side. Israel "provokes Palestinians into reacting," he said, "and it wants to either destroy Hamas or inflicts so much damage that Hamas will have to say it will never negotiate with Israel. That is exactly what Israel wants. Israel never wants a moderate negotiating partner because if there is one, pressure on Israel will grow. Hamas is willing for a settlement; Hamas stands by its word. But Israel does not want to negotiate. "[26]

Hamas has pure political intentions and passively yearns for truces and safe borders, according to Mr. Finkelstein, while the invidious state of Israel, fearing moderate Arab foes who would force it into peace, is obdurate, conniving, and bellicose. In fact, Finkelstein suggested, Israel was collectively going mad, while everyone else in the rational world yearned for Middle Eastern peace:

> I think Israel, as a number of commentators pointed out, is becoming an insane state. And we have to be honest about that. While the rest of the world wants

peace, Europe wants peace, the US wants peace, but this state wants war, war and war. In the first week of the massacres, there were reports in the Israeli press that Israel did not want to put all its ground forces in Gaza because it was preparing attacks on Iran. Then there were reports it was planning attacks on Lebanon. It is a lunatic state.[27]

And, Finkelstein concluded, after thwarting peaceful resolutions to the Gaza issue, committing genocide and massacres against innocent Palestinians, and generally destroying the property, infrastructure, and culture of the Arabs, Israel is then puzzled by the waves of enmity hurled in its direction. "And then these satanic narcissistic people throw their hands up in the air and ask, 'Why doesn't anybody love us? Why don't our neighbors want us to be here?' Why would they?" he asked, especially when Israel's ideological academic foes, like him, continuously wage a campaign of slanders, lies, and distortions against the Jewish state while apologizing for, or even lauding, the dysfunctional barbarism of Islamofacism.

If Finkelstein lives in an academic netherworld of political fantasies, conspiracies, and intellectually-imbecilic distortions of history and fact, his spiritual mentor, MIT's professor emeritus of linguistics NOAM CHOMSKY, has inhabited a similar ideological sphere, but has become an even more widely-known, an eagerly-followed academic celebrity of the Israel-hating, America-hating Left. The avuncular, shabbily-dressed professor has built an ideological following of a great magnitude, spewing forth his vitriol about the sins and errors of the West and the blamelessness of Third-world despots, revolutionaries, dictators, and genocidal monsters. In fact, historian Arthur Schlesinger wryly noted that Chomsky "begins as a preacher to the world and ends as an intellectual crook,"[28] and in the same way the Finkelstein skirts with truth, creates outright falsehoods, misrepresents the scholarship and research of others, and sees the United States and Israel through a lens of raw hatred, Chomsky shapes his odious ideology from the frenetic temper of his attenuated brain. His unctuous intellect has also enabled him to successfully straddle ideologies, so that as Professor Edward Alexander has noted, Chomsky "is among the few writers trumpeted by the leftist *Nation* magazine and the neo-Nazi *Journal of Historical Review*, by Alexander Cockburn and David Duke . . , by anti-Semitic Holocaust deniers like Robert Faurisson and David Irving and by leftwing anti-Semitism-deniers, who habitually label the murder of Jews [merely]. . . 'criticism of Israeli policy.'"[29]

The explosive power of Chomsky's animus for the imperialist West is only matched by his slavish affection and apologetics for the murderous despots of the Soviet Union, Khmer Rouge, and Viet Cong, whose barbarous excesses were, of course, predicated by the perceived oppression and exploitation of the tyranny of Western democratic states. His hatred for the United States, where he has been able to prosper and enjoy the freedom to relentlessly attack the morality and actions of his own country, is legendary, as is the invective he promiscuously uses to renounce America's forays into other parts of the world. Classics professor Bruce Thornton observed that Chomsky's anti-Americanism reflects not only an abhorrence of our nation's influence around the globe, but that, tellingly, like his fellow Leftists, "lurking within this hatred is the disdain for the American people, which is characteristic of most 'progressives' who, for all their populist rhetoric, simply can't stand the average person."[30]

Nevertheless, hegemonic, imperialist America is the unending focus of his visceral, irrational contempt. After the events of September, 2001, for instance, Chomsky coolly, off-handedly admitted that while "September 11th, 2001 was a terrible atrocity. . . [i]t's the first time in hundreds of years that massive terrorism was directed against the West." Even more important to Chomsky, though, was the necessity of shifting the discussion away from the barbarity of the terrorists who committed it and back to America and other democracies, since, he believed, "the West is the source of far worse terrorism and violence directed against others."[31] In Chomsky's fevered brain, every weak country on the planet has been victimized by American imperialism, so the al-Qaeda attacks for him were a nearly welcomed event, signaling a reversal of fortune where "for the first time in history the victims are returning the blow to the motherland."[32]

If Chomsky's vituperation against America has been a defining theme in his intellectual jihad, an obsessive, apoplectic hatred for Israel has more completely dominated his screeds and spurious scholarship. In all of his work, suggested Paul Bogdaner, an essayist who has extensively examined Chomsky's "scholarly" output, "one theme is constant: his portrayal of Israel as the devil state in the Middle East, a malevolent institutional psychopath whose only redeeming feature is the readiness of its own left-wing intelligentsia to expose its uniquely horrifying depravity."[33] Like other anti-Zionists in the West and in the Arab world, Chomsky does not even recognize the legitimacy of Israel, believing that its very existence was, and is, a moral transgression against an indigenous people. And Israeli Jews are not solely responsible for the crimes of the Jewish state; American Jews, too, in Chomsky's opinion, share culpability. "In the American Jewish community," he scolded, "there is little willingness to face the fact that the Palestinian Arabs have suffered a monstrous historical injustice, whatever one may think of the competing claims. Until this is recognized, discussion of the Middle East crisis cannot

even begin."[34] Indicting American Jews for the offenses he perceives as having been perpetrated by Israel is another way in which Chomsky allows his
rabid anti-Zionism to engulf Diaspora Jews, as well, making them morally
responsible for the crimes of the Jewish state with which they may or may
not actually even share any affinity. What is more, Jews' support of Israel, and
their abrasive and powerful presence in the world, are factors contributing
to the increase in world-wide anti-Semitism, not, of course, the malevolent
impulses and psychological defects of Jew-hating anti-Semites themselves.

"Jews in the US are the most privileged and influential part of the population," Chomsky decided. Not only that, but with the same sentiment articulated in such historical gems as the *Protocols of the Elders of Zion*, or even *The
Israel Lobby*, he asserted that Jews strove for even more omnipotence, that
"privileged people want to make sure they have total control, not just 98%
control," and that is the base reason "why antisemitism [sic] is becoming an
issue. Not because of the threat of anti-Semitism; they want to make sure
there's no critical look at the policies the US (and they themselves) support
in the Middle East."[35] What is more, the U.S.'s support of Israel, and Israel's horrible behavior toward the Palestinians, have made the Muslim world
harbor the anger that served to unleash jihadism against them. "Virtually all
informed observers agree," Chomsky condescendingly asserted in an interview, "that a fair and equitable resolution of the plight of the Palestinians
would considerably weaken the anger and hatred of Israel and the US in the
Arab and Muslim worlds—and far beyond, as international polls reveal." In
fact, he suggested, it would be a simple task to achieve this harmony between
Islam and the West if not for two obdurate superpowers, that "such an agree-
ment is surely within reach, if the US and Israel depart from their long-
standing rejectionism."[36]

Jewish power is a repellant notion for Chomsky, just as the hegemonic
might he ascribes to the terror states of Israel and America is the scourge of
peace, not the destabilizing barbarism of Islamism. The existence of Israel
not only subjugates the long-suffering Arabs, but is driving the entire globe
toward annihilation, Chomsky suggested, using the same image used by
Finkelstein, of Israel having succumbed into a kind of moral madness. Its
very psychosis had become a source of power, and the exercise of that power
would bring about global genocide. "Israel's 'secret weapon. . . ,'" Chomsky
wrote, evoking an apocalyptic vision, "is that it may behave in the manner
of what have sometimes been called 'crazy states' in the international affairs
literature. . . eventuating in a final solution from which few will escape."[37]

Chomsky is perfectly happy to use this shrill, barely rational rhetorical
technique perfected over years of vilifying Israel, one shared by his intellectual

protégé, Norman Finkelstein, as well. Both often begin their tirades against Israel by asserting that "Israel is a racist country" or "Israelis are terrorists," or the creation of Israel was "illegal;" they then contend that these views are established fact, that, as Finkelstein often claims, "these facts are not disputed," or that they are known as fact by everyone, when they clearly are not. This is a convenient technique for establishing a thesis by which one can then promote views that have nothing to do with reality, when the speaker, or writer, can build on a series of arguments whose primary thesis is flawed. If it is a given fact that Israel is racist, then any denunciation of its very being is acceptable, and indeed necessary.

Chomsky denounces Israel's identity as a Jewish state as being essentially racist on its face, and decries the very notion of its Jewishness as necessarily violating the concept of social equity by being exclusionary, elite, and, in David Duke's words, 'supremacist.' Moreover, the very crime of creating Israel on land stolen from Arabs, and these people's subsequent dispossession and subjugation, all justify for Chomsky any Palestinian "resistance" to recover usurped lands and property, including, of course, armed resistance and any form of terrorism. While he is happy to, and regularly does, ignore the murder of Jews by Palestinians, Chomsky never hesitates to point to the perfidy of Israel, and its barbarous assault on their Arab neighbors who, in his socialist fantasies, wish for nothing more than to live in peace. He draws the perverse parallel between Israelis and Nazis so frequently in his writings that, to paraphrase the wry professor Edward Alexander, he would be rendered nearly speechless if he was unable to use the epithet of Nazi against Israel in every sentence he utters. The rogue state of "Israel has tried killing, beating, gassing, mass arrests, deportation, destruction of houses, curfews and other forms of harsh collective punishment," Chomsky wrote, and yet, even in the face of this hideous, Nazi-like behavior by Israel, "nothing has succeeded in enforcing obedience or eliciting a violent response." That observation would probably come as a surprise to the families of the thousands of Israeli civilians murdered in two intifadas, or Israeli residents of southern towns who have been bombarded by thousands of rockets raining down from Gaza. In fact, Chomsky also asserted while employing his characteristic historic amnesia, "the Palestinian uprising is a remarkable feat of collective self-discipline."[38]

If imperialism itself can be classified as a type of state-sponsored "terror," as it regularly is in the morally-incoherent universe where Chomsky and other anti-Western thinkers reside, then it is quite simple to suggest, as Chomsky repeatedly does, an equivalence between the murderous acts of suicide bombers who attempt to address grievances and the legitimate self-defense of democracies whose citizens are under attack by murderous, non-state actors. Once someone has equated the rogue terror of one party with the legitimate acts of self-defense by sovereign nations, it is possible, and indeed inevitable, that he or she will start investing both actors with the same moral, and legal, standing.

More ludicrous is Chomsky's additional claim that Hamas and Hezbollah not only can claim a moral right to "resist" Israeli occupation, but that these terrorist entities, and, in fact, Islamism in general, were born as a direct result of U.S.-Israeli interference in Arab politics as a way of marginalizing domestic movements and forcing Western might upon a weak populace. "It is no secret," Chomsky said, "that in past years, Israel has helped to destroy secular Arab nationalism and to create Hizbullah and Hamas, just as US violence has expedited the rise of extremist Islamic fundamentalism and jihad terror."[39] Hamas, a group that was formed with the specific, articulated position of exterminating Jews and extirpating Israel, in Chomsky's addled brain is a benign community organization, and "the policies of Hamas are more forthcoming and more conducive to a peaceful settlement than those of the United States or Israel. . . ," who of course do nothing but create conflict and agitate for war. On the other hand, Chomsky claimed, "There is a long-standing international consensus that goes back over thirty years that there should be a two-state political settlement on the international border" and ". . . Hamas is willing to accept that as a long-term truce."[40]

That hallucinatory view would be credible, save for some inconvenient facts: first, that Hamas would not and has not ever honored a truce, and, in fact, is exempted from having to adhere to the terms of any truce by virtue of the Islamic tradition which provides for deception with non-Muslim when entering into treaties—most especially, one would think, the perfidious Jews. Secondly, and more important, Chomsky knows full well that not only is there no "international border" which would define the two states of Israel and the putative Palestine, but that Hamas's charter specifically addresses the belief that *all* of Palestine, from the Jordan River to the Mediterranean, including what is present-day Israel, is Arab land, now and forever, and must be reclaimed through jihad as a sacred Muslim duty. "Israel will exist and will continue to exist until Islam will obliterate it, just as it obliterated others before it," the charter explicitly reads. "The day the enemies usurp part of Moslem land, Jihad becomes the individual duty of every Moslem. In the face of the Jews' usurpation, it is compulsory that the banner of Jihad be raised."[41]

Chomsky's optimism concerning the political aspirations of Hezbollah is equally as ludicrous. In 2006, when he traveled to Beirut to Hezbollah's headquarters to meet with its Secretary General Sayyed Hassan Nasrallah, Chomsky was naturally impressed with the terrorist's "reasoned argument and persuasive argument that [arms] should be in the hands of Hezbollah as a deterrent to potential aggression. . . ."[42] After all, there was no trusting a heavily-armed Israel, according to Chomsky, since "Israel's *development and deployment of weapons of mass destruction* continues under U.S. aegis, as it has since the Kennedy years."[43] Nor could the United States be trusted, since its own terrorism was self-evident, at least to Chomsky. ". . . I've been writing about terrorism for the last 25 years," Chomsky wrote, "always using the official US definition, but that definition is unusable, and the reason is when you use that definition it turns out not surprisingly *that the US is one of the leading terrorist states*. And other states become terrorist or none terrorist depending on how they are relating to US goals."[44] As for Chomsky's "reasoned" Nasrallah, his wild opinions concerning Israel and the Jews are widely known, including his view that Jews "are a cancer which is liable to spread again at any moment," but "if they all gather in Israel, it will save us the trouble of going after them worldwide."[45] And in keeping with Chomsky's own pathological obsession, Nasrallah has suggested that, since the Zionist regime is nothing but a blot on mankind, "there is no solution to the conflict in this region except with the disappearance of Israel." That would seemingly be a perfect world for Professor Chomsky, but what would he then write about so fervently and with so much venomous enthusiasm?

While professors Finkelstein and Chomsky, among others, have defined their approach to academic conversations about Israel and the Arabs with tactics of excoriation, ideological attacks on Zionism, and an evident loathing of Israel's history and very existence, others in the academic war against Israel have taken a different tack. JOHN ESPOSITO, for instance, founding director of the Saudi-financed Prince Alwaleed Center for Muslim-Christian Understanding at Georgetown University, has helped to weaken Israel in a more subtle, but no less dangerous way—by becoming one of academe's foremost apologists for Islamism and Arab self-determination. In fact, The Investigative Project on Terrorism's Steven Emerson referred to Esposito "as a man who has never met a radical Muslim he didn't like,"[46] particularly because of his propensity for ignoring the growth of Islamism, coddling terror sympathizers, jihadists, and radical Muslim movements, for defending such organizations as the Muslim Brotherhood and CAIR, and for making impassioned pleas for the dismissal of charges against such individuals as convicted jihadist professor Sami al-Arian.

While Chomsky and Finkelstein's influence is substantial, and their respective fantasies about Nazi-like Israel widely-disseminated, their audiences have tended to be student groups, notably the Muslim Student Association, or other fringe radicals from the socialist, solidarity, or Marxist movements. The soft-spoken, seemingly reasoned Esposito, on the other hand, runs a well-financed center at an elite American university, has published some 35 books on Islam, and has the ear of the State Department, Capitol Hill, and policy makers—all factors which make his opinions, and influence, all the more significant and potentially damaging. Like Karen Armstrong, another scholar of Islam who has made an academic career of soft-peddling the danger of Islamism, Espos-ito has a consistent theme in his speeches, research, and books: that Islam is indeed a "religion of peace," and that the fears of nascent radicalism and a world-wide jihad are merely specters in the paranoid, bellicose minds of neo-conservatives, Islamophobes, and the Bush-Cheney Republican right. In the same way that Edward Said accused the Orientalists of using a Western, post-colonial perspective in assessing the lethal potential of radical Islam, Esposito, too, gave a nod to Said's theory, attacking scholars like Martin Kramer and Daniel Pipes for not understanding the nuances of Islam, and for their con-cern at the growing radicalization of Islamists with jihadist intentions.

In 1992, Esposito published a book, *The Islamic Threat: Myth or Reality?*, which, characteristically, made the conclusive assessment that the danger of Islamism arises, not from within the radical Muslim world itself, or from within mosques where sermons foment a loathing and mistrust of the West, but as a result of *our* incomplete understanding of the true nature of Islam. "Islam and most Islamic movements are not necessarily anti-Western, anti-American, or anti-democratic . . ," Esposito, concluded, and "they do not nec-essarily threaten American interests. Our challenge is to better understand the history and realities of the Muslim world."[47]

In his book *Ivory Towers in the Sand*, an indictment of the state of Middle Eastern studies in the university, Martin Kramer suggested that Esposito's view paralleled many supposed scholars of Islam, who were more than willing to see the evolution of Islamism as a resurgence of a type of Middle Eastern "democratization," and that critics in the West who were unable to understand the benign, rather than dangerous, potential of these movements were either Orientalists or intellectual bigots who could only see a democratic movement through Western, and therefore biased, eyes. "While other parts of the world democratized through the 1980s, the Muslim Middle East did not," Kramer noted. "To resolve this anomaly, Esposito came forward to claim that Islam-ist movements were nothing other than movements of democratic reform. . . This idea—that Americans suffered from an ethnocentric understanding of democracy—soon reverberated throughout Middle Eastern studies."[48]

The problem with this benign view of a radicalizing Muslim world, of course, was that it was tragically flawed. Political movements in the Muslim world were being energized by self-determination and an increasing commitment to exert ideological will and fundamentalist theologies—with increasingly lethal tactics of imperialistic jihad. Esposito and his fellow apologists for Islamism were busy downplaying the potential threat of radicalism, since, in their minds, ". . . Islamist violence. . . was deemed beyond the bounds of approved research [and] dwelling upon it would only reinforce stereotypes," suggested Kramer. And at the same time Esposito and others were obscuring the threat of Islamist rage, those very radicals were proving them wrong:

> . . . Despite these assurances, there seemed to be no shortage in the 1990s of Islamists still prepared to live up to orientalist expectations. Acolytes of shaykhs angry at America continued to plant massive bombs—inside the World Trade Center in New York, near an American barracks in al-Khobar, outside American embassies in Nairobi and Dar Es Salaam. Tourists in Luxor, bus riders in Tel Aviv, and pedestrians in Algiers all became the targets of lethal and indiscriminate attacks. Not all of the Islamists—perhaps not even "most" of them—had heard that violence was 'counterproductive.' Whenever such an act occurred, scholars who had promised a waning of the violence entered a state of denial.[49]

The inability, or unwillingness, to recognize imminent threats from the Muslim world has plagued Esposito's academic career, a record that might be inconsequential if not for the fact that government officials, the U.S. State Department, and others rely precisely on the expertise of such academicians to help them navigate diplomacy, international security, and military strategy. Even in the summer just before September 11, 2001, ignoring the clear pattern of recurring Islamic violence catalogued above, Esposito was still minimizing the threat of radical jihad, and blaming the West for its misperceptions and stereotyping of such questionable personalities as Osama Bin Laden, whose name, just a month later, would be forever etched on the public imagination.

Writing in the journal the *Fletcher Forum of World Affairs*, Esposito smugly commented that far from being an actual threat to the lives of innocent civilians, Bin Laden was actually good for those who found use in creating a terrorist bogeyman for their own, more sinister, political purposes. "Bin Laden is the best thing that has come along, if you are an intelligence officer, if you are an authoritarian regime, or if you want to paint Islamist activism as a threat," Esposito wrote. "There's a danger in making Bin Laden the poster boy of global terrorism and not realizing that there are a lot of other forces involved in global terrorism. . . Bin Laden is a perfect media symbol. . . As long as we focus on these images we continue to see Islam and Islamic activism through the prism of ayatollahs and Iran, of Bin Laden and the Afghan Arabs."[50] A month or so later, it turned out that, contrary to Esposito's notion that demonizing the Bin Ladens of the Arab world was the real "danger" facing the West, it was actually the exact opposite that was true.

Even after 9–11, Esposito still insisted on shifting the blame from the Islamists themselves and onto the West—and its legacy of imperialism and Islamophobia—in explaining jihadism. In the tradition of Edward Said and other mandarins in the Middle East studies establishment, Esposito reiterated his view that the answer to "why the terrorists hate us" had something to do with American actions and perceived misdeeds, not on the pathological hatreds fomented in the virulent strains of Islamism. Echoing the tradition of the pro-Palestinian apologists who point to Israeli and American policies as the cause of Arab terror, Esposito again claimed that terror strikes against the United States were due to American hegemony and failed diplomacy, that "most fundamental and important is the recognition that widespread anti-Americanism among mainstream Muslims and Islamists results *from what the United States does—its policies and actions*,"[51] not, of course, the rabid ideology which inspires a global jihad based on a drive for Islamic supremacism.

Like Chomsky and Finkelstein, Esposito also did manage to find one rogue state in the Middle East, one upon which he could heap the blame for the social and political ills of the region: it was, of course, Israel. Finkelstein and Chomsky are less delicate than Esposito, as already noted, attacking Israel forthrightly and demonizing it as a brutal, Nazi-like oppressor while simultaneously excusing the errant behavior of the ideological pathologies of Israel's foes. And like many other critics of Israeli policy, Esposito was also quick to add the United States as enabler, and co-sponsor, of Israeli malefaction. "In Israel-Palestine," Esposito wrote in *Al Ahram Weekly*, the Israel-hater's favorite state-sponsored news source, "Bush's continued failure to match his tough stand with Arafat on terrorism with an equally tough stand against Ariel Sharon's use of violence and terror to destroy the political, economic and institutional infrastructure in Palestine discredited the American Roadmap and fed extremism, a result that professional analysts (as distinct from the administration's political appointees) in the State Department and CIA would have warned him about." This passage is illustrative of the code words and misguided thinking that defines much of the anti-Israel rhetoric from the pro-Islamist and pro-Palestinian camps. First, Esposito refers to "Palestine" as if the putative sovereign nation already exists, just as all vehement pro-Palestinians do who wish to unilaterally create a state called Palestine to make legitimate the existence of this fictive people they identify as Palestinians—presumably from a nation called "Palestine" that existed before Israel. Esposito the scholar should obviously know better, and obviously does, but uses the term so that he can make the defective analogy he does in the next sentence: namely, that there is an equivalence between the terror campaign of the stateless murderer Arafat and the actions of self-defense of Ariel Sharon in protecting his nation from murder of Jews by Fatah. And what is the end result, and the most serious aspect, of the White House's failure to aggressively denounce the "terror" of Sharon as he destroys "the political, economic and institutional infrastructure in Palestine?" Not, in Esposito's mind, that innocent civilians were being murdered by the thugs of Arafat's kleptocracy. "The end result," Esposito decided, "has been the further erosion of America's moral leadership and credibility, increased anti-Americanism among many of its allies and hatred of America among extremists."[52] The U.S. and Israel, again, were conveniently blamed, and the Islamists were absolved of any guilt or complicity.

Esposito had used the perverse notion of "moral equivalency" before, notably at the September 1997 "Conference for Civilisational Dialogue" where one of the attendees, Ahmad Faiz bin Abdul Rahman, questioned Esposito about "whether we should include in the list of those Muslims who contribute, inadvertently or otherwise, to the notion that Islam equals fundamentalism which equals terrorist violence, the Sheikh al-Azhar. After all, the Sheikh had recently declared the suicide bombings in Israel to be unequivocally Islamic, in that it is a legitimate form of self defense." Instead of addressing what, to many observers, seemed to be the most troubling aspect of Islam—using theology as a justification for jihad—Esposito deflected the question, again suggesting that, as one example, Israel's defensive military actions equated to terrorism of a different stripe. Rahman recounted how:

> In a rather long winded response, Esposito explained that one man's terrorist is another man's freedom fighter; and that terrorism, as seen in the case of Israel's or the Tel Aviv regime's treatment of Palestinians, can and has been used to legitimate wanton violence and continued acts of oppression. However, surprisingly, Esposito added, 'Although I have not read or come across the actual 'fatwa', as a rule, we must not be too quick to draw upon the '*bid`a*' gun against anyone, not least of whom the Sheikh al-Azhar.'[53]

Since Israel and the United States, because of their policies, were to blame for the pathologies of the Levant, Esposito used the same strategy as other anti-Israel individuals, such as former president Jimmy Carter, and not only denounced the actions of the America and the Jewish state, but offered apologies and gave emotional support for the terror groups who are Israel's mortal foes. Terrorism expert Steven Emerson suggested that when Esposito made a statement suggesting that "some object to sitting at the same table to engage in a dialogue with Hamas or Hizballah but I see no problem with that" (as he did in the Arabic daily newspaper *Al-Sharq al-Awsat*), he not only seemed naive about the groups' real sinister intentions, but was violating the intent of U.S. laws, as well. "Esposito has made statements defending the terrorist organizations Hamas and, Hizballah," Emerson wrote. "He has also defended radical Islamist organizations including the Muslim Brotherhood. . . In his statements, Esposito seeks to portray them as political groups with legitimate goals without addressing their terrorist activity." But, stressed Emerson, "It is important to note that Esposito has repeatedly made statements to paint Hamas and Hizballah as legitimate political parties with whom the United States should reason and negotiate, *after* they each were designated Foreign Terrorist Organizations (FTOs) by the U.S. State Department."[54]

Why can Esposito seem to support the actions of Hezbollah? Because in his mind, of course, Israel is to blame, since Hezbollah's transgressions are as a result of the dreaded occupation of Shebaa Farms. "In recent years," Esposito wrote, "Hezbollah's actions in the south have been of a resistance movement. Hezbollah has made it clear that *such actions would not exist if the Israelis would pull out of the south*. Many outsiders refuse to see the Israeli occupation of Southern Lebanon as an occupation and as illegal."[55]

Similarly, like Jimmy Carter, Esposito was eager to embrace Hamas, regardless of the fact they were clearly intent on creating a purely Islamist state in Gaza and beyond, and had never even pretended to disavow terrorism as a tool for destroying Israel and killing Jews. In a 2000 interview in the *Middle East Affairs Journal*, for example, Esposito was disingenuous when asked about the violence that is the core of the Hamas ideology, using the opportunity again to shift the blame of this terrorism onto Israel, for its errant ways and ceaseless random oppression. "One can't make a clear statement about Hamas," Esposito said. "One has to distinguish between Hamas in general and the action of its military wing, and then one has also to talk about specific actions. Some actions by the military wing of Hamas can be seen as acts of resistance, but other actions are acts of retaliation, particularly when they target civilians."[56]

One has to wonder if Professor Esposito, like Jimmy Carter, has lost some independence of thought in his analyses of the Middle East and Israel, particularly since both men's professional careers and research centers are generously subsidized by extravagant Saudi largesse ($20 million in the case of Georgetown's center) and there exists an unspoken, but clear, understanding that little of the focus of whatever research comes out of those endeavors will honestly address the social and political defects of the Arab world; instead, much of the criticism will be aimed at those other favorite scapegoats instead—Israel and its foremost patron, the United States.

One of the off-campus activities in which John Esposito participated was his presidency of MESA, the Middle East Studies Association, which Martin Kramer has criticized as an organization that "now functions as a kind of union or lobby that boosts the image of Middle Eastern studies and circles the wagons against any criticism."[57] Franck Salameh, Assistant Professor of Near Eastern Studies at Boston College, is less kind in his assessment of MESA's usefulness and intellectual integrity, suggesting that the organization's leaders, the "radical wardens . . , exert a subtle, but stifling, grip over what kind of Middle East can be taught, thought, and written about in the American academy." Their obsession with the Palestinian cause, Salameh suggested, has meant that "MESA's leadership would have students of the Middle East ignore complex historical data and adhere to approved lines of group-think. The treatment of historical information, be it flouted, suppressed, fabricated, or dismissed in classrooms and faculty lounges, depends entirely on the whims and ideological predilections of the academy's keepers and the dictates of their favorite narratives."[58]

Given its ideological bias, it is not surprising that Esposito was tapped in 1988 to serve as MESA's president, a position also occupied by two other notorious academic Israel bashers, University of Michigan's JUAN COLE and Stanford's house Marxist and anti-Zionist, JOEL BEININ.

Cole, Richard P. Mitchell Collegiate Professor of History, was elected MESA's president in 2004, unsurprising for a rabid anti-Zionist who accuses American Jews of dual loyalties, equates Israel's Likud party with fascists, links the 9–11 attacks to Israeli actions, and has made the hallucinatory claim on his frenetic blog, "Informed Comment," that his frequent criticism of Israel has possibly put him under investigation by the Mossad.

After a July 2004 protest in which "tens of thousands of rightwing Israeli imperialists formed a human chain aimed at stretching between Jerusalem and Gaza to protest plans of Israeli Prime Minister Ariel Sharon to withdraw Israeli colonists from Gaza," Cole was angered that "no American media will report the demonstrations in Israel as fascist in nature, and no American politicians will dare criticize the Likud," referring to Israel's conservative party, his favorite target of excoriation. Cole, of course, is gravely concerned about the omnipotence of the dreaded 'Israel Lobby,' as his fellow travelers in the hate-Israel camp uniformly are. And not only were the political strings in Washington being pulled by the rabid Likudniks in Jerusalem, but it was their fascist policies that were at the root of the Muslim anger and humiliation that resulted in the September 11th attacks. The findings of the exhaustive 9–11 Commission, and even Osama Bin Laden's own statements, aside, Cole concludes fantastically that ". . . the fact is that the Israeli predations in the

West Bank and Gaza are a key source of rage in the Muslim world against the United States (which toadies unbearably to whatever garbage comes out of Tel Aviv's political establishment), something that the 9–11 commission report stupidly denies."[59]

Tellingly, the professor of history refers to Tel Aviv as Israel's capital, either because he is ignorant, or as a common way of refusing to recognize Jerusalem being part of sovereign Israel. And with the arrogance of the academic elite who transform their biases into fact, he dismisses the widely-accepted conclusion that jihadists attacked the United States for their anger over the presence of American troops on the Arabian Peninsula, and instead prefers the theory that the Israelis were to blame. "If the United States is hit again, as seems likely," Cole wrote, "the fascist Likud demonstrators will be in the chain of causality. . . But although the cause of Israel's own peace and security is just, the cause of colonizing Gaza and the West Bank is fascist. That shouldn't be defended by the US, and the loss of even one American life in defense of Israeli aggression and expansionism is intolerable."[60]

Cole's obsession with what he believes to be the underlying fascism of Israeli politics is only matched by his hysteria over the Likud, a political party that he compares to the actual fascists under the rule of Syria's Bashar al-Assad. While "the Likud coalition in Israel does contest elections," Cole admitted, "it isn't morally superior in most respects to the Syrian Baath. The Likud brutally occupies 3 million Palestinians (who don't get to vote for their occupier) and is aggressively taking over their land. That is, it treats at least 3 million people no better than and possibly worse than the Syrian Baath treats its 17 million."[61] That is an interesting theory, save for the inconvenient fact that the so-called "brutal" occupation has been facilitated under both conservative and liberal Israeli leaders. The three million Palestinians Cole refers to who are losing their lands to the usurping Israelis do not get to vote for their occupiers, of course, because they are not citizens of Israel, only a stateless people living in disputed territories awaiting a state. The 17 million Syrians, on the other hand, *are* actually deprived human and civil rights under the weight of their totalitarian regime, rights and privileges that Israel's own Arab and non-Jewish citizens *do* enjoy as some twenty percent of Israel's population.

In Cole's hallucinatory lucubrations, the Likud party not only subjugates the Palestinians, its tentacles also reach all the way to Washington, where its jackbooted thugs dictate U.S. policies through its neo-con puppets. U.S. involvement in Iraq, or in any incursions that might be seen to be beneficial to Israeli interests, are evidence for Cole of the dual loyalty of American Jews in government, and the essential malefaction of the Likud, who manipulates U.S. policy makers solely for the good of Israel.

The run-up to the Iraq war, Cole suggested, was simply another example of the manipulation of U.S. foreign policy under the influence of the nefarious Likud, operating in a behind-the-scenes cabal within the American government. "It is an echo of the one-two punch secretly planned by the pro-Likud faction in the Department of Defense," Cole revealed. "First, Iraq would be taken out by the United States, and then Iran. [Foreign policy specialist] David Wurmser, a key member of the group, also wanted Syria included. These pro-Likud intellectuals concluded that 9–11 would give them carte blanche to use the Pentagon as Israel's Gurkha regiment, fighting elective wars on behalf of Tel Aviv (not wars that really needed to be fought, but wars that the Likud coalition thought it would be nice to see fought so as to increase Israel's ability to annex land and act aggressively, especially if someone else's boys did the dying)."[62] This view of the inner workings of Washington is laden with wild conspiracy theories, not to mention the classically anti-Semitic allegation of Jewish power being used to fight wars to the detriment of innocent others—here with the odious Likud thinking "it would be nice" to have America start a war as a distraction for Israel's land grabs and oppression of the Palestinians, forcing nations to go to war, with "someone else's boys dying," with same detachment they might exhibit in ordering a cup of coffee.

The other now-familiar trope against Israel—that its policies blemish the international reputation of the United States—is oft-used by Cole, as well. Not only has "this aggression and disregard of Arab life on the part of the proto-fascist Israeli Right . . . gotten more than one American killed, including American soldiers," Cole wrote, but when "Ariel Sharon sends American-made helicopter gunships and F-16s to fire missiles into civilian residences or crowds in streets, as he has done more than once, then he makes the United States complicit in his war crimes and makes the United States hated among friends of the Palestinians."[63] Why Sharon might be sending gunships to randomly shoot into civilian neighborhoods receives no mention from Cole, nor is there ever acknowledgement that Israel might have the legal justification to suppress terroristic attacks on its own civilian populations—who are always the targets of Palestinian attack—as opposed to Palestinian civilians, who are fastidiously not targeted and generally die as a result of militants having set up bunkers and rocket-launching facilities inside of neighborhoods—precisely to cause the deaths of Arabs at Israeli hands to use as propaganda against the Jewish state.

Not only does this virulent anti-Israel bias inform the body of Cole's intellectual output, but he has on at least one occasion, in a Chomsky-like flourish, played wild and free with facts in making his point. Reacting to the

London subway terror bombings, Cole was eager to once again draw Ariel Sharon and Israel's brutal militarism into a theory of why terrorism was being employed against the West. "According to the September 11 Commission report," Cole wrote, "al-Qaeda conceived 9/11 in some large part as a punishment on the US for supporting Ariel Sharon's iron fist policies toward the Palestinians. Bin Laden had wanted to move the operation up in response to Sharon's threatening visit to the Temple Mount, and again in response to the Israeli attack on the Jenin refugee camp, which left 4,000 persons homeless. Khalid Shaikh Muhammad argued in each case that the operation just was not ready."[64] That is an interesting theory, except for a few inconvenient facts, as Martin Kramer and blogger Ted Badran pointed out soon after Cole published it. In the first place, Sharon had only come into office in March of 2001—hardly enough time for his "iron fist policies" to have driven the future jihadists to concoct their elaborative plan to turn passenger jets into lethal weapons against the West. Whatever insanity had inspired the September attacks obviously drew its inspiration from other dark sources, considering also that the twin towers of The World Trade Center had already been attacked as early as 1993.

But the more serious historical gaffe is Cole's mention of the Israeli incursion into Jenin as another justification used by al Qaeda for the 2001 attacks. Jenin, of course, has great symbolism in the anti-Israel imagination as the alleged location of "the massacre of the 21st century," where Israel was accused of slaughtering hundreds of innocent Palestinians. Even an odious little film, "Jenin, Jenin," has been made to help Israel-bashers to commemorate Israel's genocidal tendencies, an event and an accusation that has never gone away.

The problem with the Jenin massacre of innocent Palestinians, unfortunately, is that it never happened. In fact, Israeli troops were hunting down the perpetrators of a bloody terror bombing at a Passover service at the Park Hotel in Israel which killed thirty people and injured 140, since that and 23 earlier suicide bombing operations had been launched against Israel from a Jenin-based terror network. When the IDF operation inside Jenin was complete, the death toll was not in the many hundreds, as Palestinian propagandists and much of the gullible Western media had claimed, but only 56 Palestinians, the majority of them combatants; in addition, 23 Israeli soldiers had perished in the action, largely as a result of a decision to send in vulnerable ground troops as opposed to employing an air assault, which would have saved IDF lives but likely caused a higher death toll of the Jenin residents. So Cole's use of the Jenin event is yet more evidence that an alleged historian allows his bias and ideological impulses to inform his scholarship.

More serious, however, as Kramer pointed out, was Cole's reference to the Jenin event at all as a potential trigger for the jihad of September 2001. Why? Because the Jenin incursion took place in April 2002, *seven months after 9–11 took place*, a fact that even an undergraduate writing a term paper might have picked up in passing, even if his or her work was riddled with hatred for Israel. Apparently, facts are not necessary when an ideologue wants to make a point.

Another high-profile defamer of Israel, who shares the distinction with Cole and Esposito of having been a past president of the Middle East Studies Association, is JOEL BEININ, Donald J. McLachlan Professor of History and professor of Middle East history at Stanford University. Beinin is a self-proclaimed Marxist, whose own vocal radicalism resulted in the creation of a column in Stanford's student newspaper called "Beinin Watch." He is also a rabid anti-Zionist who follows the ideological pathways of the Coles and Espositos of the academic world by singling out Israel for criticism of its varied and frequent transgressions, all the while excusing the social and political defects of the neighboring Arab states who surround it and blaming the pathologies of the Middle East on Western imperialism and the continuing colonial impact of the U.S.'s proxy in the Levant, Israel. In fact, in those rare instances when Beinin was even willing to admit to the existence of Islamic terrorism, he was quick to find its root cause with its victims, not its perpetrators. Terrorism, Beinin wildly suggested, was a "product of postcolonial anxieties about U.S. global supremacy, and the regional dominance of the U.S. alliance [with Israel] in the Middle East,"[65] not, of course, the product of a jihadist impulse of barbaric madmen seeking to impose their own form of Islamic imperialism in the Middle East and into the West, as well.

When he did admit to Palestinian terrorism, as he did in a 2002 article he wrote during the Second Intifada, Beinin wove a fabulous tale about relatively innocent stone-throwing on the part of restless Arab teenagers that escalated into violence and the death of civilians on both sides only after Israel's disproportionate and unreasonable response to protects its citizens from being murdered. "The typical pattern for the first several weeks of the intifada was that Palestinian civilians engaged in peaceful protest marches," Beinin wrote, attempting to make the jihadists seem Gandhi-like in their non-violent approach to social change. "Toward the end of the protests," however, Beinin admits, "youths taunted and threw stones at Israeli troops . . ," causing the "soldiers [to fire] on stone-throwers and non-stone-throwers alike, rapidly escalating their responses. . . ." Why was a brutal suppression of dissent necessary by Israeli troops? According to Beinin, because it was part of Israel's nefarious strategy to be able to kill protestors "in accord with previously devised plans." And this was in response to violent protests that arose, after all, "over thirty years of occupation," more than justifying, for Beinin, armed resistance.

What is more, Beinin continued, as a result of Israel's brutal reaction to mere protest, "Secular and Islamist Palestinian factions revitalized their military wings," as if Hamas, for instance, has any other "wings" beside the primary one which was created for the specific purpose of murdering Jews and extirpating Israel. Nonetheless, Beinin concluded, with all other means exhausted, and "once it became clear that they were hopelessly outmatched by Israel's military force," only then did these otherwise peaceful "secular and Islamist factions" "resort to the strategically and morally catastrophic deployment of suicide bombers, targeting civilians."[66]

Beinin also used his observations about the Second Intifada to indict the United States for its complicity at the same time he was condemning Israel for its disproportionate response to terror attacks upon its civilians. In the same frame of mind used by Noam Chomsky in seeing America and Israel as the two most egregious, imperialistic evildoers on the planet, Beinin rarely misses an opportunity to denounce the actions of these "terror states" in defending themselves from terroristic assault. "For the last three and a half years," Beinin wrote, "the Israeli army has deployed American-supplied F-16 fighter jets, Apache helicopters, armored Caterpillar bulldozers and Merkava tanks powered by engines made in the USA in an unsuccessful effort to suppress the second Palestinian uprising." The fact that those arms tactical weapons had become an existential necessity for Israel after repeated attempts by the Arab states surrounding it to destroy it is ignored by Beinin, as if this weaponry was supplied by the U.S. and employed by Israel merely to break up crowds of rock-throwing protestors.

A heavily-armed Israel is a nightmarish image for many anti-Israel critics, used most often to further the fantasy of the Palestinian as the helpless, weak victim in the struggle between Third-world innocents and imperialists from the colonial West. Beinin's own description of "armored Caterpillar bulldozers" is particularly symbolic because it feeds the widely-held myth that the IDF randomly destroys Palestinian houses to steal the properties, as opposed to what function the bulldozers are there to serve: namely, destroying houses of terrorists, or homes that are used to store rockets and bombs, or which provide cover for tunnels for smuggling weapons. Beinin's intent, as it is for Israel-haters worldwide, is to make any defensive actions on the part of Israel seem an overreaction, regardless of how many of its citizens have been murdered or how many threats against its very existence have been proclaimed. Israel, then, is always the bully and the Palestinians, regardless of their behavior and deeds, are always the victims. "According to both Ehud Barak and Ariel Sharon," Beinin wrote, dismissively, "Israel is engaged in a war *despite the spectacularly unequal military balance in the conflict*," as if a nation reacting to unprovoked attacks on its citizens is compelled to insure that its enemy is equally armed and that the fight will be fair—something only a college professor, from the comfort and safety of his Stanford office, could possibly consider. And the worst aspect of this imbalance in forces, Beinin concluded, was that in this intifada "Palestinian civilians and the infrastructure of Palestinian society have been its principal victims."[67]

That may well have been true, but Beinin obviously overlooked the fact that Palestinian terrorists never wear military uniforms and identify themselves as combatants. In fact, not only do they strategically disguise their identities visually, they also regularly embed themselves, and their armaments, within civilian neighbors—virtually insuring that Israeli counter-attacks will cause civilian deaths, despite any attempt by the IDF to specifically avoid such occurrences. Hamas had long ago perfected this technique, which had twin benefits for them: if they hid within Palestinian residential neighborhoods they effectively shielded themselves from detection, and if it happened that Israel caused collateral damage in these same neighborhoods when seeking out militants, those deaths could be used as grisly proof of Israel's callousness and perfidy.

But Beinin even brushes aside the fact of this barbaric practice on the part of Hamas, as he did in 2009 when commenting on Israel's Operation Cast Lead into Gaza. First, Beinin made the same claim, in almost the exact language that professor Jennifer Loewenstein used, that the 8000 or 50 rockets fired into Israeli towns over years were not possibly the actual motivation for the Israeli incursion. "The Gaza operation was premeditated," Beinin incredibly announced. "It had nothing to do with rockets, terrorism, or anything the Israeli government claims."[68] What, then, was it that prompted Israel to re-enter Gaza, four years after it had disengaged from that territory and uprooted every Jew who lived there? An insatiable hunger on the part of Israel for Arab land? The inherent cruelty of Jews that inspires random attacks on a peace-loving Palestinian populace? Beinin does not say, although he is sure that it could not be reasonable that a sovereign nation might wish to protect its citizens from being murdered by non-state militants who had turned Gaza into the world's largest rocket-launching site.

Beinin *was* kind enough, however, to answer the question of why it was necessary or appropriate for Hamas terrorists to embed themselves in neighborhoods while launching attacks. "Of course Hamas hides among civilians," he said. "Gaza's a very small, densely populated place. Where else are they going to hide? "

Some ideas, said Orwell, are so stupid they could only have been thought of by intellectuals.

✒ Chapter 4

Distorting Scholarship to Discredit Israel: The Israel Lobby & Facts on the Ground

"Anti-Semitism" wrote Stephen Eric Bronner, author of the engaging book *A Rumor About The Jews*, "is the stupid answer to a serious question: How does history operate behind our backs?"[1]

For a wide range of ideological extremists, anti-Semitism is still the stupid answer for why what goes wrong with the world does go wrong. It is a philosophical world view and interpretation of history that creates conspiracies as a way of explaining the unfolding of historical events; it is a pessimistic and frantic outlook, characterized in 1964 by historian Richard Hofstadter as "the paranoid style" of politics, which shifts responsibility from the self to sinister, omnipotent others—typically and historically the Jews.

Long the thought product of cranks and fringe groups, Hofstadter's paranoid style of politics has lately entered the mainstream of what would be considered serious, and respectable, academic enterprise. One recent example, for instance, was the 2006 article "The Israel Lobby and U.S. Foreign Policy," by Harvard Professor Stephen Walt and University of Chicago Professor John Mearsheimer, which first appeared, not surprisingly, in the *London Review of Books*, and then was posted in a longer version as a working paper at Harvard's Kennedy School of Government, where Mr. Walt was also the Academic Dean.

"It is a work," said Richard Baehr and Ed Lasky in *The American Thinker*, "without a trace of balance, in essence no more than an angry polemic disguised as academic research. 'The Israel Lobby' is a long, bitter, op-ed piece given a patina of respectability because of where the authors are employed. They may feel themselves protected from criticism by tenure and their titles. They live and work in the proverbial ivory towers of an academic environment that has become an Arab-subsidized lobby against Israel."[2]

What the 83-page screed attempted to do was convince readers that America's support of Israel, both politically and financially, was out of balance with what the authors believe to be benefits derived from this troublesome relationship between the United States and the Jewish state. In fact, in the authors' view, Israel was founded on terrorism, is not a military or economic underdog that deserves or needs U.S. assistance, has made us hated internationally by Arab regimes who have their own loathing of Israel and now conflate that animus to include America, and, more recently, urged on the neoconservative-led Bush administration to go to war against Iraq—all to the benefit of Israel and causing serious damage to U.S. national interests.

What troubled observers of this type of scholarship was that, unlike its intellectually flabby predecessors from right-wing hate groups or left wing cranks, this political analysis came complete with academic respectability and the crests of Harvard and the University of Chicago, a trend that Hofstadter had himself originally found curious. "In fact," he wrote, "the idea of the paranoid style as a force in politics would have little contemporary relevance or historical value if it were applied only to men with profoundly disturbed minds. It is the use of paranoid modes of expression by more or less normal people that makes the phenomenon significant."[3]

In the Walt and Mearsheimer worldview, shared with other political "realists," there has been a troubling disjoint, in which a nation that they believed was clearly undeserving of support—Israel—continued to receive it nonetheless, at increasingly generous levels, even when all the many flaws in this largesse seemed so glaringly apparent, if only to them.

Why, then, does Israel still find sustenance and support from the U.S. despite the many defects Walt and Mearsheimer identified in its political, historical, and military character? The answer is found in the title of their piece: it is due to the Israel Lobby, an all-powerful, manipulative, and influential group whose effect is seemingly to cause otherwise rational leaders in Congress and in the White House to make irrational choices in international policy. And why is this group able to induce this irrational exuberance on the part of the U.S. government in formulating foreign policy? "The explanation lies in the unmatched power of the Israel Lobby," they wrote. "Were it not for the Lobby's ability to manipulate the American political system, the relationship between Israel and the United States would be far less intimate than it is today."[4]

The characterization of pro-Israel lobbying by organizations and high-placed government officials as "manipulation"—coercive, underhanded actions whose end result would not otherwise honestly, fairly, or reasonably be achieved—this language was the very tone that drew such immediate and thunderous denunciation of the piece. And it was a particularly incendiary bit of language when discussing Israel, a Jewish state, because it paralleled so invidiously the classic anti-Semitic canards, such as the *Protocols of the Elders of Zion*, that purport to reveal the intention of Jews to furtively rule and dominate the globe. And as happened here, there is a double insult to Jews: first, that they achieve this supposed sway over governments and other people by indirection, betrayal, and stealth; and, second, that in the end they are not only not admired for accomplishing these extraordinary, nearly super-human feats, but envied and reviled for having supposedly surreptitiously achieved them.

Some critics of the article, such as Eliot A. Cohen, a professor at Johns Hopkins University's School of Advanced International Studies, took great offense at what seemed to be evidence of this latent anti-Semitic sentiment. "Inept, even kooky academic work, then," he wrote in an op-ed in *The Washington Post*, "but is it anti-Semitic? If by anti-Semitism one means obsessive and irrationally hostile beliefs about Jews; if one accuses them of disloyalty, subversion or treachery; of having occult powers and of participating in secret combinations that manipulate institutions and governments; if one systematically selects everything unfair, ugly or wrong about Jews as individuals or a group and equally systematically suppresses any exculpatory information— why, yes, this paper is anti-Semitic."[5]

Melanie Phillips, author of *Londonistan*, minced no words when she declared in an essay, "The Graves of Academe," that the paper was "but the latest example of a poisonous pathology which has gripped the intelligentsia of the west, centred [sic] around a visceral loathing of America, Israel, the neocons and the Jews."[6]

As Hofstadter described it, the paranoid scholar sees the manipulator, in this case the Israel lobby, as an enemy, one with disproportionate and unreasonable influence. "Unlike the rest of us," however, he wrote, "the enemy is not caught in the toils of the vast mechanism of history . . . Very often the enemy is held to possess some especially effective source of power: he controls the press; he directs the public mind through 'managed news;' he has unlimited funds . . . he is gaining a stranglehold," in this case on the votes of American politicians and policy makers.[7]

Walt and Mearsheimer were nearly in awe with the ruthless precision with which the Israel lobby subordinates Congress to its iron will, having attained what they describe as a "stranglehold on Congress." "The Lobby pursues two broad strategies to promote U.S. support for Israel," the professors wrote. "First, it wields significant influence in Washington, pressuring both Congress and the Executive branch to support Israel down the line," presumably, they suggested, whether or not there is any validity or sound international policy actually involved. They then continued questioning whether American politicians can even vote their own consciences where Israel is concerned, so fearful are they of challenging the pernicious, behind-the-scenes policy makers. "Whatever an individual lawmaker or policymaker's own views, the Lobby tries to make supporting Israel the 'smart' political choice," they wrote, suggesting that members of Congress would choose political expediency and favor Israel's interests rather than voice their true feelings about Israel and protect America's national interest.[8]

Walt and Mearsheimer then revealed a remarkable discovery: that lobbying organizations actually work to have Israel's policies accepted by world opinion, that "the Lobby strives to ensure that public discourse about Israel portrays it in a positive light, by repeating myths about Israel and its founding and by publicizing Israel's side in the policy debates of the day."[9] Of course, the smarmy reference to "myths about Israel" would refer to any positive aspects of the history and political evolution of the democratic Jewish State, something than Israel haters—as well as those who have never embraced or accepted the legitimacy of Israel at all—are fond of criticizing, particularly Israel's defensive military attempts to ward off Arab aggression and equating those actions with the murderous, intentional terrorism of Hamas, Hezbollah, and the Jewish state's other jihadist foes.

More sinister in their minds, the power of the Lobby is manifested in its extraordinary ability to suppress any negative analysis of Israel's policies and America's response to them, a charge often heard on campuses by supporters of the Palestinian cause. "The goal [of the Israel Lobby]," they wrote, "is to prevent critical commentary about Israel from getting a fair hearing in the political arena,"[10] a rather remarkable assumption that assumes policy makers are never exposed to the ubiquitous, sometimes venomous, anti-Israel bellowing from the U.S. and international press; NPR; Middle East study centers which foment anti-Israel sentiment and have obsessive reverence for everything Palestinian; university campuses across the country where leftists decry Israel's policies and equate Zionism with Nazism in demonstrations, divestment efforts, speeches, and marches; and even high-visibility UN-sponsored conferences, such as the 2001 event held in Durban, South Africa which degenerated into an anti-Semitic hate fest and perfidiously announced to the world again that Zionism was racism.

This huge wave of worldwide, consistent, and oft-repeated anti-Israel, pro-Palestinian sentiment apparently never reaches the consciousness of American policy makers, Walt and Mearsheimer have concluded, because the omnipotent Israel Lobby has as its goal "to prevent critical commentary about Israel from getting a fair hearing in the political arena," 'fair' presumably meaning for the authors a critical view which would support their own negative preconceived attitudes about Israel. "A candid discussion of U.S-Israeli relations," such as the one they weave in their paper, "might lead Americans to favor a different policy."[11]

As traditionally occurs when Israel's defenders answer anti-Semitic or false charges with a vigorous defense and counter-attack, these attempts to set the record straight are often greeted with cries of righteous indignation and false charges that because the defenders of Israel are providing their own narrative, they are, in the critic's view, trying to foreclose on a honest dialogue about Israel; if one calls what appears to be anti-Semitic speech anti-Semitic, the real intent must be to foreclose altogether all discussion about Israel. Israel-haters want, therefore, to be able to roundly denounce any aspect of Israel but not be questioned on the accuracy or motive of their speech. They are therefore 'shocked, shocked' when Israel's defenders speak back to them, and often claim their free speech is being curtailed and that there is no open discussion when Israel is involved.

But Jonathan S. Tobin, executive editor of the *Jewish Exponent*, thinks that when Walt and Mearsheimer complained about the rare instances when criticism of Israel is actually effectively neutralized, this is the exception rather than the rule. "Far from suppressing academic freedom," he said, "these are merely isolated counter-attacks on the true monolith of the academy: bias against Israel. It is the 'Lobby' conspiracy-mongers who wish to repress not only those few academics such as [Daniel] Pipes and [Martin] Kramer who have the temerity to stand up for the US-Israel alliance but the free speech rights of American Jews."[12]

Harvard's Alan Dershowitz took offense at the very notion that, as the writers claimed in their paper, the Lobby is engaged in a "campaign to eliminate criticism of Israel from college campuses." "If this absurd assertion were true," said Professor Dershowitz in a lengthy and strongly written critique of the Walt/Mearsheimer piece, "it would prove that 'the Lobby' is a lot less powerful than the authors would have us believe, considering the fact that anti-Israel sentiment is nearly ubiquitous on college campuses. Mearsheimer and Walt try to have it both ways. On the one hand, the Lobby is an all-powerful force for manipulating American thought, conversation, and policy. On the other, the Lobby is ineffectual in its desperate attempt to stifle debate about Israel on university campuses."[13]

"In fact," Dershowitz went on, "the Mearsheimer-Walt *paper* may be one of the strongest pieces of evidence of the powerful culture of anti-Israeli animus on college campuses." That prevailing sentiment makes it possible, not only for such academic papers to be written, but also that they are then embraced by a willing cadre of same-thinking academics who might otherwise be more skeptical. Dershowitz quotes Caroline B. Glick, senior Middle East Fellow at the Center for Security Policy in Washington, DC and the deputy managing editor of *The Jerusalem Post*, who suggests that even mediocre and biased scholarship can pass muster if the subject is Israel:

> Walt and Mearsheimer—who are both rational men—undoubtedly considered the likely consequences of publishing their views and concluded that the anti-Israel nature of their article would shield them from criticisms of its substandard academic quality. That is, they believe that hostility towards Israel is so acceptable in the US that authors of shoddy research whose publication would normally destroy their professional reputations can get away with substandard work if it that work relates to Israel.[14]

Aware that the tone and seeming intent of their article would immediately make their actual intentions of demonizing Israel suspect, Walt and Mearsheimer made reference openly to the likelihood that their paper would be viewed as a new version of the *Protocols*. But this tactic was predictable, said Richard Baehr and Ed Lasky:

> Of course, the authors denounce anti-Semitism, attempting to inoculate themselves from accusations that they harbor such views themselves by arguing that all critics of Israel have to face such charges. That argument is ludicrous. Israel's media is dominated by critics of Israeli policies in the territories, who have been political foes of every Likud-run government in the last quarter century. The authors themselves often rely on criticism coming from Israelis and within the Israeli government to disparage Israel.[15]

In their zeal to expose the undiscovered truth about "the Lobby" in their scholarly tract, Walt and Mearsheimer participate in another typical practice by paranoid historians, namely supposedly bringing to the surface the truth about some sinister events or trends, as yet unknown to the general public.

This pattern, of trying desperately to reveal the machinations of a subversive group or groups to a world of dupes who cannot see as clearly as the paranoid historian can, is consistent with paranoid scholarship and also conspiracist inquiries.

In *A Culture of Conspiracy*, for instance, Michael Barkun suggested that "Conspiracism is, first and foremost, an explanation of politics. It purports to locate and identify the true loci of power and thereby illuminate previously hidden decision making. The conspirators, often referred to as a shadow government," in Walt and Mearsheimer's world of intrigue where divided loyalties account for pro-Israel lobbying, "operate a concealed political system behind the visible one, whose functionaries are either ciphers or puppets."[16]

The other characteristic of paranoid scholarship, as was the case here, is that the paranoid historian does not conduct his research in a methodical, objective way, with the primary intention of creating unbiased history and scholarship. He has already preordained the outcome of his research by the slant of his ideology. "The typical procedure of the higher paranoid scholarship," said Hofstadter, "is to start with . . . defensible assumptions and with a careful accumulation of facts, or at least of what appear to be facts, and to marshal these facts toward an overwhelming 'proof' of the particular conspiracy that is to be established."[17] This, of course, is the very technique used by Holocaust deniers, who conduct their research and have come to their findings in a manner similar to the way Walt and Mearsheimer come to theirs about the legitimacy of Israel and its role as an American ally and beneficiary.

In his essay "Why Revisionism Isn't," Gordon McFee seemed to echo, in the context of revisionist history, the technique used by the professors of building their case against Israel, namely, using facts, myths, and questionable scholarship (including citations from what Professor Dershowitz had identified as neo-Nazi websites) to construct their argument. In the same way that the professors began with the assumption that the Israel Lobby manipulates, unfairly, how policies toward the Jewish state evolve, wrote McFee about deniers, "'revisionists' depart from the conclusion that the Holocaust did not occur and work backwards through the facts to adapt them to that preordained conclusion." "Put another way, they reverse the proper methodology . . , thus turning the proper historical method of investigation and analysis on its head . . . To put it tritely, 'revisionists' revise the facts based on their conclusion."[18]

Walt and Mearsheimer were clearly unhappy with the continued favorable treatment Israel receives from America, and wanted to expose the subterfuge that allowed this process continue, despite what they carefully outlined as all the reasons it should not. As paranoids, they could not accept a different view of why that special relationship exists between the U.S. and Israel, namely, that it makes good sense geopolitically, that there is broad public support for Israel here, that the Jewish state is not alone in the world community to behave in ways which can be criticized, and that, despite its flaws, it has been and will continue to be a strong strategic ally and democratic, Westernized model in a part of the world surrounded by totalitarian regimes and social chaos.

That was the professors' scholarly flaw here, too—that in their ambitious effort to uncover some hidden reason for Israel's support in America, they ignored the obvious: that it may well be that the U.S. props Israel up, protects it from its enemies with money and diplomacy, and values it as a model of democracy in a sea of fanaticism, not because of an invidious, manipulative lobby forcing policy makers to make decisions against America's interests, but for an opposite, more believable reason: because it is the right thing to do and America's leaders and voters know it is the right thing to do.

Their other, more serious, academic offense is that they seem to have deliberately manipulated the substance and outcome of their 'research' as a way of justifying an ideology they possessed prior to writing the paper. And that is the gravest indictment of the paper: that it is an amalgamation of counter-factual, untrue, or exaggerated bits of data, lumped together to form a biased evaluation of Israel and its supporters. "The authors also contend that there is a 'dwindling moral case' for Israel," said Lasky and Baehr:

> To prove this point, they pull statements out of context to discredit Israel. Indeed, one of the most distressing instances of their lack of objectivity and proof of their bias is the devotion they show in scraping together every bit of innuendo, biased research, quotes out of context, and use of suspect sources, while completely ignoring even the most basic facts of the conflict, available to anyone with more than a passing interest in the topic, let alone professors who hold themselves out as "experts."[19]

Not everyone, of course, found fault with the Walt and Mearsheimer's work. David Duke, former Klansman, for one found the piece remarkably in step with his own research, saying that it "validated every major point I have been making since even before the [Iraq] war started,"[20] praise that the authors were apparently less than pleased to have received. The late Tony Judt, former professor of history and director of the Remarque Institute at New York University, who had already fatuously decided that Israel had become an "anachronism" and should be dismantled, wrote another op-ed in

The New York Times entitled "A Lobby, Not a Conspiracy" in which he tried to provide a defense for the validity and intent of the "Lobby" paper.[21] But his defense exposed his own predispositions towards Israel, according to Alex Safian, writing for CAMERA (Committee for Accuracy in Middle East Reporting in America):

> Not surprisingly, Judt's take on the matter is of a piece with his own anti-Israel fulminations. He mischaracterizes the substantive refutations of the Walt/Mearsheimer paper, including criticism from their Harvard and Chicago colleagues, as a 'somewhat hysterical response.'" He claims that the paper "draws on a wide variety of standard sources and is mostly uncontentious"—the 'wide variety' in fact being mostly cherry-picked newspaper articles containing anything portraying Israel in a bad light, along with multiple citations to extremists like Noam Chomsky, Norman Finkelstein and the holocaust-denying, Saudi-friendly *Washington Report on Middle East Affairs*.[22]

Other critics of the paper noted that the document, while focusing on Israel and how the country benefited from its cozy relationship with the United States, actually indicted not Israelis, but, as Ruth Wisse of Harvard University pointed out, American Jews. For it is that group, whether as lobbyists, politicians, media figures, or government officials, whose loyalties and true patriotic intentions are questioned by the central theme of the "Israel Lobby" piece.[23]

Baehr and Lasky suggested that while Walt and Mearsheimer questioned the motives of American Jews in lobbying on Israel's behalf, they carelessly (or intentionally) ignored the concurrent activities of the Arab world to lobby on behalf of their own nations. "The authors resent Jewish citizens who contribute to universities, Jewish critics of the media, Jewish supporters of think tanks, and, finally it seems, Jewish people in government," they wrote. "However, they seem to have no concern for or even acknowledge the magnitude of FOREIGN (Arab) donations, given by dictators who steal their own people's wealth to support hate and terror around the world, raining money down on think tanks, colleges, and media outlets in America . . . Foreign money, as long as it is anti-Israel, is worth its weight in gold (or oil). Jewish Americans who support universities are somehow tainted in their worldview."[24]

In September of 2007, Walt and Mearsheimer's original article and working paper found itself expanded to 480 pages and published as a book by Farrar, Straus & Giroux with the portentous title *The Israel Lobby and U.S. Foreign Policy*. The substance and tone of the original document had changed little; only the extent to which the stilted evidence was compiled varied from the original permutation. That the two authors were able to initially proclaim that no criticism of the Lobby or Israel is allowed by this omnipotent force, that the cabal of power-wielders effectively stifles debate and discussion about America's relationship with Israel, seemed slightly ironic, at least to some commentators like Jacob Laksin, given the fact that Walt and Mearsheimer were not only continuing to speak critically of Israel, but did so now with an even larger audience. "In the original essay, it may remembered," Laksin wrote,

> . . . the authors leveled the sensational charge that Israel's supporters in the United States, when not manipulating American foreign policy to Israel's advantage and wrenching the country into the Iraq war, posed a terrible threat to American democracy. Lurking behind every curtain, the 'Israel Lobby' was guilty not only of 'silencing skeptics'—presumably like Mearsheimer and Walt—but also of stifling debate about Israel in Congress and thereby subverting the 'entire process of democratic deliberation.' Truly, this was a force to be reckoned with.[25]

Jewish interests, with its control of media, public opinion, publishing, international negotiations and diplomacy, Congressional lobbying and influence peddling, and a "stranglehold" on voting and foreign aid allotment—this huge force completely failed in its supposed intent and ability to suppress criticism and dissent over Israel. Why? Because, as Laksin pointed out, only those who believe in the conspiratorial nature of the Lobby in the first place could ever have imagined that a work like this would ever be successful suppressed. "So, one can't help but wonder," asked Laksin, "How is it that this all-effecting lobby, with infinite powers of intimidation at its disposal, has nonetheless failed to prevent the publication of a nearly 500-page tome that purports to expose its sinister doings? To those with a less conspiratorial cast of mind than the authors, the answer seems fairly obvious. There is not now nor has there ever been an omnipotent 'Israel Lobby.'"[26]

The residual effect of a piece of scholarship like this is always uncertain, but the danger of seemingly respectable works of scholarship by legitimate academics is that their views and ideology are thereby more likely to help shape future views of students and other opinion leaders. In a *National Review Online* article, "Echoing the Moans of Anti-Israel Ghosts: Do Israel's Critics Have Anything Original to Say?" former deputy chief of mission in Israel's embassy in Washington, Lenny Ben-David, revealed that Walt and Mearsheimer's underlying thesis—the disproportionate influence on U.S. policy on behalf of Israel—had wide circulation decades ago by high-visibility policy makers. According to Ben-David, the scholars "repeat and amplify the 30- and 40-year-old opinions of two of the most prominent critics of American support for Israel a generation ago: Sen.

J. William Fulbright and George Ball, an under secretary of State in the 1960s. Curiously, the Fulbright and Ball names did not appear even once in the professors' voluminous footnotes in their original study." More important, does the legacy of this invidious questioning of the morality and ethics underlying the U.S.-Israel relationship seem to be passed on when it comes with an acceptability and veneer of respectability because of the intellectual status of the anti-Israel ideologues? "Walt and Mearsheimer were university students studying international relations and political science when Fulbright and Ball were at their peak challenging the American policies in Vietnam and the Middle East,' wrote Ben-David. "How much were the two influenced by Ball and Fulbright who, for many on campus, were heroes?"[27]

Since the publication of their book, Walt and Mearscheimer have been on a wilrwind speaking tour, frequently the guests of Arab and pro-Palestinian groups, including Muslim Student Associations on campus, who welcome the opportunity to have credible academics support their own theories about the seemingly disproportionate influence of Israel on America politics, and echo their sentiments that criticism of Israeli policies is regularly stifled in the world marketplace of ideas out of fear that the powerful and omnipresent "Lobby" will wield its far-flung powers to punish those who do not walk in lock step with its own interests—even if those interests are not beneficial or useful to America.

All the concern and intrigue engendered in this piece of defective scholarship show that the obvious, and easy, answers are not the ones the paranoid is likely to accept on face value. He is condemned by his nature to suffer in the labyrinthine schemes and conspiracies he uncovers. "We are all sufferers from history," Hofstadter concluded, "but the paranoid is a double sufferer, since he is afflicted not only by the real world, with the rest of us, but by his fantasies as well."[28]

Politically-Charged Scholarship
Facts on the Ground

In one of those ironies of questionable scholarship, just as a battle over a Barnard scholar's book about Israeli archeology had inflamed her 2007 application for tenure, heavy equipment tore away at the ancient crown of Jerusalem's 36-acre Temple Mount, Judaism's holiest site. Nadia Abu El-Haj's book, *Facts on the Ground: Archeological Practice and Territorial Self-Fashioning in Israeli Society*, originally a doctoral thesis, questioned the historical existence of a Jewish link to

Israel, and her provocative claims caused her to become the center of a fractious debate about her qualifications for tenure as a Barnard professor of anthropology.

Meanwhile, in Jerusalem during that same time, Hebrew University's Dr. Eilat Mazar, along with representatives from the Committee Against the Destruction of Antiquities, was in the Israeli High Court of Justice attempting to halt the work on the Temple Mount being conducted by the Muslim Waqf, the religious trust charged with oversight of the location. The excavation, a trench 500 meters long and 1.5 meters deep, was, according to the complainants, "causing irreversible damage to antiquities and archaeological artifacts of the greatest importance . . , [was] being carried out illegally, [and] entail[ed] damage to ground layers, some of which may have been in place since the first Temple stood there 3,000 years ago."[29]

The effrontery of that recent, but not isolated, act by the Waqf was made all the more troubling by the fact that the archeological contempt shown by the Muslim trust reflects its attitude that a Jewish historical connection to the site is only apocryphal, and that, in the same way that El-Haj denied a Jewish component to the archeology of Israel, the Waqf's oversight of the Temple Mount had contributed to an effort, in pursuit of the Palestinian nationalistic cause, to erase or obscure Judaism in the Holy Land and replace it with a Muslim historical narrative which predates a Jewish one.

Dore Gold, Israel's UN ambassador from 1997 to 1999, exposed in his latest book, *The Fight for Jerusalem: Radical Islam, the West, and the Future of the Holy City,* how many in the Muslim world, and even some individuals in the West, have begun a sinister process aimed at establishing a spiritual as well as political presence in Jerusalem for Islam, while simultaneously diminishing Jewish historical links to the city. Gold believes this trend began at the 2000 Camp David meetings when Yasser Arafat first stated loudly and publicly his breathtaking belief that there had never been a Jewish temple at the Temple Mount, and that Arafat, according to Gold, thereby tossed "a stone of historical lies into a lake and its ripples spread all over the Middle East. 'Temple Denial' became a common theme at seminars in the UAE or in Jordan in the years that followed. European professors joined this anti-biblical trend."[30]

A second, but concurrent, assault on that Jewish history, and an effective tool in the intellectual jihad against Israel fomenting on American campuses, is "post-colonial" scholarship like that of El-Haj, "the hallucinated claim," as author Stephen Schwartz puts it, "that Jewish identity is a modern, nationalist, and Zionist-imperialist 'construct' rather than a product of thousands of years of recorded history and religious tradition."[31] Post-colonialism, of course, is the holy grail of the late Edward Said of Columbia University, a way of minimizing the importance of history and scholarship by making the sweeping assertion that academic inquiry by non-Orientalists, indeed history itself, is diminished by its inherent flaw of being, as Said put it, "Eurocentric in the extreme" and defined by a imperialistic narrative imposed by Western powers on the under-developed world. Historical narratives, and the archeology by which these narratives were created, in Said's view—and in El Haj's—are mere 'constructs,' artificial recountings of history that are subject to deconstruction, inversion, and counter-factual revision. Western thought and research are no longer an alternate, meaningful scholarly means of inquiry, but defective and distorted ones that can therefore be dismissed, ignored, or relegated to discredited modes of academic study.

Thus, El Haj's scholarship and approach to archeology in *Facts on the Ground* is what she described as a school of thought that "reject(s) a positivist commitment to scientific methods . . ." and is "rooted in . . . post structuralism, philosophical critiques of foundationalism, Marxism and critical theory . . . and developed in response to specific postcolonial political movements."[32] That approach would be a novelty in scholarly pursuits in the humanities, for instance; but the rejection of the notion that objectively verifiable facts *do* exist does not result in valid scholarship, at least the type that ordinarily would exist in departments of history, archaeology, or anthropology that had not been politicized by an ideological agendas seeking to subsume facts with new, wistful narratives to achieve what Martin Kramer has termed a "reversal of history."[33]

Dr. Kramer, in fact, has had much to say about how Saidism—the postcolonial strain of scholarship that pervades and, in his view, has devalued the entire field of Middle East studies—has become the intellectual litmus test for what is accepted and promoted in teaching, writing, and, in the case of El-Haj, tenure decisions. The danger here, of course, is that once institutions like Barnard give its scholars credibility by granting tenure and supporting the publication of what would once have been considered shabby academic works, they grant academic legitimacy to the creation of what can amount to scholarly "myths." Tenure and published books reinforce and give validity to this defective scholarship, and it becomes a shared set of new values and tactics for scholarship that is judiciously protected by the very scholars who worship at its altar, a collective academic credibility that becomes "a very useful tool to those who seek to delegitimize Israel and demonize Zionism."[34]

That, of course, has been one of the chief aims of Middle East studies, and has become part of the arsenal of ideological weapons against Israel as academe has become obsessed with the Palestinian cause. "At Barnard as at Columbia," wrote Aren M. Maeir, an Israeli archaeologist from Bar-Ilan University, "certain departments appear to be so deeply in thrall to the late Edward Said, that scholarship is valued not for rigorous methodology or mastery of a body of evidence, but according to the rigor with which it conforms to the orthodoxies of post-colonialism."[35] And for El Haj, as it was for Said, those orthodoxies were crafted to delegitimize Israel and promote Palestinianism, the core purpose of *Facts on the Ground*.

Since archeology can and has established an unbroken historical link between Jews and the lands on which Israel has been created, it became the task of El Haj to re-evaluate that history, to "use post-structuralist 'discourse' to rewrite the history of ancient Israel," as Ami Isseroff, web author and director of *MidEast Web*, observed, "writing the Jews out of it, and writing the 'Palestinian Arabs' into it."[36] El Haj was not shy about revealing that she was a fervent Palestinian supporter, and her negative feelings about the Jewish state are similarly evident from the outset. To her, Israel can claim no legitimacy on a moral, political, or historic basis, and she thereby elevated and made superior the Palestinian claim to the lands of current-day Israel. In her view, Israel was an artificial "colonial settler state" built on the history and homeland of the indigenous Palestinians, and this bestowed a fundamental illegitimacy and moral flaw on the Jewish state, one that had to be obscured through the efforts of a contrived Zionist "myth" and abetted by the efforts of Israeli archeologists who selectively studied artifacts and strata in the ancient soil of the Levant in order to substantiate a viable Jewish claim to Palestine.

"This book," El-Haj announced in the first pages of *Facts on the Ground*, "analyzes the significance of archaeology to the Israeli state and society and the role it played in the formation and enactment of its colonial-national historical imagination and in the substantiation of its territorial claims."[37] Thus, ignoring the fact that her scholarly effort here has as its purpose the exact thing that she accuses Israel of—that is, creating a Palestinian state through "historical imagination"—she continually hammered home the point that the modern state of Israel is a mere construct, a colonial enterprise with no integral moral or historic value. Even more damning is her underlying theme that Israel not only has spurious historical links to biblical Palestine, but the whole sociopolitical relationship of Israel with the land there, one upon which the justification for the nation's creation was largely based, is a type of historical sham, a hoax enabled by dishonest scholarship and the manipulative work of Israeli archeologists intent on reinforcing the myth of Jewish statehood.

"The very distinctive form of Israeli settler-nationhood returns to haunt the cultural property debate," El-Haj contended, stressing continuously, as she did in this passage, that Israelis are mere settlers on this land, latter-day

Pilgrims who arrived from Europe to colonize and steal lands belonging wholly to another group. The inconvenient fact that the Palestinians as a group did not even exist until the nineteen-sixties, that they emerged as propaganda tool against Israel after the 1967 war, is, of course, ignored by El-Haj, as it is generally by pro-Palestinians everywhere. If Palestinians, according to their supporters, are to have the superior claim to the land of Palestine—that is, that *they* are the indigenous people "from time immemorial"—Israel would have to create a narrative that obscured that truth, if in fact it existed, and archeology would be the tool through which this false narrative would be cemented together. "The ongoing work of archaeology, after all," El-Haj wrote, "was constitutive of the territorial self-fashioning of Jewish nativeness out of which a settler-colonial community emerged as a national, an original, and a native one, which would thereby have legitimate claim not just to the land as a whole, but, more specifically to particular ancient artifacts that embody the Jewish nation's history and heritage."[38]

Her book was widely denounced during her tenure battle precisely because it seemed not to be authentic scholarship on archeology in the Holy Land at all, but a revisionist history based on political ideology—the notion that any historical relationship between Jews and Jerusalem, indeed to Israel itself, is merely a construct, a fiction, a professional fraud hoisted upon the world by crafty Israel archeologists who sifted through digs and artificially 'built' a historical link between the Jews and Israel, thus, of course, denying the Palestinians their own historic connection. Israel, a "colonial settler state," had to create history through selectively revealed archeological finds and, El-Haj wrote, "the colonial dimension of Jewish settlement in Palestine cannot be sidelined if one is to understand the significance and consequences of archaeological practice...." She thus disingenuously, and apparently without worrying about science, fact, or history, dismissed or ignored generations of professional archeology carried out by *actual* archeologists (which she is not), and posits in the book's most inflammatory and controversial line, that "the modern Jewish/Israeli belief in ancient Israelite origins" is a "*pure political fabrication*," an "ideological assertion comparable to Arab claims of Canaanite or other ancient tribal roots."[39]

Complicit in that fabrication were Jewish archeologists, El-Haj contended, for it was they who were able to fashion a narrative which both confirmed a connection with and justified a return to the Promised Land for diaspora Jews. "In the context of Israel and Palestine," she wrote, "archaeology emerged as a central scientific discipline because of the manner in which colonial settlement was configured in a language of, and a belief in, Jewish national return." Because colonial settlers from Europe, people with no substantial claims to the land of Palestine, could never make a moral claim for statehood and self-determination at the expense of an indigenous people, a faux history was constructed. "In producing the material signs of national history that became visible and were witnessed across the contemporary landscape," El-Haj wrote, "archaeology repeatedly remade the colony into an ever-expanding national terrain. It substantiated the nation in history and produced Eretz Yisrael as the national home."[40]

That may be El-Haj's way of wanting to appraise the history of Israel, but it unfortunately flies in the face of all scholarship on the antiquities of Israel and Palestine, and would require that the enormous intellectual output of Jewish, Christian, Islamic, and other scholars, historians, theologians, and archeologists be ignored to embrace her politically-shaped theories. In fact, Diana Muir and Avigail Appelbaum, two Barnard graduates who wrote a review of her book, felt that the "outrageous nature of this demand is breathtaking. Not only does Abu El-Haj take upon herself the privilege of dismissing large bodies of evidence, she demands that other scholars ignore or deliberately distort evidence to conform to her political bias."[41]

Of course, "distorting evidence to conform to political bias" is ubiquitous amid Palestinian propagandists, who, along with their apologists in the West, have assiduously attempted to rewrite a historical narrative with themselves as an indigenous people and Israelis as European colonial usurpers with no real connection to the land of what became Israel. So to overcome that inconvenient set of facts, El-Haj contended, Israeli-directed archeology took it upon itself to sift through a past rich with Muslim relics, but ignored them, and looked for, identified, and recorded only those findings which confirmed a historical Jewish connection to the land. "The work of archaeology in Palestine/Israel is a cardinal institutional location for the ongoing practice of colonial nationhood," El-Haj wrote with the politicized syntax of her ideological mentor, Edward Said, "producing facts through which historical-national claims, territorial transformations, heritage objects, and historicities [sic] 'happen.'"[42]

Even more pernicious was El-Haj's attempt to provide apologies for the destruction of Jewish archeological sites as understandable and legitimate impulses on the part of Palestinians who seek self-determination and attempt to throw off the yoke of Israel's colonial occupation. If archeology assigns the ownership of objects to particular people at particular times in history, the symbolism of these objects in verifying a people's, or nation's, existence can be profound—particularly when terrritory or statehood is disputed, as it is in the Israeli/Palestinian discussion. El-Haj contends that "particular objects emerge as emblems of heritage, a fundamental category for societies—for nations—'intent on finding legitimacy through history,'" such as holy sites, tombs, cemeteries, or the Temple Mount itself. "Of course," she continued, "to produce ancient objects as the heritage of the modern Jewish nation requires the assertion, or belief in, a connection (perhaps even a genealogical relationship) between 'the people . . . who created [the] artifacts in the first place and those whose identity they are seen to represent.'"[43] If this connection between these artificats, these symbolic links to a cultural past, are put into doubt—or even better, destroyed—the narrative can also be altered.

El-Haj discusses this very topic regarding the desecration of antiquities in her account of the 2000 Palestinian riots in Nablus in the West Bank which resulted in the burning and destruction of Joseph's tomb, one of Judaism's holy sites. Instead of condemning the deliberate assault on historically-significant sites—something, one might think, that any scholar of archeology would normally decry, regardless of who the perpertrators were—El Haj evaluated the event as many Palestinian supporters do in other contexts, where they excuse Arab violence and terrorism as understandable, and justified, responses to Israeli oppression and occupation. Thus, what she refers to as the mere "looting" of Joseph's tomb is an example in her mind of the use of a "weapon of the weak" (a term she lifts from James Scott) to resist oppression and to cast off Israeli occupation and the symbols and substance of its nationalistic claims. "Archaeology remains salient in this world of ongoing contestation," El-Haj suggested, making a general thesis into something that she wished to narrowly define the Israeli/Palestinian conflict. "It is a sign of colonial presence and national rights, of secularism and science, as various groups in Palestine and Israel engage in struggles to (re)configure the Israeli state and polity and to determine its territorial limits." The attack on Joseph's tomb was a taking back of history, a re-writing of a historical narrative in which the colonial occupiers, the members of the settler state, achieve social justice in what El-Haj termed "a form of resistance to the Israeli state":

> Joseph's tomb was not destroyed simply because of its status as a Jewish religious shrine. The symbolic resonance of its destruction reaches far deeper than that. It needs to be understood in relation to a colonial-national history in which modern political rights have been substantiated in and expanded through the material signs of historic presence. In destroying the tomb, Palestinian demonstrators eradicated one 'fact on the ground.'[44]

The problem with coming up with a book of archeology which defies logic and history, as El-Haj had done here, of course, is that one would have to condemn or marginalize the work of all archeologists in the field whose work had formed the basis of the historical record she was determined to negate. One of the reasons that critics opposed her being granted tenure at Barnard was precisely because she had defamed noted professionals in the field, based on anonymous sources and anecdotal evidence for which she offers the thinnest bits of evidence. In fact, one of El-Haj's fellow professors at Barnard, Alan F. Segal, Ingeborg Rennert Professor of Jewish Studies, took her to task during the tenure battle in an op-ed in the *Columbia Spectator* for what he perceived to be one of her severest scholarly offenses: "that Israelis deliberately mislabel Christian sites as Jewish and tear down churches . . . [and] that they use bull-dozers to level sites and wipe out evidence of Palestinian habitation."[45] Professor Segal finds the assertion that bulldozers have been used in "contemporary archeology" to be El-Haj's "most outrageous charge," not only because Israeli archeologists are fastidious in methodology and practice, but also, given what is happening currently atop the Temple Mount itself—one of the world's richest archeological and historical sites—it is something that the Waqf, not the Israelis, should have to answer for.[46]

Scholars and archeologists remember, for instance, the howls of outrage that arose from the Arab world in February 2007 when Israeli authorities initiated a project to rebuild a ramp to the Mugrabi Gate, an entrance to the Temple Mount plaza and the Al Aqsa Mosque platform that had been damaged in an earlier storm. Riots and protests began immediately, with accusations against Israel coming from throughout the Arab world for its "scheme" and treachery in digging under and threatening to destroy the Al Aqsa Mosque itself. The committee of Muslim scholars in Jordan's Islamic Action Front, for one, "urge[d]. . . proclaiming jihad to liberate Al Aqsa and save it from destruction and sabotage from Jewish usurpers,"[47] a spurious claim since construction was taking place well outside the Mount platform, some 100 meters from the mosque, and clearly posed no possible threat.

So while riots ensued when Israelis initiated a carefully supervised reconstruction project *near* the Temple Mount, the Muslim guardians of Judaism's holiest site have felt no compunction in brutally gouging the historic surfaces when it suits their own purposes, either in 2007 when they created a deep trench, or as they did in 1999 when they opened a gaping hole—in what is known as Solomon's Stables—18,000 square feet in area and 36 feet deep, for new mosques. Most seriously, 13,000 tons of rubble from that criminal dig, containing rich archeological remnants from the First and Second Temple periods, was scattered clandestinely in the Kidron valley dump without any professional archeological oversight and before experts could evaluate any unearthed items of significance.

At least one critic of El-Haj's book points to this illicit activity on the part of the Waqf as one bit of evidence that seems on its face to disprove her overriding belief that in fact there is *not* a preponderance of archeological evidence supporting a Jewish link to the land. El-Haj does mention the illegal excavations that have been conducted for years on the Temple Mount by the Waqf, and according to David Meir-Levy this admission points to something that El-Haj and others wish to obscure: that if there was nothing in the archeological remains that proved a Jewish link to the site, there would be no need to destroy the evidence, to de-Judaize Jerusalem. "These excavations are avowedly intended to eradicate evidence of earlier Jewish existence and activity on the site," Meir-Levy writes. "If there were no such existence, there would be no such evidence. If whatever evidence remained on the Mount were immaterial or inconclusive, there would be no need to destroy it. The very actions of the Waqf are clear attestation to the existence of what is for el-Haj and at least some of the Muslim world the very troublesome, unwelcome, and inconveniently incontrovertible evidence of Jewish life and activities and sovereignty in and around the Temple Mount in pre-Islamic times."[48]

The Arab world's own complicity in playing fast and loose with history, and obscuring the actual "facts on the ground" in its attempt to create a historical narrative conforming to its political agenda, makes El-Haj's accusations against Israeli archeologist all the more disingenuous. This includes the outrageous belief, which Yasser Arafat himself proclaimed to a startled President Bill Clinton at Camp David in 2000, and which is now heard with increasing frequency from the Arab world, that the Temple Mount was *never* a Jewish site, that despite references to it in Jewish, Christian, and Islamic scripture alike, this place in Jerusalem was, and still is, Muslim holy land.

Adding insult to injury, El-Haj widens the accusations against Israeli archeologists by contending that, in addition to obscuring the actual connections to the land of Israel, they practice an aggressive, sloppy form of archeological investigation, using crude and destructive tools, "bulldozer archeology," to obliterate the facts on the ground as they create a false narrative. "The claim that Israel practices 'bulldozer archaeology,'" noted Ralph Harrington, "is an explosive one and draws on images of ideologically-driven Israeli destructiveness that are deeply rooted in contemporary Palestinian perceptions," but it is explosive because it is part of a pattern of lies.[49] Edward Said himself had raised the specter of Israeli archeologists with their bulldozers carelessly pushing aside Palestine artifacts in their zeal to obscure a Palestinian history, a theme which was clearly resurrected by El-Haj when she wrote her study. "Even so apparently innocent a discipline such as archeology," Said proclaimed at a 2003 speech at Ewart Hall at The American University in Cairo, "which is one, of course, of the prides of Egypt, was used in

Israel and was made complicit in the making-over of the land and its markers, as if there had never been any Arabs or any other civilizations there except Israel and the Israelites . . . the traces of other more just as historical histories were ignored or simply moved away by trucks and bulldozers."[50]

In yet another example of "turnspeak," the Arab world has accused Israel of the misdeeds, lies about history, and destruction of a nationhood that they themselves are committing. It is part of a relentless and continuing effort to delegitimize Israel and finally eliminate it through a false historical narrative that is repeated in Palestinian schoolbooks, in sermons, in the Arab press, in Middle East studies programs at universities, and in the politicized scholarship and dialogue generated by Israel-haters, anti-Semites, and Palestinian apologists around the world. And when it is legitimized on campuses through the "scholarly" output of highly-politicized academics, it gives greater solace to Israel's ideological enemies, as well.

"At the heart of this . . . is a monstrous lie," said professor of Classics at Cal State, Fresno, Bruce Thornton, "the airbrushing of Jews from the history of Jerusalem, an Orwellian rewriting of history started by the Arabs and abetted by some politicized Western scholars."[51] That is the core problem with *Facts on the Ground*—that it is not a scholarly attempt to shed light on the rich archeological history of the Levant at all. Instead, it is ideology parading as scholarship; it is the work of a dilettante who is not an archeologist, never visited a dig, reads no Hebrew, and used anonymous sources and anecdotal evidence as the foundation of her research to craft what *Haaretz* columnist Nadav Shragai called a "tissue of lies"[52] about Israeli archeologists, who, perhaps lacking the political motivations that so clearly subsume El-Haj's own work, actually uncovered the true facts on the ground that shape the uninterrupted 3000-year Jewish presence in the land that became Israel.

Chapter 5

Criticism of Israel or Anti-Semitism? The Corruption of Academic Free Speech

In the campus war against Israel, a new rhetoric has evolved, one which would stun those who once considered the university as a place where civility and reasoned scholarly discourse normally occurs. Two trends have emerged, both of which are used by Israel's campus foes as a way of framing the ideological argument against the Jewish state.

One involves the gradual ratcheting up of the level of acrimony against Israel and Zionism by speakers, both faculty and students and invited guests from off campus, who appear at rallies, demonstrations, conferences, symposia, and other campus events. While most universities now scrupulously define acceptable, and unacceptable, speech and behavior on their campuses—and indeed often codify them in written speech codes and rules of expected conduct—virulent anti-Israel speech and acting out is now a common occurrence on campuses. The speech and academic output of professors has been of some concern, as well, even though one of the university's principles is enshrined in the concept of academic freedom and unbridled rights of expression for the professoriate, and that concept of freedom is often abused by radical professors who use it as a cover for outrageous and abusive "scholarship" and speech.

The other tactic in the war against Israel involves the Left's attempt to inoculate itself from the accusation of being anti-Semitic by insisting that all expression that critiques Zionism and Israel itself—no matter how incendiary, vile, or libelous—is no more than political commentary on the Jewish state. It should not be seen in any way as being couched in anti-Semitic sentiment, nor is it reasonable, in the critic's view, for them to be accused of Jew-hatred merely because they single out the world's only Jewish nation and regularly heap invective and condemnation upon it. Coupled with this attempt by Israel's foes to distance themselves from being seen as merely another generation of those who harbor animosity toward Jews is the way they have self-positioned themselves as noble and brave spokespeople who dare to name Israel's and Zionism's many sins, and, in their view, suffer for it when they confront "powerful forces" who try to stifle and prevent any criticism of Israel.

Many Muslim Student Association events held on campus, for instance, are publicized with the seemingly benign intention of furthering discussion on the troubling issues of the Middle East, but the stated purpose is also frequently to "educate people whose view of the Arab/Israeli conflict is not accurately depicted in the news media," or "is hidden from many people's notice," and to make students and others aware of the "truth" of the situation on the ground in Israel and the Palestinian territories. That "truth," of course, is something that is only true as part of the ideology of the sponsoring organization, and is based on the assumption that this person or group somehow has access to verifiable and conclusive facts, while the mainstream media, politicians, diplomats, and government officials do not.

Interestingly, most legitimate observers of media bias have substantial data to conclude that the major media outlets—*The New York Times, The Boston Globe, The Los Angeles Times*, CNN, CBS News, ABC News, Huffington Post, among them—not only do *not* suppress information that reveals the Palestinian plight, if anything, they have been relentless in their criticism of Israel. They certainly are not uniformly cheerleaders for Israel or Israeli policy, despite what those who wish to push their own pro-Palestinian, anti-Israel agenda might like to think. So the notion that pro-Palestinian views are not getting wide play already, and that the mainstream media regularly sides with Israel in its coverage, is not only naïve and conspiratorial but actually a complete inverse of the truth.

For instance, after the Lebanon War of 2006, in which Hezbollah engaged in asymmetrical warfare with Israel for 34 days, resulting in large-scale destruction within Lebanon, Marvin Kalb, of Harvard University's Shorenstein Center, wrote a report that summarized media perspectives of the conflict, with the aim of revealing any biases in the news coverage. Even though the conflict was initiated after Hezbollah kidnapped three IDF soldiers and preemptively launched missile attacks into Israeli territory, the world community, as it is wont to do, immediately began decrying Israel's use of "disproportionate response" in reacting to the aggression and seeking to suppress further Hezbollah raids. As a result, Kalb found, "on the front pages of *The New York Times* and *The Washington Post*, Israel was portrayed as the aggressor nearly twice as often in the headlines and exactly three times as often in the photos . . . Although neither *The Times* nor *The Post* stressed the theme of 'disproportionally' on their front pages, both made frequent references to it in their stories, analyses and editorial columns."[1] Kalb's conclusions when it came to broadcast coverage were not particularly favorable toward Israel either. "If you were watching American television," he wrote, "you would quickly have concluded that Fox cable news favored Israel, CNN tried to be balanced, and the three major evening news programs on ABC, CBS and NBC were more critical of Israel than of Hezbollah. It was a time of saturation coverage. In the first two weeks of the war, they ran 258 stories, an average of 18 stories a night. . . ."[2]

After the Cast Lead operation in Gaza by Israel in early 2009, the world media had a similar anti-Israel bent in describing both the military operations and the implications for Gazans, and for an eventual peace between the Palestinians and Israel. Not only did some mainstream media regularly condemn Israel's military strategy completely, but they went even further afield into editorializing, found HonestReporting.com, a web site that tracks and analyzes media coverage in the Middle East. "Many supposedly mainstream media and commentators saw no problem with [even] resorting to Holocaust imagery to make a point," its report found. "*The Independent's* Yasmin Alibhai-Brown, for example, asked: 'How many Palestinian Anne Franks did the Israelis murder, maim or turn mad?' while *Time Magazine's* front cover of a Star of David behind a wall and barbed wire, made it impossible to ignore the parallel between Israel's actions in Gaza and the Nazi Holocaust . . . *Toronto Sun* columnist Eric Margolis wrote on his personal website: 'It now seems clear the last disastrous act of the Bush administration was giving Israel a green light to launch its *final solution campaign* against the Hamas government in Gaza [emphasis added].'"[3]

So when Israel-haters spew their rhetoric and find it gains no traction in public opinion, their notion that it is due to a latent pro-Israel bias is obviously completely false. For pro-Palestinians, the reality that the whole world has not mobilized to dismantle the Zionist regime is proof enough that that pernicious pro-Israel forces must be at work to keep the status quo. What else could explain the general public's not seeing things in the same way, and not coming to the same conclusion, as the Israel-hater?

The eventual, but erroneous, conclusion that these anti-Israel ideo-logues invariably come to is that the reason their views are not widely known or accepted by the mainstream media is because of two possible reasons: either, in the popular, invidious fantasy that has inhabited the mind of anti-Semites for generations in what Richard Hofstadter called the "paranoid style of politics," the media itself is owned or otherwise controlled, and therefore censored, by Jews (thereby protecting Israel by deflecting any honest critiques); or, related to this same paranoia, peo-ple are so afraid of speaking against Israel for fear of being branded anti-Semites that they suppress their own speech, holding back criticism of the Jewish state even though they feel Israeli policies and actions, and the U.S.'s support of them, are fundamentally wrong. Those who do express their true feeling, who "fight truth to power" by condemning Israel and its treatment of the Palestinians, inevitably have to answer for their opinions when pro-Israel forces challenge them. This, of course, is something that ideologues despise: to actually have to defend their wild rants with facts. And in the Israeli/Palestinian conflict it has been very convenient for crit-ics of Israel and Zionism to claim that the cool reception their writings and utterances frequently receive in "the marketplace of ideas" is not due to the vacuity of their thought, but to the fact that, as many have stated, no criti-cism of Israel is "permitted," that there are severe consequences for those who condemn Israeli policies and behavior.

Stephen Walt and John Mearsheimer, for instance, authors of *The Israel Lobby* (discussed at length in Chapter 4), made this empty and ironic claim repeatedly as their anti-Israel book soared to the top of *The New York Times* bestseller list and they embarked on a virtual non-stop speaking tour to cam-puses, think tanks, and other anti-Semitic and anti-Israel groups who were eager to hear how criticism of Israel was a forbidden topic in academic or popular speech. The odious Norman Finkelstein, in one of his dozens and dozens of speeches on campuses around the world, cautions his audiences on the high price he pays for daring to say the impermissible, that is, for daring to criticize Israel. Clearly, he has not been cowered into silence.

Some of these forlorn spokespeople for the anti-Israel team have also appropriated the terms of campus victim groups when they describe the situ-ation they find themselves in once they have condemned Zionism, vilified Israel, or made libelous claims about "occupation," "genocide," "apartheid," "brutality," or the need for divestment. Because their ideological opponents have answered back their criticism of Israel, these Israel-haters claim that they no longer feel "safe" in expressing their ideas, that they are intimidated, or that their speech has been "chilled."

One example of this academic paranoia was Harvard's former Professor of Anthropology and of African and African American Studies, L. Roland Matory, who called upon his academic peers in a November 2006 faculty meeting to foster "a civil dialogue in which people with a broad range of perspectives *feel safe* and are encouraged to express their reasoned and evidence-based ideas [emphasis added]." And what were those "reasoned" ideas that had caused Professor Matory to feel "unsafe" on Harvard's insulated campus? Criticism of Zionism and Israel, of course, an issue about which Professor Matory had many notorious opinions, but which were being suppressed, in his view, through "widespread censorship of dissent about Israel-Palestine."[4] Professor Matory's implication was that on this one issue—criticism of Israel—the sacrosanct notion of "academic freedom" was being threatened by pro-Israel opponents who, he believed, wished to stifle any and all speech critical of the Jewish state.

But like many of his fellow travelers on the academic Left, Professor Matory made the mistake of assuming that academic freedom, and, indeed, academic free speech, is a bundle of rights that can be exercised without regard to those two other fundamental principles of higher education: academic responsibility and a fervent commitment to actual scholarship, as opposed to sheer ideology parading as what Matory referred to "reasoned and evidence-based ideas." With great regularity, academic imbecility and fraudulent scholarship has been substituted for reasoned inquiry on our campuses, and, observed Michael Rubin, a resident scholar at the American Enterprise Institute, "academic freedom is meant to protect scholarship, not replace it."[5]

Professor Matory is not the first academic to bemoan the oppressive and fearful might of pro-Israel spokespeople in stifling any criticism or discussion of Israel; and his outrage and trepidations might inspire sympathy, save for the inconvenient fact that the sheer volume and frequency of chronic, unrelenting, vitriolic, and one-sided demonization of Zionism and Israel on campuses worldwide makes Professor Matory's claims of being cowered into silence by Israel's supporters a bit disingenuous. But evidence to the contrary aside, Professor Matory, who spent his years at Harvard railing against Israel and who has since left Harvard for Duke University, determined conclusively that "Since Vietnam, Israel has become the heartbeat of U.S. foreign policy and a litmus test of what can be debated—and even of who will be allowed to speak—on university campuses."[6] What is more, Matory wildly claimed, a then-current attempt by the British Union of Lecturers to boycott Israel, which in the meantime had come under fire from Israel supporters around the world, "has its counterpart in a decades-old U.S. practice of threatening, defaming, or censoring scholars who dare to criticize Israel."[7] Professor Matory, and Jimmy Carter, Ward Churchill, and Norman Finkelstein, among other Israel critics, regularly express their shock when their rants and libels are answered back to, and they often imagine horrible oppression imminent once they have gone public with their attacks on Israel. "In my country, people tremble in the fear of losing their friends, jobs, advertising revenues, campaign contributions, and alumni donations if they question Zionism or Israeli policy," Matory ominously described, "despite the billions of our tax dollars paid annually for Israel's defense and sustenance."[8] One wonders then, if they are so concerned with possible job loss, sanctions, censure, and intellectual excommunication, why these ranters do not simply remain silent.

What Professors Finkelstein, Walt, Mearsheimer, and Matory have all apparently failed to realize is that they have *not* been silenced at all in their unrelenting attacks against Israel; in fact, the very opposite is true: they have achieved world-wide notoriety and, in some cases, wide acclaim for their views. More importantly, in their zeal to preempt the insulating benefit of this notion of "academic freedom," they have sought to deprive their ideological opponents of the same rights and protection; that is, while they want to be able to utter any calumny against the Jewish state and suffer no recriminations for their speech, they view any speech from those challenging their views to be oppressive, stifling, unreasonable, and, in the popular term used by those who frequently utter second-rate ideas, "chilling."

But the issue is far more obvious than the professors care to realize, and much less insidious. Those who speak back to ideologues such as Matory, Finkelstein, Carter, Walt, and Mearsheimer do so not to suppress criticism of Israel; academic freedom grants the professors the right to spew forth any academic meanderings they wish, but it does not make them free from being challenged for their thoughts.

"Free speech does not absolve anyone from professional incompetence,"[9] wrote Michael Rubin; and those who question divestment petitions, or critique the anti-Israel and anti-American "scholarship" parading on campuses as Middle East Studies, or contradict a former U.S. president who suggests that Israel is an apartheid nation, or answer back when a work purports to reveal a sinister Jewish cabal controlling U.S. foreign policy, or correct such notions as Professor Matory's that Israel is "quashing the rights of millions of Palestinians refugees to lands, houses, and goods stolen as a condition of Israel's founding in the late 1940s" are not stifling debate about Israel or seeking to silence their intellectual opponents. They are using *their own* academic freedom and free speech to rebut what they see as distortions, half-truths, propaganda, mistakes about history, or outright lies.

It is also convenient to assign blame to a powerful, silencing lobby for one's own failure to communicate a viewpoint in a compelling way—in the case of Israel-bashers—who either have to explain why their noxious ideology is not being accepted widely, or invent a reason why they have been punished for their radical thoughts by public ridicule, loss of tenure, or other career-altering occurrences. Norman Finkelstein assumes that his failure to receive tenure at DePaul, and his subsequent dismissal, was due to the pressure and denunciation his received from many quarters in academe, but, most significantly, from the dreaded 'Israel Lobby' that Walt and Mearsheimer were clever enough to uncover in their screed. Supporters of Finkelstein, such as University of Wisconsin student Kyle Szarzynski, found credence in the notion that the Israel Lobby regularly suppressed criticism of Israel and punished those who uttered it. In an article he wrote in the University's student newspaper, *The Badger Herald*, "Israel Lobby Censors Academic Honesty," Szarzynski specifically accused the Lobby of orchestrating Finkelstein's academic downfall because it found his views on Israel unacceptable. Finkelstein's "writings and activism penetrate the façade of conventional political discourse and expose the ugly reality of U.S. and Israeli power," Szarzynski wrote. "The result has been a backlash from the political mainstream—especially from the Israel lobby—in the form of an aggressive campaign to silence him as a public intellectual." What is more, he continued, once again using the language of victimization and oppression, "Dr. Finkelstein's case is not an isolated one. Indeed, it is indicative of an *increasingly hostile atmosphere* for pro-Palestinian and leftist academics [emphasis added]."[10]

The irony that has escaped the many extreme voices that continually rail against Israel is that much of the hostility and intimidation on campus, when it exists at all, is largely due to their own outrageous speech, teaching, and professed ideology about the Palestinian cause and the many ills of Israel. It is the incendiary rhetoric emanating from Middle East studies departments, Israel Apartheid Weeks sponsored by Muslim Student Association chapters, teach-ins and rallies where Stars of David are torn, coated with blood, or equated to swastikas, boycotts and petitions for divestment of funds from Israeli-connected businesses, or the banning of Israeli scholars from visiting other institutions—it is all of these instances in which the level of incitement and execrable speech against Israel, Zionism, and Jews is heard and where actual intimidation, harassment, and verbal oppression could be said to be occurring. The Left, and those who despise the West and love Third-world movements of resistance and self-determination, feel that they are morally superior to people with opposing views, including those who give their moral support to the Middle East's only democracy; in fact, they are contemptuous of anyone who professes not to see the need for social justice for the Palestinians, and who does not work diligently to bring an end to what they believe to be the racist Zionist regime and an elimination of the colonial project that Israel, in their view, has become.

What Leftist professors and students who demonize Israel want is to be able to exploit academic freedom to proclaim whatever slander and accusation they wish against the Jewish state—all of which they most surely believe with the utmost conviction—but without suffering any consequences as a result of their attacks. That habit is convenient because it means that what one says against Israel does not even have to be true, or reflect the reality of the politics of the Arab/Israeli conflict. It means that history and facts can be overlooked, and propaganda, which is either invented by the speakers themselves or merely promulgated by them, can be used to further marginalize Israel in the world community. Having another, contradictory voice question one's statements means that the Israel-hater would have to engage in a dialogue, in which his or her commentary could be shown to be flawed or inaccurate, as opposed to a monologue, which goes unquestioned and, when uttered by professors in the classroom, become indoctrination, not teaching.

In the view of classics professor Bruce Thornton, on-campus dialogue has been hijacked and scholarly endeavor has been politicized; the effect of this is that in only permitting one point of view, academic inquiry has been debased and substandard levels of dialogue have been introduced. "The politicization of the university has transformed academic free speech into something more like the no-holds-barred, anything-goes political speech of the town square," Professor Thornton wrote. "Ideologues have discarded the university's higher intellectual standards, deriding them as ivory-tower excuses for avoiding political engagement. This decline of academic free speech into activist politics and ideology has not even been consistent. The political prejudices of the professoriate—a continuum that starts at liberal and ends at radical leftist—have favored liberal and leftist speakers, thus narrowing the range of ideas offered to the campus community."[11]

The American Association of University Professors (AAUP) warned against this very situation on campuses where the professoriate promoted personal or political agendas instead of teaching and inquiry, a situation which increasingly occurs today, especially in highly-politicized departments in sociology, anthropology, history, and Middle East studies. The Association's "1940 Statement of Principles on Academic Freedom and Tenure" suggested that:

> Teachers are entitled to freedom in the classroom in discussing their subject, but they should be careful not to introduce into their teaching controversial matter

which has no relation to their subject . . . When they speak or write as citizens, they should be free from institutional censorship or discipline, but their special position in the community imposes special obligations. As scholars and educational officers, they should remember that the public may judge their profession and their institution by their utterances. Hence they should at all times be accurate, should exercise appropriate restraint . . . and should make every effort to indicate that they are not speaking for the institution.[12]

There is nothing unseemly about countering speech—even hateful speech—with more speech. In fact, that is at the very heart of the university's mission. Professor Matory and others claimed that they sought a greater civility on campus through reasoned academic discourse, but their real intention seemed to be to create that civility by having only their side of the discussion be heard—without the uncomfortable necessity of hearing other, dissenting views. Like many of their fellow academics, they proclaimed widely the virtues of open expression, but only for those who utter those thoughts with which they agreed.

And while academics fulminate regularly against Israel and America, give tacit support to these countries' enemies, and heap vitriol on the Jewish state and its supporters—much of it approaching or exceeding what would be considered reasonable or rational criticism of a democratic state—they regularly cloak themselves with the protective shield of "academic free speech," that sacrosanct philosophy which has come to mean that liberal academics can express themselves, even loathsomely, and expect no one to question their poisonous rhetoric or answer back with a vigorous defense from the other side. When the Left derides Israel and promotes false, biased, or hateful ideas about Zionism, the Israel government, or military policies, and defenders speak back (as they did, for instance, when Walt and Mearsheimer published their controversial study of the "Israel Lobby") and commentators call them on their defective views, the common claim is that the outspoken critics of Israel have been "silenced" by the accusation of anti-Semitism and that their free speech is being "suppressed."

Part of that problem, suggested Gary A. Tobin in his book *The Uncivil University*, is that higher education has slavishly indulged its faculty with this elevated concept of academic free speech without suggesting that with that unfettered freedom comes some responsibility to speak with judgment and restraint. "Higher education is so concerned about the preservation of academic freedom that academic responsibility is ignored," he wrote. "Anti-Israelism can flourish because the academy is afraid to confront this ideology and those who preach it for fear of going down some slippery slope that will infringe upon academic freedom. But other slippery slopes are just as profoundly damaging to the ideals of the university, including the failure to ensure both high quality and honest scholarship, adhere to principles of truth, preserve civil discourse and provide freedom from intellectual intimidation. All of these affect academic freedom, and define academic responsibility."[13]

It is perfectly acceptable for academics to question the status quo and challenge prevailing ideas as they help students to find some truth amid many ideological options; indeed, that is one of the chief roles of the university, and should be. What is not acceptable, and, in fact, is damaging the very core of higher education in its one-sided, doctrinaire approach to learning, is the pattern of lies, contortions, and mistaken assumptions endemic to discussions about the politics, military actions, and very existence of Israel. Focusing all that opprobrium on this one country, suggested Melanie Phillips, is the great tragedy of the academy, and signals a failure of the professoriate to address contemporary issues in a reasoned, balanced way, all at the expense of one nation. ". . . These are our university teachers," she wrote, "the very people responsible for shaping the assumptions of a society, whose own profound ignorance, prejudice and twisted morality are now on such conspicuous display. Rather than maintain their historic role as the disinterested custodians of truth and objectivity, university academics have become the principal promulgators of an agenda to delegitimise [sic] the state of Israel and, by doing so, delegitimise [sic] the claim to peoplehood of one people and one people alone in the world: the Jews."[14]

Moreover, while Leftist and radical professors profess to be guarding the tradition of academic freedom and free speech on their campuses, universities as a lot have been subsumed by a rank hypocrisy when it comes to actually balancing competing views from different sides of academic debates. What has been dubbed "political correctness" is actually the subversion of the stated goal of promoting the free expression of *all* views within the university community. What it has come to mean, unfortunately, is that only those views conforming to prevailing political orthodoxies are considered to be "acceptable" by the guardians of what may be said and who may say it. On most campuses today, that means that liberal professors and students of specific "victim" groups are largely responsible for defining and permitting the limits of expression, abetted by craven administrators who are worried about offending some students or in creating campuses where certain groups or individuals will feel "harassed," "intimidated," "uncomfortable," or "unwelcomed."

Of course, concern for Jewish students' well-being and emotional safety does not seem to be of any great concern by college administrations. That has meant that while Jewish students at UC Irvine, San Francisco State University, and York University in Toronto, to name a few troubling campuses, have had to endure being assaulted by waves of anti-Israel propaganda, vitriolic speeches, hate-fests, and lengthy campaigns of anti-Zionist vilification—including physical intimidation and assaults—university officials have been slow to address these incidents, nor have they taken public moral stands against the professors and students groups who have conjured up this odious brew against Israel and Jews.

That does not mean that university administrations are unaware of certain groups' concerns when their rights or "feelings" are trampled on. It *does* mean that Jewish students—like white men, Christians, conservatives, or Republicans—are not perceived as being a group needing protection; so in the greatest moral fraud perpetrated by universities claiming to be diverse and all-inclusive, diversity on most campuses today encompasses diversity of thought, as Professor Thornton put it, on "a continuum that starts at liberal and ends at radical leftist."[15] In their mission to protect the sensibilities and emotional well-being of identified campus victim groups, universities, often violating their own written guidelines and codes of behavior, have instituted speech codes to prevent what is generally called "hate speech" now, but which has become a perverse tactic to marginalize, and exclude, the speech and ideology of those with whom liberals and Leftists do not agree. Because they feel they have the moral high ground and a much more profound insight into social justice and the rights of the oppressed victim groups with whom they share an intellectual affinity, Leftists are fervent in their belief that they therefore have a right to unfettered speech to promulgate their own high-minded views. In fact, the speech of their ideological opponents, simply by virtue of the fact that it contradicts the moral principles that the Leftist holds dear, is regularly regarded as "hate speech" that can be ignored, punished, or, as happens with increasing regularity, shut down completely and excluded from the campus conversation.

Some universities have resorted to implementing speech codes as way to expunge expression that they believe will intimidate or harass certain groups on campus, which ordinarily might seem like a reasonable goal for universities to have. But the true intent of speech codes is far more sinister, as courts have regularly determined in finding them to generally be unconstitutional: the real intent of regulations governing what may be said on campus about whom is not to suppress *all* speech and attitudes, but merely those ideas with which the moral gatekeepers disagree, those ideas and political beliefs that are unfashionable.

Where did the philosophical rationale come from which allows liberals and college administrators to make the leap from purporting to endorse freedom of expression for all on their campuses, to instead reserving that right, in actual practice, only to favored groups? For many on the Left who were students and young faculty members during the 1960s, it was the influence of the Marxist philosopher Herbert Marcuse and his notion of "repressive tolerance" that changed the way intellectuals understood who should, and should not, have the right to free speech—in short, whose views should prevail in the marketplace of ideas. Marcuse realized that liberal "progressivism" could not achieve radical social and cultural change if its views had to compete on an equal plane with the conservative ideology of the Right. Why? Because in his view, the repressive force of the existing establishment could not be weakened unless its ability to control speech—and ideas—was diluted. That would only be accomplished, according to Marcuse, by favoring "partisan" speech to promote "progressive" or revolutionary change, and that speech would, by necessity, be "intolerant towards the protagonists of the repressive status quo."[16]

When political correctness first began to engulf our campuses, of course, Marcuse's legacy meant that racist or "hateful" speech was attacked as just that: speech which was unacceptable to those "victim" groups who were perceived as needing protection from freely-spoken opinions—generally members of racial, ethnic, or sexual minorities. As a result, speech codes were frequently called for to insulate such individuals from speech that was deemed to be too hateful to permit—speech that was, nevertheless, consistently recognized by the courts to be protected speech. Universities have therefore had to take a new approach in their attempts to suppress speech of whose content they do not approve. As they do, for instance, when Muslim students' sensibilities are offended when critics of Islamism come to speak on campuses, administrators now deem offensive behavior and speech to be 'harassing' and 'intimidating,' not merely expressive. On college campuses now, to paraphrase George Orwell, all views are equal, but some are more equal than others.

The moral relativism that imbues academic free speech was clearly at work on Professor Matory's campus during the tenure of Lawrence Summers as Harvard's president between 2001 and 2006. Summer's ignoble loss of his presidency confirmed the reality that, despite its claims to the contrary, academia, even at hallowed Harvard, was no longer necessarily the intellectual marketplace for open discourse and free speech, even on matters of controversy where vigorous debate and alternate views would be productive.

Widely praised by much of the student body, alumni, and some faculty members for his vision and ability to take a hard look at large financial, ethical, and managerial challenges at Harvard, Summers nevertheless was done in by a core group of Faculty of Arts and Sciences professors, scolds on the intellectual Left whose tolerance for freedom of speech and ideas seemed to be extended only to those harboring viewpoints identical to their own.

Summers' resignation, as widely known, came after dissenting faculty twice cast a "no-confidence" vote—a largely symbolic gesture—but one that sufficiently eroded his support and made further conversations untenable. The term 'no-confidence vote,' of course, has become a code word that actually represents, not in this instance a lack of confidence in Summers' managerial or leadership abilities, but rather a rigid unwillingness for certain vocal faculty to embrace ideas—some bold , some logical—antithetical to their own. Thus, 'no confidence' really means: no affinity, no discussion, and, ironically, no intellectual diversity.

One of his defining moral decisions was embodied in Summers' controversial 2002 speech in which he rejected a divestment petition to withdraw funds benefiting Israel signed by, among others, seventy-four Harvard professors, many from the College of Arts and Sciences. He observed that anti-Semitic and anti-Israel attitudes, once the invidious products of fringe groups and right-wing cranks, had begun to appear on college campuses, that "profoundly anti-Israel views are increasingly finding support in progressive intellectual communities. Serious and thoughtful people," he said in the most pointed section of his comments, "are advocating and taking actions that are anti-Semitic in their effect if not their intent."

But even as he was cautioning divestment proponents to examine the true nature of their attitudes and the ramifications of their actions, Summers, unlike his critics, was willing to let even foolish views be heard. "We should always respect the academic freedom of everyone to take any position," he said. But, he added, those who take provocative positions have to assume that their views can and will be challenged, "that academic freedom does not include freedom from criticism."[17]

One thing those on the Left despise is being questioned about their integrity, and so it was with the indignant petition-signers and their fellow travelers, who accused Summers of being intellectually oppressive and "stifling debate" by questioning the morality of their actions and raising a point about the true intent of the divestment effort: singling out Israel specifically among all nations for economic sanctions. The offended faculty never forgave Summers for expressing his opinion, engaging in intellectual inquiry, and naming them for what they were.

That same sensitivity to language about Israel and anti-Semitism did not seem to faze faculty members and liberals, however, when Harvard's

English department in 2002 invited poet Tom Paulin to speak as a prestigious Morris Gray Lecturer, and did so, according to English Department
chair, Lawrence Buell, to affirm a "belief in the importance of free speech as
a principle and practice in the academy." That, of course, is a noble and pur-
poseful role for universities, save for the fact that Paulin, poet and lecturer at
Oxford University, had been quoted articulating the odious sentiment that
"Brooklyn-born" Jewish settlers [in Israel] should be "shot dead." "I think
they are Nazis, racists, I feel nothing but hatred for them," he told Egypt's
al-Ahram Weekly. "I can understand how suicide bombers feel . . . I think
attacks on civilians in fact boost morale."[18]

Summers had also uttered forbidden speech, in the view of campus Leftists, when he urged the Harvard community, after the events of September
11th, to examine their feelings of patriotism and to undertake a reevalua-
tion of the school's 34-year ban of the Reserve Officers Training Program
(ROTC) on campus. Patriotism, Summers said at the annual Public Service
Awards presentation at Harvard's Kennedy School of Government, might
actually be a positive and virtuous emotion for a wounded nation; it was,
he thought, a word "used too infrequently" in academia. "There is a special
nobility, a special grace, to those who are prepared to sacrifice their lives for
our country."[19]

These were, one would think, not outrageous, jingoistic sentiments for a
university president to express, not long after the nation was terribly wounded
by homicidal terrorists. But to a large number of Left-leaning, anti-American
Harvard professors, these calls for patriotic spirit were an inexcusable affront
to their clearly-defined and long-standing animus to the military.

It is one thing to reject patriotism and support of the military during a
time of war and be insulted by having it suggested to you as positive things;
it is another, more incredible, act instead to embrace and encourage the
ideology of the perceived enemy of the United States. But a Harvard faculty panel felt no compunction in committing this very act when they chose
Zayed M. Yasin as a speaker at Harvard's 2002 commencement, whose provocative speech was originally titled, "American Jihad." His faculty supporters
apparently saw no insensitivity in using that incendiary term as a theme in
the months after 9/11, nor did it seem to bother them that Mr. Yasin was a
current supporter of the Holy Land Foundation, an organization that raised
funds for Hamas and that eventually was indicted by the U.S. Department of
Justice. Thus, respect for the military and patriotic zeal uttered by President
Summers was characterized as heavy-handed, inappropriate pressure; faculty
behavior, on the other hand, using a terrorist-comforting mouthpiece to castigate and scold America in an era of terrorism, was, in their view, a perfectly

acceptable technique for testing the boundaries of free speech, no matter how seemingly vile the message or intent.

This hypocrisy, not to mention a double standard, when it comes to evaluating the relative merits of speech on campuses is not limited to faculty and university presidents, either. Students, usually conservative or Republican students, often find themselves attacked and sometimes punished for exercising what should be their Constitutionally-protected right of expression In one instance of what has become a predictable and frequent assault on conservative campus publications, The Committee on Student Life at Tufts University, for instance, censured *The Primary Source*, a student magazine, for running satirical pieces that offended, in two separate instances, some African-American and Muslim students. Instead of actually creating "a place where controversial expression is embraced," and "an open campus committed to the free exchange of ideas," as described in Tufts' own student handbook, universities continue to punish what they categorize as offensive speech that does not conform to the acceptable, liberal views of politics, race, or sexuality.

While Tufts' official policy extols the merits of unfettered speech, suggesting that students "should cherish the opportunity to be learning in a place where controversial expression is embraced," it turns out that in reality that embrace is a somewhat deadly one for anyone whose controversial comments are aimed at groups perceived to be too vulnerable and sensitive to confront offensive speech and answer it with expression of their own views. The offending *Primary Source* piece, "Islam—Arabic Translation: Submission," which satirized Tufts' "Islamic Awareness Week" with a series of factual points about some of radical Islam's violent characteristics, "made the Muslim students on campus feel very uncomfortable and unwelcome," according to some of the complainants, and "was uncalled for and demean[ed] all of the work we put into our Islamic Awareness Week." The publication's punishment included the prospect of being de-funded and the requirement of thereafter having all stories and editorials signed by authors (a requirement that no other Tufts publication had), presumably so victims could henceforth know exactly which offending party to drag before the Committee for any future offenses.

Tufts' Committee on Student Life, after conducting a full investigation into the incidents, found, without sensing any contradiction in its conclusions, that while "The Committee believes that it is important for Tufts University to foster an intellectual climate in which students feel free to express their thoughts, however controversial," "we find that the MSA proved, by a preponderance of the evidence, that *The Primary Source* harassed Muslim students at Tufts, and created a *hostile environment* for them by publishing 'Islam—Arabic Translation: Submission.' The Committee found that the MSA established that the commentary at issue targeted members of the Tufts Muslim community for *harassment* and *embarrassment*, and that Muslim students felt *psychologically intimidated* by the piece [emphasis added]."[20]

There were troubling issues here, putting aside the basic question of fairness in punishing a student publication with repressive speech control because it exhibited loutish behavior. The publication was sanctioned, not because it displayed *actual* illegal harassing or intimidating behavior, but because some individuals were 'offended' or 'intimidated' by speech that they were perfectly free never to read. In fact, it was these same "victims" who provided testimony to the Committee and who provided "proof" that they were harassed by speech with which they did not agree. Students have a right to be offended by the speech—even hate speech—of their fellow students and speak back to that speech with speech of their own, but their fellow students also have a Constitutionally-protected right to be offensive, assuming that their conduct is within the bounds of the law—which the satirical publication's articles clearly were.

Nor were anti-Israel Tufts faculty members and students ever silenced in 2002 when a group of them signed a divestment petition to urge economic sanctions on Israel, an effort to destroy the viability of the Jewish State because they had decided that it was an apartheid, colonial settler nation that tramples the rights of victimized, long-suffering Palestinians. Could these very public denunciations of the Middle East's single democracy—political speech by Tufts faculty and students—have possibly been intimidating to Jewish students on campus and others who have a different, more positive view of Israel and its role in the world? Could Jewish students and supporters of Israel feel "harassed" by the anti-Israel invective that accompanies divestment petitions and harsh criticism of Israel? Yes, of course, they could have had that effect, but no one at Tufts seemed to think it necessary in this instance, when the "victims" were Jews and supporters of Israel, to create a committee to investigate any injustices perpetrated against a particular student group and what sanctions should be exercised to address those wrongs.

In those instances when controversy arises because Israel-hating or anti-Semitic professors have publicly expressed radical views, not only is there generally silence from most faculty and administrators about how these views may have harmed the collegiality of academic community, but many will reflexively defend the speech, regardless of how outrageous the content or potentially "hurtful" the message. In January of 2009, for example, a tenured sociology professor, William I. Robinson, of the University of California, Santa Barbara, sent an odious email to the 80 students in his "Sociology 130SG: The Sociology of Globalization" course. Under the heading "Parallel images of Nazis and Israelis," the email displayed a photo-collage of 42 side-by-side, grisly photographs meant to suggest an historical equivalence between Israel's treatment of Palestinians in its "occupation" of Gaza and the Third Reich's subjugation of the Warsaw Ghetto and its treatment of Jews during the Holocaust. Robinson sent the email without supplying any context for it, nor did it seemingly have any specific relevance to or connection with the course's content. Robinson's email did, however, contain the following helpful commentary:

> I am forwarding some horrific, parallel images of Nazi atrocities against the Jews and Israeli atrocities against the Palestinians. Perhaps the most frightening are not those providing a graphic depiction of the carnage but that which shows Israeli children writing "with love" on a bomb that will tear apart Palestinian children.

> Gaza is Israel's Warsaw—a vast concentration camp that confined and block-aded Palestinians, subjecting them to the slow death of malnutrition, disease and despair, nearly two years before their subjection to the quick death of Israeli bombs. We are witness to a slow-motion process of genocide .., a process whose objective is not so much to physically eliminate each and every Palestinian than to eliminate the Palestinians as a people in any meaningful sense of the notion of people-hood.[21]

In response to the inflammatory email, two students dropped the course and immediately filed a complaint with the University's Academic Senate's Charges Committee, and additionally went to two off-campus advocacy groups, the Anti-Defamation League and StandWithUs. Not surprisingly, charges of "anti-Semitism" came from some of Robinson's critics, as well as from those who believed, like StandWithUs's Roz Rothstein, that professors "should [not] be using their class roster to sell their own political opinions . . . Our concern," she said, "is that he abused his position and that it was unre-lated with his class."[22]

But many students and professorial colleagues at UCSB immediately came Robinson's defense, forming an ad hoc group called the Committee to Defend Academic Freedom (CDAF) at UCSB, "dedicated to organizing stu-dents on campus against nationwide campaigns against political repression," and also resisting what they ominously referred to as a "silencing campaign" waged against Robinson by outside forces who had undertaken a "flagrant and baseless affronts to academic freedom on this campus and to Professor

Robinson in particular." In June, five months after the University had initiated its investigation into Robinson's conduct, officials dismissed all charges and terminated the case without any negative findings against the sociology professor, and the CDAF smugly asserted that "the charge of anti-Semitism [was] made in bad faith," and that "its real purpose is to vilify and stifle any honest critiques of the state of Israel's policies and practices."[23]

Apparently Professor Robinson shared the Committee's belief that sinister outside "thought policemen" had instigated a campaign of suppression against him. Like professors Matory and Walt at Harvard, Robinson knew exactly where to assign blame for the scrutiny he had undergone as a result of his provocative email. "The Israel lobby is possibly the most powerful lobby in the United States," he told the *Daily Nexus*, UCSB's student newspaper, repeating the same accusation that is common from those who have actually acted in an anti-Semitic way, "and what they do is label any criticism of anti-Israeli conduct and practices as anti-Semitic." "This campaign is not just an attempt to punish me. The Israel lobby is stepping up its vicious attacks on anyone who would speak out against Israeli policies."[24] So in Professor Robinson's morally-incoherent mind, depicting Israeli Jews as the new Nazis who are committing genocide against the Palestinians is merely instructive content for a sociology course, but when those who believe that the comparison between Nazis and Jews is a perverse and libelous reading of historical fact answer back, it is a "vicious attack," a tactic of pro-Israel forces to deflect criticism and obscure the malignancy of their deeds. The professors and students who rallied so long and so fully behind Robinson as his case was heard recognized that the professor had the right to make those absurd utterances, as vile and as untrue as they may have been; what they forgot, or had never realized, is that he also had to be responsible for what he said, and be prepared for critics of his views to be free to express their views, as well.

The Anti-Israel 'Heckler's Veto': Shouting Down Conservative Speech

When campus radicals and Leftist professors are not moaning about how the dreaded Israel Lobby is attempting to suppress all criticism of Israel, or complaining about how any scrutiny of radical Islam, Palestinian terror, or Arab intransigency constitutes "hate speech" that will intimidate or harass Muslims, they have found other means to insure that countervailing opinions about Israel and the Palestinians are shut out. With great frequency, Muslim student groups, radical, anti-Israel professors, and even college officials themselves have taken it upon themselves to either restrict the ability of conservative or pro-Israel speakers to appear on campuses, or to deny them access to campus altogether.

In October of 2009, for example, two students groups at Washington University in St. Louis, the College Republicans and Young America's Foundation, had invited conservative author David Horowitz to deliver a speech entitled, "An Evening with David Horowitz: Islamo-Fascism Awareness and Civil Rights," and university administrators, choosing to avoid a close examination of radical Islam, cancelled Horowitz's planned appearance.

What Washington University's administration had done in this instance was essentially to exercise the "heckler's veto," shutting down speech with which it did not agree, or which it felt was too controversial for certain protected minorities on campus; but ominously, and in seeming contradiction to the school's own stated policy "to promote the free and open exchange of ideas and viewpoints, even if that exchange proves to be offensive, distasteful, disturbing or denigrating to some," this particular speech was suppressed *in advance of the event*, based on a belief that the speaker's words would possibly insult Muslim students and inflame their sensibilities.

The school officials' decision seemed to belie the University's own feckless contention, in its "Policy Statement on Demonstrations & Disruption," that it "encourages students, faculty and staff to be bold, independent, and creative thinkers," and that "fundamental to this process is the creation of an environment that respects the rights of all members of the University community to explore and to discuss questions which interest them, to express opinions and debate issues energetically and publicly, and to demonstrate their concern by orderly means."[25]

There were troubling issues here, putting aside the basic question of the fairness of denying certain students, with certain political beliefs, the opportunity to invite speakers to campus to share their views. Horowitz's speech was cancelled (and he had appeared, by his own account, on more than 400 campuses in the past), not because it might contain speech that was demonstrably false or even incendiary, but because some individuals might be 'offended' or 'intimidated' by speech that they were perfectly free never to hear.

"For me, it was . . . the content," explained the University's Dean of Students, Scott Smith, in rationalizing the decision to rescind Horowitz's invitation to speak, "particularly, the blanketed use of the term Islamo-Fascism."[26] The school was also concerned that the speech would be seen as "attacking another faith and seeking to cause derision on campus." But where does a college administration, whose own institution claims to value speech that is even "offensive, distasteful, disturbing or denigrating to some," decide that this particular topic—radical Islam—cannot and should not be spoken about?

Is this not a relevant discussion in a world where, since 9/11, over 15,000 acts of terror have been committed by murderous radicals in Islam's name? Does not an ideology which has as its aim the subjugation of other faiths and a world-wide caliphate under sharia law, and is fueled by billions in petro dollars, deserve, and, in fact, require, some critique and evaluation? And Mr. Horowitz's context for delivering his speech was also relevant; his view was that the current jihad against Israel on campuses in America and Canada was a symptom of the West's accommodation to radical Islam, and part of a wider problem caused by the Left's excuses for, and embrace of, totalitarian movements.

Mr. Horowitz always emphasized in his speeches that when he critiqued Islamo-fascism, he was not indicting all of Islam, or all Muslims, only those who used the religion as a justification for jihad. That was clearly the point of his message, and any honest listener to his speeches would think that it was. So, Washington University's notion that it had to preemptively protect the sensibilities of its Muslim students was at best condescending and at worst another way that unwritten speech codes are constructed, according to attorney and free speech expert Harvey Silverglate, to "protect ideologically or politically favored groups, and, what is more important, insulate these groups' self-appointed spokesmen and spokeswomen from criticism and even from the need to participate in debate."[27]

This obscurantism where radical Islam is being discussed—or not discussed, as the case may be—has much wider implications outside the relatively protected campus community, as Anne Bayefsky, from Eye on the UN.com, for instance, observed. Led by the Organization of the Islamic Conference, the morally-incoherent UN Human Rights Council passed a resolution in 2009, Bayefsky said, apparently embraced by the Obama administration, that "emphasizes that 'the exercise of the right to freedom of expression carries with it special duties and responsibilities . . .' which include taking action against anything meeting the description of 'negative racial and religious stereotyping.'"[28] Tellingly, and ominously, the resolution was passed to protect one religion and only one—Islam—and had as its main intention to criminalize blasphemy and essentially exculpate radical Islam by inoculating an entire religion from inspection, criticism, or condemnation.

Most disingenuous is how institutions of higher education like Washington University, while horrified by the prospect of a David Horowitz visit, use their claims of academic free speech as a cover for regularly bringing outrageous, out-of-the-mainstream views to campuses—either in student-run organizations, in course materials and teaching philosophies, in the sponsorship of festivals and cultural events, or in the person of controversial speakers and artists. For example, the concern over offending certain student groups suddenly did not have the same sense of urgency when speakers, with views certainly as controversial as Horowitz's, were enthusiastically invited to the Washington University campus, notable among them Norman Finkelstein (discussed extensively in Chapter 3), who spoke in 2007 as part of "Palestine Awareness Week," sponsored by the on-campus group Washington University Solidarity with Palestine.

Horowitz had been prevented from speaking and shouted down by ideological bullies before. In 2007 at Emory University, as a guest of Emory's College Republicans, Horowitz was scheduled to speak to an audience of some 300 people as part of that year's Islamo-Fascism Awareness Week. While boos, catcalls, and shouts of "Heil Hitler" filled the room, and protestors stood, backs turned to the stage, Horowitz attempted to deliver his speech. Finally, the hecklers, raucous members of radical groups such as Amnesty International, Veterans for Peace, Students for Justice in Palestine, and the Muslim Student Association (MSA), were sufficiently intrusive and belligerent to prevent Horowitz from speaking any further, and the speech was cancelled, as police, finally unable to calm the angry crowd, escorted Horowitz off the stage to safety.

The MSA, which, as discussed here extensively, is always eager to host Israel-loathing demagogues, has little use for the ideas of David Horowitz, nor are they receptive to Daniel Pipes, director of the Middle East Forum and founder of Campus Watch. Dr. Pipes' 2007 UC Irvine appearance, when he was scheduled to speak on "The Threat to Israel's Existence," was met with such outrageous vocal eruptions, chanting, and screaming that the event to be cancelled.

Ideological thugs were also present at the University of Chicago in October 2009 to greet Israel's former prime minister Ehud Olmert, who was invited to speak at Mandel Hall as part of the King Abdullah II Leadership Lecture series organized by the Harris School of Public Policy. Dozens of protestors inside the hall and some 100 outside, from Chicago's Muslim Student Association, Students for Justice in Palestine, as well as groups from the University of Illinois-Chicago (UIC) and Northwestern, were intent on disrupting the speech with catcalls, jeers, and outrageous threats and condemnation, and were so effective in their incivility that the planned 20-minute presentation ran nearly an hour and a half. Police had to forcibly drag a bleating protestor out the door as others hurled invectives, condemnation, and swears at Olmert, calling him a "murderer," "war criminal," and "racist." While the University's president, Robert J. Zimmer, condemned the behavior of the protestors, and suggested that their disruptive behavior was "disturbing" and inimical to "rational discourse," those anti-Israel radicals who had decided to suppress Olmert's speech felt that the former Israeli prime minister had no right to even be part of an academic conversation.

One student who had attended the speech, for instance, Frank Pucci, a political science and history major, wrote in the University's student newspaper, *The Chicago Maroon*, his view that "Ehud Olmert is not an academic who happens to have a difference of opinion that must be respected; he is responsible for the deaths of thousands. As the first protester who stood cried out, 'war crimes are not free expression.'" Not only that, Pucci claimed, but the mere fact that Olmert was invited to speak was insulting and hurtful to the campus community. In light of the grave moral injustice effected by Olmert's presence, "the only responsible course of action is for the University of Chicago to apologize to the members of the Arab, Muslim, and pro-Palestinian community for allowing such a blatant display of bias and insolence against them."[29]

While Pucci was eager to catalogue Olmert's many and various war crimes and inhuman actions— "1,400 people . . . killed in Gaza . . , an overwhelming majority of them . . . civilians," demonstrating "military incompetence at best and a massacre at worst," which "the United Nations Human Rights Council formally backed [in] a report that confirmed war crimes committed against Palestinians by Israel"[30]—tellingly absent in his retelling of Israel's conflicts in Gaza and Lebanon was any mention of Hamas and Hezbollah, respectively. Ideological enemies of Israel want to position Israel always as the brutal aggressor, a country which randomly, and without provocation or cause, wages war against innocent Arab populations. Clearly, the inconvenient truth that Hamas's charter contains an article that mandates an unending mission to exterminate Jews and extirpate Israel, for example, does not seem to have anything to do, in Pucci's mind, with Israel's 63 year-long need to defend itself and its citizenry from terrorism and Arab rage.

When confronted with the possibility that a speaker will voice ideas contrary to their own reflexive ideology, radical and Leftist campus groups often try to have the speaking event cancelled in advance by college officials, as they did in David Horowitz's case at Washington University. Rather than have to go through the intellectually inconvenient process of having to confront views other than their own, anti-Israel, anti-American groups try to demonize and marginalize the views of conservative speakers—in advance of their visits—by painting them as Islamophobes, Zionists, right wing hate-mongers, neo-cons, or Christian fundamentalists. Appeals to university administrators by these victim groups commonly claim that the prospective speaker is known for "hate speech," that his or her views are too controversial or "hurtful" for campus audiences, or, in the case of Geert Wilders, the Dutch parliamentarian who was invited to Temple University in October 2009, that the political views of a speaker are so controversial and potentially offensive to Muslims that the speaker should not even be able to speak at all—even if some students on campus do wish to hear the views.

Wilder's appearance was organized by a student group called Temple University Purpose and funded by the David Horowitz Freedom Center as part of its series of campus events across the country named "Islamo-Fascism Awareness Week." But while they seem perfectly content with inviting their own speakers who spew forth loathsome calumnies against Jews, Israel, and imperialist America, when it came to Wilders, the Muslim Student Association simply had to protest. Monira Gamal-Eldin, president of the Muslim Student Association, voiced the sentiments of victims-in-waiting on the Temple campus, those Muslim students who would be unable to bear Wilder's alternate ideas about a "stealth jihad" he feels is being waged world-wide by radical Islam. "The Muslim population at Temple feels attacked, threatened and ultimately unsafe that Mr. Wilders has been invited to voice his hate-driven opinions,"[31] Gamal-Eldin wrote in a letter to school officials as a justification for cancelling the speech. What is more, she claimed that the content of Wilder's speech, which neither she nor anyone else on campus, of course, had heard yet, was not even worthy of protection by the concept of academic free speech. Why? Because, in the view of MSA, who have "had to deal with hate speakers before," Wilder's expression would not fall under the category of acceptable speech. "What he's preaching is not free speech, Gamal-Eldin decided. "He is funneling hate toward one group of people."[32]

The MSA was correct about one thing: Wilder definitely had been focusing one group of people: Islamists, who, he believed, used the Quran and the precepts of Islam to wage jihad against the West. Some of his views, such as outlawing the Quran for its ideology of Islamist imperialism and its call for the suppression of other creeds, have met with understandable resistance from groups around the world, including in Britain where he was denied entrance to the country by officials who felt his presence might incite violence. He is also the producer of a short film, "Fitna," which many have denounced as being anti-Muslim for its vivid depictions of Islamic terrorism juxtaposed with passages from the suras of the Quran, a film that was shown at the Temple University event.

That was all too much for one Temple student, Josh Rosenthal, who saw Wilder's message not as a warning to the West of the "stealth jihad" being waged by jihadist foes bent on our destruction, but as yet another example of conservatives' fundamental "racism" and "intolerance." "'I think it's completely wrong that someone who promotes racism and intolerance should be given a platform at this university," he said. "It's hate speech disguised as free speech."[33] Many in the audience that night seemed to have shared Rosenthal's sentiment, since, after the 30-minute talk concluded and a question-and-answer session began, jeers and booing became so loud that Wilder's security team had to usher him out of the room to safety, once again shutting down a conversation in which the enemies of democracy, Israel, and Western values did not wish to engage.

In that same month of 2009, Yale University, too, ironically, had invited a speaker whose expression had already inflamed Muslim emotions around the world with the publication in 2005, by the Danish newspaper *Jyllands-Posten*, of 12 cartoons depicting the prophet Mohammed. Kurt Westergaard, one of the cartoonists whose own drawing provocatively portrayed Mohammed with a bomb in his turban, was invited to speak to students by Branford College Master Steven Smith, at what is quaintly referred to as a Master's Tea, an event promoted on the Yale campus by the International Free Press Society. Yale had more than a passing interested in the controversial cartoons, and how their publication had raised a world-wide examination of the limits of free speech and how Islam should, or should not, be accommodated in an open society. During the same week as Westergaards's visit, Jytte Klausen was also coincidentally slated to speak to the Yale community—and about the same topic. Klausen was the author of a provocative new book, *Blasphemy and Inquiry: The Cartoons That Shook the World*, which Yale University Press had agreed to publish. The book had intended to be a comprehensive analysis of the creation of the original cartoons, and an overview of how their publication in various world media inspired riots, deaths, and Muslim rage around the globe. But even the publishing process had become controversial; after the book was complete, the Yale Press decided, almost incredulously, that it would not include the cartoons themselves in a book which purported to be the comprehensive analysis of the affair, fearing, as many other media had, that re-publication of the cartoons would likely ignite violence and repercussions once again.

So in this October week in 2009—with one of the creators of the cartoons and an author who was resurrecting the cartoon discussion on campus—it was something of an imperfect storm for Yale's Muslim Student Association, who, in words regularly heard from the group at other campuses, proclaimed that they were "deeply hurt and offended" by the invitation to Westergaard. "As an institution purportedly committed to making our campus an educational environment where all students feel equally comfortable, we feel that by hosting Kurt Westergaard Yale is undermining its commitment to creating a nurturing learning environment by failing to recognize the religious and racial sensitivity of the issue," the group said. "Certainly, it would be unlikely for a white supremacist or a holocaust denier to be a distinguished guest speaker at Yale; hosting individuals who propagate hate is not only a disservice to the minorities that hate is directed towards but to the campus community as a whole."[34]

The Yale campus, of course, has had its share of controversial visitors before the Danish cartoonist and an author writing about the same incident. In 2006, Sayed Rahmatullah Hashemi, former ambassador-at-large for the Taliban, outrageously became a student at Yale, with the administration's official statement suggesting, apparently without any moral embarrassment, that they hoped that Hashemi's "courses help him understand the broader context for the conflicts that led to the creation of the Taliban and to its fall. . . . Universities are places that must strive to increase understanding."[35]

Apparently, no groups of Yale students were "hurt and offended" by a former Taliban member on campus, or in 2003 when the Afro-American Cultural Center and the Black Student Alliance invited Amiri Baraka, former Black Panther and the soon thereafter-dismissed, and embattled, poet laureate of New Jersey, to speak. It surprised and annoyed some in the Yale community that Baraka—a virulent anti-white, anti-Semitic, anti-Establishment Leftist—was invited to the University in the first place, but not Pamela George, assistant dean of Yale College and director of the Cultural Center, who drew a comparison between Baraka's hate-filled visit to that of Yoni Fighel, a former Israeli general and soldier who had come to Yale earlier that semester to engage in apolitical discussions on Middle East security and Israel.

Perhaps the comparison was made precisely because Mr. Baraka had been under assault by many who were shocked by the conspiracy-laden anti-Semitism of his poem "Somebody Blew Up America" in which he referred, among other wild claims, to Israel's foreknowledge of and complicity in the bombing of the World Trade towers. But the poem also had words to denigrate American culture, imperialism, the white race, Zionism, and other sinister powers in Baraka's cynical imagination. Though he persistently denied his anti-Semitism, earlier poems have included such descriptions as "poems like fists beating niggers out of Jocks or dagger poems in the slimy bellies of the owner-jews . . . Setting fire and death to whities as-."

But more revealing than the fact that such a seemingly anti-Semitic speaker was invited, and then celebrated, at Yale was the reaction of one student whose theory was that the only reason that there was controversy about Baraka's poetry and slurs of Jews was because—incredibly—that Jews control the press. Writing one of his regular columns in the *Yale Daily News*, Sahm Adrangi decided that, in this case, where, after all, it was only Israel, Jews, and America being slurred, "student groups who invite controversial speakers ought to be congratulated, not condemned. Contrarian thinkers and conspiracy theorists," he mused, "expose us to vantage points we rarely encounter in fellow Yalies. Their arguments are often more sophisticated than we'd expect and in debating them, we gain a deeper understanding of our own opinions."[36]

But that aside, the real lesson to be gleaned from incendiary anti-Israel speakers like Baraka "isn't really about free speech," Adrangi cautioned, "It's about how special interests manipulate the public discourse to advance their agendas." And who were those special interests who were attempting to make much ado about Baraka's poetic ravings? The Jewish press, of course. "Jews tend to sympathize with Israel more so than non-Jews. And in my three years at the *Yale Daily News*, Jewish students have comprised a majority of management positions. . . ." Adrangi was quick to point out, however, that he was not suggesting there was a conspiracy among Jewish journalists to tilt the argument in Israel's favor. "But," he asked rhetorically, and knowingly, "does the prevalence of Jews in American media, business and politics help explain America's steadfast support for Israel, whose 35-year occupation of Palestinian lands is an affront to human decency? Of course."[37]

The moral inversion that occurs so commonly on campuses has completely infected rational dialogue and scholarly inquiry. When Columbia University's president Lee Bollinger invited Iranian President Mahmoud Ahmajinedad to speak at the School in 2007, it was clear that questionable intellect and moral imbecility would not immediately disqualify someone from being an honored speaker on the most prestigious American campuses. In fact, after the speech, more than 100 of Columbia's faculty did register their protest about Ahmajinedad's appearance at the University; unfortunately, noted Bruce Thornton, "not for inviting the Iranian president, but for Bollinger's harsh introductory comments, which they deemed an appeasement of conservative critics and, in the words of one professor, the 'language of warfare.'"[38] So great was the faculty's disdain for George Bush and his incursions into Iraq, not to mention his war on terror and the use of the Patriot Act, that the faculty exhibited more concern for the stringency of the questions with which Bollinger confronted the Iranian president than they did for the fact that a great university had given a world stage to an apocalyptic madman who denies the first Holocaust at the same time he is planning the next one.

Liberal-leaning academics on American campuses seemingly hold the notion that free speech is only good when it articulates politically correct, ideologically-acceptable views of protected victim or minority groups, and that it does not offend Islam. But true intellectual diversity—the ideal that is often bandied about but rarely achieved—must be dedicated to the protection of unfettered speech, representing opposing viewpoints, where the best ideas become clear through the utterance of weaker ones. For Justice Oliver Wendell Holmes, for instance, the protection of free expression for all views was essential, not only to allow discourse of popular topics, but, even more importantly, in instances where unpopular or currently-controversial speech was deemed offensive and unworthy of being heard. "If there is any principal of the Constitution," he observed, "that more imperatively calls for attachment than any other, it is the principal of free thought—not free thought for those who agree with us but freedom for the thought that we hate."

The university officials and student groups who now try to expel all thought that they "hate;" who proclaim their desire for campuses where there will be vigorous discourse, on contentious issues, from many points of view, but allow the expression of only acceptable opinions; who label speech with which they do not agree as hateful, and demonized or shun the speakers who utter these alternate views; who vilify Israel, Jews, Zionism, and U.S. support for the Jewish state with every sort of invective, but claim that criticism of Israel is suppressed by a cabal-like "Israel lobby;" and who shout down, heckle, and bully their ideological opponents during on-campus events—all of these individuals have sacrificed one of the core values for which the university exists. In their zeal to be inclusive, and to recognize the needs and aspirations of victim groups, they have pretended to foster inquiry, but they have stifled and retarded it.

They have created what Gary A. Tobin characterized as the "uncivil university" where frequently "a 'butterfly effect' has taken place, so that, with a small shift here and there, what were once well-intentioned and vital components of the university system, such as an emphasis on academic freedom, the willingness to question the established order, a love of rigorous scholarship, and an embracing of multiculturalism, have become twisted and sometimes barely recognizable versions of their former selves. It is in this unfortunate state that ideologies and practices antithetical to the civil university have flourished on some campuses, an indication of just how far they have diverged from their purpose."[39]

And, as this otherwise noble purpose for the university has devolved, the first victim in the corruption of academic free speech has been the truth.

PART TWO
THE ANTI-ISRAEL BATTLEGROUNDS

Chapter 6

Intellectual Rot at Columbia's MEALAC & Other Middle East Studies Programs

Columbia Unbecoming

On a November night in 2004, almost four hundred students at Columbia University sat crowded in the theater of the University's Lerner Hall to watch a troubling 25-minute film that was finally being released to the public, *Columbia Unbecoming*, produced by a Boston-based Israel advocacy organization, the David Project. The film, which exposed instances of student intimidation at the hands of some professors in Columbia's department of Middle Eastern and Asian Languages and Culture (MEALAC), was brief but shocking, and revealed what many had already suspected about Columbia's program—and other Middle East studies programs elsewhere: that under the veneer of purported scholarship and high-minded academic goals, there had developed a hothouse of intellectual rot, an entire area of academic study guided by what Martin Kramer, among other critics, has called "tenured incompetents."[1]

For one of the country's great universities the film's content became something of an embarrassment, as alumni, faculty, administrators, and students began to question how an entire department—encompassing an entire area of scholarship—had devolved into such a troubling state. Were professors, under the umbrella of academic free speech, articulating one-sided, virulently anti-Israel, anti-American assessments of current politics? Did they stifle dissenting views from students in their classrooms? Were Jewish students singled out for harsher treatment, and had Columbia failed to provide adequate support systems and administrative channels through which these students could seek redress for mistreatment by errant professors? Based on the film, the answer seemed to be, yes; more troubling was the suggestion that this problem was endemic to Middle East studies programs—and the academic mandarins who oversaw them—in major universities around the country. "MEALAC is the embodiment of Columbia's Middle East Studies problem," said *Jihad Watch's* Hugh Fitzgerald: "the exclusive focus on the present at the expense of the past, the embrace of flimsy academic fads and confessional politics in place of deep and dispassionate scholarship, the teaching of narrow specialties and faculty interests couched in broad terms of post-colonialism and anti-imperialism, the fetishization of the Arab-Israeli conflict, and the reward of mediocrity."[2]

It was these characteristics of Middle East studies programs that had drawn earlier ire from critics, including the David Project's Dr. Charles Jacobs, who justified the production of *Columbia Unbecoming* on his own view that intellectual dishonesty and moral relativism had crept in to the MEALAC teaching programs in a way that compromised the academic value of the courses offered there. In fact, wrote Jacobs, "when at Columbia it is taught that the Israelis are Nazis and the Palestinians are the new Jews, and that the Jews slaughtered Arabs in Jenin, these are not 'rhetorically combative' modes of teaching [as Columbia's own investigative committee would seem to suggest]—they are blood libels, anti-Semitic provocations, deceptions, and Arabist propaganda. Will only brave Jewish students stand up and say so? Does academic freedom give professors license to teach incendiary, hateful lies?"[3]

This was, and is, the most serious aspect of the state of Middle East studies: that faculty members in these highly-politicized departments regularly were consistent in their rabid ideological approaches to assessing the contemporary Middle East, and particularly when it came to their topic of choice, the Israeli/Palestinian conflict. Critics like Martin Kramer had long observed how whole departments, with Columbia's being a prime example, had balkanized into single-minded academic enterprises defined by blatant antipathies for Israel, the United States, and the West, and regularly oblivious to the many pathologies and endemic civil and social ills of the Arab world. The lingering influence of Edward Said's concept of Orientalism had meant that academic departments of Middle East studies had become closed societies, where myopic academics, heavily imbued with postcolonial suspicions, created a world-view of Islam, the Arab world, and particularly of Israel and the Palestinians that was at odds with how other scholars—with less ideological baggage—would view the same facts on the ground.

When Columbia launched its own investigation into the charges raised by the movie, most of the findings, to the disappointment of many, related, not to the intellectual foundations upon which teaching was built, but on the manner in which selected MEALAC faculty behaved in the classroom. In other words, the ad hoc committee investigating the charges of anti-Semitism, harassment and intimidation of students, and highly-politicized and biased teaching ended up, to a large extent, dealing with recommendations for acceptable faculty protocol in dealing with students—somewhat beside the point. Yes, some of the allegations suggested that certain MEALAC professors purportedly displayed inappropriate behavior in their interaction with (Jewish) students; but the context in which this behavior occurred, and the ideology which unleashed it, was the more serious problem. Some of the disturbing testimony of students who had appeared in the film began to suggest that more was going on in classrooms than simple intellectual inquiry over divisive issues.

One of the students, for instance, Deena Shanker, had been enrolled in a spring 2002 class, "Palestinian and Israeli Politics and Societies," taught by Joseph Massad, an associate professor of modern Arab politics. Massad, whose controversial bid for tenure seemed to have been realized in the summer of 2009 after vigorous protests from within and outside Columbia, regularly espouses his loathing of Israel in fringe, anti-Semitic publications like *Counterpunch* and *The Electronic Intifada*, or in the Arab press, and never misses an opportunity to denigrate the Jewish state as a racist, colonial enterprise, a moral stain on the world without any semblance of legitimacy. He assigns blame for all of the turmoil in the Palestinian territories to the brutal Israeli regime, and ignores completely any role the Arabs states may have had in inciting violence and murdering Jews in the name of what he, and his like-minded apologists for jihadist terror, categorizes as legitimate "resistance" to occupation. In fact, in his perfervid imagination, Israelis, as he never tires as mentioning, have become the new Nazis and the Palestinians the Jews. "As Palestinians are murdered and injured in the thousands," he wrote after Operation Cast Lead in January of 2009 when Israel was defending itself against some 6000 rockets attacks from Gaza, "world powers are cheering on .., and it even happened during World War II as the Nazi genocide was proceeding." Perversely likening the barbaric aggression of Hamas from within Gaza to the efforts of Warsaw Jews to repel imminent extermination by the

Nazis, Massad obscenely suggested that "The Gaza Ghetto Uprising will mark both the latest chapter in Palestinian resistance to colonialism and the latest Israeli colonial brutality in a region whose peoples will never accept the legitimacy of a racist European colonial settlement in their midst."[4]

So unsurprisingly, when Ms. Shanker finally appeared before Columbia's ad hoc grievance committee, she had a distressing account of one particular class session with Massad:

> Professor Massad was discussing Israeli incursions into the West Bank and Gaza, but I do not remember exactly what he was saying. I raised my hand and asked if it was true that Israel sometimes gives warning before bombing certain areas and buildings so that people could get out and no one would get hurt. At this, Professor Massad blew up, yelling, "If you're going to deny the atrocities being committed against Palestinians, then you can get out of my classroom!" I don't remember exactly how I responded except saying, I'm not denying anything. I wasn't. But I was so shocked by his reaction that I don't think I said much more than that.[5]

Tomy Schoenfeld, a former student at the School of General Studies and a second student who testified before the committee, also had experienced an uncomfortable run-in with Professor Massad during "a lecture on the Israeli-Palestinian conflict given by Professor Massad in the late fall or early spring terms of the 2001–2002 academic year . . . Having found Professor Massad's views offensive and inaccurate, he chose to wait until the question and answer period before expressing his disagreement":

> I raised my hand to ask a question, and presented myself as an Israeli student. Professor Massad, in his response, asked me whether I served in the Israeli Military, to which I replied I had been a soldier. Then, to my surprise, Professor Massad asked me, "Well, if you served in the military, then why don't you tell us how many Palestinians have you killed?" I replied by saying that I did not see the relevance of that question to the discussion. Professor Massad, however, insisted, and asked again, "How many Palestinians have you killed?" I did not answer his question, and remained silent. A few minutes later, as my frustration grew, I decided to show Professor Massad how absurd was his response since it was stereotypical in nature. I raised my hand and asked Professor Massad how many members of his family celebrated on September 11th. By asking this question, I wanted to prove that stereotypes are misleading and do not contribute to an academic discussion. Professor Massad was very naturally very upset from my question, and the organizer of the event, at that point, decided to step in and stop the discussion . . . .[6]

But Massad is quite willing to invoke stereotypes and overlook history and fact when describing the malevolence of Israel and the victimization of

Palestinians. In a 2009 article in *The Electronic Intifada*, ironically entitled "Israel's Right to Defend Itself," Massad concluded that Israel, due to its fundamental racist nature and oppression of the Palestinians, has no moral, or legal, right to self-defense. In fact, in his mind, the Semitic Jews have become "white" so they can be more efficient racists in a world where darker people have historically been subjugated by the white race. ". . . The West and Israel will continue to defend Israel's right to defend itself and to deny the Palestinians the right to defend themselves," Massad wrote. "While some call this international relations, in reality it is nothing short of *inter-racial* relations wherein Jews, who since World War II have been inducted into the realm of whiteness, have rights that the Palestinians, like their counterparts elsewhere in the non-European world who are forever cast outside the realm of whiteness, do not."[7]

This notion, that white people of European descent cannot fully accept or appreciate the cultures of Third-world "colored" people, plays right into the intellectual legacy of Columbia's Edward Said, as well, since it uses the concept of Orientalism and post-colonial theory to not only blame Western hegemony for suppressing and dominating the Islamic world, but it thereby also, conveniently, exculpates Middle Eastern countries from responsibility for their cultural pathologies and radical Islamic impulses. Imperialism, colonialism, and racism are the root causes, according to Massad and his Saidian brethren, not the failure of many Arab states to confront modernity and construct civil societies. Since the concept of Orientalism—almost universally embraced in Middle East studies, and certainly in Columbia's MEALAC where Edward Said remains something of an intellectual god—was a convenient way for these academic mandarins to establish themselves as the gatekeepers of who could make judgments about Islam and the Middle East, the Palestinians naturally became what Martin Kramer referred to as the "chosen people" of Middle East studies, primarily because they were the perennial victims of the oppressive, imperial West and its proxy, Israel.

"What the Palestinians ultimately insist on is that Israel must be taught that it does not have the right to defend its racial supremacy," Massad wrote, "and that the Palestinians have the right to defend their universal humanity against Israel's racist oppression," in one of his frequent morally-incoherent linkages in which the opinion that Israel is a racist state is presented as an indisputable fact, and the intellectual leap is therefore easy to make to excuse Palestinian terror as part of this spurious "right to defend their universal humanity."

These dark ruminations against the very essence of Israel—that it is racist, murderous, callously genocidal, supremacist, soulless, and that its citizens murder and rape innocent Palestinians randomly, as if for sport, and commit atrocities at Jenin and Gaza—all this has become the blueprint for Massad's venomous ideology, and it has persistently tainted and influenced his teaching. One other example of his interaction with students is the case of Anat Malkin-Almani, a violinist who took a break from a musical career after a debilitating accident and enrolled in Middle East studies at Columbia between 1999 and 2001. While she did not appear as one of the interviewed students in *Columbia Unbecoming*, she was interviewed by the Israeli newspaper *Haaretz* in 2006, and her comments on Massad and his professorial temperament seem to confirm the observations of many who have questioned his suitability, or even qualifications, to be a professor at an Ivy League institution.

"Every week," Malkin-Almani told the *Haaretz* interviewer, "I would get e-mails about anti-Israel demonstrations, lectures that were virtually a form of incitement. The whole atmosphere in the department was hostile, and it was orchestrated by Edward Said. In one class the lecturer cited an article about how the Israelis were raping Palestinian women in the prisons and then sending them back to the territories. I raised my hand and said that no friend of mine had raped a Palestinian, and he started to shout at me." That lecturer, she later confirmed, was none other than Joseph Massad.

Malkin-Almani described how other MEALAC professors apparently shared Massad's irrationality and lack of restraint. "There were cases like that all the time," she said. "In one class I asked the lecturer where the border between East and West Jerusalem ran. He started to shout that you Israelis are so stupid, you don't know anything. All the students in the class joined him and started shouting at me. That was the routine."[8]

"In another class," she told *The New York Sun* in another interview about her experiences at Columbia, Massad "said Israelis sleep very well because they kill Palestinians. But I never killed anyone."[9] After two years, Ms. Malkin-Almani, not surprisingly, withdrew from the program and left Columbia.

A third student to be interviewed by the ad hoc committee investigating student grievances was Lindsay Shrier, who reported her experiences in 2001 in Professor George Saliba's course entitled "Introduction to Islamic Civilization." "She reported being troubled by a video that dealt with the modern Muslim world that she considered to be very one-sided," the committee's report reads, "and she was disturbed by the absence of a post-film class discussion. Ms. Shrier reports that as the class session ended she:"

> . . . approached Professor Saliba with many questions and thoughts that the documentary/video provoked. I started to challenge him on many aspects of the video and question the validity of some of its claims . . . We discussed the history of Jews in Israel . . . Saliba told me I had no voice in the debate. I was puzzled by

his comment. Then he slowly came towards me, moved down his glasses, looked right into my eyes, and said, 'See you have green eyes; you are not a Semite. I am a true Semite. I have brown eyes. You have no claim to the land of Israel.'[10]

Her final reflection on her classroom experience with this particular professor was that "Saliba wanted to intimidate me into silence."[11]

Another woman student, one who actually appeared in *Columbia Unbecoming* but whose identity was masked in the film, related an episode during which she approached Professor Saliba after a course she took with him had concluded, an event which seemed to confirm the peculiar mindset of the MEALAC faculty when it came to anyone questioning their evident biases against Israel. As she recounted in the film, the student went to Saliba and her "basic first question was something like: 'Professor, why is it that we've been in class the whole year and we've been talking about the Middle East and every time Israel comes up it's been referred to as Palestine, which is not really a politically accurate term?' and I am not even sure that I finished my sentence completely until, you know, by the time he had already started with 'Oh, so that's the ax that you have to grind? Why Israel is being called Palestine in my class? What about the plight of the Palestinians? Why isn't that what you are talking to me about? Why don't you come to me and ask me why we are not trying to help the Palestinians in the Middle East?'"[12]

Referring to territory that now encompasses Israel as Palestine, of course, is common practice for the country's enemies, and those who still wish to ignore history and deny its existence. Saliba's habit of using the term "Palestine" serves two destructive purposes, perennial tactics in the intellectual jihad against Israel: first, it suggests that the place "artificially" created and now called Israel is actually a place that was—and, in the minds of Israel's foes, still is—a "nation" called Palestine, inhabited by a people called Palestinians, whose lands were illegally appropriated by Zionists to create the Jewish state. This is an ideological practice, of course, which ignores history, and overlooks the inconvenient fact that over centuries Palestine designated a geographical area without precise boundaries or established nationhood, and that the people who were historically associated with that territory were primarily Jews, not the invented people now called Palestinians. But Saliba's constant reference to Palestine, and the omission of the word Israel, has the same intent as do the textbooks in West Bank and Gaza schools in which maps of the Middle East do not show Israel, and where Israeli towns are still noted with Arab names. It is part of a 63-year campaign to refuse to recognize the reality of the Jewish state's existence, and to deny the reality of Israel as a way of legitimizing the claims that colonial Israel exists on a nation and lands stolen from a Palestinian people.

Saliba and others repeatedly use this intellectual ploy to demonize Israel, not to mention to justify what is euphemistically referred to as legitimate "resistance" to the occupation by Zionist oppressors, a morally-incoherent way that terrorism is excused as an acceptable tool in the Palestinian struggle for self-determination. The student in the film, in her meeting with Saliba, remembered how he seemed to threaten her physically to make this point about how Israel's guilt—by even existing at the expense of the Palestinians— made aggression understandable and acceptable. "He says," she recalled, "'You know, these are preemptive strikes. If I got up to hit you right now. . .' and he start moving out of his chair . . . 'If I got up to hit you, wouldn't you hit me first?' And I said, moving my chair back slowly, I said; 'no, I wouldn't hit you first. I would walk away from you, and say, until you are ready to talk, I am not ready to reciprocate.' I walked out of a door, of which had been open the entire time, and I just saw his secretarial staff, mouths wide open . . . shocked . . . ."[13]

Saliba's outrageous verbal attacks were not restricted to students, nor did he care to even keep them private. In fact, he and another MEALAC professor, Hamid Dabashi, openly attacked Columbia's Jewish chaplain, Rabbi Charles Sheer, in the pages of *The Spectator* after Sheer had questioned, in an op-ed piece, the propriety of Saliba and other professors cancelling their classes and encouraging students to attend an April 17, 2002 pro-Palestinian rally at Low Library Plaza that would also condemn Israeli military activities in the West Bank. Sheer had long been a critic of MEALAC's perceived anti-Israel bias, and he was regularly sought out by Jewish students who had encountered intimidation, harassment, embarrassment, or aggressive teaching methods at the hands of some professors. In addition, and even more significantly, this particular rally was typical of the hate-spewing events commonly mounted by anti-Israel students and faculties, complete with such expressive guest speakers as Professor Massad, who, as he regularly did, described Israel as "a Jewish supremacist and racist state," and warned with firm moral conviction that "every racist state should be threatened."[14] Sharing the podium with his own invective was the equally notorious Columbia professor of anthropology and Latino Studies, Nicholas De Genova, who a year later, at a faculty teach-in to protest the approaching Iraq War, would almost seditiously yearn for the deaths of U.S. servicemen when he welcomed "a million Mogadishus," referring to significant losses of American soldiers in a 1993 incursion into Somalia, known as the "Black Hawk Down" incident. But at this particular anti-Israel rally in 2002, the repugnant De Genova took aim at Jews and

Israel with the obscene proclamation that "The heritage of the victims of the Holocaust belongs to the Palestinian people. The state of Israel has no claim to the heritage of the Holocaust."[15]

It was against this backdrop, and several years over which he had been fielding complaints from Jewish students about anti-Israel bias in Columbia classrooms, that Rabbi Sheer made his comments in the *Spectator*. But when Sheer had the audacity to publicly criticize professors' decisions to cancel classes so students could go to this anti-Israel hate-fest, it was all too much for Professor Saliba. In an angry letter to the *Spectator*, laced with ad hominem attacks against Sheer, Saliba bleated that he was deeply troubled by this intrusion into the private affairs of his teaching—by a religious figure, no less—that, as he wrote, "it is doubly alarming to learn from Rabbi Sheer that students are reporting to him, as he claims, what goes on in the classrooms, thus making one feel that we have been miraculously transported to some medieval theocracy, where a religious authority is re-instituting the Inquisition. . . ."[16]

Not one to let an opportunity to pass in which Israel could be indicted for its many perceived crimes, Saliba asserted his belief that attendance at the rally was important for his students since "both students and faculty could benefit from access to accurate information on the Middle East that is never reported by the newspapers 'of record' nor is it even allowed to be reported by any member of the press as Ariel Sharon's army prohibited access to the press *when he was committing his massacres in Jenin* [emphasis added]."[17] Those alleged "massacres in Jenin," of course, never occurred (as has been confirmed even by the United Nations, no friend of Israel), but are repeated, viciously, by ideologues and enemies of Israel who wish to continually defame the Jewish state, irrespective of facts. The fact that a professor at Columbia either still believes that the Jenin massacre took place, or knows it to be a lie and continues to allude to it and gives public expression to this libel, speaks volumes on the academic tenor of the entire department. Saliba is also sinister in the way that he implies that Sheer was criticizing attendance at the anti-Israel rally as a way of suppressing information about Israel's offenses against the Palestinians in the same way that Ariel Sharon tried to do regarding the Jenin event, a typical reaction to anti-Israel radicals whose belief is that the reality of Palestinian suffering is something hidden from the public and known only by them.

A second indignant Columbia MEALAC professor, Hamid Dabashi, rallied to the anti-Israel cause and produced similar invective against Sheer in a *Spectator* op-ed. Dabashi, Hagop Kevorkian Professor of Iranian Studies and Comparative Literature, also invoked the religious oppression he felt as a result of Sheer's comments, wildly conjuring up both the Crusades and the Inquisition in his convoluted imagery. "Rabbi Charles Sheer, Jewish chaplain," he wrote (in case anyone had any confusion about the rabbi's religious persuasion), "has taken upon himself the task of mobilizing and spearheading a crusade of fear and intimidation against members of the Columbia faculty and students who have dared to speak *against the slaughter of innocent Palestinians* [emphasis added]. In a succession of rude and intrusive interventions, he has launched a campaign of terror and disinformation reminiscent of the Spanish Inquisition against me," suggested Dabashi; and, in case his point had not been made about how his freedom of speech should not be suppressed, he repeated again that "none of us who have publicly spoken against the *Israeli slaughter of innocent Palestinians in Jenin refugee camps and other parts of Palestine* have broken any University rule. . . ." "Rabbi Sheer targets to denounce in his tirade," he concluded in a contorted syntax, "or subject to systematic harassment in his crusade against those of us who believe *Zionism is a ghastly racist ideology* [emphasis added]."[18]

As if to give further credence to the accounts of aggressive and inappropriate behavior toward students by professors Dabashi and Saliba, Rabbi Sheer commented in the film his suspicion that "if this is what they are willing to do to me in public, in writing, you can imagine what they are willing to do to students in the classroom."[19]

Understandably, the reaction to *Columbia Unbecoming* was immediate and explosive. Outside of the University, media coverage was extensive, given that academic in-fighting at Ivy League schools is welcome fodder for news stories and op-ed pages. Faced with a flurry of unrelenting media coverage in *The New York Sun* (which ran a series of pieces on the film and its findings, written by reporter Jacob Gershman), *The New York Times*, Fox News, *Harvard Crimson*, *The Forward*, *New Criterion*, *New York Daily News*, *Jerusalem Post*, not to mention Columbia's own newspaper, *The Spectator*, Columbia's administration realized it had a problem on its hands that could not simply be avoided. In fact, Columbia's president, Lee Bollinger, recognized that the controversy had significant, wide-ranging implications that went to the very heart of higher education: could the university continue to support the mission and behavior of one of its most visible faculties, and what type of self-examination would be necessary, given the pressure stakeholders both inside and outside the university, to straighten out the embarrassing mess in which the school found itself?

In response to the film, and as a result of increased scrutiny from Columbia's internal and external stakeholders, the University set up an Ad Hoc Grievance Committee, known as the Dirks Committee (named for Nicholas Dirks, Columbia's Vice-President for Arts and Sciences), which was given the task of looking into "the set of issues and complaints that gave rise to the current controversy."[20] There were, unfortunately, some fundamental problems, critics immediately observed, in the individuals selected to serve on the committee, specifically, as Noah Liben, a Columbia graduate who is now at the Jerusalem Center for Public Affairs, outlined in his analysis of the Committee's report:

> . . . None of its members was unconnected to the matter they had to judge objectively. Of the five, two had signed [an earlier Columbia] anti-Israeli divestment petition; one was the dissertation adviser for Joseph Massad, the professor most often accused of student abuse; one wrote in the *Financial Times* that America went to war in Iraq for the benefit of Israel and that Israel is responsible for global anti-Semitism; and one was a university administrator who ignored student complaints for months. The man who handpicked the committee, current Vice-President for Arts and Sciences Nicholas Dirks, is married to a professor, Janaki Bakhle, who co-teaches a class with Massad. Both Dirks and Bakhle signed the original divestment petition, although Dirks's name is absent from the most recently updated list.[21]

As often happens when institutions attempt to investigate their own flaws, the Dirks Committee produced what most observers considered to be a feck-less document; by its own admission, the committee did not even tackle the most imperative aspect of the controversy, namely, was scholarship and teaching in MEALAC being diluted by endemic bias, politicization, and ideology? Instead, they took on the far simpler task of trying to determine if students did, indeed, have legitimate grievances about the way they were treated and taught in Columbia's classrooms and if they had suffered "intimidation." "The majority of complaints focused on what a number of students perceived as bias in the content of particular courses," the Committee reported. And while "complaints also were lodged that particular professors had an inadequate grasp of the material they taught and that they purveyed inaccurate information," surely the critical aspect of the entire controversy and the one that was eventually avoided altogether, "*the committee judged that our charge did not encompass the examination of such matters* [emphasis added]."[22]

Many were outraged by the investigation itself, and its findings, although for different reasons.

The David Project's Charles Jacobs contended that "The report [was] deeply flawed. It considered only three incidents of professors harassing students, yet we know of many, many more. It invokes a sort of 'professors' omerta' to intimidate dissenting professors, upbraiding whistleblowers who helped students report abuse. The committee turns the tables on the complaining students, giving weight—without any proof—to claims by MEALAC professors that pro-Israel 'outsiders' invade classrooms to hector them."[23]

More importantly, Jacobs observed, and as the University had itself admitted, "The Dirks Committee simply evade[d] the main issue: how to deal with the teaching of lies and propaganda by Arabist professors who so demonize Israel that defenders of the Jewish state find themselves in a hostile environment in their classes. It achieve[d] this evasion by referring to incidents of biased, dishonest teaching in exclusively pedagogical and psychological terms."[24]

For the professors who were the subject of the investigation into teaching practices and ideology, the Dirks Committee represented something sinister, repressive, contrary to academic freedom, and, in the favorite expression of those who do not like their outrageous speech and writing to be critiqued, "chilling." Not surprisingly, therefore, Massad wrote that the effort to examine his teaching style, not to mention the content of his instruction, was the "latest salvo in a campaign of intimidation of Jewish and non-Jewish professors who criticise [sic] Israel,"[25] ignoring the fact that when he ranted about "atrocities being committed against Palestinians," what no doubt went unmentioned by him is the unrelenting terror campaign against Israeli citizens conducted by the PLO, Fatah, and Hamas. Unwilling to acknowledge that just as he is free to criticize Israel and its policies, individuals with opposing ideas are also free to challenge *his* views, Massad wildly accused certain groups of stifling academic inquiry in a sinister campaign to silence him. "Pro-Israel groups are pressuring the university to abandon proper academic procedure in evaluating scholarship," he claimed, assuming that what he produced was both proper and scholarship, "and want to force the university to silence all critical opinions. Such silencing, the university has refused to do so far, despite mounting intimidation tactics by these anti- democratic and anti-academic forces."[26]

And then, without a bit or irony, Massad came to the breathtaking conclusion that the Dirks Committee had one overriding, sinister objective: to insure that the only opinions tolerated on the Columbia campus would be pro-Israel. "This witch-hunt," he ranted, from a professorship in a department that was and is perhaps the most biased in the world against Israel, "aims to stifle pluralism, academic freedom, and the freedom of expression on university campuses in order to ensure that only *one* opinion is permitted, that of uncritical support for the State of Israel."[27]

Writing a response to Rabbi Sheer's comments in the March 10, 2003 *Spectator*, Professor Dabashi also postured as if he was on the vanguard of academic freedom, observing that "such malicious misrepresentations of my department are a deliberate attempt at silencing voices of civilized dissent and civil discourse in these extremely troubling times. They have created undue anxiety among our alumni on one hand and on the other unleashed scores of death threats against me personally, and against my colleague Professor Joseph Massad, by *lunatic thugs*." What was perhaps the most depressing part of Dabashi's rant? The promise to his readers that "None of these intimidations will be effective. *We will not be silenced*. [Emphasis added.]"[28]

Some students echoed the same paranoia that was expressed by MEALAC faculty when their pedagogy and ideology was examined. Monique Dols, for example, who at the time was a student in Columbia's School of General Studies and, tellingly, a Mid-Atlantic representative to the Campus Antiwar Network Coordinating Committee, wrote in Professor Massad's favorite publication, The *Electronic Intifada*, that "As opposed to their innocuous stated goals," the David Project and the film "have created a witch-hunt atmosphere on campus. They are trying to silence and marginalize the minority, anti-Zionist position. Rather than protecting 'academic integrity' they are waging a full frontal assault on it." What is more, she claimed, pleading the case of the victim, "The makers of this film have created an atmosphere on campus that dovetails with this national climate of racist scapegoating. It should behoove the Columbia University administration to leap to the defense of an untenured Arab professor [Massad] who is defamed and harassed out of teaching his class. Instead the administration has given credence to the politically motivated claims."[29]

Other students agreed with Charles Jacobs and others who had looked askance at MEALAC and who were disappointed both with the findings of the ad hoc committee and the reaction of professors who had been examined and who were now claiming that an academic witch-hunt was taking place. "The Orwellian McCarthyism, if you will, being practiced by MEALAC is where we should refocus the debate," wrote Sara Sebrow, then a Barnard student, in an article in the *Spectator*. "The department avoids having to deal with criticism by calling it an infringement on its academic freedom—silencing its opponents by accusing them of trying to silence it . . . The real danger of MEALAC is that opposing points of view are dishonestly recast as attacks on academic freedoms. Such an attitude not only cultivates a generation of students of the Middle East with a skewed and hate-driven education but also creates an atmosphere in which anything can be criticized except criticism of Israel."[30]

That was the precise reason that many felt disappointment with Columbia's feeble effort to assess MEALAC and to take steps to prevent the entire department from being hijacked by highly-politicized teaching and defective scholarship. Yes, the Dirks Committee's attempt to both mollify those students who felt intimidated or harassed in the classrooms of bullying professors, and then to suggest steps to prevent that behavior from occurring again, were necessary first steps. But the more dangerous aspect of Middle East studies is how the teaching from these ideologically-driven, Israel-loathing professors had become what journalist Rachel Neuwirth, in describing UCLA's program and the problems at that institution, has called "sustained academic indoctrination."[31]

Asking a student how many Palestinians he had killed, or screaming at another that she has no right to deny atrocities committed by Israel against Palestinians, may well be examples of professorial intimidation of students; at the very least, the behavior violates the collegial atmosphere that campuses seek to create to foster learning and dialogue. Those are issue of pedagogy and civility. More dangerous to academic integrity is professors who coddle terrorists, apologize endlessly for the Arab world's social pathologies, and falsely depict and condemn Israel, unrelentingly, as a racist, brutal, genocidal, violator of international law. "The issue is not whether professors should treat their students with due respect, as they should," observed Efraim Karsh, head of Mediterranean Studies at King's College at the University of London, "but whether they should be permitted, under the guise of academic freedom, to pass off personal bias and open political partisanship as scholarly fact."[32]

Columbia, tragically, had failed to address that issue head-on.

Rashid Khalidi:
Ascending The Saidian Throne

When Rashid Khalidi, late of the University of Chicago (where he had become close friends with future president and first-lady Barak and Michelle Obama), was named to fill the Edward Said Chair at Columbia, he was the perfect ideological heir to the endowed professorship named for the intellectual godfather of Columbia's, and, indeed, most departments of Middle East studies. Like Said, Khalidi was virulently anti-Israel, obsessively anti-Western, and apologetic for every defect and social pathology in the Arab world, and particularly those of his beloved Palestinians in the West Bank and Gaza.

But unlike many other academics, whose affinity for resistance movements and the strivings for social justice and the end to occupation were expressed from the safety of their office desks, Khalidi not only supported the Palestinian movement, but was an integral part of it. Said had traveled to Lebanon and was photographed taking a stand for the Palestinian cause by flinging rocks across the border at Israeli soldiers; but Khalidi's commitment to and involvement with the Palestine Liberation Organization cause went much deeper. Both Thomas Friedman of *The New York Times*, and Martin Kramer of the Washington Institute for Near East Policy, have revealed that Khalidi was a PLO operative in the years between 1976 to 1984. In 1982, in fact, Friedman wrote a piece about the PLO in which he specifically identified Khalidi as director of WAFA (Wikalat al-Anba al-Filastinija), the Palestinian press agency.

When he wrote *Under Siege: PLO Decisionmaking During the 1982 War*, Khalidi enjoyed unprecedented access to PLO archives granted to him by then-chairman Yasser Arafat, access that was offered "because [he was] a serious scholar and a Palestinian who wouldn't harm the cause," said Hassan Abdul Rahman, director of the Palestine Affairs Center in Washington in a 1991 *Chicago Tribune* article. When Khalidi's book was published, it included a fawning acknowledgement for the special treatment he had received. "Permission to utilize the P.L.O. archives," the book's inscription read, "was generously given by the Chairman of the P.L.O. Executive Committee, Yasser Arafat. To him and to the dedicated individuals working in the office of the Chairman, the P.L.O. archive and the Palestine News Agency (WAFA), who extended every possible assistance to me on three trips to Tunis, I owe deep thanks."

His close attachment to the seminal figures of the Palestinian movement has meant that Khalidi's perspective was always heavily skewed against Israel, which he perceived as the principal cause of Middle Eastern turmoil and the singular obstacle to peace and the realization of a Palestinian state. His 1997 book, *Palestinian Identity: The Construction of Modern National Consciousness*, draws a picture of the misery of the Palestinian's life, based on brutal occupation and Israeli oppression:

> The quintessential Palestinian experience, which illustrates some of the most basic issues raised by Palestinian identity, takes place at a border, an airport, a checkpoint . . . For it is at these borders and barriers that six million Palestinians are singled out for 'special treatment,' and [are] forcefully reminded of their identity . . . [E]very Palestinian is exposed to the possibility of harassment, exclusion, and sometimes worse, simply because of his or her identity.[33]

In Khalidi's mind, addled as it was with the moral relativism that is so pervasive in Leftist thought—and particularly in the cult-like post-colonial schools of thought that permeate Middle East studies—Palestinian suffering exists only as a result of Israeli oppression, never due to the rejectionist policies of the Palestinian leadership in refusing to co-exist with the Jewish state and who, instead, wage a war of propaganda and arms against it. The moral benefit to casting the Palestinians as the perennial victims, of course, is that it makes it easy for Khalidi and other apologists for terror to justify homicidal aggression against Jewish targets as a legitimate means of "resistance" to occupation—a legitimacy they claim as a right under international law.

A 2005 editorial in *The New York Sun* noted that Khalidi had stated repeatedly that the Palestinians could claim this so-called right to murder their oppressors. "In a June 7, 2002 speech he delivered before the American-Arab Anti-Discrimination Committee," the editorial pointed out, Khalidi had pronounced that " 'Killing civilians is a war crime. It's a violation of international law. They are not soldiers. They're civilians, they're unarmed. The ones who are armed, the ones who are soldiers, the ones who are in occupation, that's different. That's resistance.' " A year later, the editorial continued, Khalidi repeated the same mistaken notion when he claimed that while "Killing civilians is a war crime, whoever does it . . , resistance to occupation is legitimate in international law."[34]

It may be comforting for Israel's intellectual foes to rationalize the murder of Jews by claiming some international right to do it with impunity and a sense of righteousness. Unfortunately, however, as the Editorial Board of the *New York Sun* and other legal experts have inconveniently pointed out, Khalidi and his terror-appeasing apologists are completely wrong about the legitimacy of murder as part of "resistance" to an occupying force. Article IV of the Third Geneva Convention, the statute which defines combatants and legitimate targets in warfare, is very specific about who may kill and who may be killed, and it does *not* allow for the murder of either Israeli civilians—or soldiers—by Palestinian suicide bombers who wear no identifying military uniforms and do not follow the accepted rules of wars. Nor, certainly, does it recognize the legitimacy of launching more than 8000 random rocket and mortar attacks from Gaza aimed at civilian neighborhoods in southern Israeli towns, as has occurred since the Hamas takeover, a violation of the Geneva conventions that require "distinction" in the targeting of opponents and clearly a more salient example of "collective punishment" than, say, the Gaza blockade by Israel to suppress these attacks.

So when Professor Khalidi, a high-visibility professor at one of the world's major universities, repeats this claim that Palestinians somehow have an internationally-recognized legal "right" to resist occupation through violent means, he is both legitimizing that terror and helping to insure that its lethal use by Israel's enemies will continue unabated. Policymakers, researchers, and government officials rely on the views and expertise of Khalidi and his academic brethren in Middle East centers, and when his opinion that "under international law, resistance to occupation is legitimate" is published, as an example, in a February 25, 2005 article in *The New York Times*, it has the pernicious effect—even though it is a false claim—of perpetrating even more terrorism and the absence of peace in the Levant. Those, like Khalidi, who lend their moral support to terrorism, and who continually assign the blame for the emergence of terror as a justifiable tool of the oppressed, have helped to introduce a sick moral relativism into discussions about radical Islam and Palestinianism. In fact, they have borne out the notion that Harvard Law professor Alan Dershowitz wrote about in his insightful, but frightening, book, *Why Terrorism Works*. In the case of Palestinian terrorism, terrorism as a tactic works because instead of being repulsed when acts of terror are committed by Arabs against Jews and other civilians, Leftists and other Western apologists see terror as a reaction to a brutal and racist Zionist occupation against which weak, oppressed Palestinian victims have no other weapon. Instead of being horrified by the use of terror against innocent civilians, its very existence is evidence to the Left that the great wrongs being done to Palestinians, and their suffering and desperation, make terror necessary. Since liberals refuse to accept the idea that some people are manifestly evil and do terrible things as a result, they make the moral judgment that when terror is committed by the weak against the mighty, it is an acceptable and forgivable response to injustice and can be labeled "resistance" to oppression. That is the greatest danger in apologizing for terror and for rationalizing its use: as terror is seen to be a successful tool for the weak, and for victims of Western imperialism specifically, to demonstrate their grievances, it is likely to occur with greater frequency. Khalidi and his like-minded professors do not seem concerned with their contribution to this vicious cycle of carnage.

Professor Khalidi also plays another administrative role at Columbia; he is the Director of the Middle East Institute (MEI) at Columbia's School of International and Public Affairs, a center that receives some $300,000 in federal funding each year. It should be of great concern that an academic is being subsidized by American taxpayers who regularly expresses his support for armed struggle against a sovereign state and the murder of its citizens, and, in part, blames the United States for the failure of peace between the Palestinians and Israelis. "The entire Arab world," Khalidi wrote in the *Chicago Tribune* in 2002, "which just approved a peace plan at the Beirut summit, is in upheaval because of the bloody events in Palestine, and U.S. support for Ariel Sharon. The stability of the entire Middle East is in danger as a result not only of the ongoing violence, but of the failure of the U.S. to accept its responsibilities as the world's sole superpower."[35]

How could the United States be more effective in creating a peaceful solution to the Arab/Israeli conflict? By strong-arming Israel, of course, not by reigning in Palestinian terror, getting Hamas to recognize the Jewish state, or helping to create a civil society and social institutions to support a viable Palestinian state. In Khalidi's view, Israel's military supremacy, and America's complicity in supplying some of those arms, is the problem, not the jihadist tradition that made defensive actions necessary in the first place. "Israel is a state that has a powerful army with the awful weapons of mass destruction (many supplied by the U.S.) that it has used in cities, villages and refugee camps." And what did Khalidi think had compelled Palestinians to use their bodies as instruments of death against Israeli civilians at cafes, discos, pizza parlors, and on buses? His tendentious answer: frustration from living under occupation. "The Palestinians have no state, and no army, but only the terrible weapons of the weak: bombs, automatic weapons and knives," he lamented, "and all too many youths so desperate and hopeless after living their entire lives under occupation that they are willing to die using them against Israeli troops, settlers and civilians."[36]

And who was responsible for the power struggle between Hamas and Fatah for control of Gaza, and Hamas's eventual ascendency there? "I think that this is a direct, logical, inevitable result of American, Israeli and European policy," Khalidi told an NPR interviewer in 2007. While Khalidi graciously admitted that "the foolishness and the irresponsibility of the Palestinian leadership played an enormous role," he contended that, in the final analysis, U.S. policy had been the primary cause and "this has to be laid at the doorstep of Bush administration and Israeli government policy, [and] they almost willed this result. They refused to deal with anybody. They refused to negotiate. They refused to try and bring along the people with whom they could have negotiated, including leaders of Hamas. And this is the logical, inevitable, natural result."[37]

Professor Khalidi's foundational bias against Israel and the United States, his embrace of tactics of terror as a legitimate means of addressing grievances and achieving self-determination for the Palestinians, his misreading or intentional misrepresentation of history and international law—all of these create an ideological stew that one can hardly assess as balanced, let alone the proper intellectual temperament for an academic leader in a world-class university. That he sits in an endowed chair and oversees a sizable inflow of federal funds, as well, makes the moral incoherence of his world-view even more troubling. But this precise ideology is endemic to Middle East studies on campuses across the country, since, as Hugh Fitzgerald has observed, "many of the Middle East Studies faculty . . . appear to believe in the surpassing perfidy of the mighty empire of Israel, in the sheer nobility and justice of the 'Palestinian' cause, in the diabolical imperialist dreams of the American government, and in the crazed hatred for the Arabs and Muslims, and will to dominate, by Israel or America or the West . . ."³⁸

Middle East Studies For Sale

When Rashid Khalidi left the University of Chicago and arrived at Columbia, he became the Edward Said Professor of Middle East Studies, a chair that had already been endowed in 2000, but under a cloud of controversy. Columbia's administration at first refused to disclose who the donors had been who gave the approximate $3 million to endow the professorial chair, not a common practice in philanthropy. In a long report prepared for the Trustees of Columbia University that reviewed the on-campus incidence of anti-Israel bias and politicized teaching and sentiment that led up to the *Columbia Unbecoming* film, the group Scholars for Peace in the Middle East noted that increasing pressure was brought to bear on the Columbia administration to reveal the names of the donors who had funded the Edward Said professorship. "As 2003 wore on," the report said, "the demands for disclosure of the donor list became more persistent and widespread," and that Columbia finally relented when "it was pointed out that failure to disclose a major donation by a foreign government [above $100,000] represents a violation of New York State law."³⁹

That legal aspect of how endowed chairs, research centers, institutes, indeed, whole departments are subsidized or even created through the largesse of questionable donors became an important issue in Columbia's case, especially once the University revealed that one of the principal benefactors for the Said Chair was the United Arab Emirates. There was more than a little irony in the fact that Harvard University's Divinity School had also been pledged a $2.5 million gift in 2000 by UAE President Sheikh Zayed bin Sultan al-Nahyan for an endowed professorship in Islamic religious studies. Several of the Divinity School's students, led by Rachel Fish, began to pressure the School's dean to refuse the gift once they had uncovered questionable a relationship between Zayed and the Zayed Center for Coordination and Follow-up. Fish and her student allies "alleged that the Zayed Center, established in 1999, had hosted speakers claiming that the Holocaust was perpetrated by Zionists, not Nazis, and that Israel plotted the Sept. 11 terrorist attacks."⁴⁰ Harvard put a hold on the gift while the University diplomatically considered its options, which sent a clear message to the UAE that something was amiss; eventually the kingdom asked for a return of the donation.

Coincidentally, Rachel Fish, the student who had doggedly resisted the UAE gift, was also a staffer of *Columbia Unbecoming's* The David Project.

But where Harvard had seen the moral implications of taking money from a source whose ideology and organizational culture were at odds with the University's own, Columbia seemed to have no compunction about retaining the portion of the Said Chair endowment given by the UAE. Columbia is certainly not alone in accepting gifts from Arab states, and in that respect it shares a common thirst for funding of many Middle East study centers for professorships, research grants, institutes, bricks and mortar, and conference sponsorships and underwriting.

But that type of funding, from those types of donors, has thorny moral and ethical aspects to them. What is more, while the major Middle East centers have a long tradition, since 1958, of receiving federal Title VI funding as part of the National Defense Education Act, they have increasingly learned to rely on the largesse of Arab states, whose oil-rich royalty are increasingly willing to pay for access into and influence over American universities.

In 2005, for instance, good fortune smiled on Harvard University with the announcement of a $20 million gift from Saudi Prince Alwaleed bin Talal, with the expressed purpose, in his own words, to "bridge the gap between East and West, between Christianity and Islam, and between Saudi Arabia and the United States." The Prince, reputed to be the world's fifth richest man and chairman of the Riyadh-based Kingdom Holding Co., had been intent on "bridging the gap" for some time; he was, it will be remembered, the same individual whose intended $10 million gift to families of 9/11 victims was returned by then-Mayor of New York, Rudi Giuliani, after the Prince off-handedly mentioned that the U.S. had to "reexamine its policies in the Middle East and adopt a more balanced stance toward the Palestinian cause . . .Our Palestinian brethren continue to be slaughtered at the hands of Israelis while the world turns the other cheek."

Lest anyone doubt on what side of Palestinian-Israeli debate Alwaleed comes down, one could point to yet another donation he made in 2002: during a government-sponsored, live-broadcast telethon for the benefit of Palestinian families of suicide bomber 'martyrs' which eventually raised $100 million, the Prince himself made a pledge of $27 million to help show Saudi support for the Palestinian cause.

And Alwaleed's educational generosity was soon felt by Georgetown University, as well, with another $20 million pledge for a naming opportunity at the University's Center for Muslim-Christian Understanding, headed by John Esposito, an academic who terrorism expert Steven Emerson noted has "a history of minimizing the threat of Islamic extremism and supporting Islamist regimes and movements."[41]

One of the dangers of having entire faculties within Middle East studies centers who share the exact intellectual biases is that single, significant donors can influence entire departments, that when there is uniformity in the scholarly outlook of an entire faculty—as there clearly is in many Middle East departments—the likelihood is that large gifts from Arab states will buy conformity of thought, vis a vis the Arab/Israeli conflict, and will help insure that academic scrutiny is deflected away from some of the Arab world's own troubling problems. And academics learn that their ability to keep funding streams flowing inward is often dependent on satisfying the particular and specific expectations of private donors. Jay P. Greene, a Senior Fellow at the Manhattan Institute and endowed chair and head of the Department of Education Reform at the University of Arkansas, has studied trends and practices in Arab state donations to universities and saw some issues of concern.

First, the sheer levels of the gifts were a potential problem, since Greene "found that Arabian Gulf states (mostly Saudi Arabia, Qatar, and United Arab Emirates) give way out of proportion to their wealth. Gulf Arabs are the source of 16.44% of all foreign gifts and contracts to US universities but they represent only 1.95% of foreign GDP. That is, Gulf Arabs give 8 times more relative to their wealth than do other foreign donors."[42]

And those totals are large, Greene noted. "Gulf Arabs gave a total of $88 million to 14 US universities between 1995 and the present (if federal filings are accurate and complete)."[43] What does all that largesse buy? For one thing, academic recipients are going to shy away from any critical investigation of the donor's own political system, autocratic rule, or abuse in the social and civil rights of the citizens of those oil-rich but often economically- and socially-backward countries. Though many of the funded centers, such as Georgetown's, are established with the stated intention of helping to "build bridges" between the Christian West and Islam for the purpose of enhancing mutual understanding, in practice the centers end up serving as beachheads where Arab states can attempt to influence scholarship and indoctrinate a new generation of scholars. And those scholars become good students of the rules of the funding game, as well, claimed Greene. "Anyone wishing to be a successful graduate student and eventually a professor of Middle Eastern Studies," he said, "has to know that if they stay away from certain questions, like the abuses of authoritarian Arab regimes, and focus on other questions, like alleged shortcomings of Israel or the US, they might get several million dollars dropped in their lap."[44]

Saudi money obviously is not pouring into American universities because of the reverence the Arab world expresses toward Western higher education. There is a more pernicious aspect to this philanthropy, suggested columnist Ben Shapiro, and "the Saudi motive is clearly stated by the official Saudi English weekly *Ain-Al-Yaqeen*, in describing donations to U.S. colleges: 'The Kingdom of Saudi Arabia, under the leadership of the Custodian of the Two Holy Mosques King Fahd Ibn Abdul Aziz, has positively shouldered its responsibility, and played a pioneering role in order to raise the banner of Islam all over the globe and raise the Islamic call either inside or outside the Kingdom.'"[45] Here again is another instance of the dangerous "unholy alliance" between Islamists with a specific agenda to dilute Western institutions, and Leftists who, in accommodating radical Islam, not only enable what Robert Spencer has called a "stealth jihad," but help facilitate it.

Investigative journalist Lee Kaplan looked at alarm at Saudi giving to American universities and pointed to both the size of the gifts and the sheer number of schools that had received them:

[The late Saudi] King Fahd donated $20 million dollars to set up a Middle East Studies Center at the University of Arkansas; $5 million was donated to UC Berkeley's Center For Mideast Studies from two Saudi sheiks linked to funding Al Qaeda; $2.5 million dollars to Harvard; $8.1 million dollars to Georgetown including a $500,000 scholarship in the name of President Bush; $11 million dollars to Cornell; $1.5 million dollars to Texas A&M; $5 million dollars to MIT; $1 million dollars to Princeton; Rutgers received $5 million dollars to endow a chair. . . .[46]

Gulf State wealth has not only poured into academic programs run by and taught in by random professors whose influence and visibility is generally limited. Former U.S. presidents have also been fortunate enough to benefit from Saudi and Arab generosity, not the least of whom is Jimmy Carter, whose Carter Center at Emory University has been heavily subsidized by donations from what columnist Jacob Laksin called the "Arab Lobby," including some of the benefactors whose gifts have, as noted, have reached other Middle East studies centers, as well. For instance, Laksin revealed that Carter, like Columbia, had accepted monies from the United Arab Emirates and its then-president, Sheikh Zayed bin Sultan al-Nahyan. While Harvard's Divinity School had decided in good conscience *not* to accept a gift from Zayed, Carter apparently had no moral qualms about the source of the donation, since, as Laksin recounted, the former president "even traveled to the country to accept the Zayed International Prize for the Environment . . . , [and] having claimed his $500,000 purse, Carter enthused that the 'award has special significance for me because it is named for my personal friend, Sheikh Zayed Bin Sultan al-Nahyan.'"[47]

Another familiar face also showed up at the Carter Center with some $5 million in gifts: none other than Prince Alwaleed Bin Taleel, he of the Georgetown and Harvard $20 million donations, and following in the tradition of his uncle, the late King Fahd of Saudi Arabia, who, Laksin noted, "was a longtime contributor to the Carter Center and on more than one occasion contributed million-dollar donations. In 1993 alone, the king presented Carter with a gift of $7.6 million."[48]

That his Center has been so lavishly rewarded by Arabs may account in part for Carter's obsessive criticism of Israel at the same time he has been urging the West to embrace the thugocracy of Hamas and allow them come to the negotiating table as supposed partners in peace. He has nothing but pity for the terrible state in which the Palestinians find themselves, making it clear in his writing and public appearances that blame for their continuing misery should be assigned to heavy-handed Israeli and U.S. policy, never to the intransigent Arabs themselves. In 2006, Carter published a book about the Israeli/Palestinian conflict, *Palestine: Peace Not Apartheid*, whose inflammatory and provocative title—suggesting, libelously and falsely, that Israel was an apartheid nation—revealed very clearly about where he stood, morally and ideologically, on the issue. By accusing Israel of being the primary obstacle to peace, and by referring to the region as "Palestine" (just as do all of Israel's enemies who would prefer that the Jewish state was absent from the Levant), Carter contributes to propaganda war against Israel; and his Center, underwritten by Arab wealth, is complicit with foes who yearn for Israel's destruction.

What would compel the Saudis and other Arab states to funnel such huge waves of petrodollars into U.S. universities, part of a culture and set of Western values with which they are in fundamental opposition? Investigative reporter Lee Kaplan asked that same question, although it is obvious that he knows the answer. "One wonders why a theocratic totalitarian regime," he wrote, "where 30% of the population is illiterate and where PhDs teach that Jews use the blood of gentile children to make matzoh, would take such interest in the American educational system instead of their own."[49] Clearly, their intent is not to bring back lessons from scholars in America. Their strategy is for ideology and propaganda to go in one direction, and only one: outward from the Muslim world as part of the process to influence and eventually subvert the West.

What is the final effect of this lavish funding of professorships, research centers, conferences and symposia, and entire academic departments? According to Martin Kramer, whose book *Ivory Towers in the Sand: The Failure of Middle Eastern Studies in America* is the most comprehensive and valuable overview of the subject, the entire field of Middle East studies has been devolving; its academics are, increasingly, mediocre scholars with politicized teaching agendas all conforming to similar worldviews and political agendas, who have not only become "obsessed with the obsession" of Palestine and Israel, but have been, in Kramer's view, incompetent in their failure to see the implications of nascent Islamism and being caught completely off-guard by its transformation into lethal jihad:

> . . . The new elite in Middle Eastern studies had failed to ask the right questions, at the right times, about Islamism. They underestimated its impact in the 1980s; they misrepresented its role in the early 1990s; and they glossed over its growing potential for terrorism against America in the late 1990s. Twenty years of denial had produced mostly banalities about American bias and ignorance, and fantasies about Islamists as democratizers and reformers. These contributed to the public complacency about terrorism that ultimately left the United States vulnerable to "surprise" attack by Islamists . . . Middle Eastern studies were so heavily invested in one interpretation that few dared to challenge the collective migration from one error to another.[50]

Edward Said's corrosive concept of Orientalism had subsumed authentic scholarship in the field of Middle East studies with its nonsense of postcolonial theory, moral relativism, assignment of blame on Western imperialism for the defects of the Arab world, and a general failure to look past the isolated issues of the Arab/Israeli conflict. There were other, much more significant and relevant problems in many parts of the Arab world, where totalitarianism, theocracy, suppression of human rights, gender apartheid, economic stagnation, and a host of other pathologies were going un-discussed. But much of the academic energy of Middle East scholars was squandered on continuing the demonization of Israel while the more important task of trying to bring modernity, stability, and democracy to the Middle East was overlooked. Academics in Middle East studies programs will have to be held accountable, finally, for this lost opportunity and an intellectual tragedy of their own making.

Chapter 7

The Radicalization of California Campuses

UC Irvine: Hot Bed of Anti-Israelism

If any area of the United States can be identified as the epicenter of anti-Israelism on campus, California, the nation's most populous state, can certainly be said to have earned that dubious distinction. In fact, observers of out of control anti-Zionist and anti-Semitic activity on campuses consider California's universities to be the veritable ground zero of such vitriol, with particularly troubling and persistent problems of radical student groups, venom-spewing guest speakers, annual hate-fests targeting Israel and Jewish students, and a pervasive mood on campus in which Jewish students and other pro-Israel faculty and students experienced visceral and real "harassment, intimidation and discrimination," as a 2004 Zionist Organization of America's complaint to the U.S. Department of Education's Office for Civil Rights described the situation on one campus, the University of California at Irvine.

The situation on California campuses with regard to anti-Israelism, and even raw anti-Semitism, continues to grow in intensity and frequency, and, while it may well represent some of the more egregious examples of Israel demonization occurring anywhere today, in many ways it reflects some of the persistent and alarming issues seen elsewhere. The question is, why California?

What is it about the system of higher education in the nation's most populous state that has seen the flowering of this most noxious and insidious trend? For one thing, the state has a long tradition of radicalism by Leftist professors and students, exemplified most clearly by the free speech movement founded at Berkeley during the Vietnam War era and its attendant campus debate and violent protest. The student radicals of the 1960s have now become tenured professors, and have sway over tenure decisions, fellowships, the topics for research, and the overall tenor of scholarly inquiry on campuses. Many in California's liberal professoriate, as they do in around the country and as was discussed in Chapter 1, also embrace an essential cynicism about the West, a suspicion of capitalism, a condemnation of the military, and a general attitude that the imperialism of America and Israel continues a trend of hegemonic powers wronging Third-world victims.

Since much of the on-campus agitation against Israel is spearheaded by pro-Palestinian Muslim student groups, the fact that 20 percent of America's Muslims live in California (representing over 1,000,000 people and 3.4 percent of the State's population)[1] is likely also a contributing factor. Relevant, too, is the fact that while the age group of individuals between 18 and 29 represents only 14.1 percent of the overall U.S. population[2], in that same age group—a sizable chunk of whom are college students—Muslims represent 26.1 percent of that total.[3] The constant flow of billions of Saudi petrodollars as part of a "soft" jihad to undermine intellectual values in academe in the West has also meant that Muslim Student Associations, an offshoot of the extremist Muslim Brotherhood, have garnered strength and an impressive presence on campuses, especially in California, where, as in UC Irvine, they have essentially dominated all on-campus debate vis a vis Israel and the Palestinian cause, supplemented by generous support from this public university's pool of student funds.

In fact, even after the U.S. Office of Civil Rights had initiated their 2004 inquiry into rampant anti-Semitism on campuses—including at UC Irvine, a focus of their study—a second similar effort, the "Task Force on Anti-Semitism at the University of California, Irvine," was launched in December, 2006 by the Hillel Foundation of Orange County and staffed by local professionals, religious leaders, and academics.[4] Feeling that the federal inquiry had uncovered some troubling trends on the Irvine campus, but had delivered a somewhat feckless response to the University's administration, the Orange County task force took it upon itself to revisit some of the incidents in an attempt to show a pattern of anti-Israelism and anti-Semitism as endemic to the Irvine campus. Its stated goal was "to study, investigate and issue a report on alleged incidents of racism and anti-Semitism at the University of California–Irvine (UCI). We are not singling out any specific group. We are looking at all instances of alleged anti-Semitic and racist activity." The U.S. Office of Civil Rights, as the task force report noted, had focused more specifically on issues of discrimination based on students' national origin, and the "investigation applied narrow legally technical analysis about whether UCI violated Title VI of the Civil Rights Act of 1964 and its implementing regulations."[5] The task force came to the following conclusions, based on their own extensive interviews with students, faculty, and UCI administrators (at least those who agreed to respond to inquiries):

1. Jewish students have been subject to physical and verbal harassment because they are Jewish and support Israel;
2. Hate speech, both direct and symbolic, is directed at Jews by speakers and demonstrators;
3. An annual week-long event sponsored by the Muslim Student Union is an anti-Semitic hate fest targeting Israel and Jews using lies and propaganda dating back to the anti-Semitism of the Middle Ages;
4. Speakers who are pro-Israel and/or those who condemn speakers who espouse anti-American and anti-Israeli views are subject to disruptive behavior by Muslim students and their supporters;
5. Jewish students claim they are subject to a hostile class environment by faculty members who adopt an anti-Israel bias;
6. Materials contained in certain Middle-East Studies courses are biased and are indicative of a "leftist" orthodoxy that characterizes this area of study;
7. The UCI administration is not responsive to complaints by Jewish students;
8. Jewish students complain of a "double standard" when the administration enforces campus rules and regulations.[6]

These are troubling assessments, but not at all uncommon on campuses across the country, and in Canada and Great Britain, as well. Yet, despite the two protracted investigations into anti-Semitic activities at UCI, the incidence of hate-fests, protests, and incendiary speakers has not subsided at all.

In fact, in May of 2009, the Muslim Student Union continued its tradition of sponsorship of vile, hate-spewing events to further demonize Israel, this time an 18 day-long extravaganza hideously named "Israel: The Politics of Genocide," which preposterously proclaimed on the posters announcing the event that Israel had resulted in "61 years of illegal occupation. 61 years of statelessness. 61 years of systematic ethnic cleansing. The Palestinians have lost thousands of lives and millions of have been displaced from their homes. Despite all of this, their resolve remains steadfast, their resistance enduring, their fire unflinching. However, though Israel continues to violate international law and inflict these injustices, Palestinian blood stains our hands, too."[7] If the astounding claim is made here that the existence of Israel represents "61 years of illegal occupation" then that either exposes a sore lack of historical insight on the part of the sponsors, or, more likely, it reflects the notion held in much of the Arab world that *all* of Israel—not just the "occupied territories" gained in 1967—is "occupied" Muslim land and that Israel is therefore "illegal" and not a nation at all.

The "Politics of Genocide" event included the speaking talents of such luminaries as the vitriolic Amir-Abdel Malik-Ali, a black Imam associated with the Masjid Al Islam mosque in Oakland and frequent guest of the Irvine MSU; former Georgia congresswoman Cynthia McKinney, a member of the Free Gaza Movement and Green Party presidential candidate, who, while in Congress, when she was not frantically suggesting that the CIA and George Bush were behind 9/11, had pointed to a sinister "pattern of excessive, and often indiscriminate, use of lethal force by Israeli security forces in situations where Palestinian demonstrators were unarmed and posed no threat of death or serious injury to the security forces or to others;" Anna Baltzer, a rabid anti-Zionist, herself Jewish, who is "a relative newcomer who tours US campuses, churches and community venues denigrating Israel with baseless and propagandistic allegations;"[8] George Galloway, the former Member of the House of Commons, who, when fawning over one of his favorite tyrants, Saddam Hussein, said to him, "Sir, I salute your courage, your strength, your indefatigability," and went on to assure the sadistic dictator that "I want you to know that we are with you until victory, until victory, until Jerusalem;" and Reem Salahi, an ACLU lawyer who wrote that "Israel must be held accountable for its crimes in Gaza lest it commit larger and more egregious crimes in the future."[9]

Just to insure that no part of this scholarly event lacked profound bias against Israel, the MSU sponsors thoughtfully included a screening of the propaganda video *Occupation 101*, a film that one reviewer categorized as "a blanket excusal of violence" which was "designed to evoke sympathy for Palestinians and contempt for Israel," and whose "worst offense is its twisting of the history and facts of the conflict in order to equate the Palestinian cause with celebrated civil rights struggles around the world."[10]

So, as is typically the case whenever, and wherever, one of these "pro-Palestinian" educational events occurs, the chance that any authentic scholarly inquiry, intellectual debate, or an open discussion about real issues and solvable geopolitical problems would take place was clearly remote. Moreover, rather than actually provide some valuable insights into Palestinian culture, politics, or even their struggle for statehood, these events inevitably devolve solely into hate-fests against Israel, with condemnations, blood libels, conspiracy theories, Nazi imagery, anti-Semitic ravings, physical attacks on Jewish students, and a visceral loathing of Zionism, Judaism, and the Jewish state. There is no talk of Palestinian terrorism, the Arab's intractability in refusing many offers of Palestinian statehood, or the genocidal impulses from a sea of jihadist foes that have threatened the Jewish state from its birth, which themselves have necessitated the much-maligned security wall, checkpoints, and even occupation. Only Israel's sins are discussed, and all of the blame for the region's various social dysfunctions is laid at its feet. That is clearly the Muslim Student Union's intention and purpose in sponsoring their myriad events—vilifying Israel and Jews—and not to support the Palestinians; and all the disingenuous talk from university administrators and faculty about "academic freedom," an "open exchange of ideas," or an opportunity for learning about difficult issue either ignores or evades what is actually going on with respect to these events.

A closer look at the ideas tossed about by some of invited guests suggests both the moral incoherence and intellectual debasement that characterizes the ideological output of these events. Amir-Abdel Malik-Ali, for instance, former Nation of Islam member, convert to Islam, and cheerleader for Hamas and Hezbollah, has been a ubiquitous, poisonous presence on the Irvine campus who never hesitates to castigate Israel, Zionists, Jewish power, and Jews themselves as he weaves rambling, hallucinatory conspiracies about the Middle East and the West. In a February 2004 speech titled "America under Siege: The Zionist Hidden Agenda," for example, UCI's student newspaper, *The New University*, reported that Malik-Ali "implied that Zionism is a mixture of 'chosen people-ness [sic] and white supremacy'; that the Iraqi war is in the process of 'Israelization'; that the Zionists had the 'Congress, the media and the FBI in their back pocket'; that the downfall of former Democratic [presidential] front-runner Howard Dean was due to the Zionists; and that the Mossad [Israel's intelligence agency] would have assassinated Al Gore if he was elected [in 2000] just to bring Joe Lieberman (his Jewish vice-president) to power."

Malik-Ali used a February 2005 MSU-organized event to proclaim that "Zionism is a mixture, a fusion of the concept of white supremacy and the chosen people." He complained about Zionist control of the American media, Zionist complicity in the war in Iraq, and Zionists' ability to deflect justified criticism. "You will have to hear more about the Holocaust when you accuse them of their Nazi behavior," he warned, after railing against Zionist control of the press, media, and political decisions of the American government. And what was his vision for Israel and the Palestinians? "One state. Majority rule. Check that out. Us. The Muslims."

Speaking from a podium with a banner reading "Israel, the 4th Reich" in May 2006, Malik-Ali referred to Jews as "new Nazis" and "a bunch of straight-up punks." "The truth of the matter is your days are numbered," he admonished Jews everywhere. "We will fight you. We will fight you until we are either martyred or until we are victorious." The call to martyrdom at UC Irvine, of course, might well have fallen on willing ears, since it has become something of a perverse tradition among Muslim Student Union members, who, "in June 2004 . . . , asked UCI's graduating Muslim students to wear green sashes inscribed with the word 'shahada,' the Arabic word for the 'martyrdom' of a suicide bomber, to their graduation ceremony. Two dozen students complied with this MSU request,"[11] and have also found reason to wear green armbands at other events, including another of Malik-Ali's incendiary lectures, "UC Intifada: How you can help Palestine." Their displays and posters at their sponsored events regularly depict the Israeli flag splattered in blood and the Star of David shown to be equating a swastika, punctuated with numerous hysterical references to a "Holocaust in the Holy Land," "genocide," "ethnic cleansing," "Zionism = racism," and the oft-repeated blood libel against Jews that "Israelis murder children."

In May of 2007, the ever-present Malik-Ali hit upon a now-familiar theme of Israel defamers as part of his speaking role at a three-day event called "Israel: apartheid resurrected," where he condemned Zionists and lauded the "resistance" efforts of a terrorist organization, Hamas, in front of an adulating crowd:

> Hamas are freedom fighters, not terrorists. . . . The Zionist Jews, the Israelis, these are oppressors. There is nothing honorable about what they are doing. . . the Palestinians are paying for the crimes of the Germans. Let the Germans pay. . . . The Zionist Jew has only one fear . . . the ultimate fear of the Zionists are the Muslims. They never defeated us in history. . . . Even though we got the FBI coming down on us [Muslims], even though we got the media coming down on us, even though we have the government coming down on us, everyone . . . in terms of who are running the system; we are still not afraid of them . . . You are dealing with people who fight in the name of Allah, against your imperialism, against your colonialism, against your occupation, and against your racism. And we will not stop until we are either victorious or we are martyred.[12]

At a 2008 event, dubbed "Never Again? The Palestinian Holocaust," Malik-Ali was at his hateful best once again, standing behind a banner that read "Death to Apartheid" while he wildly contended that "The Islamic revival should only be feared by those who support imperialism, colonialism, racism, occupation . . . Groups like Hamas and Hezbollah" are not the real terrorists at all, he proclaimed. No, the actual "terrorists are the United States; the terrorists are Israel!" At the tumultuous conclusion of his ravings, Malik-Ali, joined with the MSU's president, marched with a group down the campus's Ring Road shouting out the following inventive ditty:

> "Judaism, yes! Zionism, no!"
> "Judaism, yes! Zionism, no!"
> "The state of Israel has got to go!"
> "The state of Israel has got to go!"[13]

Another odious guest speaker who regularly makes appearances on the MSA hate-fest circuit is Muhammad al-Asi, an anti-Semitic, anti-American Muslim activist from Washington, DC who has written, among other notorious ideas, that "The Israeli Zionist are [sic] the true and legitimate object of liquidation."

At a MSU-sponsored event in February 2008, "From Auschwitz to Gaza: The Politics of Genocide," which repulsively tried to draw parallels between the Holocaust and Hamas-controlled Gaza, al-Asi was a featured speaker. In his speech, he repeated the canard of Jewish control of world politics, suggesting that "Zionists or what some people call the Jewish lobby" had reduced the United States to playing "second fiddle to the Israeli government." This situation had to end, he cautioned, before the perfidious Zionists draw America into yet another war for their own benefit. "How long are we going to take the Israeli dog wagging the American tail?" he asked, rhetorically. "Now the pro-Zionist, Israeli crowd in the United States says the United States should go to war against Iran."

Just months after 9/11, al-Asi had similar invective to utter towards Jews, in the context of Israeli oppression of Palestinians. Using his favorite image of the ghetto when describing Jews, he observed that "We have a psychosis in the Jewish community that is unable to co-exist equally and brotherly [sic] with other human beings. You can take a Jew out of the ghetto, but you can't take the ghetto out of the Jew, and this has been demonstrated time and time again in Occupied Palestine." What is worse, he continued, this behavior on the part of the malicious Jews would likely continue, since "now they have American diplomats and politicians and decision makers and strategists in their pocket."

When they invite moral defectives like al-Asi to campus to engage in "dialogue" about the Israeli/Palestinian conflict, the Muslim Student Union pretends that it is merely conjuring up a critique of Israeli politics and military actions, that its criticism and vilification has nothing to do with Jew-hatred or calls for the murder of Israelis. But al-Asi himself revealed his true feelings about Jews and murder when he articulated his contorted theological explanation of an oft-cited hadith which called for the murder of Jews. While most Israel-haters now claim to make a distinction between Judaism and Zionism, to al-Asi there was obviously no difference, and the hadith call to murder Jews was, in his fervid imagination, now transferred to Zionists. At the 2008 UCI hate-fest al-Asi referred to the Islamic exhortation "'the stone and the tree will say, oh Muslim, there is a Jew behind me, come and kill him.' The context of this prophetic statement is speaking about the political, or the ideological, or the military Jew, which in the language of today turns out to be the Zionist Jew . . . Jew here means Zionist,"[14] with the implication that Zionists had become theologically-justified targets of jihad.

While the Irvine campus community has had to endure this type of rambling hate speech for years now, as is typical of many campuses controlled by Leftist thought, when those speakers with alternate views—especially conservative speakers—do manage to get invited to campuses, they are frequently denounced prior to their visits, heckled when they try to speak, and often finally escorted off stage by security personnel who fear for the speakers' physical safety. So while the Muslim Student Union is happy to take every opportunity to sponsor speakers they know will spew forth hateful rhetoric about Israel and Jews, they are less than accepting when someone like Daniel Pipes, the conservative, pro-Israel commentator, comes to UCI to speak on "The Threat to Israel's Existence," as he did in January of 2007. Not wanting any view about Israel, terrorism, and the Middle East other than their own to be heard, members of the MSU disrupted the speech by shouting over Pipes and caused the event to be cancelled.

The radical students were also caught on video tape that evening outside the lecture hall where a member of the MSU and organizer of the protest gave an impromptu speech, with the shouts of "Takbir" and "Allahu Akbar" from the crowd of supporters. "They have no future," he said. "And it's just a matter of time before the state of Israel will be wiped off the face of the earth . . . Our weapon, our jihad, our way of struggling in this country is with our tongues. We speak out, and we deflate their morale, and this is the best we can do right now. And our brothers and sisters, on the other side of the world, they're handling business in their own way. May Allah give them strength . . . ."[15]

This astounding conversation did not take place within Hamas headquarters among crazed jihadists, but on the campus of an American university by members of a taxpayer-supported student group at a public university.

The administration and some members of UCI's faculty have been complicit in enabling the takeover of campus by Muslim radicals who have a single agenda of spreading hatred of Israel and Jews. What has been the officials' characteristic response? Sadly, evasion and denial, even in the midst of the two investigations looking into the charges of anti-Semitism. Vice Chancellor of Student Affairs Manuel Gomez, for example, who attended anti-Israel events, decided not to attempt to curtail hate speech, since, as he put it, "one person's hate speech is another person's education."[16] UCI Chancellor Michael Drake was regularly called upon to forthrightly denounce what amounted to blatant hate speech emanating from MSU events, yet he regularly sidestepped any direct denunciation of the speakers, the tone of events, or the implicit anti-Semitism engendered in them.

This stonewalling frustrated many observers of the Irvine situation, specifically because some felt, like commentator Susan Estrich, that "Dr. Drake has a twisted view of academic freedom, one that allows Muslim students to engage in open anti-Semitism, to hold rallies on campus attacking Zionist control of the media, equating Jewish support for Israel with Hitler's Nazis, even (according to campus Republicans) displacing previously scheduled Young Republicans meetings with rallies denouncing Israel's right to exist."[17] When he appeared at an open forum at one of Irvine's synagogues, Congregation Shir Ha-Ma'lot, in response to a direct question on why he had not firmly, and publicly, renounced the hate speech typified by Malik-Ali at MSU events, Drake again pulled back, and did not, as other university presidents had done,[18] ever take a forceful stand against what was clearly speech and behavior not in keeping with UCI's own standards for acceptable discourse and civility. He refused to recognize anti-Semitic behavior for what it clearly was, instead claiming that "We have 1,000 guest speakers on campus every year. Could I evaluate them and say this one is anti-Semitic? I could not. What I could say is that as a person and a campus, we abhor hate speech, period."

While faculty and administrators usually found it easy to identify hate speech when it came from the College Republicans making a point about Islamofacism, or when it involved a display of the notorious Danish cartoons depicting Mohammed that inflamed Muslims worldwide (including on Irvine's campus where in March, 2006 one thousand MSU members came to loudly protest), in those instances when *Jewish* students brought their complaints of intimidation or harassment to the administration, they were regularly ignored or dismissed as unreasonable. When one Jewish student complained about the Muslim students who sported the green Hamas-inspired armbands, for example, she was accused by the Dean of Students, in a mistakenly distributed email, of being "hysterical" for pointing out that having students openly support terrorism against Jews might be inappropriate behavior. Another student recounted his dismay at witnessing "the Star of David painted with red and blood dripping out" at a MSU event." "If you want to hate that's fine," he said, "but I think that there is a clear distinction between Israel as a State and the Star of David as a Jewish religious symbol. So we went to . . . [the Dean of Students] asking if there is something that we can do . . . because it is really offensive . . . The Dean went to the Muslim Student Union with us in [Spring 2002] and asked the Muslim students, politely, to put down that kind of poster and they said no! And that's it; she said that's all what I can do!! [sic][19] Another student confirmed this hands-off, feckless attitude: "We talked to the Dean of Students. . . . She was sympathetic, but there was always, '. . . we can't do anything.'"

UC Irvine is also the home of history professor Mark LeVine, whose Marxist view of the world makes him reflexively suspicious of the United States and the West, due to their economic and military might. "[W]ar and occupation," he wrote, "are wonderful opportunities for corporations to make billions of dollars in profits, unchecked by the laws and regulations that hamper their profitability in peace time," suggesting that Israel and the United States go to war simply to generate profits from their incursions into the occupied territories and Iraq, respectively. The week after 9/11, LeVine also wrote that the barbaric acts of terror that resulted in the slaughter of America civilians were brought on this country, as they have been in Israel, because of its own oppressive actions toward the rest of the world. ". . . I fear we are more like Israelis than we realize," he wrote, "because even after extreme violence has been perpetrated against us by those whose oppression we have supported and even enforced, we refuse to engage in the honest introspection of what our role has been in generating the kind of hatred that turns commuter jets into cruise missiles."

How did the United States generate that kind of hatred? Presumably, according to LeVine, by being a culture of freedom, law, civil rights, and vibrant economic markets, something that jihadist madmen evidently find untenable in their worldview, just as the professor seemingly does. Israel, too, suffers, according to LeVine, because of its treatment of the Palestinians, behavior that makes terrorism reasonable and, in fact, inevitable. "In Israel the violence and terrorism of the latest intifada," he wrote in 2001, "cannot be understood except as emerging out of decades of occupation, discrimination and dispossession. Yet Israel continues and even intensifies these practices, safe in the knowledge that they have the power and support to ignore the roots of the conflict with Palestinians and avenge the casualties it produces daily. Forgotten in the process is the prophetic injunction to fight oppression and correct injustice, or the warning that 'those who sow injustice will reap calamity.' American tax dollars have overruled both."[20]

UC Davis: The 'Diversity of Ideas' Hypocrisy

One thing that Columbia University's 2007 invitation to Iranian President Mahmoud Ahmadinejad made clear was that questionable intellect and moral imbecility will not immediately disqualify someone from being an honored speaker at the most prestigious American campuses. What might get you disinvited, however—as it did for former Harvard president Lawrence Summers for a planned September 2007 speech at the University of California, Davis—is to have committed the unforgiveable sin of questioning the lockstep orthodoxies prevalent on Left-leaning campuses.

Summers, a prodigy who entered Massachusetts Institute of Technology at age 16, became the youngest tenured professor in Harvard history at the age of 28, and later served as Bill Clinton's treasury secretary and later as Barak Obama's economic advisor, apparently no longer warrants speaking invitations to campuses where "diversity" is held sacred—diversity, that is, strictly limited to the liberal Left's acceptable notions about race, sex, and politics. UC Davis professor Maureen Stanton, who was absolutely "stunned" when she learned that the school had invited Summers to speak, said that she "was appalled that someone articulating that point of view would be invited by the regents."

That forbidden point of view of which she spoke, of course, referred to Summers' informal remarks at a January 2004 conference on women in science in which he suggested, off-the-cuff and simply as one possible viewpoint, that the absence of women from science faculties might be linked to superior *genetically-based* quantitative reasoning on the part of men.

So for Professor Stanton, disinviting Summers became imperative since she felt it was "a symbolic invitation and a symbolic measure that [she] believe[d] sen[t] the wrong message about the University of California and its cultural principles."[21]

Most disingenuous is how universities like UC Davis, while horrified by the prospect of a Lawrence Summers visit, use diversity as a cover for regularly bringing outrageous, anti-American, anti-Israel, out-of-the-mainstream views to campuses—either in student-run organizations, in course materials and teaching philosophies, in the sponsorship of festivals and cultural events, or in the person of controversial speakers and artists. For example, the "cultural principles" that the indignant Professor Stanton so self-righteously trumpeted have managed to lapse on several recent occasions when speakers with considerably less intellectual standing than Summers were enthusiastically invited to the UC Davis campus, notable among them DePaul's Norman Finkelstein (guest of the Muslim Students Association) and, scheduled to speak that November as a guest of Students for Justice in Palestine, the notorious and academic fraud, formerly from the University of Colorado, Ward Churchill.

Churchill, who had served as chair of Colorado's Ethnic Studies Department, had defined his academic career by spewing forth anti-American, Marxist ideology and his perceived connection between the evils of colonialism, imperialism, Western genocidal impulses, and, in keeping with the theme of his UC Davis talk, "Zionism, Manifest Destiny, and Nazi Lebensraumpolitik," the oppression by Israel of the Palestinians. Particularly galling to critics was Churchill's describing the *victims* of 9/11 as people who, as part of the machinery of capitalism, got what they deserved when homicidal madmen commandeered jet planes and flew into the World Trade Center towers and the Pentagon. "If there was a better, more effective, or in fact any other way of visiting some penalty befitting their participation upon the little Eichmanns inhabiting the sterile sanctuary of the twin towers," he cruelly proclaimed in his most odious and recognized line, "I'd really be interested in hearing about it."

Churchill eventually lost his position at the University of Colorado when it was disclosed that he was not entirely forthcoming about his status as a Native American, and that his scholarship had proven, upon a closer look, to be rather spurious, not to mention plagiarized. But that oppression only served to elevate his value on the anti-American speaker roster, and he continues to receive invitations from Leftist professors and radical student groups to further demonize capitalism, imperialism, America, and Israel. "What you've got to learn is that when you push people around somebody eventually is gonna push back," he said at a February 2003 book tour speech at the First Congregational Church of Oakland, California for his ever-insightful screed, *Some People Push Back: On the Justice of Roosting Chickens*, his own explanation for the September 11th terror attacks and his indignity at America's shock that it occurred. "That's what happened on nine-one-one. That whole horrible queue, an endless line of ghosts and chickens came home to roost . . . And . . . the bully acts as if there is something grotesquely unfair and inhumane, if finally, all else having failed, someone finally pushes back."

Churchill's other favorite moral sleight of hand, a point of view that makes him a particularly attractive speaker for the Muslim Student Association, is positioning the Palestinians as the Native Americans of the Middle East, another indigenous people subject to ethnic cleansing and extermination by white imperialists intent on dispossessing them. Speaking of the "terror" unleashed against the Iraqis and Palestinians, he visualized the ghosts of these victims of Western oppression as following the aircraft destined to become weapons as they flew towards New York, Washington, and a field in Pennsylvania. "In fact," he said, "you could almost see a comet-like vapor trail of the ghost chickens trailing out behind the aircraft. Because seated most proximately to the Iraqis were the children and the adults of the Indians of the Middle East who have been systematically ground into hamburger compliments of U.S. armaments and political support and economic assistance to the state of Israel over the past 50 years. Yes, I said, Indians of the Middle East. I'm speaking now as a Palestinian of North America because there is that kind of symmetry."[22]

Eager not to miss an opportunity to invite speakers who help demonize Israel and denounce Zionism, in May of 2007 the UC Davis Muslim Students Association and Students for Justice in Palestine invited another luminary of the academic netherworld, Norman Finkelstein, who was discussed at length in Chapter 3, to present a talk titled "Israel and Palestine—Roots of Conflict, Prospects for Peace." For the MSU and the other radical groups who regularly invite him to speak at their hate-fests, Finkelstein is the perfect touchstone to enrage and incite pro-Israeli students. In fact, the UC Davis MSA had specifically sought out the incendiary Finkelstein as intellectual payback to a pro-Israel group on campus, Students for Defense of Democracies, who, in February of that year, had invited Walid Shoebat, a former PLO terrorist-turned-Zionist, to speak, much to the dismay of MSA members who were "shocked, shocked" by Shoebat's premise that Islam had bred homicidal madmen conducting jihad in its name. In fact, the MSA did everything it could to have the speech cancelled, including calling "on the FBI and Department of Homeland Security (DHS) to investigate and deport Walid Shoebat, a self-confessed 'ex-terrorist,'" as a posting on their web site put it. The statement went on, without a hint of irony or embarrassment, to suggest that such controversial speakers might mistakenly arouse passions of resentment and constitute hate speech, a consideration that apparently is not important to them when they themselves invite Jew-baiters, Holocaust deniers, and other extremists to their campus, as long as Israel is that target and not Palestinians or the Muslim world. "We also condemn the intentionally Islamophobic and erroneous association of Islam and violence that will result from the fear-mongering employed in the event's advertisements," the release went on. "We ask fellow students and community members to study the facts about Islam and reject hate-speech and propaganda."[23]

So the MSA's choice of Finkelstein the following month seemed a fitting and cruel way of inciting the Jewish students on campus, since, as Stand With Us's Roz Rothstein (herself the child of Holocaust survivors) pointed out, "Finkelstein uses his identity as the child of Holocaust survivors to gain credibility, distorting history by omitting context and defaming well-respected figures for the purpose of promoting hatred against the State of Israel and minimizing the horrors of the Holocaust."[24]

San Francisco State University: A Double Standard For Campus Speech

The fragile ceasefire between Hamas and Israel after the late 2008-early 2009 Gaza incursions may have brought a tentative peace to that region, but on campuses in California the debate over the 61-year conflict gained a new, and more insidious, momentum in the time period when Israel was defending itself from rocket attacks against its citizenry from Hamas.

San Francisco State University is not far behind UC Irvine in the ignoble way it has enabled its Muslim students' organizations to create a veritable reign of terror on campus against Jewish and pro-Israel students, while simultaneously attempting to silence voices of opposition, a situation made evident in 2008 when SFSU's College Republicans were once again pushed into the limelight for their outspoken challenges to the school's ubiquitous Palestinianism.

Playing off the indignity suffered by president Bush when an insolent Iraqi reporter hurled a shoe at the former president's head during a press conference, the College Republicans had set up a booth to let students who so wished to sign an anti-Hamas, anti-terror petition and throw a shoe at a Hamas flag. Deeply "offended" by the Republicans for daring to condemn terrorists, rather than the Israeli state in defending its civilians from genocidal attack, members of SFSU's General Union of Palestinian Students (GUPS) and socialist club overturned the table, seized the Hamas flag, and were physically aggressive enough in their assault of the Republican students to result in two of their members being put under arrest.

The outcome of this event, one would think, would be fairly straightforward, since the pro-Hamas protestors clearly violated SFSU's own rules for student behavior. But in the morally-inverted world of academia, the Republican group, for the third time, found themselves the target of punishment and censure, not their attackers, and the "offended" parties—the GUPS and the socialist club—made some breathtakingly audacious demands to the SFSU administration: the College Republicans must be punished or sanctioned for throwing shoes at the Hamas flag, and, most ominously for defenders of free expression on campus, a forum would be created to "educate" students about what forms of speech the "offended" students deemed acceptable or unacceptable. The idea that one group of college students believe they can and should decide what acceptable speech is at any given moment is a particularly chilling concept, particularly when those same students have defined their political beliefs with an unwavering support for the jihadist aggression of groups that threaten not only Israel, but the West, as well.

Two years before that, the College Republicans had held a similar anti-terrorism rally at which SFSU students were invited to stomp on the flags of Hamas and Hezbollah, and with similar punitive results: the complaining Muslim students accused the Republican group members of creating a "hostile environment" by publicly walking over the terrorist flags, which, unbeknownst to the Republican students, happen bear the name of Allah in Arabic script.

While college protestors here and abroad regularly burn, deface, and desecrate the flags of Israel and the United States—something that the courts have repeatedly upheld as Constitutionally-protected speech—only on a campus controlled by Left-leaning faculty, administrators, and radicalized students could the protest against the flags of genocidal terrorist thugs be considered, as it was here, an attempt to "incite violence," "hateful religious intolerance," and an act by those who "pre-meditated the stomping of the flags knowing it would offend some people and possibly incite violence." Thanks to the intervention of the Foundation for Individual Rights in Education (FIRE), a group that defends campus free speech, the Republican club was exonerated, but only after they had been dragged through protracted proceedings by University officials.

Were *only* the College Republicans acting out in a provocative way on an otherwise peaceful SFSU campus, they might well be rebuked for being crude and demonstrating impolite and impolitic behavior. But not only has the campus gained notoriety for the outrageousness of some of its radical protests, but the same "offended" parties who sought punishments for the College Republicans, the General Union of Palestinian Students, have continually been at the center of a succession of riots, protests, and anti-Israel, anti-American hate-fests and counter-protests at which radical speakers regularly, and with unbridled invective, denounce and demonize Jews, Zionists, Israel, Republicans, and America.

Most notorious was the Muslim student-sponsored, pro-Palestinian April 2002 demonstration that included grotesque flyers and posters depicting a dead Palestinian baby on a soup-can label imprinted with the words "Palestinian Children Meat, slaughtered according to Jewish rites under American license," echoing the centuries-old blood libel of European anti-Semitism that accused Jews of murdering Gentile children and using their blood to bake matzos—a slander that has, not surprisingly, currently gained credence in the Arab world.

It was difficult to look as this vicious poster as yet another example of campus free expression, a reality that was not lost even on SFSU's president, Robert Corrigan, who issued sincere, although feckless, comments in response to the vile message. But while he condemned the cruelty of this specific message, he was careful to spread blame around to various potential victim groups of hate speech, including the perpetrators. "In speaking as strongly as I have in this letter," Corrigan wrote, "I am doing no more than you asked — working to eliminate discrimination and combat racism. And this is just as much a protection for Muslims, Arabs, and Palestinians as it is for Jews and Israelis. I recognize that these are times of great anguish, as well as anger, and I know that one moment, one flier, does not define this group or its individual members."[25]

Not content only to mount their own vile protests against Zionism, Jews, and Israel, the pro-Palestinian student groups took it upon themselves the following month to disrupt a vigil for Holocaust Remembrance Day where some 30 Jewish students who were reciting the Mourners' Kaddish—the Jewish prayer for the dead—were shouted down by protesters who countered with grisly prayers in memory of Palestinian suicide bombers. The pro-Palestinian counter-demonstrators, armed with whistles and bull horns, physically assaulted the Jewish students, spat on them, and screamed such charming epithets as "Too bad Hitler didn't finish the job," "Get out or we will kill you," "Fuck the Jews," "Die racist pigs," and "Go back to Russia, Jews." The violence escalated to the extent that San Francisco police officers finally had to usher the Jewish students to safety off campus.

"The police could do nothing more than surround the Jewish students and community members who were now trapped in a corner of the plaza," lamented Laurie Zoloth, SFSU's Director of the Program in Jewish Studies at the time of the incident in an open letter, "grouped under the flags of Israel, while an angry, out of control mob, literally chanting for our deaths, surrounded us . . . There was no safe way out of the Plaza. We had to be marched back to the Hillel House under armed S.F. police guard, and we had to have a police guard remain outside Hillel."[26]

This atmosphere of dread and danger on campus became palpable for Jewish students and faculty. "I cannot fully express what it feels like to have to walk across campus daily," Zoloth recounted, "past maps of the Middle East that do not include Israel, past posters of cans of soup with labels on them of drops of blood and dead babies . . , past poster after poster calling out "Zionism=Racism" and "Jews=Nazis" . . . This is the Weimar Republic with brown shirts it cannot control. This is the casual introduction of the medieval blood libel and virulent hatred."[27]

Cinnamon Stillwell, the West Coast representative for Campus Watch, a web site set up to monitor abuses in Middle Eastern studies programs and politicized teaching, wrote that the University had not been decisive in confronting anti-Semitic protests and events, and "it remains to be seen whether the administration will exorcise the cancer of extremism on campus or allow it to fester. While pontificating about 'free speech,' Corrigan and the SFSU administration continue to underestimate the growing radicalism in their own backyard. As a result, what began with attacks on Jewish students has now spread outward to any students who don't share the liberal politics of the majority."[28]

In July of 2006, SFSU's General Union of Palestinian Students co-sponsored with Al-Awda, the Palestine Right to Return Coalition, yet another noxious hate-fest against Israel, this time the Fourth International Al-Awda Convention, the overarching ambition of which is to enforce the right of all Palestinian refugees to return to their former homes in what is current-day Israel, with the express purpose of demographically eliminating Israel's Jewish identity and continued existence. "Racism, tribalism, all the 'isms' we're fighting, you cannot exclude Zionism from," proclaimed Michel Shehadeh, the host of the tellingly-named "Radio Intifada," a KPFK-FM Los Angeles radio program, and one of the convention's featured guest speakers. "If struggling against Zionism isn't at the core of defining yourself as a progressive, then you're not. You cannot be progressive if you're not fighting fascism and Nazism. It's a package. You can't be selective in this."[29]

Investigative reporter Lee Kaplan, who attended the 2006 event, characterized the Al-Awda conference as "a training and strategy event to attack Jews in America and abroad with boycotts and divestment," not to mention the fact that "Al Awda also openly supports the Baath Party that funds and aids the terrorists who kill U.S. soldiers in Iraq."[30] Since Al-Awda conferences have been off-limits to Jews and other disfavored attendees, there is a serious question about why an event disguised as an educational conference but which is in reality "anti-Semitism veiled as Middle East discussion"[31] should be held at a public university, subsidized by taxpayer support.

The SFSU Al-Awda conference had two objectives as its ideological mandate: (a) "Political and material isolation of the Genocidal Zionist State of Israel"; and (b) "Political and material support of the Palestinian refugee population." Al-Awda denies the right of Israel to exist, claims it is illegitimate, and, in fact, places the rights of Palestinians under international law above any rights inherent to the national rights of Israel, a UN member nation established lawfully by the League of Nations. In Al-Awda's contorted view, Israel cannot even enter into negotiations between parties to help create a Palestinian state, and "The inalienable rights of refugees and displaced people cannot be left to 'negotiations' between Israel and the Palestinian Authority," its fact sheet read. "International law considers agreements between a military occupier and the occupied to be null and void if they deprive civilians of recognized human rights including the rights to repatriation and restitution."

More serious is Al-Awda's complete acceptance of terrorism as a justified means for obtaining the desired political ends of Palestinian nationalism. "The Convention expresses support for the struggle of the Palestinian people, currently spearheaded by the Intifada, to achieve national resistance goals . . ,"[32] its 2003 convention resolutions stated, meaning that it recognizes that widely-held but morally perverse notion that armed resistance is justified against an occupying power. Also included in those resolutions was the hallucinatory claim made only by criminals and thugs that incarcerated terrorists are in fact "political prisoners" and should be summarily released; if, as they claim, Israel is involved in "massive state terrorism" itself, it has no right to criminalize acts of resistance against it.

Al-Awda's intransigency with respect to the mere existence of Israel, and its radical stance with respect to terrorism and a desire to totally replace the current state of Israel with an Islamic Palestine, is so breathtakingly extreme that it is difficult to see how any university could look at the tone and content of this conference and pretend that it created productive dialogue or inspired positive academic debate. It is one-sided and biased to the extreme, and barely disguises the overt anti-Semitism amid its calls to dismantle what it describes as an illegal Zionist regime. Another of the conference's speakers, Lamis Jamal Deek, attorney and a member of Al-Awda New York, summed up the overriding sentiment of the movement: "There can never be a place for Zionism in the Arab world . . . Zionism will never be allowed to exist peacefully among the people. Today we again demand the end of the Zionist presence in the Arab world."[33] At least at San Francisco State University, such sentiments found a welcoming home.

Berkeley: Free Speech, Still Out of Control
After All These Years

The University of California at Berkeley's Sproul Plaza, as anyone who follows the history of academic free speech knows, has, since the 1960s, retained a storied image of the birthplace of student protest, replete with newsreels of Mario Savio and Joan Baez huddled with hundreds of disheveled students after occupying the University's administration building in a demonstration against the Vietnam War. In fact, The Free Speech Movement itself was born at Berkeley, a concept that is held as something nearly sacred on campuses where Leftist faculty and students pretend to be seeking diversity of thought but in actuality are looking to only have expressed those ideas with which they agree. How the concept of free expression had devolved at Berkeley over the last generation was made clear in November, 2000 when Benjamin Netanyahu, who at the time had been out of office for two years from his first term as Israel's prime minister, was prevented from delivering a speech when a mob of protestors screamed through bullhorns, shouted at the 2000 ticket-holders, and blocked the entrance to Berkeley's Community Theater where the speech was to be held. Police, fearing an escalation of the violence and possible harm to Netanyahu, cancelled the speech, which gratified at least one Berkeley student, Lori Berlin, whose notion of free speech was that it should only be free when uttered by those with whom she agreed, not for someone like Netanyahu, since she did not "believe in free speech for war criminals."[34]

Two years later, on September 9, 2002, Netanyahu was invited to speak at Montréal's Concordia University, with similar violent repercussions. His theme for the speech was that "the war on terror can be won with clarity and courage or lost with confusion and vacillation,"[35] but it was a message that would never be heard, since 1000 incensed anti-Israel, pro-Palestinian protestors rioted, smashed windows, threw furniture, and eventually, through their violence, succeeded in having the speech cancelled. Student Sara Ahronheim, who had tried to attend the event that evening, recounted the scene and the feelings of rage and intimidation that defined the scene:

> I rested against the wall and watched as at least a hundred (I think) red-and-green colored protesters attacked the barriers and tried to get in. Riot cops appeared, dozens of them, and went to the gate as I and a few others were herded into the building. There was yelling and chanting, drumming and fighting going on outside the doors, with hundreds of our people stuck behind the gate being abused by hundreds of violent demonstrators . . . It was the scariest feeling, because

I knew that these people wanted to hurt me and anyone who supports Israel or is Jewish . . . We could hear chanting and yelling, and the protesters began trashing the university building . . . After hours of waiting, and bomb searches by RCMP sniffer dogs, we were informed that Bibi Netanyahu could not speak after all— too much danger to him and to us . . . The scene as we exited was disgusting. Benches were overturned, papers and garbage streaked across the hallways, and broken windows. We were shoved outside directly into a huge pro-Palestinian riot, where some of our people were apparently attacked . . . On their side, they threw bottles at people's heads, screamed hatred, and tried to break the barriers down to hurt us. They started tossing pennies and coins at us—one of the oldest ways to taunt Jews by saying we're all "money-grubbing." While we sang Hatikvah arm in arm, they spat at us. Finally we decided to disperse and leave them to their hatred . . . .[36]

The protests that shut down the Berkeley appearance of Netanyahu were, thankfully, calmer, even though a well-known, incendiary Berkeley character was part the mob of angry protestors that evening: that odious individual was lecturer Hatem Bazian, a native Palestinian and one of the "101 most dangerous academics in America," according to David Horowitz in his book by the same name. On the night of the speech protest, Bazian was able to insert his favorite narrative into the evening's activities, namely, how Netanyahu, as a representative of the Jewish state, had to answer for the occupation "by settlers," in Bazian's view, "who are the most racist and fascist people on the face of the earth."[37]

Bazian, a senior lecturer in Berkeley's Departments of Near Eastern and Ethnic Studies and an adjunct professor of law at Boalt Hall School of Law, had been long notorious for his vilification of Israel, conspiracist ravings about the CIA and American government, and not only an apologist for Palestinian terrorism, but someone who was catapulted to national attention because he explicitly, and famously, called for an "intifada" on American soil at a April 10, 2004 anti-war rally. The perverse scene at the event included, according to Campus Watch's managing editor Jonathan Calt Harris, "A Catholic priest [giving] pronouncements 'in the name of Allah,' signs [being] sold proclaiming 'Support Armed Resistance [sic] in Iraq and Everywhere,' next to tomes of Marx, Trotsky and Che Guevara . . , [and] a smiling student marched carried a sign saying 'Long Live Fallujah,' and another held a Bush effigy aloft on a noose."[38] It was the perfect setting for Dr. Bazian to work the crowd and conflate the insurgency activities against American forces in Iraq with the ongoing intifada by Palestinians against Israel; and with the curious reverence for the violence of insurrection and resistance that seems to be emblematic of the

Left's attraction to terror, the Berkeley professor incited the rapturous crowd to a jihad against the United States:

> Are you angry? [Yeah!] Are you angry? [Yeah!] Are you angry? [Yeah!] Well, we've been watching intifada in Palestine, we've been watching an uprising in Iraq, and the question is that what are we doing? *How come we don't have an intifada in this country?* Because it seem[s] to me, that we are comfortable in where we are, watching CNN, ABC, NBC, Fox, and all these mainstream . . . giving us a window to the world while the world is being managed from Washington, from New York, from every other place in here in San Francisco: Chevron, Bechtel . . . Halliburton; every one of those lying, cheating, stealing, deceiving individuals are in our country and we're sitting here and watching the world pass by, people being bombed, and *it's about time that we have an intifada in this country that change[s] fundamentally the political dynamics in here* . . . They're gonna say some Palestinian being too radical—well, *you haven't seen radicalism yet!*[39]

In looking at Bazian's public exhortations and rants over the years it is clear that, for him, the Axis of Evil is comprised of the neoconservatives, Western militarism, the United States under a Republican president, and, foremost on that list, of course—and deserving opprobrium and moral scolding for impeding the Palestinian cause—are Israel, Zionists, and Jews. Writing in the Berkeley *Daily Planet* in 2002, Berkeley student Maya Aizenman noted, as one example, that "Last week's protest by university group Students for Justice in Palestine was none other than a true testament to the fact that the group has already lost its credibility and is desperately trying to gain more supporters after alienating much of campus with their repeated disruption of classes." Why was she put off by the protestor's actions, in addition to the fact that they had disrupted classes when they were censured for staging a protest against the University's rules and guidelines? Because one of the protestors, the ubiquitous Dr. Bazian, made the wild claim that the protestors had been shut down, and their freedom of speech abridged, because of enormous political pressure applied to the University by a powerful "cabal." And who, according to Bazian, comprised this sinister group? "Hatem Bazian, a leader in the MSU," Aizenman continued, "gets up on Sproul and tells the crowd 'to take a look at the type of names on the building around campus—Haas, Zellerbach and decide who controls this university.'" In other words, Bazian made the same type of claim that his academic counterparts, Stephen Walt and John Mearsheimer, made in a similar context in their book *The Israel Lobby:* that Jewish wealth and control of the media enabled Jews to control debate in the public marketplace, and successfully suppress any criticism of Israel. "Therefore when all else fails for them and they refuse to take responsibility for their own actions, they blame the Jews," Aizenman concluded. "Hey why not? It worked before."[40]

When he is not busy calling for an intifada in America or bemoaning the omnipotence of wealthy Jews in academia, Bazian had not hesitated to seek inspiration from the Koranic texts, such as the use of a particularly noxious segment which he delivered at a 1996 American Muslim Conference with the theme of creating an Islamic State of Palestine. In his book *American Jihad: The Terrorists Living Among Us*, Steven Emerson quoted Bazian as reciting to the crowd, "'In the Hadith, the Day of Judgment will never happen until you fight the Jews . . . and the stones will say, 'Oh Muslim, there is a Jew hiding behind me. Come and kill him!'"[41]

Given his proclivity for casting aspersions on Jews and Israel while he is bashing America and its Western values, Bazian should not have been surprised that some have accused him of anti-Semitism, a charge he confronted during a 2002 annual conference of the Palestinian Solidarity Movement (PSM). The PSM was, not coincidentally, established at Berkeley by Snehal Shingavi (discussed more fully below), a student radical who in 2000, while the Second Intifada was raging, had founded Students for Justice in Palestine (SJP) at Berkeley. Since the movement calls for divestment from Israel, the right of return of millions of Palestinians to their original homes in what is now Israel, the "decolonization" of Arabs lands, the end of all occupation, and a granting of the right of Palestinians to "resist" occupation through violent means, these radical activists clearly display an undercurrent of anti-Semitism in the rabid anti-Zionist rhetoric that is at the core of their movement. But one thing that causes people who are actually Jew-haters to become extremely indignant over is the charge of anti-Semitism, when, they will tell you, it is only Israel and Zionism they abhor, not Jews. In fact, the most rabid critics of Israel frequently see the accusations of anti-Semitism against them as yet another tool of Jewish influence in trying to control and stifle debate. At the Michigan conference, Bazian suggested this very thing, saying that when he and others are accused of being anti-Semitic, it is another example of how "anti-Semitism is used as a means of neutralizing the opposition so the mainstream American public will distance itself from the 'extremists.'"[42] What Bazian and his fellow travelers in the radical Left never consider, of course, is that it is more likely that the American public he speaks of "distances" itself from extremism and campaigns of terrorism against a Middle Eastern democracy, not because of the fear of engaging in anti-Semitism by condemning Israel, but more likely because a broad swathe of the American public, indeed, in the West, explicitly rejects the extremist views of individuals like Bazian and other radicals who apologize for terror, fail to acknowledge the complicity of the Arab world for the realization of a Palestinian state, and who continue to vilify Israel and accuse it of being the principal cause of the Middle East's multiple pathologies and economic and social strife.

Professor Bazian, at the same time he felt free to endlessly excoriate Israel for all crimes real and imagined, was quick, nevertheless, to demand certain accommodations for Islam and the Muslim world. In 2006, for instance, in the middle of the Muslim rage that spanned the globe after the publication of twelve relatively tame cartoons depicting the Prophet Mohammad, which first were published in September in Denmark's *Jyllands-Posten*, Bazian appeared with Berkeley political science lecturer Darren Zook at a Berkeley event to discuss the controversy. In language similar to that of the Organisation of The Islamic Conference (OIC)—which has been working diligently to criminalize blasphemy (singularly against Islam) and preempt any criticism of terrorism, radical imams who preach hatred and incite jihad, and even the type of satire evident in the series of cartoons—Bazian's view was that the West's behavior in publishing the cartoons exhibited "a lack of sensitivity many Westerners have toward the Muslim community."[43]

What is more, Bazian suggested, the fact that the West did not condemn the cartoons and suppress the universal notion of unbridled free speech in democratic societies revealed a hypocrisy based on an undercurrent of Islamophobia. "If it were a rabbi with a bomb on his head, every government in Europe would condemn the newspaper," Bazian said, dragging Jews even into this conversation, "but the fact that it was Muslim, it was not seen as wrong. It is like Europe is saying 'Do as we say, not as we do.'"[44] Bazian's notion that the West conspired to insult Islam by allowing the publication of the cartoons, even when it could be expected that the Muslim world would react apoplectically as a result, and that it would never publish cartoons insulting other faiths (rabbis, in his bizarre example), is not only disingenuous but also fails to acknowledge the very frequent, visible, and vile attacks in the world media on Judaism, Zionism, and Jews. But more to the point, Bazian fails to see that the reason no cartoons would be drawn of a rabbi, or of Moses, or another Old Testament prophet as a terrorist (or, for that matter, Baptists, Mormons, Hindus, or Episcopalians) is because Jews are not strapping explosives on their bodies and turning themselves into weapons to immolate Arab civilians on buses, pizza parlors, or discos. Rabbis are not preaching jihad in synagogues and urging their congregants to subsume the infidel and behead those who insult Judaism. They are not creating terror cells to launch attacks on London, Madrid, New York, Washington, DC, Mumbai, or any of the 15,000 terrorist attacks initiated by Islamists since 9/11 alone. That is why the cartoons depicted Mohammed as being theologically and ideologically linked to terror, not because the West had decided to be insensitive to Muslims and insult Islam—that, and to make a point about the West's dedication to the enshrined right of free expression in cultures of modernity.

Even more ironic is the fact that Bazian, who lives in the West, enjoys its freedoms and comforts, and teaches at one of the most elite educational institutions in the world where complete freedom of expression is one of the most sacred intellectual values, would have a double standard for free speech when it comes to Islam—just as the OIC did when it suggested that while it recognized the value of Western traditions of freedom of speech and expression, when it came to religions—and, specifically, Islam—there were certain "red lines" that should not, and could not, be crossed. In other words, Islam had to be accommodated in a manner in which no other faith in the world had to be, something that Islamic scholar Robert Spencer has noted is part of the "stealth jihad" underway with the intention of weakening the West from within. So while Bazian has felt very comfortable with appearing at rallies where he calls for a jihad against his own country from a podium at a taxpayer-funded public university, and where he has made a career for himself by vilifying and demonizing Israel and Jews, he sees no intellectual contradiction in suggesting that when it comes to free speech, there should sometimes be limits—except, of course, for Islam or in support of the Palestinian cause.

In May of 2002, Snehal Shingavi, 26, a fifth-year graduate student in English at Berkeley, posted his course description for a fall offering called English R1A, "The Politics and Poetics of Palestinian Resistance." The course listing, and its instructor, might never have otherwise gained any notice from the outside world, save for the two very controversial final lines included in the description for a course in poetry. The highly-politicized, biased description read:

> The brutal Israeli military occupation of Palestine, [ongoing] since 1948, has systematically displaced, killed, and maimed millions of Palestinian people. And yet, from under the brutal weight of the occupation, Palestinians have produced their own culture and poetry of resistance. This class will examine the history of the [resistance] and the way that it is narrated by Palestinians in order to produce an understanding of the Intifada . . . This class takes as its starting point the right of Palestinians to fight for their own self-determination. *Conservative thinkers are encouraged to seek other sections.*[45]

That a course like this could be conceived of and offered in a major public university indicates quite clearly the intellectual rot that has set into American higher education, particularly in instances when radicalized faculty members use their positions to insert ideology into the curriculum in inappropriate and politicized ways. This description, written ostensibly for a poetry course, reads like the Hamas charter, complete with its total indictment of Israel and the Jewish state's fundamental right to exist, and includes, more disturbingly, a pre-determined point of view that many students, especially a conservative one, would have a difficult time questioning or contradicting in class. Shingavi's warning that "conservative thinkers should seek other sections" is equally perverse, not only because it violates the very premise of education—to seek out some kind of truth through a scholarly inquiry into various points of view about a topic—but also because by excluding any alternate points of view, the professor is not teaching, he is indoctrinating. And what business does an English professor have teaching political propaganda masquerading as a study of poetry?

Mr. Shingavi, not surprisingly, scrambled to come to his own defense once outsiders demanded to know how a publically-funded university could offer a course which was so blatantly biased. But Shingavi was not to be moved. "You can have a series of debates about Israel's right to destroy Palestine," he answered back to critics who wanted to know why his discussions were obviously going to be so one-sided against Israel, "but those are not germane to the questions about how Palestinians understand themselves and how they understand resistance. I'm not restricting the class, it is merely a warning that the course has certain kinds of themes that are at its core,"[46] those "themes" presumably being that Israel is singularly responsible for all the suffering of the Palestinians, that Arabs are always victims of brutal oppression and have never contributed to their own plight, and that "the right of Palestinians to fight for their own self-determination" means that terror would always be apologized for, rationalized, and excused as an acceptable tactic in resistance against the Jewish state.

Shingavi did not have to wait until the public outcry over his poetry course brought him into to the limelight, since his antics and radical beliefs were already well known on the Berkeley campus. In the month before the course controversy, Shingavi and other members of Students for Justice in Palestine, with the cruel political theatrics for which the movement is known, chose Holocaust Remembrance Day to hold a pro-Palestinian rally on Sproul Plaza before an audience of over 1000 rapt onlookers. Demanding that Berkeley initiate a divestment campaign against companies doing business with Israel, Shingavi and his fellow radicals proceeded to occupy the University's Wheeler Hall and staged a sit in. By the end of the day's riotous activities, police had arrested 79 individuals, including Mr. Shingavi himself.

Mr. Shingavi, however, was unrepentant; in fact, after *Mother Jones Magazine* recognized the glowing idealism of Berkeley by rating it fourth in the nation for campus activism, Mr. Shingavi saw it as confirmation that his raucous activities with Students for Justice in Palestine were useful and defensible. "SJP has been a breakthrough in Palestinian activism across the country," he crowed. "We're proud of the work we're doing and that the plight of Palestinians remains in discussion on college campuses across the country."[47]

With the empty commitment of a would-be revolutionary who never has to leave the safety and comfort of an insulated campus, Shingavi, like many on the Left, feel they speak truth to power, and that they have to become even more radicalized in their cause because of government interference, police investigations, even the scrutiny of the Jewish-controlled press. That so many reject their ideologies is proof to the practitioner of Richard Hofstadter's "paranoid style of politics"—both on the far Left and the far Right—that a conspiracy of powerful players has been erected to defuse and obscure the "truth" that only the radical himself understands clearly. Shingavi, for instance, frustrated by those who began to take a closer look at radical Islam, the roots of jihadist terror, and some of the pathologies of the Muslim world that were causing its own strife, looked for sinister outside forces pitted against the Palestinian cause, against Islam, and against Muslims in general because of Islamophobia. Where did he find these sinister foes? A 2005 speech he gave, ominously entitled "The New COINTELPRO Campaign Directed at Arabs, Muslims and South East Asians," suggested that the focus on the Muslim community after 9/11 had nothing to do with any questionable activities coming out of that community; instead, it was a knee-jerk reaction of the United States and Israel to attempt to neutralize the growing political influence of Muslims. "Many Israeli centric individuals and organizations view with great alarm the increase in numbers and assertiveness of American Muslim and Arab communities," he absurdly proclaimed. Why? Because "it has potential in the long run of causing the reconsideration of the existing policies vis a vis Israel and the Middle East."[48]

One of the hapless victims of this "legal harassment campaign of the government" that Shingavi alluded to involved the case of then-South Florida University Professor, Dr. Sami Al-Arian, who was currently facing an inconvenient 49-count indictment by the U.S. justice system; according to Shingavi, this was simply a baseless prosecution "that allows the Israeli intelligence agency to submit evidence against him."[49] Many academics, including Shingavi, had come to the defense of Al-Arian, a soft-spoken professor who was teaching on a quiet American campus. The only problem was that Al-Arian, who had been witnessed exhorting, "Let us damn America, let us damn

Israel, let us damn them and their allies until death,"[50] had, in 1995, after a gruesome suicide bombing by the Palestinian Islamic Jihad that claimed 22 Israeli lives, sent out a fundraising letter seeking "true support of the jihad effort in Palestine so that operations such as these can continue."[51] So when the government finally made its case against Al-Arian, it was not because he was an innocent Muslim who had been railroaded into a confession; in fact, the court findings were quite clear: "Defendant is pleading guilty because defendant is in fact guilty. The defendant certifies that the defendant does hereby admit that the facts set forth [in the plea agreement] are true, and were this case to go to trial, the United States would be able to prove those specific facts and others beyond a reasonable doubt."[52] Only in the wild conspiracy theories of Shingavi's fevered and oppression-obsessed mind could Al-Arian have been anything but a co-conspirator in a far-reaching campaign to murder Jews in the name of Islam.

UCLA: Slanted Scholarship for Jihad

While much troubling anti-Israelism on California campuses has been driven by radical students groups, and, most often, by Muslim Students Associations, some schools have made their contribution with faculty-sponsored events, as well. The student-run events are insidious and expose a one-sided, highly-politicized approach to the Israeli-Palestinian issue; but because they are run by students (even though faculty are often eager to participate and give their moral support), frequently these hate-fests lack import and influence precisely because they are student events, and not explicitly supported by a school's faculty and administration. But when conferences and symposia are sponsored by a university—and particularly when a school's own faculty are the moderators as well as hosts—then the event takes on a greater significance, and the intellectual credibility of the institution is, and should be, at stake. Too often, these faculty-sanctioned events, when they have focused on discussion of the Israeli/Palestinian question, have evolved in much the same way as some of the student events discussed here, complete with their one-sidedness, extreme bias towards Israel and Zionism, a skewed historical perspective that considers only Palestinian concerns, and an overall attempt to demonize Israel and hold it responsible for the long-standing unrest in the Middle East.

One such event, "Human Rights and Gaza," was held at the University of California, Los Angeles on January 21, 2009, for example, sponsored by UCLA's Center for Near Eastern Studies (CNES). The stated objective of the symposium, as articulated by Susan Slyomovics, CNES's director, was to reveal the "truth" about Israel's current incursions into Gaza to protect its southern towns from unceasing rocket attacks by Hamas, a "truth," she suggested, that was hidden from the public because of slanted media coverage. But the event, according to UCLA professor Judea Pearl, father of murdered *Wall Street Journal* reporter Daniel pearl, became "a symposium . . . on human rights turned into a Hamas recruitment rally by a clever academic gimmick . . , carefully select[ing] only Israel bashers for the panel, each of whom concluded that the Jewish state is the greatest criminal in human history."[53] That approach to academic inquiry should not be acceptable at a major academic institution; in fact, the product of such symposia and conferences is frequently not scholarly analysis at all—it is pure propaganda. And, as the Zionist Organization of America noted in a letter about this event to UCLA's Chancellor, Gene Block, since the CNES receives federal funding from the Department of Education as a designated National Resource Center under Title VI of the Higher Education Act, its failure to "reflect diverse perspectives and a wide range of views and generate debate on world regions and international affairs" is actually a violation of the Federal regulations which govern such funding.[54]

But federal law aside, the more serious indictment of the event concerns the vitriolic approach the panelists—all well-known ideological enemies of Israel—took with respect to the discussion, and how their visceral hatred for Israel's policies, and specifically in this latest Gaza incursion, was made manifest in their presentations, and the insidious way the interaction with the audience of some 400 unraveled during the proceedings. One of those in room was Dr. Roberta Seid, a historian who teaches at UC Irvine and is director of educational research for the pro-Israel organization, StandWithUs. In her view, the event's highly-charged, one-sided presentation and counter-factual account of the Israeli/Palestinian conflict recalled "the anti-Semitic rabble rousing in Munich's 1920's beer halls," and amounted to "an academic lynching of Israel and the entire Zionist enterprise." Moreover, the supposed academics and experts did not engage in authentic dialogue and inquiry, but unraveled a series of charges against Israel that ignored the context of Arab implacability and unrelenting violence against Israel. To Seid, therefore, the event was not an academic symposium that was guided by a fair and reasonable investigation of facts; it was, in her view, more like a hate rally designed specifically to demonize, and dehumanize, Jews and the Jewish state:

> It felt like a Munich beer hall because to an implacably self-righteous, cheering crowd, Israel was painted precisely as Nazis used to paint the Jews: powerful, motivated solely by insatiable greed and cruelty, interlopers who don't belong

and are contaminating someone else's culture and home, violators of all norms of civilized behavior, decency and law. All their actions have had sinister motives. All attacks against Israel were either implicitly justified . . . or they were minimized. Palestinians are a "defenseless" people who, in the past 60 years, have never done anything to merit Israel's military responses . . . And the rest of the world—Middle East nations' roles and rivalries and other powerful players, such as terrorists and terrorism—were airbrushed away, producing a cartoon image divorced from all reality of an unfettered, demonic Israel—not unlike the Nazi cartoons of Jews holding the globe and pulling all the strings of history.[55]

On the panel, alongside moderator Susan Slyomovics, were Lisa Hajjar, associate professor and chair of the Law and Society program at UC Santa Barbara; Richard Falk, Special rapporteur for human rights in the Occupied Territories, professor emeritus, Princeton University, and then-visiting professor of Global and International Studies at UC Santa Barbara; and two of UCLA's own professors, in-house Israel-haters Saree Makdisi, professor of English and comparative literature, and Gabriel Piterberg, professor of history.

Professor Hajjar, according to Israeli professor Steven Plaut, "is in fact nothing more than a third-rate leftist sociologist. She has no training in law or legal studies, is not qualified as a Middle East scholar or researcher, and has extraordinarily few *bona fide* publications even in sociology."[56] But her sketchy academic credentials have not prevented her from being granted tenure at UC Santa Barbara and writing promiscuously about the innumerable flaws of the United States and Israel, particularly in their use of torture. While she is eager and always ready to critique the defense policies of democracies, she regularly glosses over or excuses the terrorism of Hamas, as she did during the symposium. Instead, she recounted how, in her view, Israel's actions in Operation Cast Lead displayed a flagrant violation of international law, exhibited the "disproportionality" prohibited by Geneva Convention rules, and used excessive force, all helping to make Israel the "enemy of all mankind." Hamas, on the other hand, even though it had by that time indiscriminately fired some 6000 rockets and mortars into civilian Israeli neighborhoods from Gaza, was never condemned by Hajjar. In fact, she had written, violent "resistance" (a euphemism for terrorism) is reasonable when conventional means of resisting are absent. "Because Palestinians are stateless and dispersed, their struggle for national rights has taken 'unconventional' forms, including guerilla warfare," one of those 'unconventional' forms presumably being the slaughter of Jewish children at pizza parlors, buses, discos, yeshivas, and on Israeli streets.

And as for Western nations' attempts to reign in terror and neutralize terrorist groups and their leaders? For Hajjar, this is nothing more than a blunt weapon against the self-determination struggle of what she terms "non-states." "The Palestine Liberation Organization (PLO), which emerged in the 1960s to lead this struggle, has been castigated by Israel, and to a lesser extent the US, as nothing but a terrorist organization. This typifies the use of the terrorist label to non-states in their struggles against states . . . ,"[57] she concluded, as if the label of "terrorist" might not be very appropriate for murderous organizations like Hamas whose charter calls for a jihad against infidels and death for every Jew on earth.

Richard Falk's appraisal of the Gaza situation, like Hajjar's, assigned all culpability to Israel, with the Gazans depicted as a peaceful group of hapless victims trapped in a nightmare created by an occupying power. These morally incoherent views are business-as-usual for Falk, whose many public comments about the fascist tendencies he perceived in the war on terror and such tools as the Patriot Act, not to mention his repeated comparisons of Israelis to Nazis, have made it quite clear that he was clearly ideologically ill-equipped to assume his UN role as an impartial observer. "The recent developments in Gaza," Falk wrote in 2007, "are especially disturbing because they express so vividly a deliberate intention on the part of Israel and its allies to subject an entire human community to life-endangering conditions of utmost cruelty. The suggestion that this pattern of conduct is a *holocaust-in-the-making* represents a rather desperate appeal to the governments of the world and to international public opinion to act urgently to prevent these current genocidal tendencies from culminating in a collective tragedy."[58] The following year, still looking for ways to condemn Israel and accuse it of perpetrating genocide, Falk wrote that while he had to admit, begrudgingly, that "certainly the rocket attacks against civilian targets in Israel are unlawful . . . that illegality does not give rise to any Israeli right, neither as the Occupying Power nor as a sovereign state, to violate international humanitarian law and commit war crimes or crimes against humanity in its response."[59]

Professor Falk, who commentator Ron Radosh has characterized as a "conspiracy mongering flake"[60] for his wild assertions that, among other things, neoconservatives in the Bush administration may have been complicit in the 9/11 attacks, used the UCLA event to once again condemn Israel's actions, brushing aside any notion that the Gaza incursions were conducted for self-defense after Hamas rockets had rained down on civilian Israeli communities since the 2005 withdrawal. Instead, he characterized Israel's restrained military response to terrorist attacks as "aggression." The idea that Israel acted in self-defense, he said, "falsifies in fundamental ways the interaction between Gaza and Israel," since Israel had been limiting the delivery of products, building materials, fuel and electricity, and other goods to Gaza, amounting to "a form of collective punishment prohibited by the Geneva Conventions and a grave breach of international humanitarian law that is itself a war crime." But Falk's charge of collective punishment against the Gazans by Israel, while dramatic, was counterfactual and a misreading of international law.

The Fourth Geneva Convention prohibits collective punishment as a way of preventing criminal penalties against *individuals* in a population as retribution for the actions of others. It was never meant to refer to economic sanctions, as was the case with Israel and Gaza. Israel, as Mr. Falk should know, was in full compliance with Article 23 of the Geneva Conventions which stipulates that Israel should not block humanitarian aid from being delivered to Gaza from other sources; but Israel was never under any legal obligation to provide that aid itself, particularly when what could be easily considered acts of war were being initiated against it from within Gaza. Nor, as Mr. Falk should also know, would Israel be required to permit building materials, fuel, or electricity to reach Hamas during the conflict, since those goods and services could be utilized by the enemy to continue its military aggression. The withholding of utilities and goods was a legal military tactic for Israel, since Article 52 of the 1977 Amendment to the Geneva Convention does not prohibit a weakening or neutralizing of an enemy's means of attack, "those objects which by their nature, location, purpose or use make an effective contribution to military action and whose total or partial destruction, capture or neutralization, in the circumstances ruling at the time, offers a definite military advantage."[61] But facts mean little to ideologues like Falk, who brushes aside the homicidal aggression of Hamas as the work of a "few militants" (not, of course, terrorists), and is compelled to weave a poisonous tapestry of lies, distortions, falsehoods, and propaganda at an academic conference where the stated, though unrealized, goal was to gain insight and reveal facts.

The day's flurry of vitriol was rounded out by two of UCLA's own faculty, both of whom maintained the strident anti-Israel rhetoric that had defined the symposiums entire proceedings. The first, professor of history Gabriel Piterberg, was born in Argentina, but because he was not only raised in and is a citizen of Israel—and even served in the Israeli Defense Forces—he is the anti-Semite's and anti-Zionist's dream spokesperson: an Israeli, and Jew, who hates Israel. His fundamental view is that the Jewish state is illegitimate, that its founding by Zionists is a classic model of colonialism where an indigenous population was "ethnically cleansed" to make way for the European settlers. Like many who are intoxicated with Palestinianism, Piterberg only has concern for Palestinian self-determination; for Israelis no such concern is forthcoming, since they are, in his view, merely interlopers on stolen land. The settlers, therefore, are the key problem to a peaceful West Bank, not the marauding thugs of Fatah and Hamas.

Piterberg spoke at a 2000 "speak-out" sponsored by UCLA's Muslim Students Association, part of something called the "National Day of Outrage," where he dismissed the concept of a two-state solution out of hand. Those illegal settlements were the principal impediment to peace and statehood, he contended, since "You can't have a Palestinian state with its own rights, when you have 150,000 Jewish extremists sitting in the middle."[62]

In 2002 Piterberg made another appearance at a campus rally sponsored by the Committee for Peace and Justice, an oddly named organization that clearly seeks peace only in a world without Israel and justice only for the oppressed Palestinians. Obviously wracked with guilt over being an Israeli and a veteran of the country's defense forces, he publicly confessed that the actions of the Zionist regime made him "ashamed and embarrassed to call [himself] an Israeli citizen." He then added the intellectually defective bit of moral relativism so often espoused by Leftist apologists for terror, namely that there is no difference between the terror of Hamas and the state-sponsored "terror" of the IDF. "If a suicide bomber is a terrorist," Piterberg exhorted, "then so is the Israeli pilot who flies an F-16 . . , even if he looks like Tom Cruise or a young Paul Newman."[63]

Saree Makdisi, professor of English and comparative literature at UCLA, and the author of the tellingly-titled *Palestine Inside Out: An Everyday Occupation*, rounded off the day's enlightened discussion with his own lurid accusations against Israel, a misrepresentation of history and facts, and a contortion of the political facts on the ground in Gaza, where the current conflict was then raging. Makdisi, the nephew of Edward Said, shared his late uncle's venomous attitudes toward Israel, and similarly believed that the Palestinians were complete victims and Israel the eternal colonial Middle East bully. The Gazans, he contended, had been jammed into their territory against their will, and the recent blockades and military strikes had decimated the population; all the long-suffering Palestinians sought was return to their lands, he proclaimed, and "every person has a moral right to go back home." Like other Israel-haters who have no use for the so-called "two-state solution," Makdisi assumed social justice could only be achieved with the creation of a single, bi-national state; in other words, a state where a Jewish identity would be subsumed by a hostile Arab majority living on the same land. The prospect of that demographic way of eliminating the

Jewish state never bothers enemies of democracy, so the disappearance of Israel would be a mere inconvenience and not of great concern—as long as justice is achieved for the Palestinians. "One people's desire to have their own state cannot deny another people's right to live in their own homes," he said, curiously referring to Israel's national self-determination merely a "desire" and the Palestinians' nationalistic yearnings as a "right." And what is more, the Palestinians are "a people that . . . have [been] brutalized for decades on end," largely as a result of Israel's "total disregard for international humanitarian law."[64]

And like his fellow traveler professor Piterberg, Makdisi makes no distinction between non-state terrorism and the defensive responses of state actors in repelling or suppressing terrorist attacks. In 2002, for example, after columnist Ellen Goodman had asked rhetorically the same, and obvious, question that many have asked about Palestinian terrorism, "What kind of adults raise suicide bombers?," Makdisi was quick to publish his fervid answer in the *International Herald Tribune*:

> What kind of adults raise the soldiers of a racist army of occupation? Suicide bombings are the terrible and deplorable recourse of desperate people who are resisting a brutal military occupation. Instead of indulging in racist platitudes about the supposed cultural failures of Palestinian parents, Goodman should reserve her sermonizing for the Israeli parents who have raised the bomber pilots who drop high explosives on densely populated neighborhoods, the snipers who murder stone-throwing children, the soldiers who prevent ambulances from saving lives, and the crews of bulldozers who raze people's homes, sometimes with their residents still inside.

In never apparently occurs to moral relativists like Makdisi that the military operations he lists in his rant are not random acts of malice. The bomber pilots he refers to were targeting terrorist cells from which Qassam rockets and mortars were continually fired into civilian neighborhoods in southern Israel; the reason Israel was, and is, forced to fire missiles into densely populated Palestinian neighborhoods was because Hamas—in violation of international law—inserted itself into the civilian population with the specific intention of drawing fire to innocents as a way of bringing condemnation, once again, on Israel; bulldozers did not enter Palestinian neighborhoods arbitrarily, but were used to destroy the homes of terrorists who did not cease their attacks on Jews. But to Makdisi, the actions were morally equivalent, and, as he wrote in an 2005 article in the *Los Angeles Times* in the context of the Iraq war, "The usual self-congratulatory contrast between 'our' civilization and 'their' barbarism has set the stage for a cycle of moralistic inquiries into the motivations of suicide bombers and the supposed duty of 'good' Muslims to restrain 'bad' ones."[65] In Makdisi's rarified universe there is no distinction between terrorist and soldier, no clash of civilizations, no certainty about which moral laws apply to human behavior. There is not even any context, historical or political, by which nations could make judgments about practical, just resolutions of disputes over land, sovereignty, and self-determination.

All of the Palestinians' woes are the result of the barbarism of Israel, and, in his view, Israel's security measures are merely tactical weapons to further subjugate Arabs, not legitimate means of protecting its citizens. Referring to Israel's separation barrier with the hideous imagery of Holocaust work camps, for example, Makdisi fumed that "the wall represents Israel's desire to fulfill Zionism's greatest dream and, finally, do away with the Palestinians, if not by outright massacre or explicit transfer then by bludgeoning them into a subhuman, animal-like irrelevance—precisely what has happened to the hapless inhabitants of Gaza, whose lives are now wasting away in the gigantic concentration camp the Israelis have built for them." Never mind that Israel unilaterally exited Gaza in 2005, uprooting every Jew living there when they did; an economically-stagnant, Jew-free Gaza under Palestinian control was still the fault of Israel. "Hermetically sealed off from the outside world by a network of electric fences and ditches—its labor force now entirely irrelevant and extraneous to the Israeli economy—Gaza is, quite literally, the largest prison on earth."[66]

Chapter 8

Radical Student Groups, Israel Hate-Fests, & Demonstrations

The Muslim Students Association & Stealth Jihad

In October 2009, in an action that seemed to give credence to notion that there was, and remains, a sinister and dangerous side to anti-Israel activism on college campuses, the U.S. Justice Department initiated an investigation into possible illegal fundraising on behalf of Hamas participated in by UC Irvine's Muslim Student Union. Based on a formal complaint by the Zionist Organization of America, the investigation would look into allegations that the far-Left, Israel-hating British MP, George Galloway, had raised funds for his Viva Palestina project, a "philanthropy" with the purported purpose of providing humanitarian need to Palestinians blockaded in Gaza, but which has been revealed as a funding device to provide cash directly to Hamas—designated as a Foreign Terrorist Organization (FTO) by the U.S. State Department, Canada, and the EU.

Galloway, who has referred to Hamas "as heroes [who] are opening the eyes of the world to the siege in the Strip," and who elevates the Palestinian cause as a sacred mission against the tyranny of Western imperialism, had attended a May 2009 event on the Irvine campus sponsored by the University's Muslim Student Union, "Israel: The Politics of Genocide," and used the opportunity not only to condemn Israel for its many alleged transgressions,

but also to raise money to assist its enemies in arming themselves to further their ambition of extirpating the Jewish state. His real intention, and the
spurious purpose of Viva Palestina's fundraising, was on full display in 2009
when Galloway presented a satchel of cash to Hamas Prime Minister Ismail
Haniyeh. At that meeting, Galloway was very clear about his true intentions
and the purpose of his charitable activities: "This is not charity," he said as he
defiantly passed the money to Haniyeh, "this is politics." What is more, he
contended at that meeting, he was fully intent on "break[ing] the sanctions on
the elected government of Palestine."[1]

Not surprisingly, UCI's Muslim Student Union, which had its own long
history of spewing hate speech and directing accusations, slanders, and vilification at Israel and Jews, was not too pleased when the FBI began its investigation into its role in facilitating the Viva Palestina fundraising. In fact, they
contended, the investigation, initiated after the formal complaint, ZOA's was
itself symptomatic of anti-Muslim bias, and yet another attempt by one of
the major members of the dreaded "Israel Lobby" to silence Israel's critics.
Hadeer Soliman, a Muslim Student Union member, writing in *New University*, UC Irvine's student newspaper, had her own take on what she contended
were false accusations about the MSU's role in the Galloway affair. The
Zionist Organization of America, she wrote, "has a long history of attacking
organizations that it deems a threat because they do not fall in line with its
extreme right-wing stances on the issue of Palestine." Viva Palestina was a
completely innocent humanitarian organization with the purest of motives,
Soliman continued, and "If anyone [was] acting illegally, it [was] the ZOA,
by seeking to discard the very principles of the First Amendment in trying
to shut us up and shut us down." In fact, according to Soliman, the current
FBI investigation had nothing to do with any real or imagined wrongdoing on the part of the MSU; it had everything to do what she perceived as
the ZOA's continuing campaign "to defame, censor and essentially eradicate
the MSU for years now. This is only the most recent attempt to silence the
MSU and restrict its constitutional right to freedom of speech, religion and
association."[2]

Subversive behavior on the part of the notorious Galloway was to be
expected, based on his long tradition of coddling up to tyrants and enemies
of Western democracies; but the collaboration of a campus student organization in helping to funnel funds for use by terrorists reveals a far more
troubling issue. In fact, the Muslim Student Association—on UCI's campus
and on some 600 other college campuses in the U.S. and Canada (with 200
affiliated chapters) since its founding in 1963 at the University of Illinois—
has a long history of bringing radical speakers and guests to campus for the

purpose of vilifying Israel, and, more ominously, for helping to facilitate the process by which, they hope, Western society and culture will be weakened and eventually replaced by Sharia law. Far from being another benign campus club involving itself with communal prayer, social events, and some political activism, the Muslim Student Association (MSA) is actually an offshoot of the Muslim Brotherhood, a radical, terroristic group founded in Egypt in 1963 with the express purpose of destabilizing democratic movements and imposing Islamism on the Middle East.

While the purported intent of MSA chapters is to provide Muslim students with some social interaction, discussion of religious practices, and programs for interfaith understanding, a look at a strategy memo from the Muslim Brotherhood reveals a far more sinister and pernicious tactical purpose for the creation of the MSA. During the 2007 trial by the Justice Department against the Holy Land Foundation for Relief and Development (HLF), which was accused of being a front used to channel funds to Hamas and other terrorist organizations, an interesting 1991 document by Brotherhood tactician Mohamed Akram, a.k.a. Mohamed Adlouni, for the Shura Council of the Muslim Brotherhood, was offered as evidence. In it, the true intent of the Brotherhood was exposed as being a subtle, gradual process of subversion, and members were advised of an overarching strategic objective to their movement: they "must understand that their work in America is a kind of grand jihad in eliminating and destroying the Western civilization from within and 'sabotaging' its miserable house by their hands and the hands of the believers so that it is eliminated and God's religion is made victorious over all other religions."[3]

The way that would be accomplished would be to establish, through "charities" and other social organizations, ideological beachheads in America—in mosques, in clubs, and, not insignificantly, on university campuses—for the purpose of spreading a fundamentalist creed of Wahhabi Islam, and with the ultimate intent being to subvert American society and values and subsume Western culture under an Islamist state. Estimates put the Saudi's "investment" in foreign aid—much of it specifically targeted to Islamic development with a heavy Wahhabi influence—at $4 billion annually, including to such organizations as the MSA. In his June 2003 testimony to the U.S. Senate's Subcommittee on Terrorism and Homeland Security, for instance, Stephen Schwartz, Senior Fellow at the Foundation for Defense of Democracies suggested that:

Shia and other non-Wahhabi Muslim community leaders estimate that 80 percent of American mosques out of a total ranging between an official estimate of 1,200 and an unofficial figure of 4-6,000 are under Wahhabi control . . . Wahhabi control over mosques means control of property, buildings, appointment of imams, training of imams, content of preaching including faxing of Friday sermons from Riyadh, Saudi Arabia, and of literature distributed in mosques . . . and organizational and charitable solicitation . . . The main organizations that have carried out this campaign are the Islamic Society of North America (ISNA), which originated in the Muslim Students' Association of the U.S. and Canada (MSA), and the Council on American-Islamic Relations (CAIR).[4]

The MSU's alliance with the likes of George Galloway demonstrates once again the group's willingness, not to mention eagerness, to align itself with radicals whose primary political agenda is to give emotional and financial support to Israel's enemies. The speakers it invites to its anti-Israel hate-fests are, almost without exception, vituperative radicals with only one view of the Arab/Israel conflict: one in which the Jewish state does not exist autonomously and is replaced with an Islamist state with Jews living again in dhimmitude. The regular references to Palestine, a future bi-national state of Arabs and Jews *in place of Israel*, the promotion of the Palestinian's so-called "right of return" by which they could effectively demographically subvert Israeli society, or the justification of terror as an international right as part of resistance to unjust occupation and oppression—all of these tropes in the ideological war against Israel have become central themes of the MSA's campus assault against Israel itself, Zionism, Jews, and America.

In this manner, the MSA's objectives parallel, and in fact are part of, the larger campaign of Islamism waged by the Muslim Brotherhood and other like-minded groups. At a 2005 speech at an MSA West Conference, one of the speakers, former UCLA MSA member Ahmad Shama, admitted as much when he told the attendees that "The reality is that the Islamic Movement is global and that part of that global aspect is that there has to be a local element to it. We have to be involved. We have to be plugged into the global Islamic Movement. *We have an obligation to make sure that our MSAs are part of the global Islamic Movement.*"[5]

The Muslim Student Association's strategy has been three-pronged in waging this propaganda war against Israel and the United States, all part and parcel of the broader, overriding purpose of weakening Western society and winning hearts and minds in the name of Islam. It involved, first, establishing chapters on campuses throughout America and Canada, ostensibly to help affirm students' Muslim identities and provide spiritual comradeship for young people to evaluate their faith. Universities, which have for decades been eager to incorporate multiculturalism into campus life as part of their institutional mandates, of course, welcomed yet another group of students with backgrounds and religious traditions different from mainstream student groups.

But as the MSA grew and widened its presence on campuses, its leadership also sought, as a second phase in its expansion, to assert itself politically, and to start to question and contradict prevailing beliefs about secularism and democracy. "It should be the long-term goal of every MSA to Islamicize the politics of their respective university," suggested the MSA's curious little tactical manual, *Starters Guide*, since "the politicization of the MSA means to make the MSA more of a force on internal campus politics. The MSA needs to be a more 'In-your-face' association."[6]

The third, and most troubling, step in asserting its influence and promoting the MSA's ideological agenda was to effect the "unholy alliance" discussed earlier in this book, which drew together the far Left, the far Right, and Islamists who, though unique in their own world views on any number of other topics, were able to coalesce their enmity and focus on common ideological foes—Western democracies in general, and Israel and America in particular. While the Saudi money pouring into Middle East study centers helped drive single-minded scholarship obsessed with the colonial oppression of Israel toward the Palestinians and its legacy of Western imperialism, generous Saudi funding simultaneously enabled the Muslim Student Association to enlist Israel-hating professors from the Left in their own efforts to hijack campus debate about the Israel/Palestine conflict, and to develop a range of tactics through which to execute their broader, long-term strategy, as they had admitted, of weakening Western society from within.

That has meant that MSA officials have regularly denied al Qaeda's role in 9/11, or alternately praised Osama Bin Laden as a heroic figure in Islamic self-determination; denounced efforts during the Bush administration to conduct operations against the war on terror; apologized for and defended Hamas and Hezbollah as legitimate forces of "resistance;" and lent moral support to radical Islamists in Iraq and Afghanistan who slaughtered American soldiers. The frequent and invidious events the MSA mounts on campuses across the country, with the ostensible purpose of creating dialogue on the Israeli-Palestinian situation, are single-mindedly aimed at demonizing every aspect of Israel's very existence, and simultaneously damning the United States for its complicity in enabling Israel to continue its oppression of Arabs in Palestine. The shrill rhetoric is stridently and consistently anti-American, anti-Israel, and, often, anti-Semitic.

The MSA is clever enough to exploit the West's reverence for free speech on campuses, as well as the protection for the views of ethnic and religious minorities, and use these as a cover for extending invitations to speakers and guests whose odious views would not even normally be part of civil academic discourse. And while they promote their events as being venues in which intellectual debate can take place concerning the politics and law of the Middle East, they assiduously suppress any views which do not conform to their own narrow world view, and never create opportunities where true dialogue takes place and opposing views can be aired—and considered—at the same time. They also have found willing co-conspirators in the ideological war against Israel and Western democracies with radical, far Left anti-war groups such as Act Now to Stop War and End Racism (A.N.S.W.E.R.), which was visible and vocal in massive anti-war rallies after the U.S. invasion of Iraq and during Israel's incursions into Gaza at the end of 2008 and early 2009. "An influential member of the International A.N.S.W.E.R. steering committee," noted a report of the Terrorism Awareness Project, "MSA maintains a large presence at A.N.S.W.E.R.-sponsored anti-war demonstrations. The pro-North Korea, pro-Saddam Hussein A.N.S.W.E.R. is a front organization of the Marxist-Leninist Workers World Party."[7] Why the alliance between unlikely partners? Because both A.N.S.W.E.R. and the MSA see the U.S. and Israel as aggressive imperialist powers who use their military strength to deprive Third-world innocents of social justice.

That hatred of America, and a reflexive tendency to see the Muslim world as a perennial victim of Western imperialism, was on full display, for instance, at a March 2003 Washington, DC rally when Lina Hashem (then Vice President of MSA National) conjoined racism and militarism in one long rant against America's incursion into Iraq:

> The true patriots are those who are out here today, rallying against this unjust, unprovoked war . . . President Bush, you cannot justify your war for oil! President Bush, it is un-patriotic of you to propose a war against a country that has already been devastated by over 12 years of sanctions! President Bush, you cannot justify defying the UN . . . As a woman of color, I am also painfully aware of the fact that many of our brothers and sisters of color, those who are disproportionately represented in the armed forces and on the frontlines, will unfortunately be shedding their blood and the blood of others in a war that is not of their choosing . . . No blood for oil! No war on Iraq![8]

Nor, in the purported interest of defending the civil rights of persecuted Muslims in America after 9/11, did the MSA hesitate to come to the defense of terror-enabling co-conspirators operating from the safety and freedom of their offices on American campuses. In 2003, for instance, when University of South Florida professor Sami Al-Arian was arrested by the Justice

Department, he was presented with a 120-page indictment that accused him of using "the structure, facilities and academic environment of USF to conceal the activities of the Palestinian Islamic Jihad," and helping terrorists to murder Israelis with funds Al-Arian was supposedly raising on behalf of widows and orphans. In the May 2006 U.S. District Court decision that found Al-Arian guilty, Judge James S. Mooney, Jr. called Al-Arian " a master manipulator" who helped planned the murder of civilians on buses, and, once the terrorist acts were successfully carried out, "saw it as an opportunity to solicit more money to carry out more bombings." After that particular bit of barbarism, Al-Arian wrote glowingly of the savagery, pointing to it as justification for future efforts to replicate the murder of Israelis. "The latest operation carried out by the two mujahideen who were martyred for the sake of God," the judge quoted Al-Arian as writing in a fundraising letter, "is the best guide and witness to what the believing few can do in the face of Arab and Islamic collapse at the heels of the Zionist enemy and in keeping the flame of faith, steadfastness, and defiance glowing."[9]

But USF's chapter of the MSA had defended Al-Arian immediately and without reservation, even claiming that the indictment against the professor was a symptom of Islamophobia after the 9/11 attacks. Presenting their view of the situation at a press conference, the MSA representatives announced:

> We come before you today on behalf of the Muslim Student Association at USF as well as the National Muslim Student Association of the U.S. and Canada to express our shock, deep concern, and plea for justice regarding the recent arrests of two USF professors, Dr. Sami al-Arian [sic] and Sameeh Hammoudeh . . . we are concerned that the USF professors were arrested for their political views.[10]

Actually, in suggesting that Al-Arian had been arrested for his political views, the MSA had been accurate in their assessment, since Al-Arian's political views seemed to comfortably incorporate the slaughter of civilians as part of his political strategy. The man the MSA defended as yet another innocent Muslim being rounded up in a reactionary hysteria after 9/11 had already made his political ideology very clear, and very public, proclaiming at one speech that "We assemble today to pay respects to the march of the martyrs and to the river of blood that gushes forth and does not extinguish, from butchery to butchery, and from martyrdom to martyrdom, from jihad to jihad."[11]

Al-Arian was also able to energize his audiences when he was a guest speaker at the October 2002 Palestine Solidarity Movement's Second National Students Conference, co-hosted by the University of Michigan's Muslim Student Association. That particular event was punctuated by triumphant chanting from the audience of the delightful refrain, in Arabic, of

"Chrad al Yahood," or "Death to Israel." In an affidavit he signed as a witness to the goings-on at the Ann Arbor event, David Herz not only confirmed that the odious chanting had occurred, but also recalled that some 100 others had shouted out additional troubling slogans, including "With blood and fire we shall liberate Palestine," "through Kalashnikovs," and that "Palestine will be free, from the River to the Sea," meaning in place of Israel, not a nation living in peace beside it.[12]

While they have a long history of vilifying Israel and America, and using these types of slanders, threats, and propagandistic lies with impunity as part of that angry discourse, the Muslim Student Association members have shown themselves to have a remarkably ironic double standard when it comes to others' right to expression, particularly when it involves a close examination of Islam or critique of the MSA's tactics in addressing the issue of the Arab/Israeli conflict. That double standard revealed itself in 2006 when the MSA, together with Muslims around the world, reacted with indignation to the publication of twelve relatively tame cartoons depicting the Prophet Mohammad, first appearing in September in Denmark's *Jyllands-Posten* and, thereafter, in newspapers in Norway, France, Germany and other countries. Adherents of 'the religion of peace' apparently felt that those who created caricatures of Mohammad, which in Islam is considered blasphemous (even if he is depicted favorably), not only had no right to freedom of expression, but had out stepped the bounds of acceptable speech specifically because it involved insulting Islam.

That Muslims' feelings had 'been hurt' and their sensibilities offended by the cartoons was certainly unfortunate, save for a few dramatic ironies that seemed to have escaped the moral self-examination of those Islamic voices calling for the suppression of free speech and a contempt for religious and civil rights in the rest of the world: namely, that while Muslims are outraged by innocuous cartoons which suggest a link between the faith of Islam and the spread of Islamofacism, they see no trace of hypocrisy in their how their indignation over this offense had deteriorated into homicidal madness—clearly devoid of religiosity, faith, and understanding—in which imams, mobs, and demonstrators throughout the Muslim world called for jihad, beheadings, and deaths for citizens in the West who supported or even tolerated the publication of the cartoons.

More ironic, still, was the fact that while Muslim Student Associations on various U.S. campuses held demonstrations to loudly condemn the cartoons as yet another instance of anti-Muslim expression, their own anti-Israel events often included odious images and language that, with an unrelentingly hateful, racist, and accusatory tone, targeted exclusively one group: Jews and the State of Israel. These depictions regularly demonized Israel, characterized its citizens as having become a new version of Nazis, showed Jews as animals and subhuman sadists manipulating the United States and subjugating the Muslim world, suggested them as controlling world media and committing any global crime for financial gain, and rendered Jews with same perverse physical traits once seen in classic European and Nazi anti-Semitism.

Hypocrisy aside, Columbia University's Muslim Student Association was a signer, along with 52 Muslim organizations (including MSA chapters from Florida Atlantic, Berkeley, Wisconsin, Jackson State, Miami, and others), of a February press release condemning the cartoons and "protesting the insult made by some newspapers citing the [sic] freedom of speech . . ," "protesting the newspapers' decisions to run the cartoons" . . , [and] "protesting the newspapers' insult to Islam."[13]

More ominously, and with the same language being used by the Organization of the Islamic Conference (OIC) at the UN's Human Rights Council in its effort to criminalize blasphemy against Islam, the signers of the press release repeated their contention that "Freedom of expression is not absolute," and that "such views can incite people to hatred" since "the cartoons malign the honor of Prophet Muhammad . . . and insult the integrity of Islam." And even though they were apparently blind to their own ideological assaults against Israel, Jews, and Zionism and totally intolerant of any criticism of Islamism, they concluded, without irony, that "insult and attacks against any group or religion should be stopped and new laws and regulations should be adopted against any violation."[14]

And at a March 2006 MSA-sponsored event at Chaffey College in Rancho Cucamonga California, the vitriolic Abdel Malik Ali, the ubiquitous, anti-Semitic, anti-American guest at many MSA hate-fests on campuses around the country, concluded definitively (but without any apparent evidence) who was behind the cartoons' publication, who the purveyor of hate actually was—the perfidious Zionists:

> The Danish government wasn't behind this. The Danish government wasn't behind this at all. It was the Zionists who were behind this. It was the Zionists . . . The Zionists did this. We knew, we knew who it was, but we had to wait for the information to come out; to come out. 'Cause Zionists don't like Muslims, you know what I'm saying?[15]

To do their own part in renouncing the invidious cartoons, UC Irvine's Muslim Student Union rallied 1000 Muslim students and led them in an inventive chant, against counter demonstrators in support of the U.S., Israel, and free speech, of "Hey Republicans Stop the Hate! All You Do Is Instigate," and

"Hey, Hey, Ho, Ho! The Prophet's Cartoons Have Got to Go!"[16] Michigan State's MSA collectively denounced the cartoons as another example of "hate speech," a view that was immediately challenged by at least one brave member of Michigan's faculty, Indrek S. Wichman, Professor of Mechanical Engineering. His opinion, which he expressed in an email to the MSA, was that the cartoons should inspire a protest, but against the excesses and barbarism of radical Islam parodied in them, not because of the insult they may or may not have caused Muslims. "Dear Muslim Association," he wrote in his email:

> As a professor of Mechanical Engineering here at MSU, I intend to protest your protest. I am offended not by cartoons, but by more mundane things like beheadings of civilians, cowardly attacks on public buildings, suicide murders, murders of Catholic priests (the latest in Turkey!), burnings of Christian churches, the continued persecution of Coptic Christians in Egypt, the imposition of Sharia law on non-Muslims, the rapes of Scandinavian girls and women (called 'whores' in your culture), the murder of film directors in Holland, and the rioting and looting in Paris France. . . . If you do not like the values of the West—see the 1st Amendment—you are free to leave. I hope for God's sake that most of you choose that option. Please return to your ancestral homelands and build them up yourselves instead of troubling Americans.[17]

That type of honest, straight-forward appraisal of the price of radical Islam did not sit well with the MSA, obviously, who immediate filed a grievance complaint with the University's administration, calling for the censure of professor Wichman and the implementation of mandatory university-wide "diversity training" (read: sensitivity inculcation by the thought police) for faculty. Michigan's craven administration, as other schools' officials are wont to do, acquiesced to the demands of one of the campus victim groups, and six months later "after lengthy negotiations with the Muslim Students Association and CAIR, announced that it would offer non-mandatory diversity training—including an Islamic awareness workshop facilitated by MSA-MSU and funded by the University—for its faculty and student body."[18]

Muslim student groups are very clear-thinking and able to identify "hate speech" when it is directed at them or at Islam. They seem to be less ready to look at their own expression and actions and see how they regularly overstep the bounds of rational discourse with their radical ideology. Whenever these excesses have been pointed out to the MSA perpetrators, of course, the reaction has been predictable: accuse the powerful Israel Lobby, and the biased Western media, of attempting to suppress any and all criticism of Israel—at the expense of the MSA's free speech. The fact that their own expression is generally so biased and slanted that it enters the realm of pure propaganda and counterfactual readings of international law and history is apparently of no consequence, nor is the notion that attempts by pro-Israel spokespeople to present a different point of view is not in itself an attempt to stifle the speech of pro-Palestinians, only to answer and challenge it.

Part of the MSA's war against truth involves their frequent efforts to prevent critical examinations of radical Islam from ever reaching campus, either from the mouths of speakers or, as happened at Pace University in New York in 2007, in a film, *Obsession: Radical Islam's War Against the West*. The provocative film, which examines radical Islam and its influence in spreading jihadist violence, was being sponsored by Pace's Hillel, which, as a courtesy, had informed the school's Muslim Students Association about the upcoming screening so that it could provide a speaker, if it wished, to offer a pro-Muslim viewpoint. Rather than accept the invitation to have a representative present at the screening, MSA president Zeina Berjaoui took it upon herself to go straight to the Pace administration with the predictable complaint that *Obsession* "says Islam is a terrorist religion," an opinion she had arrived at without the benefit of having actually ever viewed the film. But that detail aside, Pace officials immediately summoned forth Hillel's president, Michael Abdurakhmanov, and "'warned' him that because of the recent 'hate crimes' that had been committed against the Koran at Pace . . , any attempt by Hillel to show *Obsession* might result in the police being called in, and Hillel officers being investigated as possible suspects in the bias incidents. Mr. Abdurakhmanov report[ed] that, while bias incidents had been committed against Judaism as well as Islam, 'school administrators showed concern only for the sensibilities of Muslim students.'"[19]

Abdurakhmanov also had to endure a second meeting with Pace deans at which they not only reiterated their threat to "punish" Hillel if the film showing was not cancelled, but allowed the MSA president to use the meeting to upbraid Abdurakhmanov publicly for having the temerity to bring *Obsession* to campus in the first place and risk offending Islam and making Muslim students feel "uncomfortable" and "intimidated" on their campus—this after the MSA had allegedly sent a vituperative and accusatory email to Abdurakhmanov for planning the film screening, replete with some slurs against Judaism.

Pace ultimately relented, and begrudgingly agreed to allow the film to be shown later in the year, over the continuing objections of the MSA. In fact, noted David Lewis Schaefer, professor of political science at Holy Cross College, in an article he wrote on the incident, there was more than a little irony in the fact that Ms. Berjaoui was so resistant to letting a film about radical Islam be viewed. "It may help to clarify Berjaoui's perspective," Schaefer wrote, "to note that she is a Lebanese woman who told a reporter . . . that 'Hezbollah is just a resistance movement,' one that 'like Hamas, is giving the Palestinians and Lebanese a voice.' In other words, Pace has effectively allowed an apologist for Islamist terrorist groups to exercise veto power over the portrayal of Islamist terrorist groups on campus."[20] Once again, the motto of the MSA, when it comes to the issue of freedom of expression on campus, seems to be, "Free speech for me, but not for thee."

California Radicalism in UCLA's MSA

That the UCLA campus would provide a fitting home for radical thought and Israel-hatred is not surprising, given the general state of radical behavior on California campuses, as discussed in Chapter 7. Also not surprising is that student groups, primarily UCLA's Muslim Student Association, had taken a lead role in the fomenting of extreme anti-Israelism by inviting radical speakers with hard-line attitudes of anti-Americanism, anti-Zionism, and anti-Semitism, just as they had on other campuses in California and around the country.

In October of 2000, three months after the collapse of peace talks at Camp David and a month after the outbreak of the Second Intifada, UCLA's MSA took to the streets, not to denounce violence by Palestinians, of course, but to excoriate Israel's "aggression." The rally, which brought together a raucous crowd to demonstrate in front of the Los Angeles office of the Israeli consulate, was put together by two UCLA students, Arif Shaikh and Ahmed Shama, then-president of the School's Muslim Student Association. "Our solution is simple, Shama proclaimed, in between wild exhortations of "Victory to Islam!" and "Death to the Jews!" "We are not simply anarchists . . , he explained. "Our solution is the establishment of justice by Islamic means. That is the only solution to this Israeli apartheid."[21]

Nor did Shama, with the remarkable audacity that only a student could muster, have any use for diplomatic negotiations between world leaders, all of whom were deemed by him to be traitorous crypto-Zionists who had only Israel's interests at heart:

> When we see negotiations between Israeli Prime Minister Ehud Barak, who is a racist Zionist, and on the other side is Yasser Arafat, who used to be a so-called "Arab activist," but is now a racist Zionist, being mediated by Bill Clinton, who is a racist Zionist. And Hosni Mubarak, I am Egyptian, Hosni Mubarak, the President of Egypt, who is a racist Zionist. And King Hussein II of Jordan, who is a racist Zionist. When we see that a peace process is being negotiated between Zionists, mediated by Zionists, controlled by Zionists, and being portrayed in the media by Zionists, we come and we condemn all of you.[22]

Lest anyone in the crowd be still confused about his attitudes toward Israel, Shama concluded his presentation by burning an Israeli flag while chants of "Khaibar, Khaibar, O Jews, the army of Mohammed is coming for you," and "Death to Israel, victory to Islam" were heard in the street.

Also sharing the podium that day was Hamid Ayloush, a member of the Council on Islamic Relations (CAIR) and a co-sponsor of the event with the MSA, who used the opportunity to solicit charitable giving for the Holy Land Foundation Holy Land Foundation for Relief and Development (HLF), suggesting that donors support "victims and orphans." Ayloush's enthusiasm for that particular charity is not surprising, given the fact that CAIR's co-founder and Chairman Emeritus, Omar Ahmad, was named as an unindicted co-conspirator when a federal jury in 2008 found the Holy Land Foundation and its officers guilty of directing some $12 million of its funds to the designated terrorist group Hamas. Two years later, during one of the MSA's hate-fests at UCLA, "Palestinian Freedom Week," Ayloush was once again a guest speaker where he took the opportunity to draw one of his favorite comparisons—that of Israelis and Nazis. Steven Emerson, executive director of the Investigative Project on Terrorism, noted that this is a familiar pattern with Ayloush, confirmed in an email he wrote where he contended that "Indeed, the Zionazis are a bunch of nice people; just like their Nazi brethren! It is just that the world keeps making up lies about them! It is so unfair."[23]

When the UCLA MSA co-sponsored another conference of radicals in May, 2001, called "The Israeli Palestinian Crisis: New Conversations for a Pluralist Future," CAIR again was a featured organization, along with the Muslim Public Affairs Council (MPAC), which positions itself as "a public service agency working for the civil rights of American Muslims, for the integration of Islam into American pluralism, and for a positive, constructive relationship between American Muslims and their representatives." But just as CAIR publicly claims moderation and a desire to create understanding between Muslims and the West, a more sinister reality reveals that both organizations have become outspoken apologists for radical Islam and the terror groups, such as Hezbollah and Hamas, who practice it.

In 1999, for example, MPAC's executive director, Salam Al-Marayati, looked back to when "Hezbollah organized the bombing of the Marine barracks in Beirut in October 1983 killing 241 marines, the largest number of American troops killed in a single operation since the end of the Vietnam war. Yet this attack, for all the pain it caused, was not in a strict sense, a terrorist operation," he ludicrously proclaimed. "It was a military operation, producing no civilian casualties—exactly the kind of attack that Americans might have lauded had it been directed against Washington's enemies." That the murderous attack on American serviceman produced, as Al-Marayati put it, "no civilian casualties," may have given him some moral comfort in assessing the implications Hezbollah's barbarism, but American do not "laud" random attacks on sovereign states, and military operations are completely different, at any rate, than terror attacks where no motivation except jihadist ideology inspires violence and murder.

MPAC has had another questionable link to UCLA's anti-Israel, anti-Western position through its communications director, Edina Lekovic, who, while a student at UCLA, was the managing editor of *Al-Talib Magazine*, the University's Muslim Student Association publication. *Al-Talib*, with a circulation of some 20,000, as might be expected, has run stories that were stridently anti-Zionist, lauded terror organizations Hamas and Hezbollah for their resistance to Israeli oppression, and celebrated jihad as a way of destroying Israel and the West in the name of Islam. Though Lekovic has tried to obscure her past role with the radical publication, she was caught in her obfuscation in a debate on CNBC's "Kudlow & Co." with Steven Emerson[24] who questioned her about her role in producing a particularly startling July 1999 issue of *Al-Talib* with the cover story "The Spirit of Jihad." Though written a year after the embassy bombings in Tanzania and Kenya, terrorist events in which Osama Bin-Ladin's role was widely known, that issue of the magazine contained an editorial with reverent praise for Mr. Bin-Ladin and a twisted attempt to position him as a benevolent jihadist on an Islamic crusade. "When we hear someone refer to the great Mujahid [one who struggles in Allah's cause] Osama Bin-Ladin as a 'terrorist,'" the editorial read, "we should defend our brother and refer to him as a freedom fighter; someone who has forsaken wealth and power to fight in Allah's cause and speak out against oppressors. We take these stances only to please Allah."[25]

In 2001, *Al-Talib* also published a special, glossy 16-page report called "Zionism: The Forgotten Apartheid," in conjunction with UC Irvine's *Alkalima* magazine. The thoughtful editors felt compelled to produce this informative screed because, as they proudly announced, "As the Zionists continue to colonize, torture and ethnically-cleanse in the name of the 'peace process' and the Americans continue to fund them, the respective staffs of *Al-Talib* and *Alkalima* feel it to be their basic duty to expose Zionism, its evils and its effects . . . Zionist-controlled world media has been purposefully distorting and misconstruing world events too long." What is more, the report continued, it was not only Palestinians who had suffered under the oppression of Israel: unbeknownst to the entire world media, and only revealed, apparently, to the editors of this noxious pamphlet, "The Zionists have been oppressing, torturing, killing, and ethnically cleansing Christians, Muslims, blacks, whites and any other color or ethnicity you can think of."[26]

Including a section which praised the homicidal madmen who were members of Hamas and Hezbollah as "the resistance movements against Zionist aggression" and groups who benignly offer "humanitarian assistance . . . to the entire population, regardless of religious denomination, or even religion," the report also included a now-familiar catalogue of Israeli offenses, libels, contortions, and falsehoods, including:

"'Israeli' Apartheid: the chilling facts"

"'Zionist Torture Exposed"

"Examples of 'Israeli' Human Rights Violations"

"'Israel's' Nuclear Weapons: proof of their relentless terror"

"Stop U.S. Foreign Aid to 'Israel' Now"[27]

The editors even put the name of Israel in quotation marks to signify that it is merely a theoretical term created to define what is actually Palestine, that, just as in Palestinian textbooks which have maps on which Israel does not exist, the student publishers here promulgated a perverse fiction—which many in the Arab world seemingly long for—that a 63 year-old member nation of the United Nations does not, in their ideologically-skewed intellects, even exist.

Party On: Hate-Fests & Radical Celebrations and Events to Demonize Israel

To give wide visibility to their multifarious propaganda campaigns, pro-Palestinian student groups regularly mount festivals, symposia, speeches, rallies, and multi-day hate-fests where, with odious regularity, new ways are devised to further demonize Israel, Zionism, America, and Jews. Many of the events purport to offer learning opportunities to those who have not yet acquired the contorted view of the Middle East harbored by radical pro-Palestinians. Often the sponsors of these events announce that without such events, the real story of the Palestinian predicament will never be revealed, that because of the systemic bias against the Palestinians in the media— coupled, of course, with the stifling power of the Israel Lobby in screening the actuality of Palestinian suffering and Israeli malefaction—only provoca-tive, incendiary festivals and special events will enable the "truth" to finally be told.

As we have seen in the discussion of the hijacking of California campuses by radical Muslim student groups, the extremist character and the frequency of these events has increased. Why is that? First, because college officials have been painfully lax in monitoring how these events are produced and what is said at them; universities have also been hesitant to make courageous statements about inappropriate or unacceptable situations that often arise from these hate-fests and demonstrations, lest they offend Muslim students and seem to be insensitive to an identified minority group on campus. At the same time, pro-Israel groups on campus have also been passive in confronting these events directly, either with counter-demonstrations, or with direct challenges to the content and truthfulness of what is expressed. Also, while pro-Israel forces are generally content with the notion of two states "living side by side in peace," provided Israel's security interests are protected, the Palestinian movement has as part of its core ideal to emerge on the ruins and as a result of the *elimination of Zionism*, not as co-existing peace partner. So an important part of the ideological war against Israel is to negate anything positive about Zionism and Israel, and in fact to demonize them both so Israel becomes a pariah among nations, undeserving of the world's moral support. These hate-fests and repugnant speaker appearances are part of a tactical, ongoing campaign to dilute the political integrity of Israel, and to repeatedly point to its very existence as a fundamental threat to peace and Arab self-determination.

These extremist events also make good political theater, a fact not unnoticed by their sponsors, who continually find ways of being provocative, cruel, and politically outrageous as a means of bringing attention to their message—regardless of how untrue or vapid it actually is. The names given to some of these events suggest that part of the desired effect is a caustic vilification of Israel, even when the pretense is that these names define events which purport to be educational experiences. "Holocaust in the Holy Land," "The Politics of Genocide," "Israel: The Fourth Reich," "Israel Apartheid Week"—each of these inflammatory event titles represents not only a perverse inversion of historical truth and political reality, but is designed to wound Israel "through a thousand cuts" with a relentless barrage of rhetorical attacks.

Even events with the ostensible purpose of raising awareness about a piece of Palestinian history and culture, such as Stanford University's 2006 "Nakba Day Commemoration," have a second, insidious aspect. The Nakba, "the catastrophe" for Palestinians, commemorates the tragedy for Arabs of Israel's birth, and is "celebrated" at the same time that supporters of Israel mark the birth of the Jewish state. Once again, Palestinianism has defined itself by what it is, or is not, based on the existence of its malignant "other," namely, Israel. So while Jews celebrate the founding of their state, Palestinians have attempted to subvert the meaning and even the legitimacy of that day by condemning it to marking another holiday—one which they attempt to negate and demean by making it seem insidious rather than celebratory.

Presented as part of a longer Palestinian Awareness Month at Stanford, the Nakba Day event was sponsored by The Coalition for Justice in the Middle East (CJME), Muslim Students Awareness Network (MSAN), and the Outreach to Asian Immigrant Students (OASIS). Also included in the agenda was an appearance by Naura Erakat, whose U.S. Campaign to End the Occupation contends that "it is important for us to remember how so many of today's problems began and to draw strength from the steadfastness of Palestinians struggling for survival under conditions of dispossession, apartheid and occupation for so long."[28] Erakat claimed that the Palestinians, like Native Americans and black Americans, were indigenous people ethnically cleansed and dispossessed. She also dismissed the categorization of Hamas militants as terrorists, claiming instead that, like Nelson Mandela, history will one day see them as liberators. "Give me a few more years," she said, "and no one will be able to say that Palestinians are not freedom fighters."[29]

Tala al-Ramahi, a Stanford junior at the time and the coordinator for Palestine Awareness Month, while not busy reading his poetry about Palestinian suffering at the event, had also overseen the construction of several mock walls on the Stanford campus to drive home the symbolic importance that Israel's security barrier has to Palestinian apologists who claim it is used as part of a land grabbing scheme and to separate Palestinians from Jews merely for reasons of class and ethnicity, not safety. Using the customary, but false, accusation that Israel has constructed an apartheid state, al-Ramahi suggested that "The apartheid system is not merely associated with Israel's wall. The system of Israel being an exclusive Jewish homeland where there are separate laws for non-Jews is another example of Apartheid."[30]

Lest there be any doubting about the purity of the students' motives in mounting yet another attack against the Jewish state, al-Ramahi was careful to clarify the altruistic purpose of the event. This was, he wrote in the *Daily Stanford*, "not an incitement against Israel but a call for people to realize the injustices that the Palestinians have been living through every day under the Israeli occupation." Blame for the endemic social and political problems of the yet-to-be-born Palestinian state could, and should, be placed on Israel, because of its oppression and the occupation. "Many people do not realize how hard it is for Palestinians to 'build [their] communities,'" he wrote, "when their homes are constantly demolished to make way for new Israeli settlements, harsh economic restrictions are imposed on Palestinians that force them to live on less than three dollars a day and even the very freedom of movement to go to work and schools is controlled by the Israeli army."[31]

Not only that, pointed out Sam Dubal, another student, in the same edition of the *Daily*, an earlier article in the newspaper that characterized Hamas members being terrorists was actually a contortion of the truth. "'Terrorism' is, of course, a subjective term employed by those in power," he wrote, suggesting fallaciously, as those who excuse terrorism are wont to do, that terrorism is the only tool of the desperate and powerless. Mr. Dubal then used the favorite technique of apologists for terror—moral relativism—in which military actions undertaken for the legal self-defense of a sovereign nation are equated with random murderous attacks by militant thugs with their own ideological agenda. "While we accept that Hamas has used violence to further its political aims," he concluded, "we point out that the Israeli Defense Forces also uses violence, murdering innocent Palestinian civilians through raids and bombings."[32]

While Nakba Day festivities ostensibly were designed to "celebrate" a bit of Palestinian history and culture, and on its surface, at least, purported to be a benign event with no intrinsic anti-Israel sentiment, other popular events, such as the odious, now annual, Israeli Apartheid Week have as their overt purpose to further demonize and malign the Jewish state.

Initiated in 2004 at the University of Toronto, Israeli Apartheid Week (IAW) was held in 40 locations worldwide by 2008, with the stated purpose of educating "people about the nature of Israel as an apartheid system and to build Boycott, Divestment, and Sanctions (BDS) campaigns as part of a growing global BDS movement."[33] Events were held, among others, on the campuses of Berkeley, Toronto, Boston College, Yale, Michigan, and Columbia. IAW uses as its primary tactic what has been referred to the "Durban strategy," alluding to 2001 the anti-Israel hate-fest in South Africa where the member countries' representatives notoriously defined Zionism as racism. Maligning Israel as a racist state, of course, has been instrumental in raising the level of incitement on the part of critics who denounce it for setting up an apartheid social system which deprives Palestinians of basic human and civil rights based on their skin color. And having former U.S. president Jimmy Carter publish a book with the invidious title of *Palestine: Peace Not Apartheid*, as he did in 2007, seemingly also gave credibility to the apartheid slur.

In addition to the racism charge, IAW events regurgitate the other thorny issues of the Palestinian question: the "right of return" of all Palestinians to their old homes what is now present-day Israel, dismantling the security wall, and the formation of a bi-national state in which Jews, then a minority, would be but one class of citizens into whatever type of political structure that state evolved—in short, a world without Israel. Since the motive of the sponsors in producing these events seems on its surface to be pure—ending racism—the stridency of the message and the vitriol of the speakers and marketing materials of the Apartheid Week has ramped up as supporters have become emboldened by their mission. In some instances, such as at the University of Manitoba in the weeks after the 2009 Gaza incursion by Israel when sentiments ran high, posters for the event created by the Muslim Students Association were so out of bounds and extreme that school officials reigned in the perfidious marketing efforts. "One of them depicted a Jewish fighter plane targeting a baby stroller," reported a *National Post* article. "Another featured a caricature of a hooked-nosed Hasidic Jew with a star of David, pointing a bazooka at the nose of an Arab carrying a slingshot; a third one showed an Israeli helicopter with a swastika on top, dropping a bomb on a baby bottle." Even on university campuses, where the right to speak odiously and often seems to be one of the bulwarks of higher education, the grisly and explicitly anti-Semitic tone of the posters was all a little too much, the *Post* reported, and "the school forced their removal the same day."[34]

A year earlier, McMaster University had its own reservations about letting the week's events proceed, and the university's Provost and Vice-President Academic, Ilene Busch-Vishniac, informed one of its student organizations, Coalition Against Israeli Apartheid, that they were henceforth not allowed to use the phrase "Israeli Apartheid" on campus. The Coalition immediately issued a press release to denounce the decision, referring to it as an "unprecedented attack on the right to academic freedom and the right to organize," in other words, they were indignant about anyone denying them the right to spread hatred, slander, and lies against a particular nation with impunity, and without having to restrain themselves in the interest of academic honesty.

In fact, the University of Toronto administration had its own misgivings about the entire Israeli Apartheid Week concept back in 2005 when it was first proposed, and a number of groups and individuals from both inside and outside the university cautioned that the event would likely devolve into yet another anti-Israel hate-fest, and that the premise upon which the whole event was based—the notion that Israel was functioning as an example of racial apartheid—was itself baseless and should not be dignified by moral or financial support from a university. "Israeli Apartheid is a lie, it's hate, and it's a continuation of the demonization of the state of Israel and the Jewish people," Frank Dimant, vice president of Canada's B'Nai Brith, remarked at the time, asking the university to cancel the planned IAW event completely. But even though the general tenor and theme of the upcoming event was clear to anyone who honestly examined the promotional materials, university officials were adamant that any decisions on their part to derail the event would violate the principals of academic free speech and inquiry, regardless of how hateful and slanderous the message of the week's activities would be.

In a statement in which he defended the University's decision to permit the event, Deputy Provost and Vice-Provost of Students David Farrar said that despite numerous requests from opponents of the IAW to have the Arab Students' Collective's event cancelled, "We will not. To do so would violate the university's commitment to freedom of speech . . . As an academic community, we have a fundamental commitment to the principles of freedom of inquiry, freedom of speech and freedom of association . . . [T]he university has no reason to believe that the activities will exceed the boundaries for free speech. . . ."[35]

But that spirit of "freedom of inquiry and freedom of speech" seemed to be absent from the actual goings-on during the event, according to at least one attendee, Ilan Nachim. "I think it's one of the most racist presentations I've ever seen," he told the school's newspaper. "I was not allowed to express myself at any point during this evening, from beginning to end. We had our hands up, we did not open our mouths. We were not allowed to express ourselves. This is what the university calls free speech?"[36]

More seriously, by 2009 the annual event had so devolved into a racist, rabid rally that proceedings were closed to cameras and reporters, and individuals who actually attempted to participate in a dialogue about the issues being raised by the noxious event in the first place were confronted with physical intimidation and threats, encountering the dark side of pro-Palestinianism.

One of these individuals, Isaac Apter, a Jewish alumnus of the University of Toronto, recounted how he and others in the audience of one evening's events quizzed a speaker about why Hamas had persistently refused to recognize the legitimacy of Israel—did "Israel have the right to exist?"—and when the speaker side-stepped the questioning repeatedly, some audience members shouted out, "Answer the questions!" Apter found himself approached from behind by a member of a private guard retained by Students Against Israeli Apartheid, slapped in the head, yanked from his seat, and yelled at with the warning, "You shut the fuck up!" A second Jewish attendee was similarly assaulted that night by one of the hired security team and given a far more chilling warning, particularly in light of the barbaric practice of beheadings in the Middle East: "Shut the fuck up or I'll saw your head off."[37] Not only was the Jewish state being attacked and degraded throughout these events, but now non-Israeli Jews themselves were being targeted for emotional and physical assault, an unsurprising outcome of a prolonged, virulent campaign against the concept of Israel as a Jewish state.

When student behavior on campus becomes lawless or exceeds acceptable limits for the university's own civil community, administrators generally
have had little difficulty in making immediate and conclusive decisions about
what is, and is not, acceptable behavior, particularly, as we have seen, in
instances when vulnerable student groups are affected by the errant behavior of some of their fellow students. But while college officials seemed to
have found it difficult to suppress the harmful and extremist speech of Muslim students towards Jews, when innocuous, random comments were made
toward black students, as they were in 2006 at Johns Hopkins University,
the reaction from the school's leaders was immediate, decisive, and even
draconian.

When posting invitations on Facebook.com for a "Halloween in the
Hood" party to be hosted by his Sigma Chi fraternity, junior Justin H. Park,
a Korean-American, included some racist comments, crude stereotyping, and
such vivid descriptions as likening Baltimore to a "motherfucking ghetto"
and "hiv [sic] pit."[38] At the party itself, decorations included a plastic doll
bedecked as pirate with a noose around its neck, leading some to conclude,
given the party's theme, that it evoked the image of a racial lynching.

The invitation and party immediately drew condemnation from the
Black Student Union (BSU), members of the School's administration, Baltimore's chapter of the NAACP, and local media, with the not-surprising
accusation that the party was not only "offensive," but pointed to "institutionalized racism" at Johns Hopkins. Apparently, Johns Hopkins administrators found offense as well: in November, the fraternity chapter was
ordered not to have any activities for 45 days, and Park was suspended
from the University for one year and ordered to perform 300 hours of
community service, read and write "thoughtful" reviews of twelve books,
and participate in mandatory workshops on diversity and race relations.
Among his offenses?: violating the "university's anti-harassment policy,"
"conduct or a pattern of conduct that harasses a person or a group," and
"intimidation."[39]

Ironically enough, there was another Halloween affair that very year that
created some understandable controversy when student Saad Saadi came to
the house party of University of Pennsylvania President Amy Gutmann and
was photographed with her dressed as an Arab suicide-bomber, complete with
a keffiyeh, a toy Kalashnikov rifle, and sticks of fake explosives strapped to his
chest. Once the photos were made public, Gutmann was quick to proclaim
that the terrorist costume was "clearly offensive and I was offended by it," but
Saadi was never suspended, punished, let alone censured, for "harassing" or
"intimidating" certain individuals, precisely because it is perfectly acceptable

on campuses for students and faculty to embrace anti-American, anti-Israel, and Leftist sentiment and never be called on their behavior.

That double standard is particularly egregious in Canada, where strict regulations governing hate speech, and the government's aggressive forays into protecting the human rights of protected classes of Canadian society, have been the subject of much debate. So the University of Toronto's failure to distance itself from the Israeli Apartheid Week event that was born on its campus is a matter of concern, particularly as the event has taken on a more sinister and dangerous aspect, and its theme has come to include not just a call for human rights for Palestinians but for the destruction of Israel itself.

In fact, the IAW event, by singling out Israel and attacking it for its alleged racism, might well itself be a violation of Canadian and international laws. In a paper published in *Jewish Political Studies Review*, Avi Weinryb suggested that in allowing the IAW events to be held, the University of Toronto's decision "conflicts with the 2004 European Monitoring Center on Racism and Xenophobia (EUMC)'s working definition of anti-Semitism . . . which includes such examples of anti-Semitism as: Denying the Jewish people their right to self-determination (e.g., by claiming that the existence of a State of Israel is a racist endeavor), [and] applying double standards by requiring of it a behavior not expected or demanded of any other democratic nation."[40]

Other Canadian laws may well have been violated on the Toronto campus, as well. Weinryb points to a 2005 event sponsored by Muslim students in which a mock Palestinian refugee camp was built in a campus building, complete with recruiting posters, in Arabic, "calling on camp residents to support or join the terror group Islamic Jihad." The small problem with such a poster, Weinryb noted, is that Islamic Jihad is a terrorist organization specifically banned by the Canadian government, whose own statutes read that any "person who knowingly instructs, directly or indirectly, any person to carry out any activity for the benefit of, at the direction of or in association with a terrorist group, for the purpose of enhancing the ability of any terrorist group to facilitate or carry out a terrorist activity, is guilty of an indictable offence and liable to imprisonment for life." Thus, even though the group's actions in "displaying lifelike Islamic Jihad recruitment posters on campus, [have made it] possible that the organizers of IAW may have been in direct violation of federal law," Weinryb wrote, "[t]hey have yet to be taken to task for this act. Instead, they are permitted to return to campus every year to continue promoting their agenda."[41]

The University of Toronto is not only Canadian institution of higher education to become a breeding ground for anti-Israel radicalism. There were, notably, the infamous riots at Concordia University in September 2002, where mobs of marauding students smashed windows and destroyed furniture and fixtures to express their displeasure at the invitation to Benjamin Netanyahu to speak there. Toronto's York University had also recently defined itself with a rabid anti-Semitic leaning, when, in February 2009, some 100 pro-Palestinian students initiated a near-riot, as police had to be called to usher Jewish students to safety after they had been barricaded inside the Hillel offices and were "isolated and threatened" by the physically and verbally aggressive demonstrators.

York, one of Canada's largest universities, has a sizable Jewish student population, but that has not served to diffuse what has become an increasingly volatile, and distressing, problem on its campus. York's own student code of conduct, for example, specifically prohibits "threats of harm, or actual harm, to a person's physical or mental wellbeing," including "verbal and non-verbal aggression verbal abuse; intimidation; [and] harassment"[42] —all of which were clearly violated by the demonstrators' physically intimidating protests.

Parroting the morally incoherent and factually defective exhortations of Israel-haters elsewhere of "Zionism equals racism!" and "Racists off campus!," the York mob, members of both the York Federation of Students and Students Against Israeli Apartheid, demonstrated once again that what is positioned as "intellectual debate" on campuses about the Israeli/Palestinian issue has devolved into something that is not really a conversation at all. Rather, it is something more akin to an ideologically-driven shout fest with a new version of pro-Palestinian brown shirts. So York's supporters of the cult of Palestinianism apparently no longer felt even a bit uncomfortable voicing what was actually on their minds when the subject of Israel came up: when the York Hillel students were trapped inside locked offices, surrounded by an increasingly violent and aggressive mob, the intellectual "debate" that day included such invidious and raw slurs as "Die Jew–get the hell off campus."

That thuggery by anti-apartheid Jew-haters had already become something of a tradition on the York campus. A year earlier in April 2008, Barbara Kay of Canada's *National Post* reported, York's Hillel had invited then-Knesset member Natan Sharansky to deliver an address. Not content with allowing anyone with a pro-Israel viewpoint to share his or her views on campus, the Palestinian Students Association and Students Against Israeli Apartheid@ York (SAIA) used the now common tactic of intellectual bullies: they jeered at and shouted down Sharansky, spoke loudly among themselves during his talk, and generally prevented anyone in the audience from listening to the content of the speech, but not before they had articulated their own vitriol with such comments as "Get off our campus, you genocidal racist" and, for the Jewish audience members' benefit, "you are bringing a second Holocaust upon yourselves."[43]

The Palestine Solidarity Movement:
Apologists for Terrorism on Campus

A particularly nefarious series of conferences, that uses college campuses to give it credibility and mask its radical intentions, are the now-annual events sponsored by the Palestinian Solidarity Movement (PSM). First formed at UC Berkeley in 2001, and subsequently at Michigan, Ohio State, Rutgers, Duke, and Georgetown, these conferences are tactical sessions where speakers and attendees plan the strategic destruction of Israel thorough a continued campaign of de-legitimization, providing human shields in the Palestinian territories to thwart and obstruct the actions of the IDF, and to generally promote divestment, boycotts, and the other assaults through which, it is hoped, Israel will disappear and be replaced by a Palestinian state. The student arm of the communist-anarchist International Solidarity Movement, the PSM has not even attempted to hide its radical ideology, and its commitment to any means necessary—including, specifically, terror— in helping to achieve the goal of extirpating Israel. At the 2002 Berkeley event where the organization was formed, through the joint imaginations of Students For Justice in Palestine and the San Francisco chapter of the American-Arab Anti-Discrimination Committee, the guiding principle of the organization was clear from their tacit support of the Palestinian intifada against Israel: "We, the national student movement for solidarity with Palestine, declare our solidarity with the popular resistance to Israeli occupation, colonization, and apartheid," "popular resistance," of course, meaning terrorism against Jewish civilians. And lest anyone doubt where the organization stood with respect to condoning violence against Israeli targets, the resolution also stated that "as a solidarity movement, it is not our place to dictate the strategies or tactics adopted by the Palestinian people in their struggle for liberation."[44]

Unsurprisingly, then, when conferences do take place, sometimes not without controversy and criticism from concerned stakeholders both inside and outside of the respective universities, they attract outside speakers and students with caustic and extremist notions about Israel, the United States, and Western democracies in general. ISM founders Adam Shapiro and his wife, Huwaida Arraf, who presented at the 2002 Michigan conference, for instance, have stated that they "accept that Palestinians have a right to resist with arms, as they are an occupied people upon who force and violence is being used. The Geneva Conventions accept that armed resistance is legitimate for an occupied people, and there is no doubt that this right cannot be denied." They also reject the notion of "adopting the [non-violent] methods of Gandhi or Martin Luther King, Jr." because "no other successful nonviolent movement was able to achieve what it did without a concurrent violent movement."[45]

When the PSM chose Rutgers as the site of their October 2003 Third North American Student Conference of the Palestine Solidarity Movement, there was good news and bad news. The bad news was that the Rutgers administration, already aware of some of the incendiary rhetoric and extremist views of earlier conferences, opted to move the conference off campus to a Ramada Inn, in an effort to at least give the semblance of trying to distance itself from the hate-fest. The good news for PSM was that attending Rutgers at the time was 23 year-old Charlotte Kates, a law student and leader of the New Jersey Solidarity Movement, sponsor of the conference.

Like her fellow travelers in the solidarity movement, Ms. Kates had no great interest in engaging in debate about a peaceful resolution to the decades-old Arab/Israeli conflict. Instead she sought tactical approaches to dismantling Israel to facilitate the creation of a Palestinian state in its place. "All people have the right to practice their religion freely and to live in peace," she wrote, echoing the familiar tropes of the anti-Israel crowd, "but no group of people has the right to invade the land of another, expropriate that land by force, force out its indigenous residents, and create a racist, brutal apartheid structure." In addition to calling on her own university, Rutgers, to divest from companies doing business with Israel, her ambitions were even more ambitious: "Israel is an apartheid, colonial settler state," she said. "I do not believe apartheid, colonial settler states have a right to exist."[46]

More irrational, and dangerous, were Kates' views on the acceptability of intimidating Jewish students on campuses for their complicity in supporting Israel, not to mention her opinion that suicide bombings were not only acceptable, but desirable. Writing in the far-right online journal *CounterPunch*, Kates examined the palpable tension on campuses like Rutgers, where Jewish students had felt intimidated or harassed by aggressive pro-Palestinian activism. Not only was she unconcerned by that possible situation, she thought it a good thing if their discomfort grew worse by elevated levels of radical action against Israel:

> We have no desire to create an environment where racists may feel comfortable and secure in their racism; we very much want. . . . to create an environment

where it is, indeed, uncomfortable to declare oneself an unequivocal supporter of
an oppressive, racist state. It should be uncomfortable . . . There is nothing making
Jewish students afraid to be Jewish on campus; nothing that is, except for those
whose Jewish identity leads them to condemn the racist practices of the state of
Israel . . . May the tension continue to escalate.[47]

It is one thing for a campus extremist like Ms. Kates to openly admit that her
activism to destroy Israel makes people uncomfortable, and that this detail is
just an additional bi-product of her ideological war against the Jewish state.
But for university officials, who repeatedly pretend that conferences like
PSM hate-fests serve some academic purpose, that they provide a platform
for dialogue and inquiry, and that they somehow are balanced, or even educational in purpose or effect—all these notions are clearly disingenuous. And it
should be of concern to administrators, who worry so much about offending
any segment of their student body, or creating an atmosphere of intimidation
or harassment where some students will not feel "safe," that pro-Palestinian
student groups not only are causing discomfort for some students, but repeatedly do so intentionally and with some evident glee.

More unsettling for school officials should be Ms. Kates' casual attitude
toward the murder of Jews riding on buses, sitting in schools, or eating at
outdoor cafes or pizza parlors, an opinion she shares with all her fellow PSM
members. In the morally incoherent minds of those seeking "social justice"
for the Palestinians, any act committed to help realize that single goal is
somehow acceptable, including slaughtering Israelis so the Palestinians can
achieve self-determination in a Judenrein Middle East. "We support Palestinians' right to resist occupation and oppression, and do not feel that it is our
place as a solidarity movement to dictate tactics of resistance to the Palestinian people," Kates wrote, in language that should certainly cause her to be
removed from university guest lists. "Why is there something particularly
horrible about 'suicide bombing'—except for the extreme dedication con-
veyed in the resistance fighter's willingness to use his or her own body to
fight?"[48] In other words, the only tragic aspect to suicide bombings is not
the slaughter of innocent civilians at the hands of the murderer, but the desperation and hopelessness that have driven the terrorist to commit his or her
heinous act in the first place.

In October 2004, the PSM held its conference at Duke University, but,
again, not without some controversy. Based on eyewitness reports of extremist speech and radical ideas at the Ohio State and University of Michigan
conferences in prior years, the Duke Conservative Union and concerned
alumni generated an online petition with more than 90,000 names, urging

Duke's new president, Richard Brodhead, to refuse to allow the University to be used as a staging ground for the conference. There was also the issue of transparency, since PSM events were always off-limits to the press, the general public, and to those wishing to make video recordings—not surprising in light of the extremist rhetoric and calls for jihad that normally emanate from those gatherings. In fact, Students for Academic Freedom, a nation-wide campus group interested in bringing balance to higher education, petitioned Brodhead to at least make the noxious event accessible to unbiased observers, but this request was also ignored.

Some observers were also surprised when Brodhead, rather than merely remaining impartial regarding the conference, not only spoke in favor of it, but seemed to give it some legitimacy as a valuable learning event, complete with the University's imprimatur. Eric Adler and Jack Langer, two Duke graduate students at the time, wrote that "Mr. Brodhead himself, moving beyond his previous stance of avowed neutrality in the name of free expression, issued what amounted to an outright endorsement of the conference. Declining to criticize any aspect of the PSM, he asserted only that a great deal of inaccurate information was circulating on the Internet and that the 'deepest principle involved [in hosting the conference] is not even the principle of free speech. It's the principle of education through dialogue.'"[49]

That academic objective—creating learning opportunities by facilitating dialogue on contentious issues—is, of course, a reasonable one for an institution of higher education. But as President Brodhead should have known, based on the previous years' poisonous PSM conference proceedings, the purpose of these hate-fests was not to encourage dialogue about the Israeli/Palestinian conflict, but to vilify Israel for the purpose of dismantling the state. All speakers came to the conferences with a well-known and strident anti-Israel agenda, not to mention a predilection for terrorism as an acceptable tool to promote Palestinian self-determination. The human rights and security of Israeli citizens were ignored completely, and blame for all the ills of the Middle East, and the tragedy of the long-suffering Palestinians, were laid at Israel's feet.

Stephen Miller, a student member of the Duke Conservative Union, provided this first-hand account of the biased, ahistorical rhetoric that permeated sessions of the conference:

> During one of the workshops I attended at the conference, eager students were
> fed outrageous lies about Israel by ISM representatives, which then tried to con-
> vince students to join the ISM, attend a one-week training session in Palestine,
> and then begin fighting the evil Israelis, by building human walls in front of IDF

Bulldozers, interfering at security checkpoints, and tearing down the security wall. Naturally, the bulldozers were not described as targeting terrorists and bomb-making facilities, but the homes of innocent Palestinians to 'even out demographics.' The security checkpoints were described not as being used to prevent explosives for suicide bombers from getting into Israel, but for the purpose of 'humiliating and degrading Palestinians.' And the security wall was described not as for keeping out terrorists, but for maintaining 'an apartheid state,' which, as we were told during the conference's opening lecture, was actually not a fair comparison, as what the Israelis were doing was far worse than the South Africans. One of the recruiters at this session was none other than the co-founder of the ISM, who admitted that the organization worked with Islamic Jihad and Hamas. . . . [50]

Given the ideological credentials of the conference speakers, it is no wonder that President Brodhead's desire to create "educational dialogue" did not exactly come off as he might have hoped. One of the workshop leaders, for example, Fadi Kiblawi, had been involved with the PSM's Second National Conference at the University of Michigan, and while there had distinguished himself by writing in the Muslim Student Association publication a fantasy about murdering Jews and pro-Israel supporters. "The helplessness, the degradation . . . It is enough to make one want to strap a bomb to one's chest and kill those racists . . . The enemy is not just overseas. The enemy is also amongst us."[51] One scheduled speaker, Charles Carlson, whose workshop, "The Cause of the Conflict: How Judaized-Christians Enable War," was ultimately canceled, had also declared publicly the reasonableness of murdering Jews, suggesting the perverse notion that "every young Israeli is military . . . are all proper war targets," and that "each wedding, Passover celebration, or bar mitzvah [in Israel] is a potential military target."[52]

Investigative journalist Lee Kaplan, who managed to attend and record closed-to-the-public conference sessions by wearing a disguise, revealed that some of the Solidarity members are Israel-hating Jews, who exploit Jewish charities as a way of furthering the radical agendas to delegitimize Israel. One closed-door strategy session he attended, "From Birthright to the ISM: The Struggle against Roots and Walls," provided practical tips on how to deceive donors into subsidizing trips to Israel:

> Vicki Kaplan, a Duke alumna, Rann Bar-On, a conference organizer, and Jessica Rutter described how to get free plane tickets to Israel. The plans boiled to deceiving Jewish philanthropists, who provide money to send young Jews to the Jewish homeland on "Birthright" trips. Activists should apply for "Birthright" grants, then proceed to the West Bank to disrupt construction of Israel's security fence, which is the Solidarity Movement's latest project.[53]

Given the frantic debate about the many ills of Israel, surprisingly the participants did manage to see eye to eye on at least one important issue, the PSM's
fifth "guiding principle," the odious section of their charter which has led
the organization to consistently refuse to condemn terrorism. "As a solidarity movement," it reads, "it is not our place to dictate the strategies or tactics
adopted by the Palestinian people in their struggle for liberation." Though
there was some effort by conference attendees to moderate this bit of incendiary language, the initiative was voted down and the PSM's full moral support for the murder of Jews remained as one of the organization's guiding
principles.

After the conference had concluded, President Brodhead wrote an article in Duke's newspaper, *The Chronicle*, in which he applauded the open-
mindedness his academic community had displayed by allowing the event to
take place on the Duke campus, never once apparently realizing that providing a platform for extremists who seek to facilitate the murder of Jews and
the extirpation of their nation may not be the type of event worthy of such
prestige and moral purpose. "I am grateful," he wrote, "to the many individuals and groups who helped turn last week's Palestine Solidarity Movement conference into a peaceful and constructive event" and "proud to be at
a school where difficult matters are dealt with in such a mature and constructive way."[54]

In what way was the event "constructive," as Brodhead categorized it?
Because it provided a strategy for weakening the international status of Israel
and impeding its security measures against jihadist foes? Because it helped
radicals rationalize their support for terrorist organizations with the single
agenda of murdering Jews and replacing their state with an Islamist one?
Because, in contradiction to the University's own stated goal of providing
constructive dialogue, only one version of the Israeli/Palestinian issue was
ever discussed, and only one point of view and ideology was presented by all
participants? Because not only were other views not part of the organized
sessions, but other, dissenting voices were not even allowed to be present to
offer different views on a difficult issue?

Once more, well-intentioned but morally incoherent university administrations provided academic cover for extreme views—views, which if they were
held and articulated about any other group on campus other than Jews, would
be denounced as hate speech, ridiculed and marginalized by Left-leaning faculty
and students, and purged from campus with thunderous moral outrage. When
Israel and Jews are the target, however, universities have shown they stand in
solidarity, not with actual intellectual debate and academic freedom, but with
the enemies of those individuals world-wide who support the Jewish state.

Chapter 9

Campus Boycotts, Divestment & Sanctions To Destroy Israel

As more evidence that California campuses have clearly become the epicenter for anti-Israel, anti-Semitic, and anti-American activism, in 2010 in an unfortunate effort that has occurred frequently on campuses, student-led groups at both UC San Diego and UC Berkeley introduced initiatives to demonize Israel once again in the court of world opinion. One effort, disingenuously named "UCSD Divest for Peace," was aimed at divesting university funds from U.S. companies which benefit Israel and which take a "non-neutral financial stance in the occupation of Palestinian territories." The resolution calling for divestment from targeted companies was replete with well-worn anti-Israel accusations about an "occupying force [that] has engaged in collective punishment of the Palestinian populations," that enforces "a policy of settlement expansion that. . . constitutes a direct violation of Article 49. . . of the Fourth Geneva Convention," all of which "constitute a serious obstruction to achieving a comprehensive, just and lasting peace in the Middle East."[1]

The Berkeley initiative, endorsed by 41 students groups in March 2010 in a letter of support of Associated Students of UC Berkeley Senate Bill 118A, was cynically named "A Bill In Support of UC Divestment From [Israeli] War Crimes"—promoted by broader an anti-Israel effort named the "U.S. Campaign for the Academic and Cultural Boycott of Israel."

Calls for divestment from and boycotts against Israel, of course, did not begin with the latest California incarnations. But they are the continuing effort by members of the academic Left, joined happily by Islamists and other ideological enemies of the Jewish state, to prolong and enhance the demonization of Israel for the purpose of delegitimizing, weakening, and, it is hoped by these advocates, eventually extirpating Israel altogether.

Positioned as a morally upright effort to assert and protect the rights of the long-suffering Palestinians, these efforts at demonizing Israel are not, in fact, the benign gestures of peace activists and well-meaning academics in pursuit of social justice for the Palestinians. There is a far more sinister and deadly agenda which aims to create a new Palestinian state, not, as is frequently though disingenuously described as one that will exist side by side with Israel in peace, but actually as a new entity that will either economically or demographically subsume Israel—a war of propaganda, falsehoods, slanders, and distortions of history by which Israel's enemies vanquish the Jewish state with ideas rather than arms.

In fact, Gil Troy, professor of history at McGill University, recently confirmed this notion that the BDS movement is more about diminishing the stature of Israel world-wide and less about actually ameliorating some of the root problems that define the Israeli/Palestinian conflict. "The BDS debate is not about 'occupation' or borders or the peace process," Troy wrote in the *Jerusalem Post*. "The BDS campaign assails Israel's legitimacy, declaring it so odious that no one should drink any Israeli wine, no one should enjoy an Israeli film, no one should collaborate with any Israeli academic. The BDS movement is an obscene campaign of blacklisting, demonizing and slandering," which, in his view, requires that Israel's supporters "must name, shame, and reframe" in order to counteract the odious effects of the movement.[2]

Thus, on campuses today where boycott and divestment initiatives spring up in the rarified air of moral relativism, Israel is regularly, though falsely, condemned for being created "illegally"—through the "theft" of Palestinian lands and property—and thus has no "right to exist." The government is accused of a "brutal," illegal "occupation" of Palestinian lands, especially Gaza and the West Bank, of being a "colonial settler state," a Zionist "regime," a land-hungry nation building an "apartheid wall" as a further land grab, a usurper of property that was lived on and owned by a Palestinian "people" "from time immemorial." Zionism is regularly equated with Nazism, and the perceived offenses of Israel's government and military are likened to Nazi crimes against humanity; the notion is that Israel is creating a "Holocaust on the Holy Land" through "ethnic cleansing," ongoing "genocide" of Arabs, and the elimination of the rights of an innocent, "indigenous people" who merely seek self-determination and the peaceful creation of a Palestinian homeland.

Even worse, the struggle between "white" European colonial Jewish settlers in Israel and "brown" Third World Palestinians has been framed as a second coming of apartheid—Israel's occupation of the West Bank and its treatment of its own Arab citizens likened to the racist, separatist behavior that defined apartheid South Africa. That is why calls for divestment and boycotts against Israel are so appealing to the chattering class and Western "progressives" who wish to superimpose the South African model of oppression—even though it is not at all honest or accurate to do so—on Israel's own society. South African archbishop and Nobel Prize winner Desmond Tutu himself, in congratulating the UC Berkeley community for its assault against Israel, told them that "[Your predecessors] changed the moral climate in the United States and the consequence was the anti-Apartheid legislation, which helped to dismantle apartheid non-violently. Today it is your turn."[3] In fact, he added, it was a "principled stand" against "the injustice of the Israeli occupation of Palestinian land and violation of Palestinian human rights."[4]

The charge of racism against Israel, of course, has been increasingly uttered by the Jewish state's enemies, particularly after the 1975 United Nations' invidious proclamation that "Zionism is racism," thereby branding the very ideological existence of Israel as a racist act. In a campus environment where racism is the twentieth century's greatest ideological sin, the ability to brand Israel as an illegitimate and racist state was an irresistible way for liberals to find a new cause célèbre by which to nourish their own righteousness.

The racism charge against Israel has continued to be effective in demonizing the Jewish state in the world community, particularly when this indictment has been repeatedly formalized through the efforts of Non-Governmental Organizations, NGOs. One of the most egregious instances of anti-Israel activism in perpetuating the racism charge was the collective efforts of NGOs to demonize and delegitimize Israel at the Durban conference in the summer of 2001. As Robbie Sabel of the Jerusalem Center for Public Affairs recounted in a report prepared by the Center on the apartheid charge against Israel:

> The UN's World Conference Against Racism, Racial Discrimination, Xenophobia and Related Intolerance, held in Durban, South Africa, in September 2001, gave the Israel Apartheid calumny new force in international circles. The Declaration of the NGOs at the Durban meeting openly

stated: 'We declare Israel as a *racist*, *Apartheid* state in which Israel's brand of *Apartheid* as a crime against humanity has been characterized by separation and *segregation*, *dispossession*, *restricted land access*, *denationalization*, *'bantustanization'* *and inhumane acts* [*emphasis in original text*].'[5]

That same sentiment, and the identical call for the weakening of Israel and a campaign to help to make it a pariah in the community of nations, was articulated in a statement issued by the Palestinian Civil Society, an umbrella group comprised of unions, organizations, activist groups, and NGOs. Claiming that "Thirty eight years into Israel's occupation of the Palestinian West Bank (including East Jerusalem), Gaza Strip and the Syrian Golan Heights, Israel continues to expand Jewish colonies," the statement went on to proclaim that Israel's greatest offense was its racist character, that "Israel's entrenched system of racial discrimination against its own Arab-Palestinian citizens remains intact." To help dismantle the racist Jewish state, therefore, this alliance of pro-Palestinian groups and individuals expressed their intent to ". . . call upon international civil society organizations and people of conscience all over the world to impose broad boycotts and implement divestment initiatives against Israel similar to those applied to South Africa in the apartheid era. We appeal to you to pressure your respective states to impose embargoes and sanctions against Israel."[6]

In fact, of the many libels from the world community against Israel, perhaps none has gained such traction on campuses as the accusation that the Jewish state now practices apartheid, that the checkpoints, security barrier, Israeli-only roads, barricades, and other apparatus of occupation are tantamount to an institutionalized racist system which victimizes the indigenous Palestinians, just as South African apartheid oppressed and devalued indigenous blacks while stripping them of them civil rights.

This chorus of denunciation against the new apartheid regime has been given ideological and moral support, as well, by such high-visibility figures as Archbishop Tutu who, when visiting Israel, commented that "I've been very deeply distressed in my visit to the Holy Land; it reminded me so much of what happened to us black people in South Africa. I have seen the humiliation of the Palestinians at checkpoints and roadblocks, suffering like us when young white police officers prevented us from moving about."[7]

Similarly, former U.S. president Jimmy Carter instigated additional condemnation against Israel on college campuses with the publication of his book, provocatively entitled *Palestine: Peace, Not Apartheid*, which left little to the imagination about what his view toward the conflict was. In a 2006 interview on National Public Radio, for instance, he repeated the lie that Israel had usurped Palestinian land and suggested that the current system in the occupied territories was tantamount to apartheid:

> . . . The Palestinians have had their own land, first of all, occupied and then confiscated and then colonized . . .They have been severely restrained in their movements. . . The Israelis have built more than 200 settlements inside Palestine. . . Quite often the Palestinians are prevented from even riding on those roads that have been built in their own territory. So this has been in many ways worse than it was in South Africa.[8]

Former Bard professor, Joel Kovel, the rabid anti-Zionist whose personal ideology is focused on dismantling Israel completely through the creation of a single, bi-national state, was even more direct in his denunciation of Israel's existential sins, including the U.S.'s complicity in the oppression of the Palestinians under what he, too, described as an apartheid system. "The recent efforts of activists to publicize the parallels between Israel and apartheid South Africa, then, are an essential element in the one-state strategy," he told an interviewer. "The anti-Israeli-apartheid campaign is energizing forces of opposition across the world to build a powerful political movement to oppose Zionism and its lobbyists in the major capitalist/imperialist countries. This is significant because Israel simply cannot sustain itself without the support of the capitalist/imperialist powers, the United States in particular. Its current prosperity is entirely dependent on them."[9]

This kind of language helps reinforce the Left's notion that the imperialism of Western nations is once again responsible for setting up racist, oppressive caste systems in developing countries, systems that have to be dismantled through protest, resistance, and divestment campaigns. It has also formed the basis of divestment petitions which become "working documents" in the strategic vilification of Israel. A January, 2003 document created by New Jersey Solidarity and the Rutgers University Campaign for Divestment from Israeli Apartheid, "Acting for Human Rights, Taking a Stand for Justice," for instance, proclaimed that "The world, and specifically the United States, can no longer be silent about the criminal Israeli regime. Conceived by colonial powers without the consent of the indigenous Palestinian people, the State of Israel has continued to pursue its institutionalized policies of racism, discrimination and oppression."[10]

Abetted by the Arab world, which has also perennially defined Israelis as European interlopers with no racial or cultural connection to the Levant, campus Leftists are now willing to sacrifice the very survival of the Jewish state because they feel that charge of racism against Israel is more incompatible with their closely-held beliefs in a perfectible world than the rejectionist and genocidal efforts of the Arab world which in fact have necessitated Israeli security measures—the separation wall, indeed, the occupation itself—all of which are pointed at as indications of exactly how racist Israel's behavior against the Palestinians actually is.

The much-reviled security barrier, which Israel began building around the West Bank in 2005 as a tactic to reduce terror attacks on its citizenry (and which has been successful in reducing the frequency of those attacks by ninety percent), is, in the eyes of Israel's critics, not a means of defense, but what is promiscuously termed the "apartheid wall," a type of racial fence built merely to create Palestinian "Bantustans," which segregate Jews from Arabs, and which, for many, is emblematic of Israel's never-ending ambition to "steal" Arab land, disrupt Palestinian life, and expand its supremacist Zionist dream to ever-broader borders.

And the apartheid comparison is a simple and powerful way for Israel's campus enemies to heap yet another moral condemnation on the Jewish state, particularly because it reenergizes the campus liberals who made South African apartheid their cause of the moment during the 1990s. Even though Arab citizens of Israel enjoy more human and civil rights than their brethren in any other Arab nation, the apartheid accusation is effective because it once again points to the social disparity between Israelis and Third-world Arabs, Israeli citizens or not. Israel's need for self-defense, in the minds of its detractors, does not even justify the "apartheid wall," since it presumably should not have established its illegitimate state on Arab lands in the first place, nor should it be surprised when those indigenous inhabitants try to reclaim their stolen property by using terrorism as their only available tactic against an oppressive, militarily-strong regime.

History of Divestment

The rallying cry on campus to gather under the flag of the divestment movement seems to have arisen as the result of a November 2000 speech by Francis A. Boyle, a law professor at the University of Illinois. In that speech, Boyle carelessly conflated Israel's alleged racism with apartheid-like behavior and suggested, even more ominously, that the ongoing "genocide" against the Palestinians had parallels with the Nazi's own heinous offenses. "The paradigmatic example of a crime against humanity is what Hitler and the Nazis did to the Jewish People," Boyle said. "This is where the concept of crime against humanity was formulated and came from. And this is what the

U.N. Human Rights Commission is now saying that Israel is doing to the Palestinian People. A crime against humanity."[11]

Boyle's idea, to introduce a divestment campaign, was a result of his fear of potential Israeli malignancy, because, he cautioned, "if something is not done quite soon by the American People and the United States Government to stop Israeli war crimes and crimes against humanity against the Palestinian People, *it could very well degenerate into genocide, if it is not there already,*"[12] an odd fear, given the fact that some 600,000 Palestinian refugees created at the birth of Israel in the 1940s were now estimated to be some five million. So in order to prevent a new Holocaust, this time perpetrated against Palestinians by Jews, Boyle exhorted campus groups to initiate divestment efforts against Israel and the compliant forces in Washington that enabled it:

> You students can go out, research what the anti-apartheid movement did in this country, and your predecessors starting twenty years ago, and do the exact same thing here. You have to. If you want to see peace in the Middle East, you're going to have to go out and do something because so far the United States Government is not an honest broker. They never have been. I have been at these negotiations. I can tell you that the United States fully supports whatever Israel wants.[13]

It turns out that Professor Boyle did not serendipitously come to the divestment movement in a moment of moral indignation during which he was suddenly struck by the suffering of the Palestinians. In fact, as Accuracy in Academia discovered in a report they compiled on Boyle, the professor, whose other intellectual oddities include a belief that the U.S. government was involved in a conspiracy behind 9–11 and that the U.S. also invaded and conquered Hawaii, not only sympathized with the Palestinian cause from afar, but was one of its key strategists. As a freshly-minted graduate student, the report revealed, "Boyle went to work for the Palestine Liberation Organization (PLO) from 1987–1989 while they were still a U.S.-designated terrorist group. Once that tenure ran out, Boyle served as the legal advisor to the Yasser Arafat-led Palestinian Delegation from 1991–1993." The report further noted that Boyle "continued to advise Palestinian leadership during his formulation of the student BDS movement in the Fall of 2000."[14]

Apparently, Boyle's call for action did not go unheeded. By 2002, in the University of California system, for example, "more than 140. . . professors, including 68 from UC Berkeley, signed a petition calling on the university to divest from Israel, joining professors at Harvard, MIT, Princeton and Tufts University who [had] taken similar action." Princeton's divestment web site included the now-familiar trope about the perfidy of Israel, authored by Richard Falk, former Albert Milbank Professor of International

Law and Practice at Princeton and now United Nations Human Rights Rapporteur in the Occupied Territories, who claimed at the time that "to divest from companies profiting from business with Israel at this time is to express solidarity with victims of massive crimes against humanity and to call upon Israel to respect U.N. authority and the elemental rules of international law by withdrawing from occupied Palestinian territory."[15] By repeating these calumnies against Israel, it was thought, a universal loathing of the state would gradually evolve, an objective clearly stated by the divestment effort's proponents.

Methods were also put into place by divestment proponents which helped solidify the movement, and enabled campaigns on different campuses around the country to speak in a unified, consistent voice. Some of these were detailed manuals, or guidebooks, written by individual BDS groups, but shared with others so that tactical approaches could be compared, built upon, and disseminated widely among those intent on weakening the Jewish state.

One example, *Fighting the New Apartheid: A Guide to Campus Divestment From Israel*, written by Fayyad Sbaihat of the University of Wisconsin Divestment from Israel Campaign Project of Al-Awda Wisconsin, revealed the sinister rhetoric and tactical execution of the divestment proponents. Its purpose, Sbaihat wrote, was "to provide a scaffold for those beginning divestment campaigns." To accomplish that, the guide suggested that "In order to be successful, the divestment from Israel campaign must focus on addressing the deep-rooted issues of Israel's racism and ethno-religious centricity rather than debating facts on the ground that can prove illusive when one attempts to build a case around them," particularly the inconvenient "facts on the ground," such as those which recognize perennial Arab hostility to Jews and the state of Israel, homicidal terrorism committed by Palestinians against Israeli citizens, and the intractability of Palestinian leadership in entering into fruitful negotiations, accepting any peace settlements, or being maximal about their list of demands. Realistic political debate, and the actual facts on the ground, are regularly ignored and glossed over by anti-Israel activists, with the only discussion focusing on the malefactions of Israel, and Israel alone. Why? Because, the guide suggested, "the ultimate goal of a successful divestment campaign, such as the case with Apartheid South Africa, is to cause the isolation of the racist state economically, socially, culturally, and diplomatically in the international arena. Israel must be characterized a pariah state for serious rethinking of its policies and practices to take place on a high level, likely caused by the rise of a new peace movement."[16]

This approach has apparently been successful for Israel's enemies, since every time Israel was vilified or demonized, and its reputation tarnished in the court of world opinion, a concurrent event took place: namely, the elevation of the Palestinian cause as one deserving support from those with an interest in social justice. "Divestment campaigns and requests for institutional divestment," the guide observed, "provide debate material that places Palestine solidarity groups in the most favorable position to present their case. No other form of activism has generated as much debate and attention towards the plight of the Palestinians as does divestment. No other approach has presented the Palestinian struggle in a more positive light than does divestment." Focusing the world's attention on the defects of Israel's fundamental being would be the most effective strategy, and, the guide instructed, divestment activists should insure that "the argument is more directed towards questioning the nature of the exclusively-Jewish nature of Israel and the racist policies that allow the existence of such a project. This argument is far more effective and winnable than that of debating specific events and facts."[17]

Strategies/Methods of Divestment

This core sentiment has come to define the Boycotts, Divestment, and Sanctions movement, the notion that the repeated defamation of Israel will result in its eventual expulsion from the supposed civilized community of nations. But the call for divestment is merely a tactic through which Israel will be marginalized, and eventually extirpated, as a pariah state with no moral justification for existing. Thus, those pro-Palestinians, who give public expression to notions of "social justice" for everyone in the Middle East but actually mean justice for the Palestinians alone, and not to Israelis, admit, when pushed, that the sole underlying purpose of their calls for divestment is the eradication of Israel with a Palestine in its place.

Some radical academics broaden the significance of Israel's errant behavior by pointing to it not only as a moral issue demanding a just resolution, but as the principal obstacle to peace in the Middle East and the chief cause of terrorism against Israeli and Western targets. Writing in support of a divestment campaign on the Dearborn campus of the University of Michigan in 2006, for instance, two of the school's professors, David Skrbina and William Thomson, made the claim that unrest throughout the Middle East could be laid at Israel's door—and at America's, too, for its support of the rogue state. "The problems in Iraq, Iran and the rest of the Middle East have many causes," they wrote, "but one issue is of singular importance: U.S. support for the Israeli occupation of Palestine. This occupation, and the resulting apartheid-like structure, create[s] conditions under which violent reactions are inevitable." What is more, they suggested, using a moral inversion in which Jews are blamed for the virulent Jew-hatred which targets them, Muslim rage will Jews are blamed for the virulent Jew-hatred be aimed at the United States as well as, deservedly, at Israel. "As long as we continue to support Israel without pressing for a just resolution to the occupation, we will be seen by the Muslim and Arab world as accomplices to crimes against the Palestinian people." The solution in the professors' minds was divestment, because "The occupation is both immoral and illegal; it encourages retaliatory violence, and the University ought not be party to it in any way."[18]

Examples of Divestment Campaigns on Five Campuses

The web site of Rutgers University's divestment effort, coordinated by New Jersey Solidarity, echoed the same vilification of Israel and call to destroy the Jewish state. With not a single word about Palestinian terrorism and 6 years of Arab intransigence, divestment proponents singled out Israel as the sole evil-doer. "Today, Israel, backed by billions of dollars in United States tax monies and billions more in investment and economic participation by US-based corporations," the web site read, "continues its military onslaught, denial of human rights and racist, apartheid rule against the Palestinian people."[19]

Brown University's 2005 divestment effort was spearheaded by the Democratic Solidarity Committee and Brown Alumni for Divestment who used similarly incendiary language, as reported in the *Brown Daily Herald*, that "claim[ed] 'Israel = White Supremacy;' the groups [also] wrote that 'any Zionist—that is anyone equating Jewish identity and heritage with defense of the state and ruling class of Israel—is an accomplice of white supremacy and empire.'" Using the tired language of the far Left who see the invisible hand of racism and imperialism as the culprits of all Third-world conflict, the divestment proponents said they "would 'not relent until the undemocratic institutions on this campus are shaken; we will not stop until our tuition is no longer used to support injustice here and overseas in Palestine.'"[20]

Columbia University's divestment experiment took a slightly different, seemingly more benign, tact: instead of calling for a complete divestment from *any* firms doing business with Israel, their petition made, in their minds, an important distinction: only firms connected to the Israeli military would be targeted:

> Divestment campaigns currently are underway at a number of universities (Harvard-MIT, Princeton, Yale, California, Pennsylvania, Tufts, Cornell, Illinois, North Carolina. . .), but our campaign is different. It demands not a general divestment from all companies doing business with Israel but instead a targeted divestment from companies that manufacture and sell arms. We focus on a

fundamental feature of the current conflict: the use of force against the civilian Palestinian population living under Israel's military occupation.[21]

Of course, no acknowledgement was forthcoming as to the reasons why "the use of force against the civilian Palestinian population" existed as part of daily life for Israeli citizens as well as Arab ones; that is, that Israel's so-called "brutal occupation" and its military incursions were necessitated by Arab aggression and terrorism, and the use of force had not been a random occurrence based on the whims of a sadistic Israeli military. In fact, by targeting firms which supply arms to Israel, the Columbia divestment effort was not more morally sound at all; the participants were actually helping to achieve what Israel's Arab foes have long-wanted, a militarily-weak Israel whose defenseless citizens could be massacred and, in the favorite exhortation of jihadist foes, "driven into the sea." More ironically, the Columbia divestment proponents fell into the morally-convenient trap which ascribed the root cause of terrorism not where it belongs—with the homicidal madmen who perpetrate it in the name of jihad—but once again to Israel, due to its very presence in the Levant. "Given our opposition to all forms of terror," the Advisory Committee's petition read, the effort "seeks an end to a colonial-type occupation that reinforces the positions of those who see terror as a solution."[22]

Yale University's divestment initiative was not as generous with Israel as Columbia's; instead, the effort, led by Students for Justice in Palestine at Yale, had a far more transparent and openly announced intent, according to students Daniel Fichter and James Kirchickis, who wrote a column in opposition to the campaign in the *Yale Daily News*. The agenda, they wrote, was "to abolish the Jewish state. Activists leading the divestment campaign at Yale have repeatedly stated their belief that Zionism, the belief in Jewish national self-determination, is inherently racist and that the only way to bring peace to the region is to eliminate Israel."[23]

The way that would be effected, as was, and still is, the goal of divestment in general, was to make one of the core demands that Israel must recognize the so-called Palestinian "right of return" before efforts at achieving divestment would cease. This right, which Palestinians, and their Western enablers, claim is based on UN Resolution 194, meant to protect citizens who had been expelled from their lands by guaranteeing their legal right to return to that land after the conflict ended that displaced them.

For that very reason, of course, enemies of Israel, who wish to destroy the State from within by flooding it with Jew-hating Arabs, adamantly insist that they are protected by this right and wish to exercise it as part of final negotiations; supporters of Israel, of course, can never allow this spurious "right" to be exercised, since it will, as historian Efraim Karsh of King's College has put it, result in the demographic "subversion" of Israel and lead to the end of a Jewish state.

So when divestment petitions included the unquestioned right of return of all Palestinian refugees into present-day Israel before sanctions would cease, they were clearly insisting on a course of action that would require Israel to commit demographic suicide and eliminate its own Jewish character, a point not lost on Mr. Fichter and Mr. Kirchickis in their *Yale Daily News* column. "The Yale divestment petition," they wrote, not only "may be the only one in the country that neglects to condemn Palestinian terrorism, [but] demands the non-negotiable 'return' of 4 million Palestinians into the state of Israel, and calls for an immediate, unilateral Israeli withdrawal from the entire West Bank, Gaza Strip and Golan Heights. . . The divestment campaign trusts that the admittedly genocidal Palestinian terrorist organizations and their sponsors in the Arab world will stop killing Jews the minute Israel cedes to their maximal demands.[24]

While divestment efforts on campuses around the country eventually sputtered and failed to gain traction with university administrators, alumni, trustees, and other stakeholders, in 2009, members of Students For Justice in Palestine (SJP) at a small liberal arts college in Massachusetts, Hampshire College, seemed to have finally coaxed a feckless administration to acceding to their demands for divestment from companies doing business with Israel. The announcement by the president and board of trustees was hailed by the SJP as a victory for the divestment effort, since, they stated in one of the organization's press releases, Hampshire had "become the first of any college or university in the U.S. to divest from companies on the grounds of their involvement in the Israeli occupation of Palestine."[25]

Well, not exactly. Unfortunately for SJP and the College's president and trustees, a graduate of Hampshire happened to be the son of Harvard Law School professor Alan M. Dershowitz, the prolific and relentless defender of anti-Israelism on campuses. His answer to the divestment decision was expressed straightforwardly in an op-ed he wrote with the title: "Hampshire Divests from Israel, So Contributors Should Divest from Hampshire." "Until now," Dershowitz wrote in the widely-circulated opinion piece, "every American university administration has categorically rejected this attempt to single out Israel in a world filled with massive human rights abusers. But Hampshire caved in to student and faculty pressure and as Board of Directors agreed to divest from these six companies along with a series of others that did not meet the standards of Hampshire College."[26]

Administrative Responses to the Campaigns

The Hampshire College example was unique in that, at least in principle, college officials had adopted the ideological approach of divestment proponents. Far from being universally embraced by college administrators—who, with their trustees, actually made the final decisions on whether or not to commit a university to divest from companies doing business with Israel—the divestment efforts at all other campuses were eventually dismissed, ignored, and marginalized, though not without considerable pushback from disgruntled radical faculty and students. Harvard's then-president Laurence Summers, for example, delivered a controversial 2002 speech in which he rejected a divestment petition to withdraw funds from Israel signed by, among others, seventy-four Harvard professors. He observed that anti-Semitic and anti-Israel attitudes, once the invidious products of fringe groups and right-wing cranks, had begun to appear on college campuses, that "profoundly anti-Israel views are increasingly finding support in progressive intellectual communities. Serious and thoughtful people," he said in the most pointed section of his comments, "are advocating and taking actions that are anti-Semitic in their effect if not their intent."

Even as he was cautioning divestment proponents to examine the true nature of their attitudes and the ramifications of their actions, Summers, unlike his critics, was willing to let even foolish views be heard. "We should always respect the academic freedom of everyone to take any position," he said. But, he added, those who take provocative positions have to assume that their views can and will be challenged, "that academic freedom does not include freedom from criticism."[27]

The University of Pennsylvania's president, Judith Rodin, also refused to allow her university to be part of a divestment campaign, seeing the inherent bias and unfairness in singling out the Middle East's only democracy:

> Because Penn defends freedom of expression as a core academic and societal value, we will not use the power of the University either to stifle political debates or to endorse hostile measures against any country or its citizens. Divestiture is an extreme measure to be adopted rarely, and only under the most unusual circumstances. Certainly, many countries involved in the current Middle East dispute have been aggressors, and calls for divestment against them have been notably absent.[28]

Columbia University's president, Lee C. Bollinger, who would years later be subject to considerable criticism for inviting Iran's Mahmoud Ahmadinejad to campus to speak, where divestment was concerned, spoke firmly and with conviction. "As President of Columbia," he said, "I want to state clearly that

I will not lend any support to this proposal. The petition alleges human rights abuses and compares Israel to South Africa at the time of apartheid, an analogy I believe is both grotesque and offensive."[29]

Like other fair-minded individuals, these university leaders were able to see through the charged rhetoric and disingenuous talk of ending racism and alleged apartheid, and saw the divestment movement for what is was, and is: a cynical, morally-corrupt attempt by Israel's deadly foes to appeal to well-meaning people with a false charge of racism on Israel's part, but who are actually seeking ways to vilify and defame the Jewish state with the ultimate intention of bringing about its destruction.

The Academic Boycott of Israel

It is one thing to make a moral stand against Zionism and a perceived brutal Israeli state by urging companies to refrain from doing business with the country. It is a far more personal, and damming, step to then take a further moral step and make the judgment that Israel should be cut off economically, culturally, and politically from the family of nations by imposing boycotts on it to further vilify and defame it. Current calls for boycotts against Israel, of course, are but another tactical continuation of the original Arab boycott of 1945 through which the Arab League Council attempted to shun Jews economically and cause them irreparable harm in doing so.

Calling for economic boycotts against Israel does have its tangible benefits for the Jewish state's foes: it weakens Israel's productivity and economic stability at the same time it marginalizes the country in the international marketplace. But calling for divestment against Caterpillar, United Technologies, General Electric, ITT Corporation, Motorola, and Terex (as the Hampshire College petition did) is impersonal; and while it could theoretically help to eventually destabilize and weaken Israel's economy, for the divestment proponents, it lacked a personal connection. What these anti-Israel activists needed was a more direct assault on Israel's thought-leaders and intelligentsia; what would be effective in the latest salvo against Israel, they thought, would be a boycott, not simply against business interests that supported the IDF, but against the academic counterparts of the proponents themselves—the faculty and researchers of Israeli universities.

The academic boycott notion drew its inspiration from the odious anti-Israel hate-fest in 2001 portentously named the "World Conference Against Racism" in Durban, South Africa, but which devolved into a much-sought opportunity for attendees to single out for opprobrium one—and only one—nation for criticism: Israel. The following year, in the aftermath of Israel's 2002 Operation Defensive Shield incursion, British professors mounted the first formal effort to boycott Israeli institutions of higher learning. That April, some 120 academics representing 13 countries signed an open letter, stage-managed by Hilary and Steven Rose, professors at the City and the Open universities, in Britain's *Guardian* newspaper.

Hilary Rose was quick to draw a parallel, as boycott proponents are fond of doing, between the apartheid of South Africa and those same practices that she, and others, felt was prevalent in Israel, as well. She commented at the time that while boycotting sporting events helped weaken the South African regime, that same approach would have to be refined in Israel's case.

In July of 2002, the very personal nature of the academic boycott effort was ratcheted up a notch when Mona Baker, professor at the University of Manchester Institute of Science and Technology, who had proudly told *The Telegraph* that she "deplore[d] the Israeli state," fired two employees of academic journals she published, Dr. Miriam Shlesinger and Professor Gideon Toury, specifically because they were Israeli Jews. The morally-indignant Ms. Baker could no longer abide Israel's behavior among all the nations of the world. The Jewish state's malefaction knew no limits, and "Israel has gone beyond just war crimes," she posited. Moreover, despite data which indicated that Palestinians enjoyed one of the most robust birth rates in the world, Ms. Baker did not hesitate to suggest the very likely genocide—indeed, something of a Holocaust—they might face as a result of Israel's apartheid regime. "It is horrific what is going on there. Many of us would like to talk about it as some kind of Holocaust which the world will eventually wake up to, much too late, of course, as they did with the last one."[30]

That type of disingenuous talk about Israel, of course, is not at all uncommon among its world-wide foes who like to slander the Jewish state with calumny, lies, distortions, and overstatement whenever possible. What was unique about this boycott was that, for the first time, it focused on the moral responsibility of academics in Israeli universities, and made them culpable and responsible for the actions of their government. "The academic boycott specifically is based on several premises," Baker wrote on her web site announcing the boycott. "One is that, to date, 'the vast majority of Israeli academics have been carrying on their business as usual for the past 35 years oblivious to what is happening to their Palestinian counterparts, not to mention to the Palestinian nation as a whole,' just as Israeli society on the whole is content to sanction the apartheid policies of its government."

She called on Israeli academics to put "strong pressure on their government to rapidly end its inhumane treatment of the Palestinian people . . , not only because it is the moral and rational thing to do, but also," in a bit of academic psychobabble, "because their society's own insecurity stems from Israeli colonial oppression of the Palestinians." Finally, she asserted, if professors did not do the right thing and fully distance themselves from government policies that Baker and her fellow travelers from afar found morally unacceptable, they would not be worthy of recognition by the international community of scholars and would be punished, collectively, for Israel's transgressions. "Anything short of forthright public condemnation of the crimes committed by one's government and society against other human beings," she wrote, "almost literally on one's doorstep is nothing short of complicity," something that would not henceforth be tolerated by right-thinking individuals such as she.[31]

The Roses' and Ms. Baker's efforts found eager supporters, both in Europe and in the United States, and in fact seemed to have inspired a recurring initiative in English universities, with academic boycotts first called for in 2005 by the Association of University Teachers, and, in 2007, by Britain's University and College Union, representing some 120,000 members. Why Israeli academic institutions? Because, the boycotters said, "Israel's 40-year occupation has seriously damaged the fabric of Palestinian society through annexation, illegal settlement, collective punishment and restriction of movement,"[32] that there exists a "complicity of Israeli academia in the occupation" (which Mona Baker had also pointed out), and therefore academics in a State which behaved this way would have to be shunned from joint intellectual pursuits, research, and teaching.

But this notion of the "complicity of Israeli academia in the occupation" was flawed in at least two respects. It, first, exonerated academics in Britain or America for any misdeeds committed by their own governments, for which, by the same standard that the boycotters apply to Israel, they as concerned citizens and scholars should have to answer. Many in the international community, the Palestinians and their supporters chief among them, for example, found great offense in and disagreed with Western incursions into the Middle East during the Gulf War, and with later forays into Afghanistan and Iraq as part of the war on terror and the dissolution of Saddam Hussein's maniacal and bloody rule. Faculty on American and British campuses would hardly have been content to have been deemed "complicit" with the decisions to invade Arab states merely because they lived in those countries whose leaders had decided to take that political course of action.

Secondly, making Israeli academic complicit in the actions of their government, "the vast majority of [whom] have been carrying on their business as usual for the past 35 years oblivious to what is happening to their Palestinian counterparts," as Mona Baker put it, ignored the reality that, as is the case on

European, Canadian, and America campuses, many Israeli professors veer to the Left politically and many, incredibly, share the same virulent anti-Israel, anti-Zionism sentiments so proudly touted by the boycott supporters. In fact, some 358 members of the faculties of Israeli universities were signers of an online petition which announced proudly how, as they wrote, "We wish to express our appreciation and support for those of our students and lecturers who refuse to serve as soldiers in the occupied territories."[33] When Israel finally retaliated against Gazan rocket fire in late December of 2008 and early into 2009, the anti-Israel academics were in full force once again—not denouncing the ceaseless barrage of Hamas rocket fire that had terrorized civilians in southern Israeli towns for six years, of course, but to denounce and vilify Israel for having the audacity to protect its citizens from being murdered as they slept in their homes.

Taking a cue from a similar effort by the anti-Israel wing of the education union in Britain, the Ontario chapter of the Canadian Union of Public Employees (CUPE) used the Gaza conflict to make the smarmy announcement that, "as a protest against the December 29 [2008] bombing of the Islamic University in Gaza," it would introduce a resolution seeking to ban Israeli academics from speaking, teaching, or conducting research at Ontario university campuses. Acceding to an appeal from the Palestinian Federation of Unions of University Professors and Employees, Sid Ryan, president of CUPE Ontario, announced that the union had decided, no doubt after thoughtful and troubling deliberation, that it was "ready to say Israeli academics should not be on our campuses unless they explicitly condemn the university bombing and the assault on Gaza in general."[34]

Apparently it had not dawned on union members that demanding loyalty oaths or proclamations of one's political ideology as a prerequisite for scholars on campuses is usually something of an anathema, particularly since Leftists in American and Canadian universities ordinarily cannot contain themselves when extolling the virtues of academic freedom and free speech when they wish to rail against imperialism, the war on terror, capitalism, neocons, or Israel. In fact, some academics clearly have no problem deciding for Israel that it should continue to let its civilians be targets for Qassam rockets while Hamas jihadists randomly sought to murder Jews. When Israel was concerned, the standard of how nationhood defines itself somehow changed.

"Clearly, international pressure on Israel must increase to stop the massacre that is going on daily," chimed in Janice Folk-Dawson, chair of the CUPE Ontario University Workers Coordinating Committee, adding that since now Palestinians were dying, and not Jews, she wanted "to add CUPE voices to others from around the world saying enough is enough."[35] When

Hamas thugs were murdering fellow Palestinians in their violent takeover of Gaza in 2006, slaughtering families in their homes, throwing opponents off the rooftops of buildings, nearly decapitating other terrorists with machine-gun fire to their necks, or torturing and hanging perceived traitors in front of their families, neither Ms. Folk-Dawson nor Sid Ryan apparently were apparently concerned enough at that point to say "enough is enough."

Israel's incursions into Gaza to crush Hamas aggression also had an energizing effect on American academics. Seeming to give proof to Orwell's observation that some ideas are so stupid they could only have been thought of by intellectuals, yet another group of academics—this time in the United States—followed Britain and Canada by ignobly launching an academic boycott of Israel. What was called "The U.S. Campaign for the Academic & Cultural Boycott of Israel" sought to enjoin "participation in any form of academic and cultural cooperation, collaboration or joint projects with Israeli institutions that do not vocally oppose Israeli state policies against Palestine," "promot[e] divestment and disinvestment from Israel by international academic institutions," and support "Palestinian academic and cultural institutions directly without requiring them to partner with Israeli counterparts as an explicit or implicit condition for such support."[36]

These strident anti-Israel initiatives did not proceed with criticism, however. In fact, in the wake on the first British union's push for an academic boycott, leaders of American universities were quick to denounce the effort as anathematic to the core principles of higher education and academic free speech. A full page advertisement published in August 2007 by the American Jewish Committee in *The New York Times*, for instance, included the names of nearly 300 university presidents who supported the theme of the ad voiced by Columbia President Lee Bollinger, "Boycott Israeli Universities? Boycott Ours, Too!" "If the British UCU is intent on pursuing its deeply misguided policy," Bollinger wrote, "then it should add Columbia to its boycott list, for we do not intend to draw distinctions between our mission and that of the universities you are seeking to punish. Boycott us, then, for we gladly stand together with our many colleagues in British, American and Israeli universities against such intellectually shoddy and politically biased attempts to hijack the central mission of higher education."[37]

Duke University's President, Richard H. Brodhead, saw "the proposed academic boycott of Israeli universities. . . as a threat to all institutions of higher education, and I condemn it as such. All ideas are not equal, but it is a foundational principle of American life that all ideas should have an equal opportunity to be expressed. . . The idea of forbidding partnerships and exchanges with Israeli universities and scholars contradicts the high value we place in the pursuit of knowledge on our own campus and in the importance of robust intellectual integrity more broadly."[38]

But not all shared some of the clear-headed thinking of university leaders and pro-Israel students. David Lloyd, a professor of English at the University of Southern California, who had organized the U.S.-led boycott effort with 14 other academics, told an Israeli newspaper that "The initiative was in the first place impelled by Israel's latest brutal assault on Gaza and by our determination," echoing the CUPE's similar assertion, "to say enough is enough." And as had become the familiar paranoia of the brave scolds of Israel who saw themselves speaking truth to power, professor Lloyd proclaimed his surprise that the effort even took off, given the formidable power of the omnipotent "Israel Lobby," not to mention the high price critics of Israel invariably had to pay for speaking out against the Zionist regime. "The response has been remarkable," Lloyd told *Haaretz*, "given the extraordinary hold that lobbying organizations like AIPAC exert over U.S. politics and over the U.S. media, and in particular given the campaign of intimidation that has been leveled at academics who dare to criticize Israel's policies."[39]

A slightly different twist on the academic boycott occurred in March 2011, in this instance when South Africa's University of Johannesburg decided to sever research ties with Ben-Gurion University in Israel "on the grounds of [Ben-Gurion] University's complicity in Israeli apartheid."[40] The boycott sponsors proudly claimed that the effort had garnered the "support of over 400 South African academics, including 9 South African Vice-Chancellors and Deputy Vice-Chancellors; 11 Deans and Vice Deans; 19 Heads of Department; 175 University Professors and 125 Academic Doctorates," all of whom felt that it was necessary to end the working relationship between the two academic institutions, even though it had been characterized as 'merely the continuation' of a 'purely scientific co-operation.'"[41] The high-visibility anti-Zionist, Archbishop Desmond Tutu, also lent his name to the petition drive.

Earlier, in 2010, the Senate of University of Johannesburg had put Ben-Gurion on notice: either it could come into compliance with a new set of moral guidelines, or the cooperative research program between the two institutions would be terminated. UJ's language was forthright, and suggested that BGU shared complicity with the racist policies of the Israeli government and support of its military, both of which would disqualify it from further involvement with UJ:

1. BGU's research project 'will not entail any activity, including teaching and research, which has any direct or indirect military implications or contributes to the abuse of human rights.'

2. 'One or more Palestinian universities' must be included in the
    existing UJ-BGU agreement if relations were to continue.

As many boycotters do, the South African version proudly asserted that
it stood in solidarity with the Palestinians, and that the perceived abuses of
human rights by Israel necessitated the call for a boycott in the first place.
"The Israeli occupation of the Palestinian territories has had disastrous effects
on access to education for Palestinians," the boycott's web site read. "Palestinian students face immobilisation [sic], poverty, gendered violence, harassment
and humiliation as a result of Israeli policy and actions,"[42] all which, particularly given South Africa's own involvement in apartheid at the time the joint
venture between the two schools was initiated, made the continuing relation
untenable. But the boycott call created a dangerous precedent in academia
once more, since it clearly defined a new moral imperative for faculty members; that is, it made all faculty members at a given institution complicit in the
political views and ideologies of the *government* of the country in which those
faculty members taught—whether or not individual faculty members even
shared the political beliefs of their government in the first place.

That type of political "litmus test" has always been an abhorrent concept
to academicians, particularly those in America who well remember the days
of the Cold War when perceived sympathy for Communism and insufficient
America patriotism threatened careers and caused widespread intimidation
through the halls of academe. That the justifiable urge to resist such broad-
brush indictments of whole faculties is now being ignored in the name of
"solidarity" with the Palestinian cause should, of course, be of great concern to those who feel that the core of academic freedom and free speech is
an assumption that one's political allegiances—assuming that they are not
brought into classrooms as propaganda or politicized scholarship—should
not condemn an individual to censure, condemnation, or academic "exile,"
which is precisely what the academic boycotts against Israeli scholars does.

The more troublesome aspect of the BDS movement in general, however, is that, in its obsession with the perceived defects of Israel, and Israel
alone among nations, the movement exposes a more sinister strain of what
many believe is blatant anti-Semitism, anti-Zionism that has as its inspiration
and in its effect a hatred of Jews. BDS efforts are always initiated with the
morally-upright motivation to stand in solidarity with the Palestinian cause,
to help the Palestinians to achieve self-determination and statehood. But that
same outcome for Israel is never the concern of BDS supporters. They care
little for Jewish self-determination, the security of Israeli civilians, a thriving
Israeli economy, or even, as is often made clear by what seems to be the core

intent of the BDS movement, whether Israel even continues to exist at all. The efforts to weaken Israel militarily and economically, not to mention to flood it with millions of Palestinian refugees as part of the "right to return" movement, show that the BDS efforts are tactically designed, not to modify Israel's behavior, but to threaten its very existence, to destroy the Jewish state.

The BDS movement has gained much of its traction on campuses, and has helped generate a flood of anti-Israel activity, including "Israel Apartheid Weeks" and other anti-Israel hate-fests; Palestinian Solidarity Movement conferences where participants apologize for terrorism against Jews and plot ways to hobble with Israeli security; politicized scholarship against Israel; radical Muslim Student Associations with their retinues of Israel-hating guest speakers; and a general air of hostility and venom against Israel that is so intimidating and palpable that many Jewish students—whether they actually care about Israel or not—feel unsafe on their own campuses.

Because the BDS movement against Israel frames its ideology as a repeat of the world-wide effort to weaken, and eventually dismantle, South African Apartheid, the movement has blossomed on campuses, where impressionable and idealistic students (along with many Left-leaning faculty) are easily drawn into a movement that is purportedly designed to alleviate the suffering of an oppressed people living under Israeli apartheid. The problem, of course, is that Israel's society is not a racist system at all, but a Western-style democracy with carefully guarded human and civil rights for all of its citizens, But the ability to transform covert anti-Semitic feelings in a cause for a dispossessed Third-World victim has proved to be irresistible for liberal academics and pro-Palestinian Muslim groups who want to shroud actual enmity towards Jews and Israel as a morally-upright campaign to end racism. Where blatant anti-Semitism is still not generally accepted in the educated West, the demonization of the state of Israel can pass, not for what it often is—anti-Semitism—but instead as true concern for the victims of a brutal, colonial, racist occupying power that must be dismantled for Palestinian self-determination.

Writing in response to a divestment campaign initiated by ACUS Berkeley after Israel's Operation Cast Lead into Gaza, Hanan Alexander, Goldman Visiting Israeli Professor at UC Berkeley and Professor of Philosophy of Education, University of Haifa, observed that the well-meaning supporters of divestment actually caused more harm than good through their efforts, most of which was not unintended. Moreover, many of the manifestations of the BDS movement's efforts serve to create an on-campus atmosphere where classic anti-Semitic tropes and libels re-emerged as a "new" anti-Semitism disguised as criticism of Israel.

The divestment supporters, Alexander said,

> ... stand accused of seeking to deny Israel the basic human right of self defense by singling out Israel rather than opposing arms sales in general; of seeking to deny Jews the right to cultural self-determination in a country of their own by minimizing Hamas treachery and supporting its aim to destroy Israel as a Jewish and democratic state; of seeking to deny Jews self respect by attributing to the Jews alone the power to resolve the Israel-Palestine conflict; asserting a false analogy between democratic Israel and Apartheid South Africa; shamelessly asserting the vicious libel that the IDF intentionally targets innocent Palestinian children; and of seeking to deny supporters of Israel the right to feel welcome at their own university by ignoring hundreds of students who have complained that this initiative marginalizes them.[43]

Insightful commentator Melanie Phillips, in speaking specifically about the British lecturer union's call for a boycott, but with a sentiment that can be applied broadly to the academic boycott movement itself, lamented how those academics, with a long tradition of learning, had incredulously shamed that legacy and that their action, as she puts it, "represents a profound betrayal of the cardinal principle of intellectual endeavour, which is freedom of speech and debate."[44] The act of condemning Israel's universities, of excluding them from the fellowship of the international academic community, was, and is, Phillips thought, a disgraceful calumny that contradicted all those values that the university should, and usually does, hold dear. By proposing that Israeli scholars be banned from universities' "marketplace of ideas," from vigorous inquiry and debate, those who have called for academic boycotts against Israel are violating what should be the core precepts of the academy: bringing in many views so that the better ones are revealed, and not suppressing dissent based on whose views and ideology are currently in favour. In trying to weaken and destroy Israel, and make it a pariah in the world community of scholars, educators everywhere are violating one of the highest precepts of education, one which they normally protect and see as one of their guiding moral and intellectual principles.

Chapter 10

How To Reframe The Story About Israel & Why We Must: A Prescription For Change

A s discussed throughout this book, the university's war against Israel has been pervasive and intensifying, promulgated by the active partic-ipation both of Leftist faculty and radical Muslim student groups on campuses where the long-suffering Palestinians have replaced South African blacks as the Left's favorite victim group—whose behavior, however violent and politically irrational, is excused as justifiable in a 63 year-old campaign to demand that Israel grant the Arabs self-determination and social justice.

Coupled with that form of what Islamic scholar Robert Spencer calls "stealth jihad" has been the subtler, but equally destructive process through which Middle East study centers, institutes, professorial chairs, conferences, and publications have been richly subsidized by Saudi largesse; in the past 30 years, for example, the Saudi royal family has funneled $70 billion into universities in the West whose purpose, while ostensibly to create mutual understanding, is in reality to create scholarship and teaching that is almost uniformly designed to demonize Israel, advance the Palestinian cause, and undermine Western values and international influence—while apologizing for and helping to enable the spread of Islamism.

The other, related, trend of anti-Israelism on campuses—and, indeed, off campuses as well—is that derision of Zionism and the denunciation of Israel has become a convenient way for anti-Semites to mask their true prejudice against Jews by claiming that their problem is only with the policies of Israel, not with Jews themselves. While classic anti-Semitism is no longer considered acceptable in most Westernized societies, especially in the aftermath of the Holocaust, Jew-haters (and some liberal, Israel-hating Jews themselves) have found a convenient and effective way to mask their true feelings: they single out the world's only Jewish state for condemnation and hold it to a standard higher than they do for any other nation, not coincidentally including those Arab states and the Palestinians themselves, against whom Israel is perpetually and unfairly compared in action, self-defense, and self-determination.

The many anti-Israel events, narratives, attitudes, and deep-seated animus throughout academe, as recounted here, is not only a serious problem but is gaining momentum and an ever-more virulent tenor, particularly when Israel initiates measures to defend itself; in fact, in those instances when it does take defensive action—in the 2009 Cast Lead operation into Gaza, for example—the level of denunciation Israel receives from the world community rises exponentially. So the greater the existential threat to Israel, the greater the level of excoriation against it for attempting to ward off assault and the murder of its civilian population. The moralists of the world, and especially those on the Left, seemingly only have compassion when Jews are dying victims, not when they are politically and militarily strong and able to protect themselves from genocidal impulses that are ever-aimed in their direction.

Indeed, the problems cataloged in this book show no sign of abating, and the academic enemies of Israel, in fact, have become more emboldened as time has gone on. Why? Because it no longer requires intellectual or moral bravery to condemn and attack Israel. A pervasive anti-Zionist ideology informs the Arab world. Saudi-funded Muslim Student Association chapters have hijacked identity politics on campuses, ratcheting up the level of vilification with radical speakers, hate-fests, and the psychological, and sometimes physical, intimidation of Jewish students. Middle East studies programs, many also funded by Saudi largesse, serve as on-campus incubators for endemic anti-American and anti-Israel "scholarship," and students in classrooms taught in by these radical professors must willingly absorb the propaganda and historical contortions they are taught, sometimes attempting to bravely speak back to autocratic professors protected by tenure and craven administrations unwilling to take a moral stand.

Former professors and other academics move from campus to the State Department in a revolving door, bringing with them the bundle of their biases against Israel and the West, complete with a whole set of apologetics for the many self-inflicted pathologies of the Middle East that are likely to be blamed instead on Israel and the United States. Meanwhile, much of a biased or gullible world press regularly contorts the facts of the Israeli-Palestinian conflict, revealing an ignorance of history, an anti-Israel slant to commentary and news coverage, and a willingness to promulgate an Arab narrative which makes the Palestinians blameless for their own current state.

With anti-Israel invective increasing at an alarming rate, and given the world's continuing obsession with Palestinianism, how can the university's war to defame and weaken Israel be moderated? What can be done by stake-holders—both within and outside the campus—to change the conversation about Israel? To help mollify its indefatigable critics? To work towards famil-iarizing students and scholars with the actual narrative of the Jewish state to help inspire positive attitudes towards Israel? To shift the harsh critique of the many perceived defects of Israel's politics and military strategy away from the Jewish state alone and on to the Arab world for its own complicity in creating much of the pitiful conditions in which the Palestinians now find themselves?

That will be a difficult process, fraught with challenges and requiring constant efforts to change long-held beliefs and deep-set emotional attitudes, but it is imperative that the task be undertaken. This tactical approach should include a broad campaign to shift public perceptions about Israel. It should also make the university accountable for its teaching and programs which deal with the Middle East, and Israel particularly. More important, universities must be made to examine how radical professors and students have violated the spirit and intent of what Jonathan Tobin has called "the civil university." The civil university is a place where scholarly inquiry can take place, and competing arguments can be tossed about in the marketplace of ideas, but without creating acrimony, enabling the demonization of certain unpopular ideas, or allowing the creation of an educational environment where Jewish, or pro-Israel, students are specifically targeted and feel ostracized, intimi-dated, harassed, belittled, or otherwise uncomfortable in a place where they should feel at home.

What follows are some specific recommendations to help to end the uni-versity's jihad against Israel and Jews:

1. *Reveal Palestinianism for what it truly is and demonstrate how its foundational ideology is incompatible with peaceful coexistence with Israel*

Pro-Palestinians have been very successful, worldwide, in promoting the false narrative of the Palestinians being an indigenous people in the Levant

who were tragically and ruthlessly dispossessed by Jews with the founding
of Israel in 1948. Even though it has been Arab genocidal aggression toward
the Jewish state that has defined the 63 year history of Israel, Israel is now
seen as the political bully, a colonial oppressor of a weak indigenous people
wanting nothing more than to be able exercise their own self-determination.
In fact, the brutal occupation, the "apartheid wall," checkpoints, humiliation,
and firm military rule by Israel are often seen as the key inciters of violence,
not only throughout the Middle East, but also beyond—up to and including
being seen as one of the proximate causes of jihadist strikes against Europe
and the United States. This compelling, those false, narrative has resonated,
as seen, in the halls of academe which has made the Palestinians emblematic
of the Third-world oppressed peoples who need moral and ideological support from their sympathizers in the West. At the same time, Israel's actions
have been characterized as Nazi-like, genocidal, and racist, making it seem
like the most brutal and aggressive state on earth, causing ethnic cleansing
and grim death tolls among its Arab victims.

   All of these accusations, of course, have the intended effect of perpetuating the image of Israel as the world's bloodiest, most militaristic, and law-
breaking rogue nation, incessantly creating high body counts and spilling
Muslim blood. The problem with this assessment, even though it is widely
held and actively promulgated by Israel's enemies who obsessively focus
on the Arab/Israeli conflict as the key impediment to world peace, is that
it is a complete inversion of fact. University of Bremen's Professor Gunnar
Heinsohn and Daniel Pipes, director of the Middle East Forum, for instance,
recently compiled statistics on all world conflicts with an excess of 10,000
deaths since 1950, just after Israel was created. Despite the libelous accusations of the United Nations, the EU, Arab leaders, and Israel-hating professors on campuses, the statistics show that a number of other bloody conflicts
actually deserve the designation of "genocide," ethnic cleansing," or even
"holocaust," and that the total, though still tragic, number of deaths of Arabs
and Jews in Palestine over a tumultuous 58-year period totaled 51,000—only
the forty-ninth most deadly conflict.

   Those who ceaselessly condemn Israel for its many crimes against humanity in defending itself from Palestinian aggression have apparently conveniently
forgotten, or wish to overlook, say, the 400,000 deaths in Somalia since 1991;
900,000 fatalities in Rwanda; one million deaths in Saddam Hussein's 1980-88
war with Iran; the 1,900,000 souls who have perished, and continue to die, in
Sudan; or the 100,000 or more who have died in Iraq since 2003 alone.

   So while the significance of the Israeli/Arab conflict looms large in the
world's imagination, as a way of sensationalizing the conflict and demonizing

Israeli military power, Heinsohn and Pipes noted that the total deaths there "amount to just 0.06 percent of the total number of deaths in all conflicts in that period. More graphically, only 1 out of about 1,700 persons killed in conflicts since 1950 has died due to Arab-Israeli fighting,"[1] indicating that neither the particularity of that conflict nor the lethality qualify it for the obsessive attention Israel's detractors are fond of heaping upon it.

More revealing, as the two study authors report, is that Muslim deaths disproportionately occur at the hands of co-religionists, that while "some 11,000,000 Muslims have been violently killed since 1948, of which 35,000, or 0.3 percent, died during the sixty years of fighting Israel, or just 1 out of every 315 Muslim fatalities . . , over 90 percent of the 11 million who perished were killed by fellow Muslims."[2]

These are pertinent facts which would help to put the Israeli/Palestinian conflict in perspective, and defuse some of the incendiary emotions around it and Israel's perceived villainy in perpetrating it. So, too, would exposing the disingenuousness with which Palestinianism has evolved into an ideological "cult" that seemingly represents self-determination of a people seeking nationhood, but is actually a tool devised in the 1960s by the Yasser Arafat and his Soviet patrons as a way of masking the true Arab intention of "liberating" Palestine by destroying, not living beside, Israel. It is interesting that campus supporters of the Palestinian cause, not to mention the Arabs themselves, have always used the tactic of demonizing and delegitimizing Israel as a way of facilitating the creation of their own state. Instead of paying attention to state building—creating a civic society of laws, personal liberties, economic viability, and the other necessary foundations of nationhood—the Palestinians and their enablers have merely expected their state to evolve in the vacuum that a disappearing Israel would create.

Those academics who would define themselves as pro-Palestinian have thought that the process of Palestinian self-determination required only a negating of Israel, not constructive steps at trying to help build a social, political, and economic infrastructure for its new state. Journalist Khaled Abu Toameh, for example, suggested that pro-Palestinian activists, "people . . . found mostly on university campuses in North America and Europe," believe that "inciting against Israel on a university campus or publishing 'anti-Zionist' material on the Internet is sufficient to earn them the title of 'pro-Palestinian.' But what these folks have not realized is that their actions and words often do little to advance the interests of the Palestinians." In fact, Abu Toameh observed, these campus activists not only achieve little of actual benefit to the Palestinian cause, they often mar the struggle for statehood with their tactics. "If anyone is entitled to be called 'pro-Palestinian,'" he said, "it is those who are publicly campaigning against financial corruption and abuse of human rights by Fatah and Hamas."

The acting out and vitriolic language against Israel that so often defines campus anti-Israelism may make the activists feel good about themselves for striving for social justice, but, Abu Toameh contended, these are hollow efforts, that "[i]nstead of investing money and efforts in organizing Israel Apartheid Week, for example, the self-described 'pro-Palestinians could dispatch a delegation of teachers to Palestinian villages and refugee camps to teach young Palestinians English. Or they could send another delegation to the Gaza Strip to monitor human rights violations by the Hamas authorities and help Palestinian women confront Muslim fundamentalists who are trying to limit their role to cooking, raising children and looking after the needs of their husbands." What was Abu Toameh's conclusion about this misdirected effort to support the Palestinian cause? "What is happening on the U.S. campuses," he wrote, "is not about supporting the Palestinians as much as it is about promoting hatred for the Jewish state. It is not really about ending the 'occupation' as much as it is about ending the existence of Israel . . ," and "we should not be surprised if the next generation of jihadists comes not from the Gaza Strip or the mountains and mosques of Pakistan and Afghanistan, but from university campuses across the U.S."[3]

There is another important aspect in the intellectual and moral lapses of those who have promulgated the cult of Palestinianism at Israel's expense: in their zeal to support Palestinian nationalism, a jihadist ideology articulated quite plainly in the founding PLO Covenant, these extremist pro-Palestinians have never comes to terms with the supremacist, millenarian nature of that document and the ideology articulated in it. In other words, observed Islamic scholar Andrew G. Bostom, despite the West's fondness for considering Mahmoud Abbas and his Fatah party "moderates" with whom constructive negotiations can take place, the founding documents upon which the Palestinian authority was built and still operates do not allow for one sliver of engagement with Israel, or one bit of recognition of its legitimacy or viability—now and forever.

Bostom referred to a 1979 work by Yehoshafat Harkabi, *The Palestinian Covenant and its Meaning*, in which Harkabi was pessimistic in that he finally could not "help feeling that the Covenant is an ugly document according to its stand. It is not a manifesto of an extreme, lunatic fringe fraction, but the essence of the outlook of the center and mainstream of the Palestinian movement." In other words, when Jimmy Carter, or Sara Roy, or John Esposito, or Norman Finkelstein urge Israel and its Western allies to engage with Hamas, or even Fatah, and believe that these groups have moderated their position—vis a vis Israel—they are either being disingenuous because they know that such moderation will never be forthcoming, or they have been duped as a result of their own naiveté and unrealistic expectations. The fantasy about Israel and a new Palestinian state "living side by side in peace" is just that—a fantasy that animates the minds of the Left and those who believe in the politics of good intentions. But Harkabi contended that the Palestinian charter "is a document of arrogance, without a sign of humility that should be the lot of the human condition [and] it is completely expressed in absolute terms, without traces of any relativity;" for precisely that reason, there can never be ideological accommodation with the Zionist regime the Arabs so despise.

The PLO Covenant, Harkabi wrote,

> . . . represents an egoistic stand that does not show the slightest consideration for the adversary, nor any trace of recognition that he too may have a grievance, a claim and justice. The Palestinian movement claims absoluteness and 'totality'—there is absolute justice in the Palestinian stand in contrast to the absolute injustice of Israel; an unqualified Manichaean division of good and evil; right is on the Palestinian side only; only they are worthy of self-determination. . . .[4]

Every one of the Covenant's articles, Harkabi noted, is defined "by one-sidedness; the Palestinians arrogate rights that they are not prepared to grant to their rivals. There is no ray of light in Zionism; it is totally depraved." Moreover, he contended, while they endlessly condemn the moral defects of Zionism, "Palestinians bathe in self-righteousness, conferring on themselves spiritual virtues and moral values." The approach has meant that suicide bombers who murder Jewish civilians are elevated, after death, to the status of shahids, martyrs, precisely because their actions were predicated on the radical Islamist aggression that has been imbued with a holy purpose. "The Covenant," Harkabi concluded, "is a document of arrogance, without a sign of humility that should be the lot of the human condition; it is completely expressed in absolute terms, without traces of any relativity."[5]

2. ***Be able to differentiate between legitimate criticism and discussion about Israel and its policies towards the Palestinians, and thinly-disguised anti-Semitism using anti-Israelism or anti-Zionism as a cover***

In a speech he gave in 2004 to the Organization for Security and Cooperation in Europe (OSCE) Conference on Anti-Semitism, Israel foreign minister and former Society dissident, Natan Sharansky, offered what he thought was a useful technique for distinguishing between legitimate

criticism of Israel and anti-Semitism, which sometimes seems to be the oper-
ant factor behind the thin veil of anti-Israel rhetoric from some of the Jewish
state's critics and foes.

Sharansky made the distinction by using what he called "the 3 D test."
"The first D is the test of *demonization*," he said, and "today, the most sophisticated form of demonization is demonization of the Jewish State. For example,
the comparisons of Israelis to Nazis and of the Palestinian refugee camps to
Auschwitz . . . can only be considered anti-Semitic . . . But even those who
seek to place the blame on Israel cannot legitimately compare these camps
to Auschwitz and the other Nazi death camps. This is a clear cut case of
demonization."

"The second D is the test of *double standard*," Sharansky continued, so
"we must ask whether criticism of Israel is being applied selectively. If Israel
the only democracy in the Middle East is condemned by the Human Rights
Commission for the violation of human rights more than all the many dic-
tatorial regimes existing over the past 50 years together, it means that a different yardstick is used towards Israel than towards other countries. And a
different yardstick means a double standard and a double standard means
anti-Semitism."

Finally, Sharansky observed, was the final D, "the test of *delegitimization*," "embodied in the world-wide efforts to question aloud whether Israel
should even be recognized as a state, if, in fact, it has a "right to exist" at all,
given the moral lapses it is accused of exhibiting." "Today," Sharansky said,
[anti-Semites] are trying to deny the legitimacy of the Jewish State. While
criticism of an Israeli policy may not be anti-Semitic, the denial of Israel's
right to exist is always anti-Semitic."[6]

In 2003, a group of academics called Scholars for Peace in the Middle
East published a position paper, as anti-Semitism began showing itself on
campuses in the wake of the Second Intifada, in which they tried to specifically identify events and instances when anti-Semitism, as opposed to mere
critiquing of Israel or Zionism, revealed itself. When radical cleric Imam
Muhammad al-Asi visited the campus of UC Irvine in 2001 as a guest of
the Muslim Student Union, as one example, he spewed forth the notion that
"The Zionist-Israeli lobby . . . is taking the United States government and
the United States people to the abyss. We have a psychosis in the Jewish
community that is unable to co-exist equally and brotherly with other human
beings. You can take a Jew out of the ghetto, but you cannot take the ghetto
out of the Jew."[7] This is not merely academic discourse about the politics
of the Middle East; something entirely different was going there, and raw
anti-Semitism and ethnic attacks on Jews regularly occur under the cover

of anti-Israel rhetoric on behalf of the Palestinians. But that type of conversation has no place on campus, just as a well-intentioned, but equally prejudiced, lecture about how African-Americans are destroying America because of their lifestyles, criminality, and immorality would never be allowed to be uttered anywhere near a university.

But what SPME called "academic anti-Semitism" had taken hold, and the organization identified some ways it manifests itself:

1. Firing and refusing to hire Israeli academics
2. Boycotting Israeli academic meetings
3. Harassment, assault, and menacing of Israeli and non-Israeli Jewish academics and students
4. Academic journals' refusal to consider the work of Israeli scholars for publication.
5. Petitions to universities to divest from companies that are based in or supply goods or services to Israel.
6. Denial of campus access to legitimate Jewish student organizations, such as Hillel
7. Cancellation of invitations to Israeli or non-Israeli Jewish speakers, often on the grounds that the speaker's presence on campus may lead to a riot
8. Inviting speakers known to be associated with terrorist groups and known to have advocated murder of Israeli or non-Israeli Jews
9. Failure to prevent or control mob action against Israeli and non-Israeli Jewish speakers and legitimate student groups, such as Hillel

The rhetoric that accompanies these actions includes:

1. Justification and even encouragement of acts of terror against Israel's civilian population as acts of liberation from oppression.
2. Charges that Israel practices apartheid and colonialism.
3. The equation of support for Israel and Zionism with Nazism, Fascism, Racism and Apartheid.
4. Claims that the United States supports Israel only because of coercion from American Jews.
5. Questioning the right of Israel to exist at all.[8]

Sometimes this "academic anti-Semitism" is blatant, as in the case of al-Asi and his ravings about the depravities of Jews everywhere because of the perfidy of Israel and Zionism. In other instances, it is more discreet, even nuanced, because it is coated with a scholarly veneer and therefore made more acceptable in the marketplace of ideas, as was the case with Walt and Mearsheimer's *The Israel Lobby*.

Despite the high profile nature of much of this academic anti-Semitism, university administrations, with a few exceptions, have been loath to address the issue head-on. Harvard's president Laurence Summers did decry anti-Israel activities on his campus at the time that he asserted that such efforts (in this instance divestment) "were anti-Semitic in effect if not in their intent." Columbia's Lee Bollinger, similarly, showed moral uprightness when he characterized his institution's attempt to launch a divestment campaign against Israel as "both grotesque and offensive."

But university officials have characteristically been morally blind when it comes to identifying anti-Semitism on campuses—disguised as anti-Israelism—and denouncing it for what it actually is. This craven moral approach is troubling, not only because it allows true anti-Semites to escape condemnation for their utterances and venomous attacks on Israel and Jews, but also because diversity-obsessed universities are normally hyper-sensitive and vigilant in immediately responding to hate speech or prejudice when other victim groups are involved.

In 2002, for example, racist slurs were discovered on dorm walls at the University of Mississippi, including such imaginative epithets as "Fucking Nigger" and "Fucking Hoe Nigger," thoughtfully accompanied by chalked graffiti describing body parts and an incendiary depiction of a lynching. Commentator Michelle Malkin noted that Ole Miss's reaction was immediate, severe, and self-righteous—even though it turned out that the vandalism had actually been perpetrated by three African-American students as a hoax to prove some perverse point. Nevertheless, just after the incident, "[b]lack students," Malkin wrote, "organized a 'Say No to Racism' march and demanded more protection against white-on-black harassment. They blasted the school's president for not apologizing quickly enough for the racial slurs. The school's 'Minority Affairs' director demanded that the university establish 'programs and procedures' to ensure racial sensitivity and prevent hate crimes . . . Activists called for criminally prosecuting the perpetrators under state felony laws or federal hate crime statutes,"[9] all because, in this instance of identity politics, it was clear to the university what appropriate boundaries were.

Another hoax in 2007, this time at George Washington University with Muslim students as the presumed target, indicated once again that university administrations can act with moral clarity when they want to, as long as the alleged victims are not Jewish students. Flyers announcing Islamo-Fascism Awareness Week, supposedly distributed by GW's Young America Foundation, the student sponsor of the event, were crudely headlined with "HATE MUSLIMS? SO DO WE!!!" The clearly satirical flyers also depicted what appeared to be a Middle Eastern man with "lasers in eyes," "venom from mouth," "hatred for women," "a suicide vest," and a "hidden AK-47." As had happened in the Ole Miss incident, the creators of this distasteful flyer were not YAF members at all, but a group of seven Muslim and liberal students who were evidently trying to make a point about their belief that the Islamo-Fascism Awareness Week event was somehow "racist."

But just as the Ole Miss campus community had immediately reacted to the presumed offense against a victim group, George Washington officials stepped over one another in their zeal to denounce the hateful sentiment contained in the flyer. Steven Knapp, George Washington's president, publicly decried the flyer, commenting that "There is no place for expressions of hatred on our campus. We do not condone, and we will not tolerate, the dissemination of fliers or other documents that vilify any religious, ethnic, or racial group." Bridgette Behling, GWU's assistant director of the Student Activities Center, similarly excoriated the YAF, asking of them something that, tellingly, had never been required of any of the Muslim Student Association chapters across the country which regularly bring rabid anti-Israel, anti-American speakers to their respective campuses: that they would have to draft "a statement which states that you will not allow hate speech to be a part of any of YAF's events, literature, written or verbal communication planned for Islamofacism Week [sic]. This statement should also include your plan for preventing these things from happening as well as the consequences for these things happening. It is important that we have this document should any further incidents occur as we move forward."[10]

If universities do not or cannot see that what they describe as mere critiquing of Israel and Zionism has frequently devolved into raw anti-Semitism, and that the prevalence of this hatred on campus is causing discomfort and intimidation to Jewish students, there has to be a significant reassessment of academia's failure to provide a truly inclusive learning environment for its entire student bodies, not just its preferred victim groups. No one is expecting, or even asking for, an end to serious discussion about the Israeli/Palestinian conflict; but to allow egregious, hate-inspired speech and actions to occur as part of that discussion is to enable true anti-Semites to slither into the academy under false pretenses.

"Criticizing Israel is not anti-Semitic, and saying so is vile," observed *The New York Times'* Thomas L. Friedman in an op-ed entitled "Campus Hypocrisy." "But singling out Israel for opprobrium and international sanction— out of all proportion to any other party in the Middle East—is anti-Semitic, and not saying so is dishonest."[11] It is time for academia to acknowledge the distinction.

3. *Insist that university officials take a firm moral stand against virulent
    anti-Semitism and anti-Israelism in campus events and that they do
    not facilitate these types of events due to their own biases and ideology*

Boards of trustees, alumni, parents of students, and other stakeholders of
universities have abandoned their responsibility to insure that campus communities are kept free of hate speech, violent behavior, intimidation of students,
or other actions that adversely affect learning and living, regardless of how the
perpetrators of these offenses claim to be protected by academic free speech.
University officials at many of the universities examined in this book have clearly
failed to uphold their own regulations and student codes, presumably designed to
protect all within the academic community from serious intellectual, psychological, or physical harm. In fact, universities' failure to create "safe" academic environ-
ments may constitute a violation of federal law. An April 2006 report by the U.S.
Commission on Civil Rights entitled "Campus Anti-Semitism," and prepared in
response to the volatile situation at UC Irvine, for example, found that "[m]any
college campuses throughout the United States continue to experience incidents
of anti-Semitism, a serious problem warranting further attention," and that "[w]
hen severe, persistent or pervasive, this behavior may constitute a hostile environment for students in violation of Title VI of the Civil Rights Act of 1964,"[12]
something that should be of deep concern to university officials.

In fact, the ability of Jewish students to be protected from harassment,
intimidation, and bias in the context of discussion about the Israeli/Palestinian
conflict, both in the classroom and on campus grounds, may be closer to
realization due to legal developments underway as this book goes to press. At
the University of California, Santa Cruz, after years of witnessing "Professors, academic departments and residential colleges at UCSC [who] promote
and encourage anti-Israel, anti-Zionist and anti-Jewish views and behavior,"
a lecturer there, Tammi Rossman-Benjamin, filed a 2009 civil rights action
with the U.S. Department of Education's Office for Civil Rights, arguing
that UCSC had created a "hostile environment" for Jewish students. Since
Jews had never been recognized as a protected group under Title VI, the suit
had stalled; but in 2011, a "change in policy at the U.S. Office of Civil Rights
(OCR) affirmed that Jewish students were protected under Title VI [and] the
OCR announced that it would investigate Rossman-Benjamin's complaint,
the first such investigation under the new policy."[13] That the OCR would
finally adopt a policy that looks at anti-Semitism on campus as behavior
that would be subject to Title VI remedies is a potentially seismic change in
how university officials will be compelled to address complaints by Jewish

students and others who have previously found themselves subject to abuse and vilification. Institutions of higher education will no longer be able to ignore conditions on their campuses that may well result in the loss of federal funding if they are unable, or unwilling, to mitigate the "hostile environment" that unchecked anti-Israelism and anti-Semitism can create.

On her own campus, Rossman-Benjamin had observed an odious pattern of bias and radicalism against Israel and Jews, under the guise of a scholarly critique of Israeli policies, a process in which, she said, "Professors, academic departments and residential colleges at UCSC promote and encourage anti-Israel, anti-Zionist and anti-Jewish views and behavior, much of which is based on either misleading information or outright falsehoods."[14]

Rossman-Benjamin's descriptions of the behavior and rhetoric she had witnessed over years finally resonated with OCR:

> Rhetoric heard in UCSC classrooms and at numerous events sponsored and funded by academic and administrative units on campus goes beyond legitimate criticism of Israel. The rhetoric–which demonizes Israel, compares contemporary Israeli policy to that of the Nazis, calls for the dismantling of the Jewish State, and holds Israel to an impossible double standard–crosses the line into anti-Semitism according to the standards employed by our own government . . . The impact of the academic and university-sponsored Israel-bashing on students has been enormous. There are students who have felt emotionally and intellectually harassed and intimidated, to the point that they are reluctant or afraid to express a view that is not anti-Israel. Some students have stayed away from courses that they would otherwise be interested in taking, because they know that the courses will be biased against Israel and intolerant of another legitimate point of view . . . Since at least 2001, faculty members and students have brought these and similar problems to the attention of numerous UCSC administrators and faculty. To date, the administration and faculty have largely ignored the problems. In some cases, administrators and faculty have publicly denied that there are problems and even repudiated those who have had the courage to raise them.[15]

More to the point, it was not only the presence of this virulently anti-Israel, anti-Semitic speech and action that was of significance, but the fact that it was singularly directed, unceasingly, at one group of students: Jews. And what was more, Rossman-Benjamin added, "no other . . . group on campus has been subjected . . . to such hostile and demonizing criticism."[16]

Another serious issue is the frequent lapses in good judgment by university leaders when discussion about Israel and the Palestinians is involved,
including, at times, officials' participation in, apologetics for, or complicity
with some of the egregious anti-Semitic and anti-Israel behavior recounted
in this book. Private colleges and universities do not have to answer to the
same federal laws that govern the way student rights are protected at public universities, although many do strive to grant Constitutionally-protected
rights to their students, nevertheless.

But public universities, such as the University of California at Irvine, the
location of some of the most blatant anti-Israelism, are required to adhere
to federal law governing any intimidation, harassment, or physical danger
their students might experience on campus. That protection was apparently
not of great interest to Manuel Gomez, UC Irvine's Vice Chancellor for Student Affairs, who not only did nothing to try to moderate the hatred spewing
forth from Muslim Student Union events at UCI, but even excused some
of the incendiary speakers, claiming on one occasion, incredibly, that "one
person's hate speech is another person's education." In a report prepared by
the Orange County Task Force on Anti-Semitism at UC Irvine, a follow-up
to the U.S. Office of Civil Rights' own report, Vice Chancellor Gomez was
shown to have displayed an equally unbalanced approach when dealing with
the rampant anti-Semitism on his own campus, even as he was diligent in
facilitating Muslim student hate-fests. "Several testimonies spoke about the
Vice Chancellor's non-responsiveness if not outright hostility toward Jewish students," the Task Force found. "They spoke of an anti-hate rally that
resulted from the destruction of a cardboard Wall put up on campus by the
MSU. All organizations were invited, except for Jewish organizations . . . The
Jewish students were outraged when the Vice Chancellor not only attended
the rally, but also chose to speak at the rally as well."[17]

This type of institutional complicity with anti-Israel excesses is unacceptable, and even dangerous, since academic leaders who facilitate this vile
hatred and bigotry help to legitimize it and give Israel's mortal enemies solace
by entering into the "unholy alliance" with the Left mentioned earlier. By
offering the cover of "academic free speech" to radical groups who sponsor or
host events on their campuses, university officials are made morally culpable
by furthering hate speech and anti-Semitism, as was John F. Burness, Duke
University's Senior Vice President for Public Affairs and Government Relations, when he pushed for the invidious Palestinian Solidarity Movement's
2004 conference at Duke. As discussed fully in Chapter 8, based on eyewitness
reports of extremist speech and radical ideas at previous PSM conferences,
the Duke Conservative Union and concerned alumni generated an online

petition with more than 90,000 names, urging Duke's new president, Richard Brodhead, to refuse to provide a venue for the event.

Brodhead not only refused to criticize any aspect of the PSM, but disingenuously claimed that the "deepest principle involved [in hosting the conference] is not even the principle of free speech. It's the principle of education through dialogue."[18] And Vice President Burness was not only the PSM's point man on campus, but he effectively ran interference for the group when outside criticism came flooding in to protest the event.

During one of the closed-to-reporters conference sessions which Burness attended, he noticed the presence of investigative reporter Lee Kaplan from *FrontPage Magazine*, and subsequently wrote a note to David Horowitz, *FrontPage's* publisher, complaining that Kaplan had committed a severe ethical breach of "journalistic integrity" by furtively recording strategy sessions where conference participants were refining tactics to help facilitate terrorism and the destruction of the Jewish state—sessions, Burness said, "which the sponsors had declared off limits to the media."

David Horowitz responded to Mr. Burness, suggesting that the real issue was not the fact that Mr. Kaplan had been able to infiltrate conference proceedings which the radical PSM had clearly wanted no one on the outside to hear, but that Burness, and by extension Duke University, were at fault for letting this morally-challenged hate-fest take place at all. In Horowitz's view, Burness's questioning of the ethics of a reporter covering a university-sponsored event missed the broader, more pertinent point:

> We are not after all discussing an academic conference at Duke concerned with intellectual matters of inquiry and interpretation . . . We are discussing a convention of radical and violent groups, practiced in the art of hate, who have been brought together for the purpose of dismantling and destroying a democratic state that was created as a refuge for the pitifully few survivors of one of the great crimes against humanity in recorded history . . . In this matter, you and the Duke administration have gone out of your way to make possible and to defend at every turn a conference organized by individuals who are driven by a hatred of Jews and who are dedicated to the destruction of the state of Israel by any means necessary—including the murder of innocent civilians, which the attendees went on record refusing to condemn.[19]

Horowitz continued with another key point: many Duke alumni and other concerned stakeholders had warned Brodhead, as noted, of the pernicious character of the PSM event and the group's questionable history at earlier conferences held at other universities. In fact, the Duke administration claimed that those reports were unfounded, and that no evidence existed which would prove the bad intentions of the PSM event and show it to be unworthy of an academic veneer. "If you had been successful in policing those who came to attend the conference," Horowitz concluded in his letter, "Lee Kaplan would never have been allowed to take his tape recorder in to these sessions and the organizers would be able to present their next conference . . . in the same deceptive way they presented this one. And administrators like you would be able to claim that there was no evidence that would be anything but an 'open dialogue' and academic discussion of issues in the Middle East."[20]

4. ***Urge university officials to eliminate the double standard for academic free speech, and to not permit the notion of academic freedom to be abused by extremists pushing a biased ideological agenda***

While coddling selected victim groups and granting them unlimited expression as a purported way to further diversity of thought, college administrators have regularly denied those same rights and privileges to groups deemed not to deserve or need them, namely, conservatives, Christians, Republicans, heterosexuals, white males, or those who seek a strong defense against radical Islamism and terrorism aimed at Western democracies, principally the U.S. and Israel. Universities continually give lip service to how much they embrace the notion of "academic free speech," using it as a license to permit both professors and outside speakers to hurl invectives at the Left's favorite targets, while simultaneously sheltering designated victim groups from any kind of critique or examination. Universities do that by designating speech they do not like—speech against perceived minority groups—as "hate" speech, further proscribing it with punitive speech codes, rigid codes of conduct, or other regulatory vicissitudes emanating from the campus "thought police." In the Israel/Palestinian debate this has had the pernicious effect described earlier in which outrageous extremists and academic cranks are regularly invited to speak against Israel, Jews, and the United States, but when conservative speakers like Daniel Pipes, David Horowitz, or even Benjamin Netanyahu are invited to speak about radical Islam or Israel, their speeches are interrupted or cancelled entirely because the speakers are accused of being Islamophobes, racists, or purveyors of "hate speech."

But institutions of higher education cannot allow this practice to go on any longer. Either a university has to have a policy which says that *no* guest speakers with extreme ideologies will be invited to campus at all—regardless of where on the political spectrum they fall—or, alternatively, they have to decide that *any* speaker, with whatever beliefs, is free to come to campus, but he or she must then be granted the right to present their speech without interruption or unreasonable protest. Those students and faculty who feel that the content of a particular speaker's speech will offend, intimidate, or otherwise bother them are free not to attend; but universities have consistently let radical students with competing ideologies decide what may be said when, and by whom. If opponents of a particular speaker disrupt, heckle, or riot as a tactic for having a speaker's appearance cancelled, they should be expelled from the event or arrested, as necessary, so that willing listeners can hear the speaker's point of view. University administrators have been hesitant to refuse Muslim student demands that certain disfavored speakers even be allowed on campus, for fear of offending the students' sensibilities. But that is a dangerous and hypocritical role for academia to play, suggested classics professor Bruce Thornton. "For here is an important lesson in political philosophy," Thornton wrote, "if you are going to enjoy the right to free expression and expect that right to be protected, as the Muslim students do, then you must acknowledge and respect someone else's right to do the same. You cannot carve out an exception and call it 'hate speech,' a dishonest term created by the diversity commissars to criminalize and stigmatize whatever speech they find politically or ideologically distasteful. And you cannot be allowed to intimidate those others who are exercising their own free-speech rights."[21]

Legal scholar Kenneth L. Marcus, Executive Vice President and Director of the anti-Semitism Initiative at the Institute for Jewish and Community Research and former director of the U.S. Commission on Civil Rights, also accuses universities of using what he calls "First Amendment opportunism" when they provide moral cover for extremist speech on campus with which they seemingly agree, but seek to criminalize other speech on the same campus when it is deemed hate speech by those who disagree with its point of view—its content. In the context of allowing radical anti-Israel, anti-Semitic speakers to degrade the educational environment for Jewish students, the question for Marcus is: "When a state university permits the creation of a hostile environment for certain students, can it really hide from harassment claims behind the First Amendment, when the university actively controlled each of the elements which ultimately created the environment?"[22]

University officials are well aware that it is impermissible for them to knowingly contribute to the creation of a "hostile environment" for any of their students, so when they accede to requests for radical speakers to come to campus, they avoid any legal culpability by hiding behind the convenient shield of academic free speech. "Much of the rhetoric, and some of the legal argument, surrounding campus harassment," wrote Marcus, "and especially campus anti-Semitism . . . consists of agenda-driven efforts, varying in degree of success, to change the topic from harassment to free speech in a context in which the First Amendment is at least arguably inapplicable. These efforts

are fraught with social, legal, and political significance, as they mark a struggle to shift the boundaries of constitutional discourse in a way that could
increase some protections while decreasing others."[23]

But university officials well know that academic freedom is a right but also
a responsibility, and the university, for instance, is certainly not compelled to
offer free speech rights to those outside of the university who come to campus as invited guests. It is not incumbent on universities to offer a soapbox to
anyone, or to use student or taxpayer funds to pay for them, merely because
these speakers wish to make their opinions known and certain students would
like them to be heard. The notion of academic freedom was conceived of as
a way that enabled faculty members to explore intellectual topics without the
fear of offending prevailing orthodoxies. It was never meant to offer outsiders
the unrestrained opportunity to spew forth any quality of ideas on campus,
a right that they would, however, enjoy in the public marketplace where all
speech, in theory, enjoys First Amendment protection.

So when administrators allow fringe extremists, with no authentic academic credentials, to speak on campus and vilify Israel and Jews, and then justify those appearances with talk of "academic free speech" or having created
a "learning experience," they are being disingenuous at best, and are possibly
even violating civil rights law. "From the perspective of antidiscrimination
law," Marcus concluded, "the question here is not whether anti-Zionism is
anti-Semitism, has become anti-Semitism, crosses over into anti-Semitism,
or is a veil for anti-Semitism. Rather, the question is whether specific incidents create a sufficiently hostile environment for Jewish students to deny
them equal educational opportunities. Parsing the matter in this way shows
how high the bar is, and it also focuses us on what the stakes are."[24] When
university leaders watch Jewish students being escorted to safety by the police
from York University or San Francisco State University, they might well have
considered just how high those stakes can be.

5. ***Insist that Middle East studies programs and centers be assessed to
   insure the quality and reveal any inherent bias in their scholarship***

Martin Kramer has long been pointing to the intellectual rot in Middle
East studies programs, made worse with the influx of Saudi funds, which inevitably buys a scholarly world view that airbrushes the defects of Arab totalitarian regimes, ignores radical Islam, and focuses obsessively on the perceived
evils of Zionism, imperialism, and Israel and the United States in hobbling
the evolution of what would otherwise evolve as Middle East democracies.
In fact, Kramer believes that the current body of Middle East scholarship is
guilty of a type of academic malpractice, that the failure to notice the growth

of Islamism and the threat of jihad, the reverence for the Palestinians and the hatred of everything Israeli, and the unfounded optimism that civil societies would emerge in the Arab world all indicate a field of study that is rife with shoddy scholarship, ideology, and identity politics.

Fraught with a mistrust and marginalization of Orientalists who they felt were incapable of analyzing the Middle East accurately through a prism of Western biases, the mandarins of the Middle East Studies Association, and department chairs in programs across the country, boxed themselves in with a Saidian brew of political correctness, postmodernism, and multiculturalism that prevented an honest assessment of the Middle East and its various social pathologies, including nascent Islamism. Had scholars honestly assessed the changing political climate of the region, they may have helped diplomats and policy makers in Washington, who were subsidizing, courtesy of American taxpayers, Middle East studies through Title VI, National Defense Education Act, funding.

Middle East studies also failed because of its singular obsession with Israel and the field's leadership role in promoting the cult of Palestinianism. Kramer surveyed scholarly papers submitted for review in MESA conferences between 2002 and 2005 and found, for example, that "more papers are devoted to Palestine than to any other country. There are ten times as many Egyptians as there are Palestinians, but they get less attention; there are ten times as many Iranians, but Iran gets less than half the attention. Even Iraq, America's project in the Middle East, still inspires only half the papers that Palestine does."

What is worse, Kramer noted, is that each of these scholarly studies "reveals itself to be elaboration of Palestinian nationalist ideology, 'academized' into 'discourse' by grad students and post-docs . . . This same kind of nationalism, practiced in any other field, would be dismissed as primitive pap. But exceptions are regularly made, and standards are regularly suspended, for crudely apologetic and celebratory analysis applied to (and by) Palestinians. Of course, no one dares to call any of this work mediocre, which is why so many mediocre pseudo-academics produce it."[25]

This politicization of Middle East studies did not go unnoticed by all scholars in the field, however, and in 2008 the Association for the Study of the Middle East and Africa (Asmea) was formed as a counterforce to MESA, the single, powerful academic association that had previously represented the interests, and shaped the scholarship, of professors in the field. Asmea was cofounded by Bernard Lewis, the august professor emeritus of Near Eastern studies at Princeton University, whose exemplary academic credentials were directly brought into question by Edward Said in his influential 1978 book

Orientalism. Lewis was exactly the type of Western scholar of the Middle East who for Said was the typical Orientalist, an individual who studied the East through a biased prism of a Western worldview and sensibility. Professor Lewis and some of his fellow Orientalists formed the new association precisely so they could start to take back Middle East studies from the ideologues who now hold tenured chairs at Georgetown, Columbia, Stanford, and elsewhere where Saidian post-colonial theory is still the prevailing academic trend. Because Said's approach assumed a defective West and a guiltless East, scholarship from that field, as noted by Kramer and others, such as Daniel Pipe's Campus Watch, has been rife with bias, conspiracy theories, and contortions of history and fact; and, according to Kramer, "post-Orientalists have made Middle Eastern studies into a mere dependency of the social sciences and relegated themselves to the dubious duty of proving the universality of the latest theories propounded by the trendiest academic celebrities."[26] More seriously, the so-called experts on the Middle East never saw warning signs for 9-11, continue to apologize for terrorist groups like Hamas and Hezbollah, and have never been alarmed by the rising tide of Islamism that inspires worldwide jihad. Universities must evaluate the ideology that informs their Middle East studies programs and centers, and insure that there is some kind of intellectual balance within them. Funders, both private and public, must make continued subsidization contingent on some sweeping changes to reclaim the integrity of scholarship in the field of study.

6. *Rank universities according to their records in providing an educational setting where pro-Israel and Jewish students are not intimidated or harassed*

U.S. News & World Report has created something of a franchise for itself by publishing yearly rankings of business schools and other college programs, guides that highlight the strong programs of certain schools, give visibility and a marketing lift to the chosen schools, and which are used by prospective students to select from various programs. With the same methodology but for a different purpose, the Foundation For Individual Rights In Education (FIRE), a non-profit organization that helps students and faculty preserve their civil rights on campus, in 2009 introduced its own ranking system for colleges and universities, which it published in a full-page ad in *U.S. News & World Report's* "America's Best Colleges" issue. "These Red Alert institutions," FIRE's web site said, "have displayed a severe and ongoing disregard for the fundamental rights of their students or faculty members and are the 'worst of the worst' when it comes to liberty on campus. Students should think twice before attending these schools."[27] Schools that makes FIRE's list include institutions with designated free speech zones or restrictive speech codes, codes of behavior that deprive students of Constitutional rights of speech and assembly, or schools that impose mandatory "sensitivity" or morals indoctrination on resident students as a precondition for enrollment.

A ranking system—one with negative rankings as opposed to positive ones—has been useful for FIRE to raise awareness about egregious restrictions on student speech and behavior on university campuses, and such a ranking system should be introduced to "grade" the performance of colleges and universities in addressing the problems of anti-Semitism and virulent anti-Israelism documented here. Students, and parents and donors as well, could then make an assessment about how comfortable a pro-Israel or Jewish student might feel attending a particular school, and parents and alumni could also make personal determinations about their involvement, based on how successfully an institution was committing itself to a fair discourse about the Middle East. When the Orange County Task Force on Anti-Semitism at UC Irvine prepared its final report, it included recommendations that might well assist students and other stakeholders in making a decision on whether or not to attend that school, and the model would be useful elsewhere— particularly since it also puts the respective school on notice that its decisions and moral behavior have been revealed—in short, that there is accountability for the conditions administrators allow to exist on their campus.

For example, the Orange County Task Force suggested that "Students with a strong Jewish identity should consider enrolling elsewhere unless and until tangible changes are made. It is incumbent on UCI to make itself a hospitable environment, not the Jewish students." Additionally, since there seemed to be one set of rules about student behavior for Muslim students and another set for all other student groups, the Task Force also recommended that "The University should refrain from selective enforcement of its rules and regulations, including its 'Code of Conduct.' If it does not intend to enforce its regulations, the University should eliminate them. Those that remain should be enforced uniformly and fairly." Finally, as if to issue a strong warning about potential consequences for the university if modifications were not made in a way that seemed equitable and acceptable for a public institution, the final recommendation noted that "The Jewish organizations and the Jewish benefactors should be aware that their continued support of an anti-Semitic campus is, in the end, counterproductive and works against their own interests. They should hold the University and its Chancellor accountable."[28]

Dr. Manfred Gerstenfeld, chairman of the Board of Fellows of the Jerusalem Center for Public Affairs, had another novel and potentially useful approach to university rankings, as part of his "counterattack strategy . . . in the fight against boycotts of Israeli academics." Dr. Gerstenfeld's idea was "to propose ranking all universities in the world according to how much they promote evil. Heading the list would be those that promote genocide and murder. They are the logical candidates for universal boycott. The result will be that those Arab and, in particular, Palestinian universities where teachers and students call for genocide, murder, and racism will be among the main universities to boycott."[29] The outright promotion of "genocide and murder" is not extremely prevalent at U.S. universities, but several—Michigan, Duke, Rutgers, and Berkeley, for instance—did play host to the odious Palestinian Solidarity Movement conferences at which the extremist attendees justified and plotted strategy for "resistance" to Israeli occupation, which means, of course, the murder of Jewish civilians.

7. *Answer back to anti-Israelism and anti-Semitism—forcefully, quickly, and repeatedly*

British statesman and philosopher Edmund Burke once famously observed that "All that is necessary for the triumph of evil is that good men do nothing," and that sentiment is applicable today to the problem of the vilification of Israel and Jews on campuses, particularly since jihadists, with their own genocidal intentions, have also decided to play a role in this campaign of the delegitimization of the Jewish state.

Many pro-Israel students and faculty, Jews and non-Jews alike, have been slow to speak back forcefully and defend Israel when it is attacked on campus in speeches, classrooms, student newspapers, conferences, and other venues. Some are merely disinterested because they are out of touch with Middle East politics, and do not participate either way. Some are reticent so they do not draw attention to themselves, lest they be attacked for not showing concern for the Palestinian plight. Others have been cowered into silence because they are afraid of retribution, censure, humiliation, or physical attack.

But speaking back in defense of Israel is necessary and vital, particularly given the sheer bulk of propaganda, lies, distortions of history and fact, and alternative narratives which have been artfully constructed by Israel's mortal foes. In fact, Dr. Gerstenfeld believed that when "the battle on campus" is waged, "counterattack is the best defense,"[30] and the usefulness of that strategy has not been lost on a wide range of Israel's protectors, drawn from academia, business, non-profit organizations, and public life.

Web sites such as Daniel Pipe's Campus Watch have been aggregating articles and surveys of Middle East studies programs, and the faculty who teach in and run them, for the purpose of revealing some of the intellectual rot endemic to the field, and to expose egregious faculty behavior, corrupt scholarship, and outrageous writings and speeches that emanate from these programs. Leftist faculty who see themselves "reviewed" on Campus Watch have naturally accused Pipes' efforts as being a new form of academic McCarthyism, but their protestations are probably due to having been revealed as the intellectual defectives they often are. Former liberal-turned-conservative David Horowitz publishes *FrontPage Magazine*, an online journal that has as its mission to expose liberal bias and extremism in college education, the dangers of Islamism, and the issue of the campus war against Israel and Jews.

Horowitz's Terrorism Awareness Project, which sponsors on-campus events at universities around the country, is another attempt to bring conservative, pro-Israel speakers to campus to counterbalance the vitriolic rhetoric spewed forth by Israel-hating radicals who denounce Jewish power, Zionism, imperialist America, and a catalog of assorted villains. "The sad truth," the Project's web site reads, "is that America generally is sleepwalking through the war on Terror [sic] and our universities are doing something even worse: allowing an unholy alliance to form between the forces of terror and the forces of anti Americanism." Horowitz's goal is to confront this stealth jihad directly by helping to make students aware of the danger of it, and "to publicize and combat activities on campus ranging from the propaganda of pro-terrorist front groups such as the International Solidarity Movement to curricular distortions of disciplines such as Peace Studies."[31]

Dr. Gerstenfeld suggested that in the campus battle to defend Israel from its defamers, it would be useful to use the tactics of "counterattack, ridicule, exposure, name and shame, monitoring, documentation, mobilizing lawyers for arguing and legal actions, seeking allies, and others."[32]

Sometimes those tactics come from Harvard Law School's prolific and intellectually-energetic Alan Dershowitz, a tireless defender of Israel who regularly answers back to assaults from anti-Israel ideologues. His book, *The Case For Israel: Democracy's Outpost*, has now been made into a documentary film which is screened on campuses around the country. He offers to debate any critic of Israel, anywhere, as he did with Jimmy Carter after the former president published his odious book, *Palestine: Peace Not Apartheid* (although Carter cravenly declined the opportunity to debate his libelous claims against Israel).

Islamic scholars Daniel Pipes and Robert Spencer, both pro-Israel, regularly examine in articles and books the ideological bases for jihad and seek expose its role in fomenting protests against Israel which are positioned as mere criticism of the Jewish state's politics. Middle Eastern scholars such as Efraim Karsh and Mitchell Bard try to diffuse the power of counter-factual Arab propaganda that attempts to rewrite history in a way that strengthens the Palestinian claim to the Holy Land, while simultaneously wiping away any moral or historical justification for the creation of Israel.

And student-led, grassroots organizations have also been created to push against the rising tide of anti-Israelism. The David Project, the Boston organization which produced the controversial film *Columbia Unbecoming*, also teaches college students how to defend Israel and answer back when attacks on the Jewish state are made. Also contributing to defense of Israel on campus are the 33 organizations under the umbrella of The Israel on Campus Coalition (ICC), all of whom "are dedicated to working collaboratively to assist students in fostering support for Israel on the college campus." One of ICC's participating organizations, which includes The David Project, is Stand With Us, whose goal is "to give students powerful materials that clearly show the facts about what's really going on in the Middle East and keep alumni informed about what's happening on campus." The Simon Wiesenthal Center, an ICC affiliate organization, has created a Campus Outreach division to serve "colleges and universities by teaching about and confronting anti-Semitism, hate and terrorism, promoting human rights and dignity, standing with Israel, and celebrating diversity and tolerance." Scholars for Peace in the Middle East seeks a peace "in the Middle East [that] is consistent both with Israel's right to exist as a sovereign Jewish state within safe and secure borders, and with the rights and legitimate aspirations of her neighbors [Its] mission is to inform, motivate, and encourage faculty to use their academic skills and disciplines on campus, in classrooms, and in academic publications to develop effective responses to the ideological distortions, including anti-Semitic and anti-Zionist slanders, that poison debate and work against peace."

Part of the reason that anti-Israel factions have managed to be so successful in their mission to denounce and demonize Israel is the lack of balance in the conversation about the competing efforts at self-determination by Israelis and Palestinians. Pro-Israel students and faculty, secure in the righteousness of their Zionist cause (even if they are often aware of some of the troubling moral issues with the lingering occupation), have been slow to make a strong case for Israel on campus. The pro-Israel narrative, also, has never been articulated as anti-Palestinian rhetoric—other than a call for a cessation to Arab terrorism. In other words, those supporting Israel rarely try to justify the Jewish state's existence by pointing to the inherent political deficiencies and moral failures of Palestinian nationalism; as a result, pro-Israel demonstrations on campus, when they occur at all, are usually benign calls for peace, good faith negotiations, an end to terror attacks, and a request that the Arab world recognize Israel's right to exist.

The university's jihad against Israel and Jews is a grim reminder that the world's oldest hatred has not yet vanished; in fact, either because of the widespread negative attitudes towards Israel, or simply due to a lingering, poisonous Jew-hatred in the Arab world and, increasingly, in the West, as well, Jews once again are witness to libels, denunciation, demonization, and slurs against Judaism, against Zionism, and against Israel itself, the Jew of nations.

This hatred appeared on campus when it was promulgated by Leftist professors with a reverence for Palestinian victimization, and Muslim student groups with a foundational, theological hatred of the Jewish state. It spread a result of being enabled by craven administrators who allowed their campuses to be hijacked by radicals with the purported objective of elevating the Palestinian cause, but whose actual purpose was promoting their own noxious agenda for vilifying and eventually eliminating Israel.

The manifestations of these on-campus hatreds have been obvious and ugly: ripped Israeli flags drizzled with blood; Stars of David juxtaposed with swastikas; charges of apartheid, racism, and genocide leveled against Israelis and assigned also to their proxies, American Jews; accusations of dual loyalties, with American Jews accused of undermining American interests with the furtive purpose of assisting Israel; physical threats against Jewish students; and blood libels which transform Israelis into murderous, subhuman monsters who almost gleefully shed Arab blood in their insatiable quest for land which, their critics say, they neither deserve nor for which they have any legitimate claim.

The campus war against Israel is also indicative of the devolution of higher education, where scholarship has been degraded by bias and extremism on the part of a Leftist professoriate with a clear political agenda that enlists Israel as the new villain in a world yearning for social justice. University leaders and other stakeholders have been noticeably feckless in moderating this radicalism, either because they are unaware of how whole fields of study have been hijacked by academic frauds and morally incoherent scholars, or because they sympathize with the intellectual approach of their faculties and have become complicit with the production of pseudo-scholarship, academic agitprop, and disingenuous "learning experiences" which have a one-sided, biased approach to understanding the Middle East, and particularly the Israeli/Palestinian conflict.

That all this is taking place in the rarified air of college campuses, where civil discourse is the expected norm and scholarly inquiry is the anticipated intellectual product, makes the seething hatreds and bias against Israel and the Jews all the more unexpected and morally dangerous. Only six decades after one of the most horrific crimes against humanity that saw the murder of some six million souls, the same unsettling tropes against Jews are being restated, this time often targeting the Jewish state that arose, in part, from the ashes of the Holocaust. One would hope this battle would not have to be waged again, that college students, Jews and non-Jews alike, would not have to be confronted with "the longest hatred" once again, this time conflated with the very survival of a tiny democratic Jewish state, precariously coexisting amid a sea of jihadist foes who seek its very elimination.

Israel in some respect has become the canary in the mine of Western civilization, and its survival, or elimination, may well presage the end result of the "clash of civilizations" that political scientist Samuel Huntington first alluded to in the 1990s. The campus Left may have become critical of Israel out a purported concern for the oppressed Palestinians, with whose suffering they identify; but the larger question, and the more dangerous one, is why Israel has become the obsession of radical Islamists, and how their millennial hatred for the "Little Satan" will inevitably morph into a broader jihad against the United States, the "Great Satan," as well—not merely because of the United States' support for Israel, but because both nations are comprised of infidels.

One would hope, too, that a new generation of college graduates— who enter the world as journalists, politicians, diplomats, professors, even parents—would not have been poisoned during their college experience with distortions about Israel and its history, that young people do not learn about the Middle East by "marinating in hatred," as commentator Mark Steyn put it, and leave their universities after graduation despising, distrusting, and vilifying a nation for no other reason than it happens to be lived in by Jews.

ð Notes

Chapter 1

1. Gabriel Schoenfeld, *The Return of Anti-Semitism*, San Francisco: Encounter Books, 2004.
2. Phyllis Chesler, *The New Anti-Semitism: The Current Crisis and What We Must Do About It*, San Francisco: Jossey-Bass, 2003.
3. Edward Baehr and Ed Laksy, "Stephen Walt's War With Israel," *The American Thinker*, March 20, 2006. http://www.americanthinker.com/2006/03/stephen_walts_war_with_israel.html.
4. Chessler.
5. Alan Charles Kors and Harvey A. Silverglate, *The Shadow University: The Betrayal of Liberty on America's Campuses*, New York: The Free Press, 1998.
6. Charles J.Sykes, *A Nation of Victims: The Decay of the American Character*. New York: St. Martin's Griffin, 1993.
7. Jay Bergman, "Liberal Colleges Need a Different Kind of Diversity," *Hartford Courant*, October 20, 2002.
8. Jamie Glasov,*United in Hate: The Left's Romance with Tyranny and Terror*. Los Angeles: WND Books, 2009.
9. Ibid.
10. James Burnham, *The Suicide of the West: An Essay on the Meaning and Destiny of Liberalism*, Washington, DC: Regnery Publishing, 1985.
11. Juan Cole, "Have Arabs or Muslims Always Hated Jews?" *Informed Comment*, December 14, 2004: http://www.juancole.com/2004/12/have-arabs-or-muslims-always-hated.html.
12. Joseph Massad, "Israel's Right To Defend Itself," *The Electronic Intifada*, January 20, 2009: http://electronicintifada.net/v2/article10221.shtml.
13. Ramin Afshar-Mohajer and Evelyn Sung, "The Stigma of Inclusion: Racial Paternalism/Separatism in Higher Education," New York: New York Civil Rights Coalition, 2002.

14. Daniel B. Klein and Charlotta Stern, "How Politically Diverse Are the Social Sciences and Humanities?" Santa Clara, CA: Santa Clara University, 2003.

15. Ruth Wisse, *If I Am Not For Myself: The Liberal Betrayal of the Jews*, New York: The Free Press, 1992.

16. Jewish Virtual Library, "Khalid Abdul Muhammad," *Jewish Virtual Library*, August 25, 2011: http://www.jewishvirtuallibrary.org/jsource/anti-semitism/Khalid.html.

17. Robert Spiro, "Black Students' Attack on Pipes Misguided," *Yale Daily News*, November 7, 2003.

18. David Horowitz, *Unholy Alliance: Radical Islam and the American Left*, Washington, DC: Regnery Publishing, 2004.

19. Ibid.

20. Ibid.

21. National Association of Scholars, "The Scandal of Social Work Education," Princeton, NJ, 2007.

22. Ibid.

23. Ron Radosh, "The Real Agenda of the New Student Left," *FrontPage Magazine*, April 12, 2002: http://www.frontpagemag.com/Articles.Read.aspx?GUID=BAF95ED1-E3AC-427F-B2DF-AE4FD5732628

24. Bruce Thornton, "High Anxiety: How modernity feeds Arab anti-Semitism," *Private Papers*, December 20, 2006: http://www.victorhanson.com/articles/thornton122006PF.html.

25. Mark Strauss, "Antiglobalism's Jewish Problem," *Foreign Affairs*, November 12, 2003.

26. Ibid.

27. Ibid.

28. Hollander.

29. Glasov.

30. Joel Beinin, quoted in David Horowitz, "Joel Beinin: Apologist for Terrorists," *FrontPage Magazine*, May 19, 2006. http://archive.frontpagemag.com/readArticle.aspx?ARTID=4357.

31. Joel Kovel, "Zionism's Bad Conscience," *Tikkun Magazine*, September/October 2002.

32. Andrew Dalack and Julia Eden Ris, "A blueprint for conversation," *The Michigan Daily*, April 10, 2007: http://www.michigandaily.com/content/viewpoint-blueprint-conversation.

33. Tzvi Fleischer, "The far Left and radical Islamist international alliance," *The Australian*, June 8, 2006. Quoted at: http://www.camera.org/index.asp?x_context=7&x_issue=11&x_article=1151.

34. Paul Hollander, "The Left's Love Affair With the Palestinians," *Front-Page Magazine*, November 6, 2003: http://www.travelbrochuregraphics. com/extra/the_lefts_love_affair_with_the_palestinians.htm.

35. Wisse, *If I Am Not For Myself: The Liberal Betrayal of the Jews*.

36. Ibid.

37. Ibid.

38. Ibid.

39. Zachary Hughes, "Noam Chomsky's Support for Hezbollah," Committee for Accuracy in Middle East Reporting in America (CAMERA), July 20, 2006, quoting Chomsky: http://www.camera.org/index.asp? x_context=7&x_issue=11&x_article=1151.

40. Jennifer Lowenstein, "If Hamas Did Not Exist," *CounterPunch*, January 1, 2009: http://www.counterpunch.org/loewenstein01012009.html.

41. Tony Judy, "Israel: The Alternative," *The New York Review of Books*, October 23, 2003: http://www.nybooks.com/articles/archives/2003/oct/23/ israel-the-alternative.

42. Richard Falk, "Slouching Toward a Palestinian Holocaust," *ZNet*, July 5, 2007: http://www.zcommunications.org/slouching-toward-a-pales-tinian-holocaust-by-richard-falk.

43. Hamid Dabashi, "For a Fistful of Dust: A Passage to Palestine," *Al-Ahram Weekly*, September 23-29, 2004: http://weekly.ahram.org. eg/2004/709/cu12.htm.

44. "Israel embarks on PR face-lift," *The Washington Times*, December 5, 2006, quoting David Saranga.

45. Melanie Phillips, "Academic Inti-fad-a," *FrontPage Magazine*, April 13, 2005: http://archive.frontpagemag.com/readArticle.aspx?ARTID=8976.

Chapter 2

1. James Dorsey, "Wij zijn alleen Palestijn om politieke reden," *Trouw*, March 1977.

2. Bat Ye'or, "Arafat's Legacy for Europe," *FrontPage Magazine*, November 16, 2004: http://archive.frontpagemag.com/readArticle. aspx?ARTID=10558.

3. Ibid.

4. Bat Ye'or, Interview by Jamie Glasov, "The Palestinianization of Europe," *FrontPage Magazine*, April 26, 2007: http://archive.frontpagemag.com/ readArticle.aspx?ARTID=26359.

5. Bruce Thronton, "The Civilizations of Dhimmitude," *Private Papers*, March 26, 2006: http://victorhanson.com/articles/thornton032605.html.

6. Julian Perez, "Divest now from a racist government," *Yale Daily News*, November 15, 2002: http://www.yaledailynews.com/news/2002/nov/15/divest-now-from-a-racist-government.

7. Desmond Tutu, "Apartheid in the Holy Land," *The Guardian*, April 29, 2002: http://www.guardian.co.uk/world/2002/apr/29/comment.

8. Jimmy Carter, Interview on National Public Radio, "Palestinians Under Occupation," December 14, 2006.

9. Eugene Gu, "On Apartionalism — Nationalist Apartheid," *Stanford Daily*, March 5, 2007: http://www.stanforddaily.com/2007/03/04/op-ed-on-apartionalism-nationalist-apartheid.

10. Joel Kovel, "The One-State Solution: Zionism and the future of Israel/Palestine," *Briarpatch Magazine*, July 20, 2007: http://briarpatchmagazine.com/articles/view/the-one-state-solution-zionism-and-the-future-of-israelpalestine.

11. New Jersey Solidarity; Rutgers University Campaign for Divestment from Israeli Apartheid, *Divestment for Israeli Apartheid: Acting for Human Rights, Taking a Stand for Justice*, 2003: http://www.rutgersdivest.org/whydivest.html.

12. Humza Chowdhry, "The Holocaust of our era," *Spartan Daily*, March 18, 2008: http://spartandaily.com/2.14808/letter-to-the-editor-the-holocaust-of-our-era-1.1935770.

13. Hanadie Yousef, "Israel's pullout from Gaza is a charade," *The Tartan*, October 17, 2005: http://thetartan.org/2005/10/17/forum/palestine.

14. Nicholas Guyatt, "A colonizing power," *Daily Princetonian*, April 23, 2002: http://www.dailyprincetonian.com/2002/04/23/5011.

15. Chowdhry.

16. Paul Pryce, "Israel promotes imperialism," *The Badger Herald*, September 27, 2006: http://badgerherald.com/oped/2006/09/27/israel_promotes_impe.php.

17. David Horowitz, "Gaza: Red-Letter Day For Arab and Leftist Jew-Haters," *FrontPage Magazine*, August 18, 2005: http://archive.frontpagemag.com/readArticle.aspx?ARTID=7556.

18. Edward W. Said, *Orientalism*, New York: Vintage Books, 1979.

19. Edward W. Said, "East Isn't East: The Impending Age of Orientalism," *The Times Literary Supplement*, February 3, 1995.

20. Martin Kramer, *Ivory Towers in the Sand: The Failure of Middle Eastern Studies in America*, Washington, DC: The Washington Institute for Near East Policy, 2001.

21. Said, *Orientalism.*
22. Bruce Thronton, "Golden Threads: Former Mulsim Ibn Warraq Stands Up For the West," *City Journal*, August 17, 2007: http://www.city-journal.org/html/rev2007-08-17bt.html.
23. M. Shaid Alam, "How To be a Good Victim," *CounterPunch*, August 27-28, 2005: http://www.counterpunch.org/2005/08/27/how-to-be-a-good-victim.
24. Said, *Orientalism.*
25. Kramer.
26. Ibn Warraq, *Defending the West: A Critique of Edward Said's Orientalism*, New York: Prometheus Books, 2007.
27. Hamid Debashi, "For a Fistful of Dust: A Passage to Palestine," *Al-Ahram Weekly*, September 23, 2004: http://weekly.ahram.org.eg/2004/709/cu12.htm.
28. Mariam Moustafa, "Palestinian Plight Puts a Pall on the Party," *New University*, May 12, 2008: http://www.newuniversity.org/2008/05/opinion/palestinian_plight_puts_a153.
29. Lee Kaplan, "Princeton's Anti-Israel Jihad," *FrontPage Magazine*, January 24, 2005: http://archive.frontpagemag.com/readArticle.aspx?ARTID=9847.
30. Charles Jacobs, "Becoming Columbia," *The Spectator*, April 11, 2005: http://www.columbiaspectator.com/vnews/display.v/ART/2005/04/11/4259dce9c9205.
31. Ruth Wisse, "Anti-Semitism on Campus," *The Wall Street Journal*, December 13, 2002: http://isurvived.org/2Postings/Anti-Semitism_Wisse_Ruth.htm.

Chapter 3

1. Ruth R. Wisse, *If I am Not For Myself: The Liberal Betrayal of the Jews.*
2. David Solway, "Jewish Self-Hatred for Dummies," *FrontPage Magazine*, February 18, 2009: http://archive.frontpagemag.com/readArticle.aspx?ARTID=34091
3. Tony Judt, "Israel: The Alternative," *The New York Review of Books*, October 23, 2003: http://www.nybooks.com/articles/archives/2003/oct/23/israel-the-alternative.
4. Tony Judt, "In Defense of Academic Freedom," Conference at University of Chicago, October 12, 2007.
5. Schoenfeld, *The Return of Anti-Semitism.*

6. Marc H. Ellis, "Post-Holocaust Jewish Identity and the Academy," *Media Monitor Networks*, May 7, 2001: http://www.mediamonitors.net/marcellis1.html.

7. Ibid.

8. Joel Kovel, "The One-State Solution: Zionism and the future of Israel/Palestine," Interview by Hassan Husseini, *Briarpatch Magazine*, July 20, 2007: http://briarpatchmagazine.com/articles/view/the-one-state-solution-zionism-and-the-future-of-israelpalestine.

9. Scott Jaschik, "Anti-Israel Prof Loses Post at Bard," *Inside Higher Ed.com*, February 19, 2009: http://www.insidehighered.com/news/2009/02/19/kovel.

10. Glen Reynolds, "Kent State Professor Julio Cesar Pino," *Instapundit.com*, April 18, 2002: http://www.pajamasmedia.com/instapundit-archive/archives/001013.php.

11. Candace deRussy, "Professor Jihad," *FrontPage Magazine*, March 7, 2007: http://97.74.65.51/readArticle.aspx?ARTID=25691.

12. Mike Adams, " "Pino 911," *Town Hall.com*, September 14, 2007: http://townhall.com/columnists/MikeAdams/2007/09/14/pino_911.

13. *RateMyProfessors.com*, Julio Pino—Kent State University: http://www.ratemyprofessors.com/ShowRatings.jsp?tid=46629&page=1.

14. Mark LeVine, "We Are All Israelis Now?" *AlterNet.org*, September 15, 2001: http://www.alternet.org/story/11513.

15. Jennifer Loewenstein, "If Hamas Did Not Exist," *CounterPunch Magazine.com*, January 1, 2009: http://www.counterpunch.org/loewenstein01012009.html.

16. Sara Roy, "Israel's 'victories' in Gaza come at a steep price," *Christian Science Monitor*, January 2, 2009: http://www.csmonitor.com/Commentary/Opinion/2009/0102/p09s01-coop.html.

17. Norman Finkelstein, *Beyond Chutzpah: On the Misuse of Anti-Semitism and the Abuse of History*, Berkeley, CA: The University of California Press, 2005.

18. Omar Bartov, "A Tale of Two Holocausts," *The New York Times*, August 6, 2000: http://www.nytimes.com/books/00/08/06/reviews/000806.06bartovt.html.

19. David Greenberg, " Anti-Semitism—And Not very Good Anti-Semitism at That," *BeliefNet.com*: http://www.beliefnet.com/Entertainment/2000/09/Anti-Semitism-And-Not-Very-Good-Anti-Semitism-At-That.aspx.

20. Edward Alexander, "Academics Against Israel: Martin Jay Explains How Jews Cause Anti-Semitism," *NATIV Online*, Ariel Center for Policy Research.org, 2003: http://www.acpr.org.il/ENGLISH-NATIV/issue1/alexander-1.htm.

21. Roz Rothstein, "Beware the Finkelstein Syndrome," *The Jewish Journal of Greater Los Angeles*, June 8, 2006: http://www.jewishjournal.com/opinion/article/beware_the_finkelstein_syndrome_20060609.

22. Norman Finkelstein, "Speaking Engagements," *Norman Finkelstein.com*: http://www.normanfinkelstein.com/?norman_finkelstein=see_him_live.

23. Middle East Media Research Institute, "American Political Scientist Norman Finkelstein: 'Israel Has to Suffer a Defeat,'" *MEMRI.org*, February 20, 2008: http://www.memri.org/report/en/0/0/0/0/0/0/2575.htm

24. Norman Finkelstein, "Edited Remarks on Hizbullah and Israel," Interview on Future TV, Lebanon, *American Rhetoric.com*, January 20, 2008: http://www.americanrhetoric.com/speeches/normanfinkelsteinmemritvfuturelebanon.htm.

25. Khaled Abu Toameh, "Haniyeh: Hamas will liberate Palestine," *Jerusalem Post*, December 14, 2009: http://www.jpost.com/servlet/Satellite?cid=1260447436498&pagename=JPost/JPArticle/ShowFull.

26. *Today's Zaman*, Interview: "Norman Finkelstein: Israel is committing a holocaust in Gaza," December 18, 2009: http://www.todayszaman.com/tz-web/detaylar.do?load=detay&link=164483.

27. Selcuk Gultasli, "Norman Finkelstein: Israel is committing a holocaust in Gaza," *Today's Zaman*, January 19, 2009: http://www.todayszaman.com/tz-web/detaylar.do?load=detay&link=164483.

28. Arthur Schlesinger, Letter to the Editor: "Truman's Speech & Noam Chomsky," *Commentary Magazine*, December 1969: http://www.commentarymagazine.com/article/trumans-speech-noam-chomsky.

29. Edward Alexander, "Noam Chomsky's Hatreds," *FrontPage Magazine*, May 6, 2006: http://97.74.65.51/readArticle.aspx?ARTID=8760.

30. Bruce Thornton, "Debunking the Ayatollah of Anti-Americanism," *FrontPage Magazine*, August 4, 2004: http://97.74.65.51/readArticle.aspx?ARTID=12023.

31. Noam Chomsky, Interview LBC-TV, May 23, 2006: http://memritv.org/clip/en/1152.htm.

32. Paul Bogdanor, "The Wit and Wisdom of Noam Chomsky," *PaulBogdanor.com*, quoting Chomsky *from La Jornada*, September 15, 2001: http://www.paulbogdanor.com/chomsky/quotes.html.

33. Bogdanor, quoting Chomsky, "The Devil State: Chomsky's War Against Israel," *PaulBogdanor.com*, http://www.paulbogdanor.com/chomsky/bogdanor.pdf.

34. Noam Chomsky, *Peace in the Middle East? Reflections on Justice and Nationhood*, New York: Pantheon Books, 1974.

35. Noam Chomsky, "Anti-Semitism, Zionism, and the Palestinians," *Variant*, October 11, 2002: http://www.variant.org.uk/16texts/Chomsky.html.

36. Merav Yudilovitch, "Apocalypse near (Part one)," *Yedioth Ahronoth*, August 4, 2004: http://www.ynetnews.com/articles/0,7340,L-3286204,00.html.

37. Noam Chomsky, *Fateful Triangle: The United States, Israel and the Palestinians*, London: Pluto Press, 1999.

38. Noam Chomsky, "Scenes From the Uprising," *Z Magazine*, July 1988: http://www.chomsky.info/articles/198807—.htm.

39. Marev Yudilovitch, "Apocalypse Near (Part two)," *YnetNews.com*, August 4, 2006: http://www.ynetnews.com/articles/0,7340,L-3286214,00.html.

40. Noam Chomsky, LBC-TV Interview.

41. "The Covenant of Hamas: Main Points," *Israel Ministry of Foreign Affairs*, August 18, 1988: http://www.mfa.gov.il/MFA/MFAArchive/1980_1989/THE+COVENANT+OF+THE+HAMAS+-+MAIN+POINTS+-+18-Aug-8. htm.

42. Noam Chomsky, Interview Al Manar TV, May 13, 2006.

43. Chomsky, *Fateful Triangle: The United States, Israel and the Palestinians*, p. 21.

44. "Noam Chomsky: 'Hezbullah's insistence on keeping its arms is justi-fied': MIT prof met with Nasrallah at terrorist HQ in May," *Militant Islam Monitor.org*, July 20, 2006: http://www.militantislammonitor.org/article/id/2143.

45. Hassan Nasrallah, *Daily Star*, October 23, 2002, cited in "Quotes from the Islamic World," *Target of Opportunity.com*: http://www.targetofop-portunity.com/political_quotes_islam.htm.

46. Steven Emerson, "Worst Approach to Counter-terrorism Yet," *IPT News*, September 18, 2007: http://www.investigativeproject.org/474/worst-approach-to-counter-terrorism-yet.

47. John L. Esposito, *The Islamic Threat: Myth or Reality?*, New York: Oxford University Press, 1992.

48. Kramer, p. 22.

49. Ibid., p. 45.

50. Esposito, "The Future of Islam," *Fletcher Forum of World Affairs*, 2001, pp. 19, 32.

51. Esposito, "It's the Policy, Stupid: Political Islam and U.S. Foreign Pol-icy," *Harvard International Review*, May 2, 2007: http://hir.harvard.edu/its-the-policy-stupid. Emphasis added.

52. Esposito, "History Lessons From John L. Esposito," *Al Ahram Weekly*, July 22-28, 2004: http://ics.leeds.ac.uk/papers/vp01.cfm?outfit=pmt&folder=1393&paper=1697.

53. Ahmad Faiz bin Abdul Rahman, "Islamo facists at UN for 'Islamopho-bia 'seminar—Kofi 'Inane' hosts John Esposito and Hani El Banna

at the 'United Nazis,'" *Militant Islam Monitor*, September 19, 1997: http://www.militantislammonitor.org/article/id/337.

54. Steven Emerson, "John Esposito: Defending Radical Islam," *Investigative Project on Terrorism.com*, Accessed December 20, 2009: http://www.investigativeproject.org/documents/misc/304.pdf.

55. "John Esposito: Reputation vs. Reality," *IPT News*, September 30, 2009: http://www.investigativeproject.org/1443/john-esposito-reputation-vs-reality. Emphasis added.

56. Ibid.

57. Kramer, p. 124.

58. Franck Salameh, "Seeking True Diversity in Middle East Studies," *FrontPage Magazine*, January 16, 2008: http://97.74.65.51/readArticle.aspx?ARTID=29553.

59. Juan Cole, "200,000 Israeli Fascists Demand Colonization of Gaza," *Informed Comment.com*, July 26, 2004: http://www.juancole.com/2004/07/200000-israeli-fascists-demand.html.

60. Ibid.

61. Cole, "Dual Loyalties," *Informed Comment.com*, September 9, 2004: http://www.juancole.com/2004/09/dual-loyalties-many-readers-have.html.

62. Cole, "Pentagon/Israel Spying Case Expands: Fomenting a War on Iran," *Informed Comment.com*, August 29, 2004: http://www.juancole.com/2004/08/pentagonisrael-spying-case-expands.html.

63. Cole, "Have Arabs or Muslims always Hated Jews?" *Informed Comment.com*, December 14, 2004: http://www.juancole.com/2004/12/have-arabs-or-muslims-always-hated.html.

64. Cole, "Iraq Comes to London," *Informed Comment.com*, July 8, 2005: http://www.geocities.com/martinkramerorg/Documents/ColeLondon.htm. Cole actually removed the passages referring to Jenin after discovering his error, so the existing web page on his blog no longer contains the Jenin misinformation but Martin Kramer archived it here.

65. Joel Beinin, "Is Terrorism a Useful Term in Understanding the Middle East and the Palestinian-Israeli Conflict?" *Project Muse*, Winter 2003: http://www.why-war.com/files/85.1beinin.pdf.

66. Beinin, "The Good War," *The Nation*, May 31, 2004: http://www.thenation.com/doc/20040531/beinin/print?rel=nofollow 4/13/2009.

67. Ibid.

68. Cinnamon Stillwell, "The Professor's Obsession," *FrontPage Magazine*, June 2, 2009: http://archive.frontpagemag.com/readArticle.aspx?ARTID=35066.

Chapter 4

1. Stephen Eric Bronner, *A Rumor about the Jews: Antisemitism, Conspiracy, and the Protocols of Zion*, New York: Oxford University Press, 2003, p. 140.
2. Richard Baehr and Ed Lasky, "Stephen Walt's War with Israel," *American Thinker*, March 20, 2006: http://www.americanthinker.com/2006/03/stephen_walts_war_with_israel.html.
3. Richard Hofstadter, "The Paranoid Style in American Politics," *Harper's Magazine*, November 1964. pp. 77-86.
4. John J. Mearsheimer and Stephen M Walt, "The Israel Lobby and U.S. Foreign Policy," White Paper, Cambridge: Kennedy School of Government, Harvard University, 2006.
5. Eliot A. Cohen, "Yes, It's Anti-Semitic," *Washington Post*, April 5, 2006.
6. Melanie Phillips, "The graves of academe," *MelaniePhillips.com*, March 24, 2006: http://www.melaniephillips.com/diary/archives/001643.html.
7. Hofstadter, 1964.
8. Mearsheimer & Walt, 2006.
9. Ibid.
10. Ibid.
11. Ibid.
12. Jonathan S. Tobin, "The Paranoid Style of Politics: The Chasm Between Main Street Acedmia and Main Street America Grows," *Jewish Exponent*. March 30, 2006: http://www.jewishexponent.com/article/2893/.
13. Alan Dershowitz, "Debunking the Newest–and Oldest–Jewish Conspiracy: A Reply to the Mearsheimer-Walt 'Working Paper'": White Paper, Cambridge: Harvard University, 2006.
14. Caroline B. Glick, "The Jewish Threat," *Jewish World Review*, March 24, 2006: http://www.jewishworldreview.com/0306/glick032406.php3.
15. Baehr & Lasky, 2006.
16. Michael Barkun, *A Culture of Conspiracy: Apocalyptic Visions in Contemporary America*, Berkeley: University of California Press, 2003.
17. Hofstadter, 1964.
18. Gordon McFee, "Why Revisionism Isn't," *The Holocaust History Project*, May 15, 1999: http://www.holocaust-history.org/revisionism-isnt.
19. Baehr & Lasky, 2006.
20. Ruth Wisse, "Israel Lobby," *The Wall Street Journal*, March 22, 2006: http://online.wsj.com/article/SB114299039902704761.html?mod=opinion&ojcontent=otep.
21. Tony Judt, "A Lobby, Not a Conspiracy," *New York Times*, April 19, 2006: http://www.nytimes.com/2006/04/19/opinion/19judt.html.

22. Alex Safian, "Tony Judt, *The New York Times*, and the anti-Israel bandwagon," Committee for Accuracy in Middle East Reporting in America, April 19, 2006: http://www.camera.org/index.asp?x_context=2&x_outlet=35&x_article=1116.

23. Wisse, 2006.

24. Baehr & Lasky, 2006.

25. Jacob Laksin, "'Israel Lobby' Redux," *FrontPage Magazine.com*, September 4, 2007: http://www.frontpagemag.com/Articles/Read.aspx?GUID=C747D4E8-003D-4454-8E35-589E6B5743F9.

26. Ibid.

27. Lenny Ben-David, "Echoing the Moans of Anti-Israel Ghosts: Do Israel's Critics Have Anything Original to Say?," *National Review Online*, September 4, 2007: http://www.standwithus.com/pdfs/flyers/wm_Lenny%20Ben-David_NRO.pdf.

28. Hofstadter, 1964.

29. Nadav Shragai, "Digs, lies and the Mugrabi bridge," *Haaretz,*, November 2, 2007.

30. Jamie Glasov, "The Fight For Jerusalem: An Interview With Dore Gold," *FrontPage Magazine*, February 22, 2007: http://www.frontpagemag.com/Articles/Read.aspx?GUID=0f4c5809-00bd-4c9b-9b6e-34329a5a77e2.

31. Stephen Schwartz, "Politicizing Archaeology in the Holy Land: The Revisionism of Barnard College's Nadia Abu El-Haj." *Family Security Matters.org*, March 21, 2007: http://www.familysecuritymatters.org/challenges.php?id=818521.

32. Nadia Abu El-Haj, *Facts on the Ground: Archaeological Practice and Territorial Self-Fashioning in Israeli Society*, Chicago: University of Chicago Press, 2002.

33. Martin Kramer, "What do the financial crisis and U.S. Middle East policy have in common?," *Sandbox*, November 26, 2008: http://sandbox.blog-city.com/what_do_the_financial_crisis_and_us_middle_east_policy_hav.htm.

34. David Meir-Levy, "'Facts on the Ground:' Nadia Abu el-Haj's New Salvo in the Arab Propaganda War Against Israel." *Solomonia.com*, August 15, 2007: http://www.solomonia.com/blog/archive/2007/08/david-meirlevy-facts-on-the-ground-nadia.

35. Aren M. Maeir, "Freedom of Speech or Freedom of Slander?," *Columbia Spectator*, September 21, 2007: http://www.columbiaspectator.com/2007/0920/freedom-speech-or-freedom-slander.

36. Ami Isseroff, "Nadia Abu El Haj Versus Written History and the Scientific Method," *ZioNation Blog*.com, November 6, 2007: http://www.zionism-israel.com/log/archives/00000443.html.

37. El-Haj, 2002.

38. Ibid.

39. Ibid. (*emphasis added*)

40. Ibid.

41. Diana Muir and Avigail Appelbaum, "Review of Nadia Abu el-Haj's *Facts on the Ground; Archaeological Practice and Territorial Self-Fashioning in Israeli Society*," *History News Network*, May 31, 2007: http://hnn.us/roundup/comments/25976.html.

42. El-Haj, 2002.

43. Ibid.

44. Ibid.

45. Ibid.

46. Alan F. Segal, "Some Professional Observations on the Controversy about Nadia Abu El-Haj's First Book," *Columbia Spectator*, September 21, 2007: http://www.campus-watch.org/article/id/4171

47. Jonathan Lis, "Arab League blasts Temple Mount dig for 'altering features' of Jerusalem," *Haaretz*, November 2, 2007: http://www.haaretz.com/news/arab-league-blasts-temple-mount-dig-for-altering-features-of-jerusalem-1.212416

48. Meir-Levy, 2007.

49. Ralph Harrington, "Bulldozer archaeology?: Excavation, earthmoving and archaeological practice in Israel," *Harringtonmiscellany.wordpress.com*, 2007: http://harringtonmiscellany.wordpress.com/essays/bulldozer-archaeology.

50. Edward W. Said, "Memory, inequality, and power: Palestine and the universality of human rights," *Journal of comparative poetics*, January 01, 2004.

51. Bruce Thornton, "The Stink: What makes the worst lies in the Middle East acceptable?," *Victor Hanson.com*, February 18, 2007: http://victorhanson.com/articles/thornton021807.html.

52. Nadav Shragai, "Group petitions court to stop Muslim dig on Temple Mount," *Haaretz*, September 9, 2007: http://www.haaretz.com/news/group-petitions-court-to-stop-muslim-dig-on-temple-mount-1.229104

Chapter 5

1. Marvin Kalb and Carol Saivetz, "The Israeli-Hezbollah War of 2006: The Media As A Weapon in Asymmetrical Conflict," Shorenstein Center For Press & Public Policy, Harvard University, 2007.

2. Ibid.

3. Honest Reporting, "The Gaza War in Review," *HonestReporting.com*, 2009: http://www.honestreporting.com/articles/45884734/critiques/The_Gaza_War_in_Review.asp.

4. J. Lorand Matory, "Israel and Censorship at Harvard," *Harvard Crimson*, September 14, 2007: http://www.thecrimson.com/article/2007/9/14/israel-and-censorship-at-harvard-since.

5. Michael Rubin, "Academic Standards, R.I.P.," *FrontPage Magazine*, June 14, 2005: http://archive.frontpagemag.com/readArticle.aspx?ARTID=8272.

6. Matory, 2007.

7. Ibid.

8. Ibid.

9. Rubin, 2005.

10. Kyle Szarzynski, "Israel lobby censors academic honesty," *The Badger Herald*, September 11, 2007: http://badgerherald.com/oped/2007/09/11/israel_lobby_censors.php.

11. Bruce Thornton, "Ideology Trumps Truth on Campus," *City Journal*, November 25, 2007: http://www.city-journal.org/html/eon2007-11-21bt.html.

12. AAUP, 1940 Statement of Principles on Academic Freedom and Tenure, *American Association of University Professors.org*: http://www.aaup.org/AAUP/pubsres/policydocs/contents/1940statement.htm.

13. Gary A Tobin, et al, *The UnCivil University: Politics & Propaganda in Higher Education, San Francisco:* Institute for Jewish & Community Research, 2005.

14. Melanie Phillips, "Academic Inti-fad-a," *FrontPage Magazine*, April 13, 2005: http://www.frontpagemag.com/Articles/Printable.aspx?GUID=48F96755-7354-42FB-847E-DD6F30B100C0.

15. Thornton, 2007.

16. Herbert Marcuse, et al, *A Critique of Pure Tolerance*, Boston: Beacon Press, 1969. pp. 95-137.

17. Lawrence H. Summers, "Address at Morning Prayers," Harvard University, September 17, 2002: http://www.harvard.edu/president/speeches/summers_2002/morningprayers.php.

18. Robert F. Worth, "Poet Who Spoke Against Israel Is Reinvited to Talk at Harvard," *The New York Times*, November 21, 2002.

19. Lawrence H. Summers, "Ask Not...," *Wall Street Journal Opinion*, November 2, 2001: http://online.wsj.com/article/SB122660480302325303.html.

20. Tufts University, "Outcome of the Committee on Student Life's Hearing of Complaints Brought by David Dennis and the Muslim Student

Association Against *The Primary Source*," Medford, MA: Tufts University, 2007: http://www.thefire.org/public/pdfs/5e4f4b4bdadd652d41a4 25c952c43e49.pdf.

21. Maane Khatchatourian and Jenna Ryan, "Officials Investigate Questionable Email," *Daily Nexus*, May 21, 2009: http://www.dailynexus. com/article.php?a=19071.

22. Elliott Rosenfeld, "Investigation of Professor Forges Ahead," *Daily Nexus*, June 4, 2009: http://www.dailynexus.com/2009-06-04/investigation-of-professor-forges-ahead.

23. Committee to Defend Academic Freedom at UCSB, "CDAF-UCSB Response to Case," 2009: http://sb4af.wordpress.com/robinson-case/ charges-responses/cdaf-ucsb-response.

24. Rosenfeld, 2009.

25. Washington University in St. Louis, "Policy Statement on Demonstrations & Disruptions," http://wustl.edu/policies/demonstrations-and-disruption.html.

26. Kelly Dunn, "Horowitz Speech Rejected by SLU," *The University News*, October 1, 2009: http://media.www.unewsonline.com/media/ storage/paper953/news/2009/10/01/News/Horowitz.Speech.Rejected. By.Slu-3790132.shtml.

27. Alan Charles Kors and Harvey Silverglate, *The Shadow University: The Betrayal of Liberty on America's Campuses*, New York : The Free Press, 1998.

28. Anne Bayefsky, "You Can't Say That," *The Weekly Standard*, October 5, 2009: http://www.weeklystandard.com/Content/Public/Articles/000/ 000/017/043ytrhc.asp.

29. Frank C. Pucci, "War crimes are not free expression," *Chicago Maroon*, October 20, 2009: http://www.chicagomaroon.com/2009/10/20/war-crimes-are-not-free-expression#.

30. Ibid.

31. Dafney Tales, "Temple U. uneasy as anti-Islam figure is set to speak," *Philadelphia Daily News*, October 20, 2009: http://articles.philly.com/2009-10-20/news/24987482_1_student-groups-geert-wilders-temple-campus.

32. Brian X. McCrone, "Anger, support for Geert's visit," *Metro International*, October 20, 2009: http://www.metro.us/us/article/2009/10/21/05/1032-85/ index.xml#.

33. Associated Press, "Anti-Islamic Dutch Lawmaker Speaks at US College," *The New York Times*, October 21, 2009.

34. Paul Needham and Esther Zuckerman, "Cartoon controversy returns to campus," *Yale Daily News*, September 30, 2009: http://www.yaledaily-news.com/news/2009/sep/30/cartoon-controversy-returns-to-campus.

35. John Fund, "Taliban Man at Yale," *Wall Street Journal*, March 23, 2006: http://www.opinionjournal.com/diary/?id=110008127, March 23, 2006.

36. Sahm Adrangi, "Not just another conspiracy theory: manipulating anger," *Yale Daily News*, February 26, 2003: http://www.yaledailynews. com/news/2003/feb/26/not-just-another-conspiracy-theory-manipulating.

37. Ibid.

38. Thornton, 2007.

39. Gary A. Tobin, et al, 2005.

Chapter 6

1. Martin Kramer, *Ivory Towers On Sand: The Failure of Middle Eastern Studies in America*, Washington, DC: The Washington Institute for Near East Policy, 2001.

2. Hugh Fitzgerald, "Crisis at Coumbia: That Awful Mess on Morningside Heights," *Campus Watch*, April 14, 2005: http://www.campus-watch.org/article/id/1943.

3. Charles Jacobs, "Becoming Columbia," *Columbia Spectator*, April 11, 2005: http://www.columbiaspectator.com/vnews/display.v/ART/2005/04/11/4259dce9c9205.

4. Joseph Massad, "The Gaza Ghetto Uprising," *The Electronic Intifada*, January 4, 2009: http://electronicintifada.net/v2/article10110.shtml.

5. Columbia University, "Report of the Ad Hoc Grievance Committee," New York: Columbia University, 2003.

6. Ibid.

7. Joseph Massad, "Israel's Right To Defend Itself," *The Electronic Intifada*, January 20, 2009: http://electronicintifada.net/v2/article10221.shtml.

8. Martin Kramer, "Suffering in Silence at Columbia," *Sandbox by Martin Kramer*, January 10, 2006: http://sandbox.blog-city.com/suffering_in_silence_at_columbia.htm.

9. Alec Magnet, "Former Columbia Student: Massad's Bullying, Anti-Israel Stance Led Her to Drop Out," *New York Sun*, January 13, 2006: http://www.nysun.com/article/25831.

10. "Report of the Ad Hoc Grievance Committee," Columbia University, 2003.

11. Ibid.

12. *Columbia Unbecoming*, 2004.

13. Ibid.

14. Xan Nowakowski, "Students Organize Sit-In To Support Palestinians,"

Columbia Spectator, April 18, 2002: http://www.columbiaspectator. com/2002/04/18/students-organize-sit-support-palestinians.

15. Ibid.
16. George Saliba, "Letter to the Editor," *Columbia Spectator,* May 1, 2002.
17. Ibid.
18. Hamid Dabashi, "The Hallowed Ground of Our Secular Institution," *Columbia Spectator,* May 3, 2002.
19. *Columbia Unbecoming,* op. cit.
20. Noah Liben, "The Columbia University Report on Its Middle Eastern Department's Problems: A Methodological Paradigm for Obscuring Structural Flaws," Jerusalem, Israel: Jerusalem Center for Public Affairs, 2005.
21. Ibid.
22. Columbia University, Report of the Ad Hoc Grievance Committee," New York: Columbia University, 2003.
23. Charles Jacobs, "Becoming Columbia," *Columbia Spectator,* April 11, 2005: http://www.columbiaspectator.com/vnews/display.v/ ART/2005/04/11/4259dce9c9205.
24. Ibid.
25. Joseph Massad, "Intimidating Columbia University," *Al-Ahram,* November 4-10, 2004: http://weekly.ahram.org.eg/2004/715/op33.htm.
26. Ibid.
27. Ibid.
28. Dabashi, op. cit.
29. Monique Dols, "'Columbia Unbceoming' In the Clear Light of Day," *The Electronic Intifada,* November 5, 2004: http://electronicintifada.net/ v2/article3296.shtml.
30. Sara Sebrow, "MEALAC Profs: It's Time To Talk," *Columbia Spectator,* November 3, 2004: http://www.columbiaspectator.com/vnews/ display.v/ART/2004/11/03/4188660d11cc1.
31. Cinnamon Stillwell, "UCLA's Politicized Middle East Studies Professors," *FrontPage Magazine,* November 13, 2007: http://archive.frontpagemag.com/readArticle.aspx?ARTID=28813.
32. Efraim Karsh, "Columbia and the Academic Intifada," *Commentary,* July-August 2005: http://www.commentarymagazine.com/article/ columbia-and-the-academic-intifada.
33. Rashid Khalidi, *Palestinian Identity: The Construction of Modern National Consciousness,* New York: Columbia University Press, 1997.
34. Editorial Board of *The New York Sun,* "Right of Resistance?," *The New York Sun,* March 14, 2005.

35. Khalidi, "Basic Truths From Both Sides of the Conflict," *Chicago Tribune*, April 3, 2002: http://www.chicagotribune.com/news/opinion/oped/chi0204030173apr03.story.

36. Ibid.

37. Khalidi, "Are Palestinian Leaders Shortsighted?" Interview with John Ydstie, National Public Radio, June 16, 2007.

38. Fitzgerald, "Crisis at Coumbia: That Awful Mess on Morningside Heights."

39. Scholars for Peace in the Middle East, "Background and Analysis of the Columbia University Administration's Response to Columbia Unbecoming," 2005.

40. Stephen M. Marks, "Harvard Returns Gift to Arab President," *The Harvard Crimson*, July 30, 2004: http://www.thecrimson.com/article.aspx?ref=503246.

41. Steven Emerson, "Wolf to Georgetown: Detail Use of Saudi Millions," *Investigative Project on Terrorism News*, February 15, 2008: http://www.investigativeproject.org/607/wolf-to-georgetown-detail-use-of-saudi.

42. Jay P. Greene, interview by Jamie Glasov, "Why Arabian Gulf States Donate to U.S. Universities," *FrontPage Magazine*, June 9, 2008: http://archive.frontpagemag.com/readArticle.aspx?ARTID=31241.

43. Ibid.

44. Ibid.

45. Ben Shapiro, "King Fahd's Plan to Conquer America," *TownHall.com*, December 20, 2002: http://www.townhall.com/columnists/benshapiro.

46. Lee Kaplan, "The Saudi Fifth Column On Our Nation's Campuses," *FrontPage Magazine*, April 5, 2004: http://frontpagemag.com/Articles/ReadArticle.asp?ID=12833.

47. Jacob Laksin, "Jimmy Carter and the Arab Lobby," *FrontPage Magazine*, December 18, 2006: http://archive.frontpagemag.com/readArticle.aspx?ARTID=1001.

48. Ibid.

49. Kaplan, op. cit.

50. Kramer, *Ivory Towers on Sand*.

Chapter 7

1. Zogby International, 2000.

2. U.S. Census Bureau, 2001.

3.   Zogby International.

4.   Orange County Task Force on Anti-Semitism at UC Irvine, "Report of the Orange County Task Force on Anti-Semitism at UC Irvine," 2008. p. 13.

5.   Ibid.

6.   Ibid.

7.   Muslim Student Union of UC Irvine, "Israel: The Politic of Genocide," 2009: http://www.msu-uci.com/?cat=1&paged=3.

8.   Steven Stotsky, "Chomsky Lite: Anna Baltzer Joins anti-Israel Campaigns," Committee for Accuracy in Middle East Reporting in America, *CAMERA.org*, October 10, 2008: http://www.camera.org/index.asp?x_context=2&x_outlet=118&x_article=1548.

9.   Reem Salahi, "Israel's Crimes in Gaza," *The Electronic Intifada*, March 2, 2009: http://electronicintifada.net/content/israels-crimes-gaza/8102.

10.   Stotsky, Film Review: "Occupation 101," *CAMERA.org*, January 5, 2008: http://www.camera.org/index.asp?x_context=2&x_outlet=118&x_article=1415.

11.   John Perazzo, "The Muslim Student Union—On Campus," *RightSideNews.com*, November 14, 2007: http://www.rightsidenews.com/homeland-security-archives/the-muslim-student-union-on-campus.html.

12.   Anti-Defamation League, "Imam Amir Abdul Malik Ali," *ADL.org*, June 15, 2007: http://www.adl.org/israel/malik_ali.asp.

13.   Brad A. Greenberg, "Files of Fact and Fiction: Academia vs. Israel," *Jewish Journal of Los Angeles: The God Blog*, August 22, 2008.:http://www.jewishjournal.com/thegodblog/item/files_of_fact_and_fiction_academia_vs_israel_20080821/.

14.   Anti-Defamation League, "Mohammad al-Asi," *ADL.org*, February 14, 2008: http://www.adl.org/israel/al_asi.asp.

15.   Ruet Cohen, *Ruet Cohen Blogspot*, February 1, 2007: http://video.google.com/videoplay?docid=5158780407631950723.

16.   Cohen, "Jewish Students Discuss Vandalism With Chancellor," *Campusj.com*, October 24, 2006: http://concerneducistudent.blogspot.com/2007/06/chancellor-drake-didnt-tell-full-truth.html

17.   Susan Estrich, "The Most Corrupt Man in California," *Creators.com*, September 14, 2007: http://www.creators.com/opinion/susan-estrich/the-most-corrupt-man-in-california.html.

18.   For example, Lawrence Summers, then president of Harvard, gave a controversial 2002 speech in which he rejected a divestment petition to withdraw funds from Israel signed by, among others, seventy-four Harvard professors. He observed that anti-Semitic and anti-Israel

attitudes, once the invidious products of fringe groups and right-wing cranks, had begun to appear on college campuses, that "profoundly anti-Israel views are increasingly finding support in progressive intellectual communities. Serious and thoughtful people are advocating and taking actions that are anti-Semitic in their effect if not their intent."

19. Task Force on Anti-Semitism at the University of California, Irvine, 2006.

20. Mark LeVine, "We Are All Israelis Now?", *AlterNet.org*, September 15, 2001: http://www.alternet.org/story/11513.

21. Stanley Kurtz, "Summers Disinvited," *NationalReview.com*, September 15, 2007: http://www.nationalreview.com/corner/148785/summers-disinvited/stanley-kurtz.

22. Ward Churchill, speech in Oakland, California, February 22, 2003: http://www.ratical.org/ratville/CAH/WC022203.txt.

23. UC Davis MSA Web Site, February 1, 2007.

24. Roz Rothstein, "Beware the Finkelstein Syndrome," *The Jewish Journal of Greater Los Angeles*, June 8, 2006: http://www.jewishjournal.com/opinion/article/beware_the_finkelstein_syndrome_20060609/.

25. Robert A. Corrigan, "President's Message: 'Hate speech is not free speech,'" *San Francisco State University.edu*, April 12, 2002: http://www.sfsu.edu/~news/response/nohate.htm.

26. Quoted in John Podhoretz, "Hatefest By The Bay," *New York Post*, May 14, 2002.

27. Facing History and Ourselves, "Antisemitism: The Power of Myth - A Student Movement,", *FacingHistory.org*, May 1, 2008. http://www.facinghistory.org/resources/facingtoday/antisemitism-the-power-myth-1.

28. Cinnamon Stillwell, "SFSU's Legacy Of Intolerance," *San Francisco Chronicle*, December 14, 2004.

29. Joe Eskenazi, "Vitriolic anti-Israel gathering held at SFSU," *San Francisco Chronicle*, July 21, 2006.

30. Lee Kaplan, "Opening a Door for Al-Awda," *FrontPage Magazine*, May 24, 2007: http://archive.frontpagemag.com/readArticle.aspx?ARTID=26712.

31. Kaplan, "Palestinian Radicals at UC Riverside," *FrontPage Magazine*, April 25, 2007: http://archive.frontpagemag.com/readArticle.aspx?ARTID=26256.

32. Discover the Networks, "Al-Awda: Profile," *DiscoverTheNetworks.org*: http://www.discoverthenetworks.org/Articles/alawdaprof.html.

33. Eskenazi, op. cit.

34. Zev Chafets, "Bibi Given an F at Berkeley," *New York Daily News*, November 30, 2000.

35. "Riot at Concordia," *Aish.com*, September 16, 2002: http://www.aish.com/jw/s/48884942.html.

36. Ibid.

37. Judith Scherr and John Geluardi, "Hundreds protest Netanyahu," *Berkeley Daily Planet*, November 29, 2000: http://www.berkeleydailyplanet.com/issue/2000-11-29/article/2388?headline=Hundreds-protest-Netanyahu--By-Judith-Scherr-and-John-Geluardi-Daily-Planet.

38. Jonathan Calt Harris, "A Berkeley Prof's "Intifada" Against America," *FrontPage Magazine*, April 15, 2004: http://archive.frontpagemag.com/readArticle.aspx?ARTID=13395.

39. "An Intifada in This Country," *LittleGreenFootballs.com*. April 11, 2004: http://littlegreenfootballs.com/weblog/?entry=10615.

40. Maya Aizenman, Letter to the Editor, "Pro-Palestinian group stoops to new low," *The Berkeley Daily Planet*, May 6, 2002: http://www.berkeleydailyplanet.com/issue/2002-05-06/article/11791?headline=Pro-Palestine-group-stoops-to-new-low.

41. Steven Emerson, *American Jihad: The Terrorists Living Among Us*, New York: The Free Press, 2002.

42. Quoted in Harris, op, cit.

43. Kyle Crawford, "Lecturers Dissect Cartoon Controversy," *Daily Californian*, February 17, 2006: http://archive.dailycal.org/article/23327/lecturers_dissect_cartoon_controversy.

44. Ibid.

45. Roger Kimball, "The Intifada Curriculum," *Wall Street Journal*, May 9, 2002.

46. Tanya Schevitz, "Cramped speech at UC Berkeley," *San Francisco Chronicle*, May 10, 2002: http://articles.sfgate.com/2002-05-10/bay-area/17543159_1_uc-berkeley-free-speech-movement-students.

47. Maren Lane, "Campus Activism Rankings Place UC Berkeley Fourth," *Daily Californian*, October 22, 2002: http://archive.dailycal.org/article/9904/campus_activism_rankings_place_uc_berkeley_fourth.

48. Abdus Sattar Ghazali, "New counter intelligence operation directed at Arabs, Muslims and South East Asians," *The Milli Gazette Online*, April 16-30, 2005: http://www.milligazette.com/Archives/2005/16-30Apr05-Print-Edition/163004200566.htm.

49. Ibid.

50. Staff of the *St. Petersburg Times*, "Sami Al Arian, In His Words," *St. Petersburg Times*, February 21, 2003: http://www.sptimes.com/2003/02/21/TampaBay/Sami_Al_Arian__in_his.shtml.

51. Ibid.

52. Robert Spencer, "The New Alger Hiss," *Human Events*, April 23, 2008: http://www.humanevents.com/article.php?id=26168

53. Judea Pearl, "Daniel Pearl and the Normalization of Evil," *Wall Street Journal*, February 3, 2009.

54. Klein, Morton A. Klein and Susan B. Tuchman, "ZOA Letter to the Chancellor of UCLA Regarding Gaza Symposium," *Doc's Talk Blog.com*, April 17, 2009: http://docstalk.blogspot.com/2009/04/zoa-letter-to-chancellor-of-ucla-re.html.

55. Roberta P. Seid, "Reviving 1920s Munich Beer Halls at UCLA, Courtesy of California Taxpayers," *StandWithUs.com*, February 9, 2009: http://www.standwithus.com/app/iNews/view_printer.asp?ID=810.

56. Steven Plaut, "The Jihadnik Prof at UC-Santa Barbara," *FrontPage Magazine*, December 1, 2005: http://archive.frontpagemag.com/readArticle.aspx?ARTID=8437.

57. Hajjar, quoted in Plaut, op. cit.

58. Richard Falk, "Slouching Toward a Palestinian Holocaust," *Middle East*. June 29, 2007. Emphasis added.

59. Falk, "Israel's War Crimes," *The Nation*, December 29, 2008.

60. Ron Radosh, "The Disgrace of *The Nation*," *PajamasMedia.com*, January 2, 2009: http://pjmedia.com/ronradosh/2009/01/01/the-disgrace-of-the-nation.

61. Michael I. Krauss, "Collective Punishment and Newspeak," *American Thinker*, February 24, 2008: http://www.americanthinker.com/2008/02/collective_punishment_and_news.html.

62. Cinnamon Stillwell, "The Islamic and Radical Agenda Are United," *Dafka.org*, February 7, 2008: http://www.dafka.org/news/index.php?pid=4&id=1645.

63. "Allegations fly at Middle East," *Daily Bruin*, April 11, 2002: rally http://www.dailybruin.com/index.php/article/2002/04/allegations-fly-at-middle-east.

64. Seid, op. cit.

65. Saree Makdisi, "Brutality that boomerangs," *Los Angeles Times*, July 29, 2005: http://articles.latimes.com/2005/jul/29/opinion/oe-makdisi29.

66. Makdisi, "Said, Palestine, and the Humanism of Liberation," *Critical Inquiry*, Winter 2005: www.geocities.com/martinkramerorg/Documents/MakdisiSaid.pdf.

Chapter 8

1. Investigative Project on Terrorism, "IPT Report Documents Viva Palestina's Hamas Support," *IPT News*, October 8, 2009: http://www.investigativeproject.org/1453/ipt-report-documents-viva-palestinas-hamas-support.

2. Hadeer Soliman, "Defending the Muslim Student Union," *New University*, November 2, 2009: http://www.newuniversity.org/2009/11/opinion/defending-the-muslim-student-union.

3. Mohamed Akram, "An Explanatory Memorandum on the General Strategic Goal for the Brotherhood in North America," *The Investigative Project on Terrorism.com*, May 19, 1991: http://www.investigativeproject.org/document/id/20.

4. Steven Schwartz, "Terrorism: Growing Wahhabi Influence in the United States," Testimony before the U.S. Senate Committee on the Judiciary, June 26, 2003: http://www.globalsecurity.org/security/library/congress/2003_h/030626-schwartz.htm.

5. Ahmad Shama, Speech: "Global Islamic Movements," Striving for Revival: Student Activism for Global Reformation: 7th Annual MSA West Conference, University of Southern California, January 14-17, 2005. Emphasis added.

6. Muslim Students' Association of the U.S. and Canada, *MSA Starter's Guide: A Guide on How to Run a Successful MSA*, Washington, D.C.: Muslim Students' Association of the U.S. and Canada, 1996.

7. The Terrorism Awareness Project, "The Muslim Student Association & The Jihad Network," Los Angeles: David Horowitz Freedom Center, 2008.

8. Eric Stakelbeck, "Islamic Radicals on Campus," *FrontPage Magazine*, April 23, 2003: http://97.74.65.51/readArticle.aspx?ARTID=18601.

9. *United States of America v. Sami Amin Al-Arian*, 8:03-CR-77-T-30TBM, s.l.: United States District Court, May 1, 2006.

10. Jonathan Dowd-Gailey, "Islamism's Campus Club: The Muslim Student's Association," *Middle East Quarterly*, Spring, 2004: http://www.meforum.org/603/islamisms-campus-club-the-muslim-students.

11. Thomas Ryan, "Lobby for Terror," *FrontPage Magazine*, April 28, 2004: http://archive.frontpagemag.com/readArticle.aspx?ARTID=13238.

12. David Herz, Affadavit, December 9, 2002, s.l.: http://netwmd.com/anti-ism/affidavit.pdf.

13. The Terrorism Awareness Project, op. cit.

14. Militant Islam Monitor, "52 Muslim groups in the United States condemns cartoons as "insult to Islam" warns Muslims of places 'not to attack,'" *Militant Islam Monitor.org*, February 20, 2006: http://www.militantislammonitor.org/article/id/1670.

15. Abdel Malik Ali, Speech "War on Terrorism or War on Islam?" Chaffey College, Rancho Cucamonga, CA. March 1, 2006.

16. Aaron Hanscom, "Seeking Moderate Muslims," *FrontPage Magazine*, April 1, 2006: http://97.74.65.51/readArticle.aspx?ARTID=5363.

17. Neal Boortz, "CAIR Upset About Email," *Boortz.com*, April 25, 2006: http://boortz.com/nuze/200604/04252006.html.

18. The Terrorism Awareness Project, op. cit.

19. David Lewis Schaefer, "Defenders of Intolerance, Enemies of Free Speech," *National Review.com*, January 17, 2007: http://article.nationalreview.com/?q=NmJhNGI2NGRjMzBkMjAxYmJjZDM2N2M0MDIxMmExNTU=.

20. Ibid.

21. Quoted in Anonymous, "UCLA Sponsors of Terrorism," *FrontPage Magazine*, April 4, 2003: http://97.74.65.51/readArticle.aspx?ARTID=18870.

22. Ibid.

23. Steven Emerson, "CAIR," *Jewish Journal of Los Angeles*, November 16, 2006, quoting Ayloush.

24. Steven Emerson, "MPAC in Denial About Radicalization of Muslim Youth?," *The Counterterrorism Blog.com*, May 23, 2007: http://counterterrorismblog.org/2007/05/lekovics_lie.php.

25. Daniel Pipes, "MPAC, CAIR, and Praising Osama bin Laden," *FrontPage Magazine*, June 1, 2007: http://archive.frontpagemag.com/readArticle.aspx?ARTID=26821.

26. Jackie Vayntrub, "Anti-Zionist pamphlet insulting," *Daily Bruin*, November 20, 2003: http://www.dailybruin.com/index.php/article/2003/11/anti-zionist-pamphlet-insultin.

27. Anonymous, op. cit.

28. U.S. Campaign to End the Israeli Occupation, "Nakba Day," *End the Occupation.org*: http://www.endtheoccupation.org/article.php?list=type&type=278.

29. Marie-Jo Mont-Reynaud, "Muslims Protest Palestinian Anniversary," *Stanford Daily*, May 10, 2006: http://www.stanforddaily.com/2006/05/10/muslims-protest-palestinian-anniversary.

30. Ibid.

31. Tala Al-Rahami, "Nakba Day article troubling," *Stanford Daily*, May 11, 2006: http://www.stanforddaily.com/2006/05/11/nakba-day-article-troubling.

32. Sam Dubal, "Daily's event coverage misleading," *Stanford Daily*, May 11, 2006: http://www.stanforddaily.com/2006/05/11/dailys-event-coverage-misleading.

33. Israel Apartheid Week, *Israel Apartheid Week.org*: http://apartheidweek.org/en/about.

34. Craig Offman, "Campuses awash in tension over Israel apartheid week," *National Post*, March 2, 2009: http://www.nationalpost.com/story.html?id=1343206.

35. Graham F Scott, "Apartheid: Is this the Israel you know?," *The Varsity*, February 3, 2005, p. http://thevarsity.ca/articles/15158.

36. Ibid.

37. Offman, op. cit.

38. Annika Carlson, "Campus Informer," *Campus Progress.org*, November 27, 2006: http://www.campusprogress.org/features/1298/campus-informer-november-27-2006.

39. John Hopkins University, "University Statement on Investigation of Fraternity," *JHU.edu*, October 30, 2006: http://www.jhu.edu/news/home06/oct06/frat.html.

40. Avi Weinryb, "The University of Toronto: The Institution Where Israel Apartheid Week Was Born," *Jewish Political Studies Review*, December 2008.

41. Ibid.

42. York University, "Code of Student Rights and Responsibilities: Community Standards for Student Conduct on Campus," *YorkU.ca*: http://www.yorku.ca/oscr/standards.html.

43. Barbara Kay, "York University must get serious about taking back their campus from anti-Zionist radicals," *National Post*, April 16, 2008: http://network.nationalpost.com/np/blogs/fullcomment/archive/2008/04/16/165656.aspx.

44. Anti-Defamation League, "Palestine Solidarity Movement: Backgrounder," *ADL.org*, October 6, 2004: http://www.adl.org/israel/psm.asp.

45. Adam Shapiro and Huwaida Arraf, "Why nonviolent resistance is important for the Palestinian Intifada: A Response to Ramzy Baroud," *The Palestine Chronicle*, January 29, 2002.

46. Andrea Peyser, "Rutgers Gets an F For Putting Anti-Semitism 101 on the Schedule," *New York Post*, July 9, 2003, quoting Kates: http://www.nypost.com/p/news/rutgers_gets_for_putting_anti_semitism_UoQpvdLny8gHzzo7TMvOdN.

47. Charlotte Kates, "Tension on Campus: A Call to Silence," *CounterPunch.org*, December 4, 2002: http://www.counterpunch.org/2002/12/04/a-call-to-silence.

48. Jewish Action Taskforce, "International Solidarity: A Terrorist Protection Movement," *JAT: The "Jewish Action Taskforce.org*, http://jat-action.org/ISM_info.htm.

49. Eric Adler and Jack Langer, "The Intifada Comes to Duke," *Commentary*, January 5, 2005.

50. Discover the Networks, "Palestine Solidarity Movement," *DiscoverThe Networks.org*, November 10, 2000: http://www.discoverthenetworks.org/groupProfile.asp?grpid=6611.

51. Fadi Kiblawi, "A Perspective on Palestine while High on Vicodin," *Al-Risalah*, June 24, 2001.

52. Adler and Langer, op. cit.

53. Lee Kaplan, "Inside Duke's Hate Fest," *FrontPage Magazine*, October 29, 2004: http://97.74.65.51/readArticle.aspx?ARTID=10792.

54. Quoted in Adler and Langer, op cit.

Chapter 9

1. "Resolution in Support of Peace and Nuetrality Through UCDivestment From U.S. Corporations Profiting From Occupation," May 2010

2. Gil Troy, "Center Field: Delegitimizing the delegitimizers," *The Jerusalem Post*, November 12, 2009.

3. Ariella Charny, "UC Berkeley and the Israel divestment bill," *Tufts Daily*, May 3, 2010. http://www.tuftsdaily.com/uc-berkeley-and-the-israel-divestment-bill-1.2257399.

4. Nobel Peace Prize, Discover The Networks, http://www.discoverthenetowkrs.org/groupProfile.asp?grpid=6979.

5. Robbie Sabel, "The Campaign to Delegitimize Israel With the False Charge of Apartheid," Jerusalem Center for Public Affairs, 2009.

6. Palestinian BDS National Committee (BNC), "Palestinian Civil Society Call for BDS," July 9, 2005: http://www.bdsmovement.net/call.

7. Desmond Tutu, "Apartheid in the Holy Land," *The Guardian*, April 29, 2002.

8. Jimmy Carter, "Palestinians Under Occupation," National Public Radio, December 14, 2006.

9. Joel Kovel, "The One-State Solution: Zionism and the Future of Israel/Palestine," *Briar Patch Magazine*, August 2007.

10. Solidarity, New Jersey, and Rutgers University Campaign for Divestment from Israeli Apartheid, "Divestment from Israeli Apartheid: Acting for Human Rights, Taking a Stand for Justice," 2003.

11. Francis A. Boyle, "The Al-Aqsa Intifada and International Law." November 30, 2000: http://www.mediamonitors.net/francis4.html.

12. Ibid. (Emphasis added.)

13. Ibid.

14. Alana Goodman, "Academic Front for PLO," *Academia.org*, August 19, 2009. http://www.acadmia.org/academic-front-for-plo.

15. Anti-Defamation League, "Anti-Semitic/Anti-Israel Events on Campus," *adl.org*. May 14, 2002 http://www.adl.org/campus/campus_ incidents.asp.

16. Fayyad Sbaihat, "Fighting the New Apartheid: A Guide to Campus Divestment From Israel," June 9, 2008, http://alawda.rso.wisc.edu/ docs/divestguide.pdf.

17. Ibid.

18. David Skrbina; William Thomson, "Consider divestment from Israel and Palestine," *Michigan Daily*, March 30, 2006.

19. Rutgers Divest, 2003. http://www.rutgersdivest.org

20. Christopher Chan, "Brown University rejects Israel divestment proposal," *Brown Daily Herald*, March 3, 2005.

21. Advisory Committee on Socially Responsible Investing, Statement to the Community Hearing, November 13, 2002.

22. Ibid.

23. Daniel Fichter; James Kirchick "The truly extremist side of divestment," *Yale Daily News*, November 18, 2002: http://www.yaledailynews. com/article.asp?AID=20843.

24. Ibid.

25. Global BDS Movement, "Hampshire College becomes first college in U.S. to divest from Israeli Occupation!" February 12, 2009: http:// bdsmovement.net/?q=node/301.

26. Alan Dershowitz, "Hampshire Divests from Israel, So Contributors Should Divest from Hampshire," Hudson New York, February 13, 2009. http://www.hudsonny.org/2009/02/hampshire-divests-from-israel-so-contributors-should-divest-from-hampshire.php.

27. Quoted in Jeff Jacoby, "Summers' truth-telling," *The Boston Globe*, September 26, 2002.

28. Judith Rodin, "On the Divestment Debate: Countering Hatred and Intimidation with Knowledge," *University of Pennsylvania Almanac*, October 22, 2002. http://www.upenn.edu/almanac/v49/n09/divestment. html

29. Quoted in Columbia University Divestment Campaign 2002.

30. Charlotte Edwardes, "Fury as academics are sacked for being Israeli," *The Telegraph*, July 7, 2002. http://www.telegraph.co.uk/news/worldnews/

middleeast/israel/1400609/Fury-as-academics-are-sacked-for-being-Israeli.html.

31. Mona Baker; Lawrence Davidson , "The Boycott of Israeli Academic Institutions," *MonaBaker.com*. http://www.monabaker.com/ontheboycott.htm.

32. University and College Union, "Motion 30: Boycott of Israeli Academic Institutions," 2007: http://www.uculeft.devisland.net/motion-30-ucu-congress-2007.html.

33. Michael Yudkin; Denis Noble, "A Repugnant Proposal," *The Guardian*, May 30, 2007: http://www.guardian.co.uk/commentisfree/2007/may/30/boycottn.

34. Steve Janke, "CUPE in full retreat from Ryan proposal," *National Post*, January 14, 2009. http://www.nationalpost.com/m/story.html?id=1177344&s=Related+Topics&is=Pat%20Daley&it=Person.

35. CUPE Local 3903, "Sid Ryan and Paul Moist on Gaza bombings," January 5, 2009: http://www.cupe3903.tao.ca/?q=node/893.

36. Elizabeth Redden, "Israel Boycott Movement Comes to U.S.," *Inside Higher Ed*, http://www.insidehighered.com/news/2009/01/26/boycott.

37. American Jewish Committee, "U.S. Colleges Declare: "Boycott Israeli Universities? Boycott Ours, Too!" August 8, 2007. http://www.ajc.org/site/c.ijITI2PHKoG/b.2818289/apps/nl/content2.asp?content_id=%7B9AC09B2C-EAAC-43BE-8794-DAF0B3646E20%7D&notoc=1.

38. Richard Brodhead, "Statement by President Richard H. Brodhead Condemning Proposed Boycott of Israli Universities," July 27, 2007.

39. Raphael Ahren, "For first time, U.S. professors call for academic and cultural boycott of Israel," *Haaretz*, January 29, 2009: http://www.haaretz.com/hasen/spages/1059775.html.

40. University of Johannesburg, UJ Petition, March 23, 2011: http://www.ujpetition.com/2010/09/south-african-academics-support-call.html.

41. Ibid.

42. Ibid.

43. Hanan Alexander, "Israel is not on trial in the Divestment Movement — its proponents are," *JPost.com*, May 2, 2010. http://cgis.jpost.com/Blogs/classbattles/entry/israel_is_not_on_trial.

44. Melanie Phillips, "Academic Inti-fad-a," *FrontPage Magazine*, April 13, 2005. http://archive.frontpagemag.com/readArticle.aspx?ARTID=8976.

Chapter 10

1. Gunnar Heinsohn and Daniel Pipes, "Arab-Israeli Fatalities Rank 49th," *FrontPage Magazine*, October 8, 2007: http://97.74.65.51/readArticle. aspx?ARTID=28394.

2. Ibid.

3. Khaled Abu Toameh, "On Campus: The Pro-Palestinians' Real Agenda," *Hudson New York.org*, March 24, 2009: http://www.hudsonny. org/2009/03/on-campus-the-pro-palestinians-real-agenda.php.

4. Andrew G. Bostom, "The 'Moderate' Palestinian Faction's Vision," *Andrew Bostom.org*, May 29, 2009: http://www.andrewbostom. org/blog/2009/05/29/the-%e2%80%9cmoderate%e2%80%9d-palestinian-faction%e2%80%99s-vision, quoting Harkabi.

5. Ibid.

6. Natan Sharansky, Speech by Minister Natan Sharansky, Head of the Israeli Delegation to the OSCE Conference on Anti-Semitism, Israeli Ministry of Foreign Affairs, April 28-29, 2004: http://www.mfa.gov.il/MFA/ Anti-Semitism+and+the+Holocaust/Documents+and+communiques/ Minister+Natan+Sharansky+-+OSCE+Conference+on+Anti+Semitism +Apr+2004.htm.

7. Anti-Defamation League, "Anti-Semitism at UC Irvine," *ADL.org*, May 18, 2009: http://www.adl.org/main_Anti_Israel/Anti-Semitism+at+UC+Irvine.htm?Multi_page_sections=sHeading_3.

8. Contreras, Ruth, et al, "Anti-Semitism in Academia," *Scholars For Peace in the Middle East.net*, March 20, 2003: http://spme.net/cgi-bin/articles. cgi?ID=32.

9. Michelle Malkin, "Hate crime hoax at Ole Miss," *Jewish World Review*, December 18, 2002: http://www.jewishworldreview.com/michelle/ malkin121802.asp.

10. Ben Johnson, "Who's Behind the Censorship of Islamo-Fascism Awareness Week," *FrontPage Magazine*, October 10, 2007: http://97.74.65.51/ readArticle.aspx?ARTID=28441.

11. Thomas L. Friedman, "Campus Hypocrisy," *The New York Times*, October 16, 2002: http://www.nytimes.com/2002/10/16/opinion/campus-hypocrisy.html?pagewanted=1.

12. U.S. Commission on Civil Rights, "Findings and Recommendation of the United States Commission on Civil Rights Regarding Campus Anti-Semitism," April 3, 2006: http://www.usccr.gov/ pubs/050306FRUSCCRRCAS.pdf.

13. Edward S. Beck, et al, "U.S. Office of Civil Rights will Investigate Title VI Complaint by SPME Board Member Rossman-Benjamin, Alleging

Discrimination against Jewish Students at UC Santa Cruz: SPME Board To Endorse Investigation and Revise 2002 Statement on Intimidation-Free Campuses," Scholars for Peace in the Middle East, 2011.

14. Ibid.

15. Ibid.

16. Ibid.

17. Orange County Task Force on Anti-Semitism at UC Irvine, "Report of the Orange County Task Force on Anti-Semitism at UC Irvine," 2008, p. 13.

18. Eric Adler and Jack Langer, "The Intifada Comes to Duke," *Commentary*, January 5, 2005: http://www.commentarymagazine.com/article/the-intifada-comes-to-duke.

19. Lee Kaplan, "Inside Duke's Hate Fest," *FrontPage Magazine*, October 29, 2004: http://97.74.65.51/readArticle.aspx?ARTID=10792.

20. Ibid.

21. Bruce Thornton, "Nothing Nuanced: Academic 'diversity' speak gives pass to jihad, anti-Semitism and censorship," *Victor Hanson.com*, March 16, 2006: http://victorhanson.com/articles///thornton031606.html.

22. Kenneth L. Marcus, "Higher Education, Harassment, and First Amendment Opportunism," *William & Mary Bill of Rights Journal*, 2008: http://scholarship.law.wm.edu/wmborj/vol16/iss4/5.

23. Ibid.

24. Ibid.

25. Martin Kramer, "MESA: The Academic Intifada," *Sandstorm*, November 21, 2005: http://www.geocities.com/martinkramerorg/2005_11_21.htm.

26. Ibid.

27. Foundation for Individual Rights in Education, "FIRE's Red Alert List," *FIRE.org*, August 25, 2009: http://thefire.org/index.php/article/10963.html.

28. Orange County Task Force on Anti-Semitism at UC Irvine, op. cit.

29. Manfred Gerstenfeld, "How to Fight the Campus Battle against Old and New Anti-Semites: Motifs, Strategies, and Methods," *Institute For Global Jewish Affairs*, December 1, 2009: http://www.jcpa.org/JCPA/Templates/ShowPage.asp?DRIT=3&DBID=1&LNGID=1&TMID=111&FID=624&PID=0&IID=3188&TTL=How_to_Fight_the_Campus_Battle_against_Old_and_New_Anti-Semites:_Motifs,_Strategies,_and_Metho.

30. Ibid.

31. Terrorism Awareness Project, *TerrorismAwareness.org*: http://terrorismawareness.org/news.

32. Gerstenfeld, op. cit.

❧ Resources

Organizations

AIPAC (The American Israel Public Affairs Committee)
For more than half a century, the American Israel Public Affairs Committee has worked to help make Israel more secure by ensuring that American support remains strong. From a small pro-Israel public affairs boutique in the 1950s, AIPAC has grown into a 100,000-member national grassroots movement.

(202) 639-5198
membership@aipac.org
http://www.aipac.org/index.asp

CAMERA (Committee for Accuracy in Middle East Reporting)
Founded in 1982, the Committee for Accuracy in Middle East Reporting in America is a media-monitoring, research and membership organization devoted to promoting accurate and balanced coverage of Israel and the Middle East. CAMERA fosters rigorous reporting, while educating news consumers about Middle East issues and the role of the media.

P.O. Box 35040
Boston, MA 02135-0001
(617) 789-3672
campus@camera.org
http://www.camera.org/index.asp

CUFI On Campus
CUFI On Campus, a Christians United for Israel National Initiative, seeks to develop Christian student leaders to educate and raise awareness on their campus and mobilize students toward specific, action-based activities to support Israel.

P.O. Box 1307
San Antonio, TX, 78295
(210) 477-4714
http://www.cufioncampus.org/

Charles and Lynn Schusterman Family Foundation

The Charles and Lynn Schusterman Family Foundation is dedicated to helping the Jewish people flourish by supporting programs throughout the world that spread the joy of Jewish living, giving and learning. In North America, the Foundation aims to provide multiple avenues for Jewish young people to forge and deepen their connections to Israel, to learn about modern Israeli history, politics and society and to advocate on behalf of Israel in their schools and on their campuses. Additionally, the CLSFF works to advance the standing of Israel in academia and to strengthen the areas of Israel engagement and pre-collegiate Israel education

Jen Kraus
Program Associate (202) 289-7000
Fax: (202) 289-4983
jkraus@schusterman.org
http://www.schusterman.org

David Horowitz Freedom Center

The DHFC's mission is to defend the principles of individual freedom, the rule of law, private property, and limited government. It further seeks to defend free societies in the war against their enemies, and to reestablish academic freedom in American schools. The DHFC is supported by 100,000 contributors and publishes Front-pageMagazine.com, an online magazine featuring articles on "the war at home and abroad," which receives approximately a million visitors per month.

David Horowitz Freedom Center
P.O. Box 55089
Sherman Oaks, CA 91499-1964
(800) 752-6562

Hillel—The Foundation for Jewish Campus Life

The largest Jewish campus organization in the world, Hillel: The Foundation for Jewish Campus Life provides opportunities for Jewish students at more than 500 colleges and universities to explore and celebrate their Jewish identity through its global network of regional centers, campus Foundations and Hillel student organizations.

Doron Rubin
Jewish Agency Israel Shaliach
drubin@hillel.org

Institute for Jewish & Community Research

The Institute for Jewish & Community Research, San Francisco (IJCR) is an independent think tank devoted to creating a safe, secure, and growing Jewish community. The organization provides research to the Jewish community and the general society, utilize our information to design and develop innovative initiatives, and educate the general public and opinion leaders. The Institute conducts research on religious prejudice using surveys and other tools, and specifically examines anti-Semitism and anti-Israelism in America's educational systems, assessing how prejudice impacts elementary, secondary, and higher education.

Kenneth Marcus
Executive Vice President & Director
The Anti-Semitism Initiative
info@jewishresearch.org
(415) 386-2604 (http://www.jewishresearch.org/index.htm)

Investigative Taskforce on Campus Antisemitism (ITCA)
The Investigative Taskforce on Campus Antisemitism (ITCA) is committed to addressing antisemitism at institutions of higher education across the United States. As a non-profit research group, ITCA investigates and documents specific incidents of anti-Jewish bigotry and their effect on Jewish students, faculty and staff.

http://www.campusantisemitism.org

Media Watch International (MWI)
Media Watch International (MWI) is an independent, non-profit organization dedicated to advancing Israel's image by promoting accurate, impartial media coverage of, and providing timely, factual information about, Israel and the Middle East.

Sharon Tzur
Executive Director
(212) 439-7855
Sharon@mwio.org
http://www.mwio.org

Scholars For Peace in the Middle East (SPME)
Scholars for Peace in the Middle East is an independent, faculty-driven, not-for-profit "big-tent" grassroots community of scholars with well over 50,000 academics and members on over 3500 campuses worldwide. Over 40 of these campuses now have their own and chapters are forming in a number of countries as well. Its mission is to inform, motivate, and encourage faculty to use their academic skills and disciplines on campus, in classrooms, and in academic publications to develop effective responses to the ideological distortions, including anti-Semitic and anti-Zionist slanders, that poison debate and work against peace. SPME welcomes scholars from all disciplines, faiths groups and nationalities who share our desire for peace and our commitment to academic integrity and honest debate.

http://spme.net/index.html

Simon Wiesenthal Center Campus Outreach
The Simon Wiesenthal Center is often the first to speak out on numerous issues that are germane to the world at large. The aim of the Campus Outreach division is to do this "in miniature" at colleges and universities by teaching about and confronting anti-semitism, hate and terrorism, promoting human rights and dignity, standing with Israel, and celebrating diversity and tolerance.

Rabbi Aron Hier, Director of Campus Outreach
(310) 772-2478
iact@wiesenthal.com

Stand With Us

The goals of StandWithUsCampus.com are to give students powerful materials that clearly show the facts about what's really going on in the Middle East and keep alumni informed about what's happening on campus.

Roz Rothstein
Executive Director
(310) 836-6140
Fax: (310) 836-6145
info@standwithus.com

The Israel Project

The Israel Project (TIP) is an international non-profit organization devoted to educating the press and the public about Israel while promoting security, freedom and peace. The Israel Project provides journalists, leaders and opinion-makers accurate information about Israel.

Meagan Buren
Director of Research and Training
(202) 857-6671
meaganb@theisraelproject.org
http://www.theisraelproject.org

The Israel on Campus Coalition

The Israel on Campus Coalition (ICC) is a partnership of the Charles and Lynn Schusterman Family Foundation and Hillel: The Foundation for Jewish Campus Life, in cooperation with a network of national organizations committed to promoting Israel education and advocacy on campus.

http://www.israelcc.org/
info@israelcc.org

The David Project

The David Project Center for Jewish Leadership is a non-profit educational organization whose mission is to promote a fair and honest understanding of the Arab-Israeli conflict. We work to develop educated, skilled and courageous leaders to combat this growing animus, to advocate effectively for Israel on the campuses, in high schools, with churches, and in the general community. We work to bolster the Jewish community's response with effective training, easy to implement campaigns, and a spirit of collaboration with other community agencies.

Aviva Roland, Campus Coordinator
(617) 428-0012
ar@davidproject.org
www.davidproject.org

Films

The Case for Israel: Democracy's Outpost
This documentary presents a vigorous case for Israel-for its basic right to exist, to protect its citizens from terrorism, and to defend its borders from hostile enemies-in a highly accessible multimedia format. Alan Dershowitz has achieved international distinction as one of Israel's most prominent and articulate advocates.

http://www.thecaseforisrael.com/

Hate Speech on Campus
The 45-minute film, *Hate Speech on Campus*, profiles the rise of toxic, anti-Israel speeches being made at U.S. colleges and universities.

http://www.standwithus.com/STORE/?CID=2

Obsession: Radical Islam's War Against the West

http://www.obsessionthemovie.com

Web Sites

CAMERA: Committee for Accuracy in Middle East Reporting in America
A media-monitoring, research and membership organization devoted to promoting accurate and balanced coverage of Israel and the Middle East. CAMERA fosters rigorous reporting, while educating news consumers about Middle East issues and the role of the media. A non-partisan organization, CAMERA takes no position with regard to American or Israeli political issues or with regard to ultimate solutions to the Arab-Israeli conflict.

campus@camera.org
http://www.camera.org

Campus Watch
Campus Watch, a project of the Middle East Forum, reviews and critiques Middle East studies in North America with an aim to improving them. The project mainly addresses five problems: analytical failures, the mixing of politics with scholarship, intolerance of alternative views, apologetics, and the abuse of power over students. Campus Watch fully respects the freedom of speech of those it debates while insisting on its own freedom to comment on their words and deeds.

http://www.campus-watch.org

Discover the Networks
This website describes the networks and agendas of the political Left.

http://www.discoverthenetworks.org

FrontPage Magazine
http://frontpagemag.com/category/front-page

Honest Reporting
To ensure Israel is represented fairly and accurately "'HonestReporting'" monitors the media, exposes cases of bias, promotes balance, and effects change through education and action. When media bias occurs, our worldwide base of subscribers takes action by contacting news agencies, drawing issues of bias to their attention, and requesting changes.

action@honestreporting.com
http://www.honestreporting.com/

The Jerusalem Center for Public Affairs
Israel's growth and survival are dependent on its winning the war of ideas. The challenges that Israel faces today are not only military. They extend to the United Nations, the mass media, foreign universities, and non-governmental organizations. In this environment, what is needed is not just better public relations, but also a rigorous analysis of the issues being exploited by Israel's adversaries who question Israel's legal rights. In response, the Jerusalem Center seeks to present Israel's case and to highlight the challenges of Islamic extremism and global anti-Semitism.

jcpa@netvision.net.il
http://www.jcpa.org/JCPA/index.asp

Jihad Watch
Jihad Watch is dedicated to bringing public attention to the role that jihad theology and ideology play in the modern world and to correcting popular misconceptions about the role of jihad and religion in modern-day conflicts. By shedding as much light as possible on these matters, we hope to alert people of good will to the true nature of the present global conflict.

http://www.jihadwatch.org

MEMRI: The Middle East Media Research Institute
MEMRI explores the Middle East through the region's media. MEMRI bridges the language gap which exists between the West and the Middle East, providing timely translations of Arabic, Persian, Turkish, Urdu-Pashtu media, as well as original analysis of political, ideological, intellectual, social, cultural, and religious trends in the Middle East.

http://www.memri.org

MEForum – The Middle East Forum

The Middle East Forum, a Philadelphia-based think tank, seeks to define and promote American interests in the Middle East. The Middle East Quarterly provides in-depth analyses. Campus Watch critiques Middle East studies in North America. Islamist Watch focuses on the lawful promotion of radical Islam. The Legal Project protects public freedom of speech in this subject area.

http://www.meforum.org

Terrorism Awareness Project

http://terrorismawareness.org

❧ Index